Ancient Egypt

'*Ancient Egypt* is a book of unusual ideas and fresh assessments provided by a scholar who has closely examined a variety of sites in Egypt. . . . The very considerable virtues of the book derive not only from Kemp's fresh approach to the rich mosaic of ancient Egyptian life, but also from the wide range of evidence he deploys in support of his arguments.'   *The Times Literary Supplement*

'This study of ancient Egypt is a healthy combination of meticulous scholarly argument and imagination. . . . It is the first Egyptological study to find a satisfactory way of accommodating into the flow of Egyptian art history those works of art and architecture which, although clearly dated to various times throughout the dynastic period, retained the spirit of Predynastic art.'   *Apollo Magazine*

'. . . this fine book is consistently informative, provocative and stimulating; its vision of Egypt, even without the Pharaohs and their oriental glamour, will not fail to enthrall a more general reader seeking the best academic introduction.'   *Antiquity*

Ancient Egypt presents a comprehensive reassessment of Egyptian society written from an archaeological perspective, based on new excavation evidence and reinterpretation of existing material. Barry Kemp explores the great shaping forces of ancient Egyptian civilization: political myth and ideology, the presentational devices of charismatic rule: and, as well, the tempering effects on people of political and economic experience.

Barry Kemp is Reader in Egyptology at the University of Cambridge. He is the Field Director of the Egypt Exploration Society's excavations at el-Amarna.

Ancient Egypt

ANATOMY OF A CIVILIZATION

Barry J. Kemp

London and New York

First published in 1989 by
Routledge
Reprinted in 1991

First published in paperback in 1991
by Routledge
11 New Fetter Lane, London EC4P 4EE
Simultaneously published in the USA and Canada
by Routledge
a divison of Routledge, Chapman and Hall, Inc.
29 West 35th Street, New York, NY 10001

Typeset by Columns of Reading
Printed in Great Britain by TJ Press (Padstow) Ltd.,
Padstow, Cornwall

British Library Cataloguing in Publication Data

Kemp, Barry J. (Barry John)
  Ancient Egypt: Anatomy of a civilization.
  1. Civilization. History, 3100 BC–332 BC.
  I. Title
  932.01

Library of Congress Cataloging in Publication Data

  Kemp, Barry J.
  Ancient Egypt

  Bibliography : p.
  Includes index.
  1. Egypt – Civilization – To 332 B.C. I. Title.
  DT61.K44   1991   932   91–18484

  ISBN 0–415–01281–3 (hbk)
  ISBN 0–415–06346–9 (pbk)

Contents

Acknowledgements

Thanks are due to the following for permission to reproduce photographs and line drawings: Philipp von Zabern: Plate 3; The Egypt Exploration Society: Plates 10 and 11; Figure 92.

The drawings for Figures 3, 6, 40, 70, and 78 were made by B. and S. Garfi.

Introduction

How should we study the society of man? The decision is ours. No rigidly prescribed system tells us what to do. We can follow convention and run together a series of chapters on geographical background, history period by period, religion, art, literature, institutions, and so on. This scheme will satisfy our natural craving for logic and order. It will create areas of knowledge which match the broad subject divisions of our system of education, where culture is an accumulation of observations and judgements grouped around a conventional scheme of topics. If we do this and leave our study there, however, and the society that we are studying is significantly different from our own, we will be left with only a glorified catalogue of exotic characteristics. We may feel satisfied in having extended our knowledge, and the results may even attract us at a deeper, emotional level by their very strangeness. But we will be in danger of losing sight of an important fact: a fact so simple and so fundamental that it seems banal to repeat it.

Past and present, we are all – readers of this text and ancient Egyptians alike – members of the same species, *Homo sapiens*, equipped with a brain that physically has remained unchanged since our species emerged. We all share, and have in the past shared, a common consciousness and substratum of unconscious behaviour. We all face now, and have faced in the past, the same basic experience: existing as a uniquely important individual, looking out into a world that recedes away from the circle of daily life to a wider society of common culture and institutions, to more distant and 'foreign' societies lying beyond, all within the context of earth and heavens and the powers of luck, fate, destiny, the will of supernatural beings and now, in our modern age, the immutable forces of scientific laws. We live and keep our reason by virtue of the way that our minds select from the ceaseless flood of experiences that crowd around and flow past us from birth to death and arrange them into patterns for us. Those patterns, and the responses that we make – fleetingly in speech and more permanently in the shape of institutions and monuments – are our culture. Culture begins as a mental therapy to protect us from being overwhelmed by the information that our senses collect, classifying some elements as important and others as trivial. Through it we make sense of the world.

Accumulated learning has given us, in the twentieth century AD, an immense advantage over our predecessors in technology and in the range of mental skills by which we can explore the universe and create a multiplicity of logical images. But we must not mistake this for increased intelligence. Intelligence is not knowledge. It is the ability to cast into logical shape such knowledge as one has. Within the framework which the ancient Egyptians created to cope with the phenomenon of personal consciousness – the spheres of existence which recede away from every person – we must assume that they were as intelligent (or as unintelligent) as ourselves. That is the crucial message of biology, of the fact that we are all of the same species. Progress has not made us into superior beings.

When we look at ancient Egyptian civilization we are clearly facing the product of a mental outlook very different from our own. But how far is this because it is ancient? Is there something special about 'the ancient mind'? Does it reflect an outlook more different than is present, say, in oriental (i.e. far eastern) religions and philosophies? There is no easy scale for measuring degrees of difference in such things. Oriental religions and philosophies often have a far more extensive literature and a more coherent form of presentation than ancient Egyptian religion, which relied a great deal on pictorial symbol to convey its message and which grew up in a world where, in the absence of serious rivals, no one felt the need to develop a more cogent and complete form of communication. Persuasion was never necessary. But this is a matter of presentation rather than of substance. The main difference is one of history. Oriental religions and philosophies have survived to come to terms with and to take their places in the modern world, are thus directly accessible to outsiders, and have found within their own ranks apologists to teach outsiders. If we have the diligence and time we can learn their languages, live amongst the people themselves, absorb their culture, and generally immerse ourselves to the point where we can recreate the mental processes in our own minds. And, equally, the reverse is true. Indeed, the oriental world has shown a much greater ability to enter the western mind than vice versa.

This ability to cross cultural boundaries is an important demonstration of the ultimately common nature of human consciousness. All avenues of perception are present in each one of us, but the use we make of them, and the value that we give to them, vary according to our culture.

With ancient Egyptian thought the principal difficulty, then, is circumstantial. Successive cultural changes of great magnitude – the incorporation of Egypt into the Hellenistic world, conversion to Christianity, the coming of Islam – long ago annihilated ancient Egyptian thought as a living process, and led to the loss or destruction of most of its literature. Much that was understood immediately by symbol or by word association has vanished for ever. Although some Greek visitors attempted to record their impressions of aspects of Egyptian religion, Egyptian priests failed to develop in time a sufficient interest in explaining their beliefs in cogent form to outsiders, a process which would, in itself, have led to significant internal modifications. Egyptian thought cannot, therefore, be recreated as a living intellectual system. This is, however, an accident of history rather than a sign of how, being 'primitive', it had to be superseded by something else. In south and south-east Asia – the 'Orient' proper – this did not happen. A basic continuity has allowed extended developments to take place of intellectual systems which, whilst rooted in the ancient past, have grown to become important elements of the modern world. Judaism and Christianity have done the same, but are themselves part of western culture. They do not appear strange to us, despite having originated amongst a group of ancient Egypt's neighbours. We can, as it were, walk in and out of their thought processes without being too aware of their strangeness because their language and images are a part of the process by which, from birth, we in the west classify reality.

Though their status, or the power of their attraction, is much reduced, the ways of thinking that we encounter in ancient sources are still with us. They manifest themselves in many ways. Collectively we may call them 'basic thought'. We remain sensitive and responsive to symbols, particularly when they relate to group identities: from school ties to national flags and anthems, portraits of leaders, the costumes and architecture of legal courts. In times of stress there rises to the surface of our consciousness the acceptance that sentient power resides in inanimate phenomena and things, from the weather to immovable objects that we curse. And throughout our lives our imagination hovers all the time between taking in and interpreting reality and heading off into worlds of myth and fantasy. I am aware as I write this book that I am creating in my own mind images that I hope correspond to the way things were in ancient Egypt. I also know that the more I try to make sense of the facts, the more what I write is speculative and begins to merge with the world of historical fiction, a modern form of myth. My ancient Egypt is very much an imagined world, though I hope that it cannot too readily be shown to be untrue to the original ancient sources. My speculation is restrained partly by professional considerations – I wish to remain true to the sources – and partly, no doubt, because of the scholastic nature of the mind that I have. If I possessed a freer and more creative imagination, the same image-forming processes that I use to make sense of ancient sources might turn instead to creating worlds that were as different as possible from reality. The writer gifted in this way is able to create complete mythologies and imagined worlds that live on in the mind as vividly as if we had experienced them as real places. Indeed, the twentieth century has seen a flowering of fantasy literature in which invented mythologies play a key part. They are written and read for entertainment (so one hopes: there is a conspicuous borderline category of modern literature which, whilst fantasy, seeks credibility – the Bermuda Triangle/ 'Facts that baffle the scientists' genre) but this reflects the change in the value that we place on such things. The burden of man is to carry around in harness with the means to survive this inner world of imagination: of an infinity of invisible places, beings, situations, and logical relationships. We call some of them religion, some of them day-dreams, some of them products of artistic powers or scholarly or scientific insights, but in truth we separate the endless spectrum of images into categories by only arbitrary distinctions, and fail in the end to agree on what it all means.

Retracing the steps of this creative side to basic thought begins in a deceptively simple way, in the figurative language of personification and metaphor. 'But at my back I alwaies hear/Time's winged Chariot hurrying near' (Andrew Marvell, AD 1621–67, 'To his Coy Mistress'). This was written as poetry and we need not take it as anything else. But our minds can choose to pursue the imagery. Take the chariot. It is a symbol of motion, and common observation shows that time and motion are related, in that, over an interval of time, motion decays without an infusion of energy so making the perpetual motion machine an impossibility. In saying they are 'related', however, we are borrowing an English word which is more commonly used in talking about families and their 'relations': uncles, sisters, and so on. We have already stepped into the quicksand world of language-game. The modern world encourages us to pursue an interest in the way that time and motion are related through the study of thermodynamics. But we could, in a fanciful way, make the creature that supplies the motion for 'Time's winged Chariot' into the personification of Motion itself: perhaps a female centaur-like creature. Through the extension of meaning provided by the English word 'related' we could, in a shorthand way, say that Motion was the daughter of Time, or his wife, depending on how we viewed the logic of their relationship – unequal or equal in status. We could go on in the manner of nineteenth-century artists to create an allegorical painting. But at the end we would be judged to have done no more than indulge in a playful idea. We can afford to dismiss this kind of speculation because the growth of rational knowledge has opened up, in this case in physics, a much more complex, satisfying and creditable avenue for our interest in time and motion. But multiplicity of avenues of speculation – choice in myths – was one thing that the ancients did not have. They could make, as we still can, playful mental associations. Often they arose from accidental similarities in words – puns – to the extent that we can say that their religious thought was built around language-game. But they attached to them a very different scale of values. Such things became fragments of serious truths.

The ancient Egyptians did not develop an interest in time and motion. They did, however, develop a great interest in the concept of the universe as a balance of two opposing forces – one directed towards order, the other towards disorder. The myth of Horus and Seth (discussed in Chapter 1) was their figurative attempt to capture, in logical form that could be expressed by the words and images at their disposal, the intellectual sensation that this was a great hidden truth. It was their escape from the terrible feeling of knowing something yet not being able to find a way of saying it fully. We underestimate the intellectual grasp of reality in the ancient world if we take myth and symbol only at their face values, as curious images and odd fragments of tales that do not quite make sense. In rejecting the written and symbolic language of ancient myth as having no rational validity, we should not be too quick at the same time to throw out the ideas or sensations which lay behind. They, too, may well be part of basic thought, and universal.

The survival in the modern mind of the same avenues of thought that were open to the ancients supplies part of the mental apparatus by which we can make sense of the past. We can rethink ancient logic. But it creates an interesting pitfall, in that it is hard to know when to stop. Let us take a specific example. In front of the great Sphinx at Giza stands a temple of unique design without a single inscription to tell us what it meant to its creators. Our only means of finding out is to try to see it in terms of what we know of ancient Egyptian theology. So two German scholars have interpreted it thus: two cult niches on east and west were for rituals dedicated to the rising and setting sun, and two pillars in front of each niche signified the arms and legs of the sky-goddess Nut. The centrepiece of the temple is an open court surrounded by colonnades with twenty-four pillars. These pillars represented the twenty-four hours of the day and night. If we suppose, for a moment, that we could make direct contact with the ancient builders and ask them if this is correct, we might obtain a yes or a no answer. But we might also find them answering: we hadn't thought of that before, but it's true none the less, a revelation, in fact. They could answer thus because Egyptian theology was an open system of thought in which free association of ideas was very prominent. We really have no way of knowing in the end if a set of scholarly guesses which might be quite true to the spirit of ancient thought and well informed of the available sources ever actually passed through the minds of the ancients at all. Modern books and scholarly articles on ancient Egyptian religion are probably adding to the original body of thought as much as simply explaining it in modern western terms. We, as scholars, are now unwittingly and usually unthinkingly carrying forward the evolution of Egyptian religion.

Because of the common and oceanic character of mind, as well as the similarity of the situations in which individuals and societies find themselves, the aim of studying past societies should really be the same as that of studying present societies which are different from our own. Because time has destroyed so much of the evidence from the distant past historians and archaeologists must spend much more time on technical matters just to establish basic facts that in contemporary societies can be observed directly. Archaeological excavation is one such technical approach. But interest in the methods of research must not blind us to the fact that the passage of time makes no difference to the ultimate goal: that of studying the variations of mental pattern and behavioural response which man has created to come to terms with the reality around him. Chronology enables us to follow changing patterns over time and to chart progress towards our own modern world. But too great a concern with 'history' – with dates and the chronicling of events – can become a barrier to seeing the societies and civilizations of the past for what they really were: solutions to the problems of individual and collective existence which we can add to the range of solutions apparent in the contemporary world.

In saying 'charting progress' we are aligning ourselves to a particular belief: that mankind is set world-wide upon a course towards the universal triumph of western reason and values, and that old ways generally are superseded by new ways, which are better. We can accept that this is true for technology and for the rational understanding of material phenomena. But rational knowledge has proved to be far more fragile than knowledge about the deeper meaning of things that people feel is conveyed by religion. The latter kind has a staying-power and a vigour that suggest that it lies close to the heart of the human intellect. It is part of basic thought. Anyone who doubts this should ponder on one of the most significant developments in the contemporary world: the re-emergence of Islamic ideology as both a politically and an intellectually powerful force. For millions of people this is a newly validated pattern which makes sense of the world and creates an acceptable ideal for society. It is an alternative as vigorous and confident as any product of the western tradition of reason derived from classical Greece. It joins the astonishing range of mental devices for achieving a common end: how to structure reality. Nor need we look so far afield for examples of humankind's happy acquiescence in the mix of reason and myth. The incorporation into modern western culture, via the Judaeo-Christian tradition, of a sacred landscape based on the geography of second millennium BC Palestine and surrounding lands is, in its way, as bizarre an intellectual phenomenon as any. But since we see it 'from the inside' we accept its incongruity, even when we do not properly believe in it. And if we do believe, then a spectrum of accommodation between science and Christianity is available to provide support. The human mind is a wondrous repository as rich as any museum in intellectual relics with no shortage of guidebooks to make what is strange seem familiar. Provability by strict logic is only an incidental and essentially professional criterion for the acceptability of a piece of knowledge. All people's knowledge of most things – their everyday 'working knowledge' – is throughout akin to myth, and is in part truly myth. We cannot afford to be too dismissive of myth or patronizing about it, for it is an inescapable facet of the human mind.

The fact that rational knowledge is not steadily and inexorably replacing, or eroding, or crowding out non-rational beliefs and the atavistic ideologies and symbols of political power, we can attribute to the nature of mind. We are not like libraries or computers, with empty storage space waiting to be filled up. We cope with new knowledge by creating little myths, or mental models, from it. The process is the creative side to basic thought. We are not accustomed to use the word 'myth' in this way, to refer to ultimately rational bodies of knowledge. We use phrases like 'being vaguely or generally aware of', 'having a smattering of knowledge of'. I have in my own mind a host of patches of knowledge of this kind: the workings of the internal combustion engine, the nature of electricity, and so on. Many of the facts are probably wrong, some of the elements misunderstood, and in general the pictures must be woefully incomplete. If I am truthful with myself much (perhaps all) of my knowledge of my special field – Egyptology – rests on the same basis. The ideas that have driven this book forward certainly are. But, if I wish, I can relate my little myths, my mental models, to a huge parent body of information stored in books and other kinds of sources. This is the crucial difference between what we might term 'rational myth' – my ludicrously inadequate working 'knowledge' of nuclear physics – and irrational or original myth. Progress gives us choice in our myths, and the power to discard those that we find inappropriate.

Ancient cultures (and surviving primitive cultures) reveal the workings of our basic mental processes, shorn of the complex cladding that modern knowledge has wrapped around them. They also reveal that complex societies have arisen and run successfully for long periods without much true knowledge of the world at all. This is because of a third element in the human make-up (additional to myth and knowlege): intuitive strategies for survival. The ancient Egyptians illustrate this in several areas. They possessed no knowledge of economics as an abstract subject. Yet they behaved intuitively as 'economic man', something discussed in Chapter 6. Likewise in politics. Most of us are still the same. We have access to huge bodies of factual knowledge and informed theory on economics and politics, and will possess rational myths on these subjects. But in our daily lives we will act out instinctive survival strategies which may even run counter to our rational selves, or to our myths.

To understand culture – our own and others' – we must understand something of the human mind. Culture is the manifestation of the local and particular ways in which mind arranges the world of personal life and the world beyond. The world beyond is made up partly of society – perceived fragmentarily in glimpses and through reading and hearsay – and partly of an unseen logical framework which, for the most part, philosophers create in their minds in an attempt to find an ultimate order and meaning and which others – the rest of us – study, revere, use or are just vaguely aware of as myth. The two elements of the wider world – palpable society and intellectual framework – in practice intermingle constantly. So the rules of society frequently reflect or are reinforced by a set of codified ideas, an 'ideology'.

In theory, since differences in personality and in local and temporal setting combine to ensure that no two people are ever quite the same, there have been as many cultures as there have been human beings. But a key element of basic thought is a wish, or at least a willingness, to be part of a broader group with a distinctive identity, founded in language, religion, citizenship, guild, local society, shared subjugation, or the notion of belonging to a state. In offering a means of identity it is one of the most powerful and alluring sources of mental order. It provides a ready-made answer to the question: who am I? In practice culture is a collective phenomenon. Creative minds strengthen the bonds of identity by means of myth and symbol, fashioning ideologies. Ambitious individuals create from the framework a basis of power, establishing systems of conduct which direct the energies and resources of others. The history of the world is not an account of the development of innumerable pools of merging cultures and points of consciousness. The history of man is the record of his slow subjugation to polities of increasing size, ambition, and complexity. When these polities are small and 'primitive', we are accustomed to call them chiefdoms. When large, hierarchical, and incorporating many specialist groups, they become states. The state, ancient and modern, provides both the most practical framework within which we can study culture, and is itself, at the same time, one of the most conspicuous aspects of culture. The nature of the ancient Egyptian state and its wealth of devices – myth, symbol, and institution – to manipulate the minds and to direct the lives of its people are at the centre of this book.

It is a feature of many modern treatments of the origin of early states to work, as it were, from the bottom upwards, starting with a group of standard topics: population pressure, agricultural improvements, the appearance of urbanism, the importance of trade and information exchange. The state, by this view, arises autonomously from, or with broad anonymous interrelations between, groups of people and their environment, both the natural and the socio-economic. States are, however, built on the urge to rule and on visions of order. Although they have to work within the constraints of their lands and people they generate forces, initiate changes, and generally interfere. In looking at the state, therefore, we should keep to the forefront of our minds this generative power that works from the top downwards and from the centre outwards. Our subject will be primarily the instruments by which this is done, and, just as important, the ideology from which they spring. The history of mankind is as much a history of ideas as of behaviour. The archaeologist must not forget this even if his own sources, the material remains of past societies, tell him little on this topic that is explicit. Egypt provides rich evidence for two powerful and complementary visions: an explicit ideology of rule and corporate unifying culture which gave the state its identity, and an implicit model of an ordered society maintained by bureaucracy. The first two parts of this book deal with each in turn.

The Egyptian setting in space and time

Although the underlying purpose of this book is to use ancient Egypt as a pointer to certain basic aspects of human thought and organization, one cannot escape from the specific circumstances of Egyptian culture (or of any other culture which one may choose for broader illustrative purposes). Indeed, it is often in the details that some particular facet is most forcefully illustrated. It is thus necessary next to set the civilization of ancient Egypt within its context of place and time.

Egypt's civilization developed in one of the largest arid desert areas in the world, larger than the whole of Europe. It was possible only because of the River Nile, which crosses an almost rainless desert from south to north carrying the waters of Lake Victoria more than 3,000 miles to the Mediterranean Sea. In ancient times Egypt was just the last 700 miles of this waterway, the stretch that begins at modern Aswan and the set of rapids known as the First Cataract. Along most of this course the Nile has scoured a deep and wide gorge in the desert plateau, and then built on its floor a thick layer of rich dark silt. It is this deep carpet of silt which has given the valley its astonishing fertility and transformed what might have been a geological curiosity into a densely populated agricultural country.

The Nile Valley proper ends in the vicinity of Cairo, capital of Egypt since the Arab invasion of AD 641. To the north the river flows out from the valley into a large bay in the coastline, now entirely choked with the same rich silt, to form a wide, flat delta over which the river meanders in two branches, the Damietta on the east and the Rosetta on the west. Anciently the branches numbered more than two. The delta now represents about two-thirds of the total arable land in Egypt. The striking twofold division into valley and delta creates a natural boundary for administration particularly when viewed from Cairo or its ancient forebear, the city of Memphis. The ancient Egyptians recognized this by giving to each part a distinctive name and treating them as if they had once been independent kingdoms. These names are conventionally translated as 'Upper Egypt' for the valley, and 'Lower Egypt' for the delta.

This is, however, something of an over-simplification. Upper Egypt has its own internal division in the vicinity of Asyut. This is apparent partly from observing the course of history, which has tended to reveal this division at times of internal weakness, and partly from topography. North of Asyut the west bank becomes broader, the western cliffs fade into a low escarpment, and the land is watered not only by the main course of the river but also by a winding parallel offshoot, the Bahr Yusef (Figures 1 and 88). Because of its distinctive character the term Middle Egypt is often used for the valley north of Asyut. The delta is topographically much more of a unity, but nevertheless tends to be seen by its inhabitants as having an eastern and a western side, the former joining the vital land-bridge to Asia across the Sinai Peninsula.

The arable lands of valley and delta today present a flat, unvarying landscape of intensively cultivated fields, crossed by irrigation and drainage canals, and studded with towns and villages half-hidden by groves of palm trees, and increasingly displaying signs of rapid growth and modernization. The transition from fields to desert is abrupt and striking. Civilization visibly ends along a clear line. On the east the desert plateau above the valley gradually rises to a distant range of jagged hills and mountains bordering the Red Sea, while on the west it stretches for a distance of more than 3,000 miles to the Atlantic Ocean, an empty, silent, windswept land of gravel and sand.

The Nile receives two tributaries, the Blue Nile and the Atbara, both rising in the high, mountainous plateau of Ethiopia. The heavy summer rains in Ethiopia swell enormously the volume of these tributaries, and sweep down them a heavy load of

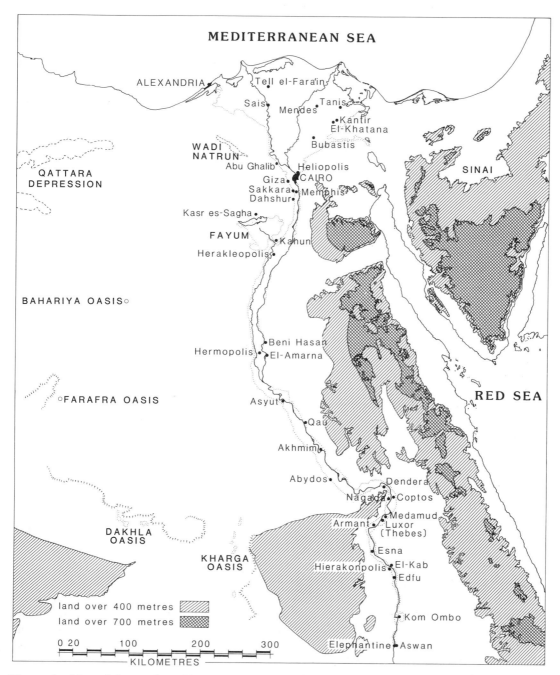

Figure 1 Map of the northern Nile Valley showing ancient Egyptian sites.

sediment, rich in minerals. In the times before the elaborate hydraulic controls which have been applied since the middle of the nineteenth century of our era this surge of water was sufficient to flood the Egyptian valley and delta, transforming the country into a long shallow lake, towns and villages remaining on low islands linked by causeways (Plate I).

As the current was checked some of the silt settled on to the land and was left behind when the waters receded in October and November. If crops were then sown in the thick wet mud, the moderate sunshine of autumn and winter would have ripened them by March or April with little or no need for further watering. Then, after the harvest in summer, the ground dried and cracked, enabling aeration to take place, which prevented waterlogging and the excessive accumulation of salt. These three seasons formed the basic divisions of the ancient Egyptian calendar: *Akhet* (inundation), *Peret* (growing), and *Shemu* (drought).

It was an ideal natural cycle but one that human ingenuity could still do much to improve. Earthen banks could be raised to enclose large basins where the farmer could allow the waters to remain for a period before releasing them back into the river. Water could be raised mechanically to irrigate areas above the normal reach of the flood, or in summer, when the river was at its lowest, to irrigate the fields for a second crop or to maintain kitchen gardens through the year. Beyond this the waters of the Nile could be spread further and more efficiently by the creation of a system of irrigation and drainage canals, controlled by locks, and ultimately, as has been the case since the opening of the High Dam at Aswan in 1970, by damming back most of the volume of the flood and letting it out gradually so that the river level remains constant and never overflows its banks. In building up a picture of ancient society it is necessary to consider how far along this path of improvement the Egyptians went.

The answer appears to be: not very far at all. The need was not there. The idea of using the fertile land to grow cash crops to be sold for profit abroad (as has happened in modern times with cotton and sugar) was far from the ancient way of thinking. Population grew only slowly and by the time of the late New Kingdom had probably not exceeded 4 to 5 million, a very modest total by today's standards. When we examine the ancient sources they suggest a very elementary picture of land management. The state remained very interested in the annual yield of the land for the purpose of collecting rents and taxes: this much is clear from ample written sources. But the same sources say little or nothing about irrigation. The implication is that this was a local matter outside government control. It suited everyone concerned to maintain the banks around the basins, and the annual filling of these by the flood left sufficient moisture in the soil for a single grain crop. There was a professional interest in the maximum height of each year's inundation. Records of this were carved on suitable markers: Nilometers or temple quays. But there is no evidence that the figures were used in calculations to assess crop yields, although people must have been very well aware of the consequences of flood levels either much higher or much lower than the average.

Modern irrigation in Egypt involves not only regulating the flow and availability of water from the Nile via networks of canals, but also the use of machines for lifting it up to ground level. Nowadays a range of machines is to be seen. Anciently there was only one: the *shaduf*, a device of simple construction, a pivoted, horizontal pole with a counterweight at one end and a bucket or its equivalent suspended at the other

Plate 1   View of the city of Asyut at the height of the inundation, photographed early in this century. From L. Borchardt and H. Ricke, *Egypt: Architecture, Landscape, Life of the People*, Orbis Terrarum, 1930, p. 119.

(Figure 2). It occurs in tomb scenes from the late 18th Dynasty (*c.* 1350 BC) onwards, but even then only in scenes of men watering gardens. In earlier versions, before the 18th Dynasty, the method was even cruder. We see water brought to gardens in pairs of pottery jars slung from yokes on the shoulders of men (Figure 3). In such scenes we are clearly dealing not with the irrigation of farmland for the production of a main crop of cereal or flax, but with the watering of only a limited amount of land out of reach of the flood, and confined to vegetable- and flower-beds and orchards maintained all the year round. This evidence serves to reinforce the argument that main-crop cereal agriculture was a matter of a single annual crop dependent upon moisture left in the soil after the inundation.

The importance of appreciating this is not just that it provides the background picture to life in ancient Egypt. It has sometimes been thought that organized society – civilization – in Egypt and elsewhere arose from the need for collective effort to control rivers to allow agriculture to develop. In the case of ancient Egypt one can state that this was not so. The origin of civilization is not to be sought in something so

Figure 2 Cultivating perennial gardens and orchards: the improved New Kingdom method, using a *shaduf*. The top scene shows a simple *shaduf* being used to irrigate a garden beside a shrine. The man (his dog behind him) stands on the bank of a canal and pulls down the vertical pole to dip the suspended bucket into the water. The long pivoting beam of the *shaduf* rests on a tall brick pillar, and has a rounded counterweight of mud at its opposite end. The bucket of a second *shaduf* is being emptied at the right-hand edge of the picture. Tomb of Ipy, Thebes, *c.* 1250 BC, after N. de G. Davies, *Two Ramesside Tombs at Thebes*, New York, 1927, Plate XXIX. In the bottom scene a more complicated *shaduf* is shown in operation. It stands beside a well (at the right-hand edge of the picture), over which projects a platform for the operator. This man is emptying the bucket into a raised trough which passes through the brick *shaduf*-pillar and runs down to irrigate an orchard. Tomb of Neferhotep, Thebes, *c.* 1340 BC, after N. de G. Davies, *The Tomb of Nefer-hotep at Thebes*, New York, 1933, Plate XLVI.

Figure 3 Cultivating perennial gardens: the original method. Water is carried to the square growing-beds in pairs of pottery jars suspended on wooden yokes. On the right a man kneels planting a lettuce in a hole made with a stick. Tomb of Mereruka, Sakkara, *c.* 2300 BC, after P. Duell, *The Mastaba of Mereruka* I, Chicago, 1938, Plate 21 (redrawn by B. Garfi).

simple. It is true that modern Egypt is maintained by an elaborate irrigation system. This is necessary, however, only because of the massive increase in population that has occurred in the last two centuries.*

Modern Egypt is an Arabic-speaking country, predominantly Islamic in religion, and secular in laws and institutions, the product of 1,300 years of Arab rule and influence since the first Arab invasion of AD 641, modified by the country's Mediterranean position. Even by the time of the Arab conquest, however, the ancient Egypt of the Pharaohs lay far in the past. We can formally recognize its end with the conquest of Egypt by Alexander the Great in 332 BC, which initiated three centuries of rule by Macedonian kings (the Ptolemies) who managed to live in Greek style in Alexandria whilst still posing as Pharaohs for the benefit of the more traditionally minded parts of the country. The last of the line was Queen Cleopatra VII (*the* Cleopatra). Subsequently, as a province first of the Roman and later of the Byzantine Empire, Egypt became a fervently Christian country. The Christian legacy in modern Egypt is the Coptic Church. Its language, no longer spoken but preserved in liturgy and in scriptural translations, is the language of ancient Egypt shorn of hieroglyphic writing.

These three great infusions of outside culture – Hellenistic Greek, Christian, Arab – effectively destroyed the indigenous Nile Valley culture of ancient times, sometimes by a process of gradual modification, sometimes by deliberate attack. Modern knowledge of ancient Egypt is, therefore, the result of reconstruction by scholars. It has two main sources: study of ancient evidence revealed by archaeology, and careful reading of the accounts of classical times.

In the early days of Egyptology one of these accounts provided a ready-made framework of history and chronology, which is still universally accepted. It is a set of

* The best introduction to the geography of ancient Egypt is K. W. Butzer, *Early Hydraulic Civilization in Egypt: a Study in Cultural Ecology*, Chicago, 1976.

summaries of a now-lost History of Egypt written in Greek in the third century BC by an Egyptian priest, Manetho. Despite inaccuracies introduced by copyists, Manetho's access to temple archives gives his work a degree of detail and authority which has stood the test of time. In particular, his division of Egyptian history into thirty dynasties or ruling families (to which a thirty-first was subsequently added) still provides the basic framework of history. For convenience, however, modern scholars have grouped Manetho's dynasties into broader units, as follows:

Early Dynastic Period (or Archaic Period)	
(1st–2nd Dynasties)	3050–2695 BC
Old Kingdom (3rd–8th Dynasties)	2695–2160 BC
First Intermediate Period	
(9th–11th Dynasties)	2160–1991 BC
Middle Kingdom (12th Dynasty)	1991–1785 BC
Second Intermediate Period	
(13th–17th Dynasties)	1785–1540 BC
New Kingdom (18th–20th Dynasties)	1540–1070 BC
Third Intermediate Period	
(21st–24th Dynasties)	1070–712 BC
Kushite (Sudanese)/Assyrian rule	
(25th Dynasty)	712–656 BC
Saite Period (26th Dynasty)	664–525 BC
Late Period (27th–31st Dynasties)	525–332 BC
Conquest by Alexander the Great	332 BC
Death of Queen Cleopatra VII	30 BC

Before the 1st Dynasty came a period of advanced Neolithic culture often called the 'Predynastic'. This lasted for somewhat less than a millennium although its roots in earlier Neolithic cultures extend back to the seventh millennium BC. For the Predynastic of Upper Egypt more than one set of terms is currently in use for the succession of individual cultural phases. The older scheme ran from the Badarian through the Amratian to the Gerzean and then, via a somewhat ambiguous transition, to the 1st Dynasty. Subsequently Amratian and Gerzean were often replaced by the terms Nagada I and Nagada II, which still left the transitional period undefined. A redivision was proposed some years ago, which recognizes three Nagada phases: I, II, and III, and this has found much favour amongst scholars. They are, however, phases of culture, defined by styles of pottery and so on. Politically it is clear that with the last century or two of the Predynastic we are dealing with 'kings', and a useful general term for them is 'Dynasty 0'.

Predynastic and Dynastic Egypt together cover around 3,500 years. Although the pace of change in the ancient world was exceedingly slow compared to that of modern times, its effects are apparent within this span of time. Anyone writing about ancient Egypt must be careful not to mix sources from the different periods too much. Indeed, it is one of the themes of this book that a changing ideology was disguised by being presented always in conservative forms, and that this has led to a modern myth that the ancient Egyptians were more conservative in their thinking than other ancient peoples. The scope of this book extends no further than to the end of the New Kingdom, except in citing a few specific sources from later periods. Even within this reduced time-span Egyptian society changed noticeably. One obvious break occurs between the Middle and New Kingdoms. I have deliberately not allowed chronology and history to intrude too conspicuously into my text, yet it has been necessary to reflect the passage of time. I have sought a compromise by concentrating on the society of the earlier periods, down to the end of the Middle Kingdom, in Parts I and II (Chapters 1 to 4). Part III (Chapters 5 to 7) draws principally on the New Kingdom.

Part I
Establishing identity

1
The intellectual foundations of the early state

In the modern world the state is the universal unit of supreme organization. No part of the land of planet Earth does not belong to one. Like it or not, most people are born members of a state, even if they live in remote and isolated communities. The stateless are the disadvantaged of the world, anachronistic. Its powers have grown so inescapable that, at least in the English language, the word 'state' has taken on a sinister overtone.

What are the roots of this condition, this vast surrender by the many and presumption by the few? Man has recognized the state as an abstract entity only since the time of the classical Greeks. But the real history of the state is much longer. If we move further back in time to the early civilizations – of which Egypt was one – we can observe the basic elements of modern states already present and functioning vigorously, yet doing so in the absence of objective awareness of what was involved. The existence of the state was either simply taken for granted or presented in terms which do not belong to the vocabulary of reason and philosophy which is our basic inheritance from the classical world. We must accordingly make allowances if we are not to miss important truths. Essentially we must not confuse substance with language. The growth in the mechanisms of the state, as with other products of the mind, has been a process of addition. The ideas and practices which we associate with more modern times have been grafted on to a core which has remained fixed and basic since the appearance of the first states in the ancient world. The study of ancient history exposes this core and thus the bedrock of modern life.

Fundamental to the state is an idealized image of itself, an ideology, a unique identity. It sets itself goals and pursues them by projecting irresistible images of power. These aid the mobilization of the resources and energies of the people, characteristically achieved by bureaucracy. We can speak of it as an organism because although made by man it takes on a life of its own. Ideology, images of earthly power, the enabling force of bureaucracy, these are some of the basic elements of states both ancient and modern. They contain and reinforce the roles of the state's leaders as effectively as they do those of its people, and bear it onwards in times of weak leadership. These are themes which will recur throughout this book.

Ideology has become one of the great shaping processes of modern times. It is the distinctive filter through which a society sees itself and the rest of the world, a body of thought and symbol which explains the nature of society, defines its ideal form, and justifies action to achieve that ideal. We might consider using the word with strictest regard to its origin only to refer to the political philosophies of the nineteenth and twentieth centuries AD, of which Marxism supplies the paradigmatic example. Because of their immediate earthly concerns ideologies might also appear to contrast with religions which appeal primarily to the spiritual condition of individuals and their redemption. But this convenient contrast between ideology and religion reflects the viewpoint of modern western culture. Islam and Judaism, for example, are concerned equally with personal righteousness and with the form that human society should take on earth. Both prescribe a complete way of life, including a code of law. With ancient speculative thought we move to a state of mind which could envisage the forces behind the visible world in terms only of divine beings and their complex interactions. For the Egyptians the ideal society on earth, though not formulated in the manner of a modern treatise, was a fundamental reflection of a divine order. It was, however, liable to disturbance by incautious kings and so required constant care and attention through ritual and pageant, as well as through occasional more forceful reminders. It seems entirely appropriate to use the term ideology to cover their vision of the state, embedded within theology yet politically valid and constantly stated in powerful symbolic terms. It was a consciously created framework within which the Pharaonic state functioned.

Yet it was not the sole source of order. Egyptian bureaucracy came to express an implicit ideology of social ordering which was never raised to the level of a fully formulated conscious scheme. This implicit ideology of social order (as distinct from the explicit ideology discussed in this chapter) will be explored in Chapters 3 and 4.

Egyptian ideology stressed three themes: continuity with the past, a mystic territorial claim of unity over geographical and political subdivisions, and stability and prosperity through the wise and pious government of kings.

The Egyptians' view of the past

Ideology requires a past, a history. For a dynamic ideology of change, such as Marxism, the past has to be unsatisfactory, an imperfect time whose shortcomings are the spur for action, for revolution. The past exists in order to be rejected. More commonly, however, societies embrace the past, or some parts of it, with respect. History makes the detailed tracery of a myth of the past which provides a model for the present. Ancient Egypt belongs firmly in this category. It knew its own past, and fitted its images within the myth-world of ideology.

The past for the ancient Egyptians had a straightforward and rather prosaic course. No epic narrative of events spanned past generations, no great theme or tale of destiny urged a moral on the living. The past was a model of order, a continuous and almost exclusively peaceful succession of reigns of previous kings, each one handing the throne on to his successor in a single, direct linear sequence. This mirrored how things really were during the 'great' periods of peace and stability. It also reflects, incidentally, an elementary view of what history is about – namely the succession of kings – that still has wide popular currency.

Continuity emerges most explicitly from the lists of dead kings which the Egyptians themselves compiled. The majority derive from the New Kingdom, by which period the Egyptians had accumulated a millennium and a half of history.[1] The best known is to be found carved in fine low relief on one of the inner walls of the temple of King Seti I at Abydos (c. 1290 BC; Figure 4). At the left end of the scene stands Seti I himself, accompanied by his eldest son Rameses (later Rameses II), in the act of making offerings. The beneficiaries of the offerings, as the accompanying text makes clear, are seventy-five royal ancestors, each represented by a single cartouche, together with King Seti I himself, owner of the seventy-sixth cartouche, and whose own twin cartouches are then repeated nineteen times to fill the bottom row completely. The order of the cartouches appears to be more or less correct historically, but numerous kings are omitted, primarily those from periods of internal weakness and division. As Figure 4 shows, the largest group (thirty-nine of them) covers the earliest kings, whilst the next seventeen cartouches belong to the immediately ensuing kings who were weak in power but legitimate in status and were perhaps represented by a mini-list or set of statues in the old Osiris temple at Abydos which lay not far away. The whole scene represents a particularly generous version of a common temple cult of royal ancestors. Normally the cult focused on individual statues placed in a temple by individual kings. At Abydos a list of names achieved the same end, more comprehensively but also more economically. Correct chronological order was not essential, however. Another king list, in the temple of Amun-Ra at Karnak, and of the reign of Tuthmosis III (c. 1490–1439 BC), represents each of a list of sixty-one kings by a picture of a statue rather than by a simple cartouche.[2] But with this list the kings appear not to be in correct chronological order.

An interesting extension to the scope of this royal ancestor cult occurs in the tomb of a high official at Sakkara of the reign of Rameses II, an overseer of works named Tenroy.[3] At the centre of the scene is a list of fifty-seven cartouches of earlier kings, in correct order. Tenroy asks them in a prayer to grant him a share of the daily offerings which were made to them in the temple of Ptah at Memphis. A similar mixture of expectation and reverence doubtless underlies other New Kingdom tomb scenes where offerings and prayers are made to deceased kings. The tomb at Thebes of the priest Amenmes (Figure 4), for example, shows him worshipping the statues of twelve New Kingdom Pharaohs regarded as legitimate, plus the founder of the Middle Kingdom, Nebhepetra Menthuhotep II. Again the chronological ordering is correct.

Although these lists are relatively late, the practice of honouring named royal ancestors was an old one. The pious regard shown by kings of the 12th Dynasty towards members of the preceding 11th Dynasty, whose power they had usurped, also reveals that the search for continuity in kingship could transcend the political details of dynastic succession.[4]

The fact that most lists put their selection of kings into correct chronological order reflects a natural Egyptian inclination towards the keeping and archiving of administrative records. The archival element is very evident in the lists of the Palermo Stone (Figure 5). This name is given to a group of fragments of a black basalt slab, evidently carved after the end of the 5th Dynasty (c. 2350 BC). Most of the design consists of horizontal rows of compartments, each one separated by a vertical line with

about 75 years omitted   about 250 years omitted

56 kings from Menes (between 850 and | 955 years = Dynasties 1-8)

9 kings (c. 270 years = Dynasties 11, 12)

9 kings (c. 245 years= Dynasty 18, omitting 5 discredited rulers)

Rameses I
Sety I
(Dyn. 19)

names of Sety I   repeated 19 times

Queen Ahmose-Nefertary   Menthuhotep I/II   (Ahmose)   Amenhetep I   Tuthmosis I   Tuthmosis II   Tuthmosis III

Amenhetep II   Tuthmosis IV   Amenhetep III   Horemheb   Rameses I   Sety I

Figure 4 *Above.* Legitimizing the present by revering an edited version of the past: King Seti I (and Prince Rameses) present offerings to the names of kings made up into a single continuous sequence which connected Seti I to Meni (Menes), the earliest king of whom the Egyptians had a firm record. In the accompanying diagram the names have been divided into blocks representing periods of legitimate rule as interpreted by the priests of Abydos. The gaps in 'real' time and history, visible to ourselves, were periods to which a stigma was attached. The weighting of the list towards kings of earlier periods is striking, presumably because this gave a more intense feeling of antiquity. The weighting has been partly achieved by including the kings of the 8th Dynasty, whose ephemeral reigns continued the rule of the great Memphite kings of the Old Kingdom, but in reduced circumstances. Temple of Seti I at Abydos (*c.* 1300 BC). *Below.* Private reverence of the ruling house and its ancestors, by Amenmes, the chief priest of an image of the cult of the long-dead King Amenhetep I, called 'Amenhetep of the Forecourt'. Amenmes lived in the time of Rameses I and Seti I. From his tomb at western Thebes, after G. Foucart, *Le Tombeau d'Amonmos*, Cairo, 1935, Plate XIIB, itself a copy made in the nineteenth century by Thomas Hay.

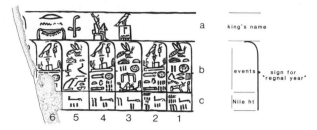

Figure 5   A section of the Palermo Stone recording events in six years of King Nynetjer of the 2nd Dynasty. His name is written in line 'a'. The compartments in lines 'b' and 'c' are divided by vertical lines, curved at the top and with a small projection to the right placed half-way down. Each of these lines is in fact the hieroglyph used to write the word for "year" (see also Figure 20F, p. 60). The compartments are further divided into two horizontal rows, 'b' and 'c'. Row 'b' summarizes in hieroglyphs the main events of the years: (1) Appearance of the King, 2nd Running of the Apis-bull. (2) Processional tour of Horus (i.e. the king), 8th time of the enumeration. (3) Appearance of the King, 3rd time of the Festival of Seker. (4) Processional tour of Horus, 9th time of the enumeration. (5) Appearance of the King, Offering. . . .goddess Nekhbet. . .Djet-festival. (6) Processional tour of Horus, 10th time [of the enumeration]. The biennial rhythm of the king's official life, built around an enumeration of the country's wealth every second year (probably an early kind of Domesday record), is striking. The lowest row of compartments (c) contains an exact measurement of the height of the Nile flood: (1) 3 cubits, 4 hands, 3 fingers (1.92 metres); (2) 3 cubits, 5 hands, 2 fingers (1.98 metres); (3) 2 cubits, 2 fingers (1.2 metres); (4) 2 cubits, 2 fingers (1.2 metres); (5) 3 cubits (1.57 metres); (6) destroyed. The variation in height, in this five-year span amounting to 0.78 metres, would affect crop yields in higher-lying fields.

curving top, which is, in fact, the hieroglyphic sign for 'regnal year'. Each of the compartments contains a summary of the principal events in a single year of kings whose names run across the top of the appropriate block of compartments. The events tell us what things the Egyptians of the time thought were important. They are a mixture of religious festivals, creation of statues of the gods, occasional warfare, regular taxation, and, in a separate subdivision, the precise height of that year's Nile flood. The Palermo Stone portrays an interest in the deeds of the past, adding an intellectual cladding to the bare lists of kings, yet one which still remained in harmony with the ideal. We can assume that this kind of chronicle provided the basis for the later summary lists of kings. It must itself have been compiled from several different sources, since there is only limited consistency in the kind of things recorded line by line, and in the length of the entries.

Administration and piety towards great royal ancestors do not provide a complete explanation for this interest, however. The records at their disposal enabled the Egyptians to measure past time, and offered them the prospect of an intellectual journey to the point where time met the cosmos. The most vivid expression of this is found in another king list, again from the New Kingdom, but this time written on papyrus and now in the Turin Museum.[5] Originally it listed around 300 names of kings, and the aim of its compiler was completeness. No king seems to have been too minor or short-reigned for inclusion. The Palestinian kings who formed the Hyksos Dynasty were included, even though they did not merit having their names written in cartouches. This, in fact, was a remarkable concession to reality: tacitly admitting a break in the succession of legitimate kings just for the purpose of attaining completeness. Against each king in the Turin list was written the precise length of his reign, sometimes to the exact day. At certain points a summary of numbers of kings and total length of reigns was inserted. Thus at the end of what we now call the 8th Dynasty, a summary of 958 years from the reign of King Menes, the first name of the lists, was provided.

If this was all the Turin king list did, it could be classed as an elaborate administrative device. The compiler of the list attempted, however, to continue back in time beyond the reign of Menes. It is here that the modern and the ancient mind part company. Beyond history modern man has placed prehistory: the record of human society in a world without writing, an anonymous place where names and deeds are unknown. Such a state of affairs was inconceivable to the ancients. But this did not prevent curiosity about what had gone before the first recorded king. The Turin list devoted more than one column of its text to this. Immediately before Menes came several lines which summarize the collective reigns of 'spirits', not given individual names, and before these, and heading the whole compilation, a list of deities. The name of each is written in a cartouche, as if a king, and followed by a precise length of reign. In the case of the god Thoth, for example, this is 7,726 years.

From the whole Turin list one could trace in direct line the royal succession from a period when the gods had ruled as kings, and from the completeness of the data gain the added satisfaction of calculating exactly the entire period involved. On consulting it, the ancient scribe could have known the age of the world since the time of the first creator god and he would have seen how the kings of the past and their great monuments fitted within this majestic scheme. The rigid linearity of this view of time is brought out in detail from the way that overlaps of whole dynasties at times of internal division are ignored, and the reigns simply placed end to end, and all figures added together for grand totals.

Continuity of orderly kingship was the principal image which the past projected. It was something satisfactory to contemplate by itself, and failed to provoke an interest in the writing of narrative history which explained people and events in terms that posterity would understand. But a few reigns had a certain 'flavour'. Sneferu of the 4th Dynasty, for example, was later regarded as the archetypal good king from the distant past.[6] Rameses II was likewise a model for his successors. 'You shall double for me the long duration, the great kingship of King Rameses II, the great god' prayed Rameses IV some sixty years later (the prayer failed: he died in his seventh regnal year).[7] Khufu (Cheops), builder of the Great Pyramid, on the other hand, acquired a reputation for cruelty and arrogance, which appears in a collection of stories (Papyrus Westcar) apparently written in the late Middle Kingdom.[8] It reappears in Manetho's History and in the narrative of Herodotus.[9] Whether this was a true reflection of his character, or an imagined consequence of having been the builder of the largest of all the pyramids, is something we can no longer tell. Papyrus Westcar tells the story as a prelude to introducing the ultra-pious kings of the succeeding 5th Dynasty, the point evidently being that by arrogant and offensive behaviour Khufu brought doom to his house. The reigns of other kings from the distant past who were thought not to have maintained the ideal standards of kingship were likewise made the settings for didactic discourses. King Pepy II, last king of the 6th Dynasty, is one example: he is apparently credited with homosexuality in a later tale.[10] A king with an unsavoury reputation probably provided the setting, now lost, for the lengthy set of lamentations on disorder of the sage named Ipuwer.[11]

At this point we must draw a distinction in our sources. Texts of this nature, recorded only on papyrus, were the speculative literary products of the scribal elite, part didactic, part entertaining, not meant as statements of theology. It was from the same educated elite that the 'theologians' were drawn. But we should not imagine two sets of people, one with a less respectful view of the past. An attitude that looks disrespectful to us can be found in papyri narrating events in the lives of the gods. In one such story the goddess Isis ('a clever woman. Her heart was craftier than a million men') schemes to discover the secret name of the sun-god Ra, depicted as an old man who succumbs to the pain of a snake bite and reveals his hidden name to Isis.[12] The text is complete, for once, and its purpose is clear: it provides 'historical' authority for using the story itself as a cure for scorpion sting. What was admissible in formal theological contexts, and what was permissible in literary scribblings, would have been a matter of clearly understood taste. The reputations of Khufu and Pepy II did not exclude them from the formal king lists. What this limited 'licence' or intellectual freedom achieved were settings in which the lessons of bad kingship could be expounded for the court, including the king, to ponder on. Furthermore, the existence of periods of disorder and injustice served as a warning and gave credence to the role of the king as maintainer of order and justice.

There was, however, a limit. We know, from modern researches, of a period of internal unrest culminating in civil war between two contemporaneous ruling families, the 9th and 11th Dynasties, of Herakleopolis and Thebes respectively. This was the First Intermediate Period. Later Egyptians treated it circumspectly. The founder of the principal breakaway group, King Khety of the 9th Dynasty, later became, like Khufu, the object of unfavourable anecdote, preserved in the copies of Manetho. The entry for this king, in fact, summarizes neatly the anecdotal, moralistic view of history: 'King Achthoes [the Greek form of Khety], behaving more cruelly than his predecessors, wrought woes for the people of all Egypt, but afterwards he was smitten with madness, and was killed by a crocodile.'[13] There is no hint here of the political opportunism which must have given Khety and his family temporary control of the Egyptian throne, soon disputed by a rival dynasty based at Thebes. No later text that we know of used the setting of provincial breakaway or warring dynasties directly. In the immediately ensuing period (the Middle Kingdom) thoughtful men composed literary texts which dwelt on the nature of a disorderly society, but within them they kept historical reality at a distance. The First Intermediate Period was not used directly to point to a moral. One device put the description of disorder into a prophecy uttered by a priest at the court of the long-dead but highly regarded King Sneferu, of the early 4th Dynasty.[14] The disorders of this unspecified future time are terminated by the saviour-like arrival of a King Ameny, whose historical model was probably Amenemhat I, first king of the 12th Dynasty. The lamentations of the sage Ipuwer were another product of the same mood, but its dramatic pictures of social upheaval conspicuously lack historical names and events.

By the time of the New Kingdom a second period of internal disorder had occurred, again culminating in a civil war: the Hyksos Period. But here the circumstances were very different.[15] The Hyksos were Palestinian kings who had taken over the Delta. Since this was a period of rule by foreign kings eventually ejected by military force from Egypt it was legitimate to see it as an unfortunate aberration from the ideal picture of the past. Even the Turin list accepted this: the Hyksos kings appear, but shorn of royal titulary and cartouches, and provided instead with a sign which categorized them as foreigners. In one remarkable temple text, Queen Hatshepsut, herself a successful usurper of the early 18th Dynasty, presented the Hyksos Period as a time of disorder from which she had saved Egypt, ignoring the half-century of peaceful and prosperous rule of her 18th Dynasty predecessors. Here the theme of royal responsibility for deliverance from chaos was used with a vengeance. It was permissible in a formal text because the Hyksos Period could be explained away, unlike the First Intermediate Period.

Departures from the picture of the ideal past were few, and (the Hyksos Period excepted) confined to individuals. More typically the past was the fount of authority and authenticity. A characteristic image is provided by King Neferhotep of the 13th Dynasty (c. 1750 BC), piously visiting 'the house of writings', examining the 'ancient writings of (the creator-god) Atum' in order to discover the correct form for a new statue of Osiris, laid down by the gods themselves at the beginning of time.[16] With a similar reverence for ancient forms Egyptian artists retained the original shapes of hieroglyphs with scarcely any modification for 3,000 years. The general continuity of style in art and architecture owes itself to the careful reproduction of codified styles created in the Early Dynastic Period and Old Kingdom. But there was an element of self-deception in this. Significant changes of ideals and forms did occur, and these must reflect intellectual development, something directly apparent from written sources also. The whole modern scholarly apparatus of art history in Egyptology is based upon the premise that style did change from period to period. Thus the brooding, careworn images of kings in Middle Kingdom statuary conveyed a very different message from the idealized youthful images of the Old Kingdom.[17] King Neferhotep's new statue of Osiris would have been recognizably a product of the craftsmanship of its time. Indeed, the 'writings' that the king examined can have specified the nature of the ancient image in only general terms, such as the precious materials of which it was composed. The Egyptians could not have put into words a description of the style of a statue. The same was true of architecture. The New Kingdom saw a major reappraisal of temple architecture in which, at least as it relates to the royal mortuary cult, we must recognize significant shifts in meaning. Change did occur, but on the whole tastefully and reverently through retention of the basic vocabulary of traditional forms, sometimes reinforced by appeals to the past. More will be said on this in later chapters.

On occasions the exploitation of the past could be quite elaborate. In the next section of this chapter an extract from an important mythological text will be quoted, known as the Shabaka Stone.[18] In its preamble King Shabaka of the 25th Dynasty (712–698 BC) claims to have copied the text from an ancient worm-eaten document, and it is, indeed, written in a very archaic style. For a long time scholars accepted Shabaka's claim at its face-value, and set the original composition of the text as far back as the 3rd Dynasty. More recently it has become widely accepted that although the themes of the myth belong to the mainstream of Egyptian thought, this particular composition is relatively late, perhaps even of Shabaka's time. As for its archaic style, there is good evidence to show that in the Late Period scribes had a working knowledge of an archaic form of the language, and could compose in it. An appeal to antiquity, and sometimes a cloaking in antique forms, made new ideas or new interpretations of old ideas, more acceptable. The past was a cultural womb.

The myth of the state

The kings of the lists shared one title in common: all were kings of Upper and Lower Egypt, the two archetypal geopolitical divisions of valley and delta. In this title lay a powerful expression of unity. Again, however, we find the Egyptians shying away from the unpleasant realities of politics. Order versus chaos is a theme which occurs in various guises in Egyptian thought. It was, as we have seen, a theme of kingship. Several reflective texts of the Middle Kingdom (including the lamentations of the scribe Ipuwer) dwell on the nature of a disordered world, making the king responsible for its cure, but these, as noted above, belong to a tradition of limited free speculation at court. At the level of formal ideology division and disunity were seen not in terms of potential fragmentation into multiple territories, or into the topsy-turvy chaos of the admonitions of Ipuwer. That would have given too much weight to a disturbing possibility. Instead a symbolic dualistic division was proposed. This appealed to the Egyptian love of symmetry, as reflected throughout their art and architecture, but more seriously the idea of two originally separate kingdoms provided a safer and more respectable basis for the king's unique unifying role than a greater number of lesser units, or a wider condition of anarchy. It also matched the general geographical division of the country into two halves, although real political history shows up internal divisions along different lines.

The elaboration of this aspect of kingship was as much pictorial as written. The Egyptians excelled in strong and direct visual symbolism. In this they were helped by the nature of hieroglyphic writing. Most hieroglyphic signs stood for groups of consonants, so that pictures of things could be used to write other words which had the same sequence of consonants even if pronounced differently. It is as if, in modern English, we chose the picture of a leaf to write all words with the sequence of consonants *l* and *f*: thus, *leaf, life, loaf, laugh,* and a*loof.* (Context and additional signs when necessary prevented ambiguity.) This dissociation between sign and meaning was boldly exploited by artists. And it remained a characteristic of the writing system that, although at an early date a cursive form of writing (hieratic) was developed, in formal contexts artists lovingly retained all the detail and natural form of the originals so that the roots were never lost. Artists could thus take hieroglyphic signs standing for abstract concepts and work them as tangible objects into artistic compositions whilst retaining congruity of style. This emblematic use of hieroglyphs contributed a visual element to theological language game. It is an important characteristic of the Egyptian art style, as is the restraint with which it was exploited. In any one composition only a very few signs would be treated in this way, giving a clear and immediate message.

A good set of examples which summarizes the basic ideology of the Egyptian state is carved in low relief on the sides of ten limestone statues of King Senusret I of the early 12th Dynasty (1971–1928 BC) from his mortuary temple at el-Lisht (Figure 6).[19] Down the centre runs a segmented vertical sign that is actually a stylized picture of a windpipe

Figure 6 The source of political order and stability: the reconciliation of conflicting powers epitomized by the gods Horus (left) and Seth (right), in whose reconciliation is subsumed the political divisions of Egypt (cf. Figure 17, p. 51). The reconciliation is symbolized by the tying together of the heraldic plants of Upper and Lower Egypt around the hieroglyphic sign for 'unification'. Throne base of Senusret I (1971–1928 BC) from his pyramid temple at el-Lisht. J.-E. Gautier and G. Jéquier, *Mémoire sur les fouilles de Licht*, Cairo, 1902, p. 36, Fig. 35; K. Lange and M. Hirmer, *Egypt: Architecture, Sculpture, Painting in Three Thousand Years*, third edn, London, 1961, p. 86 (prepared by B. Garfi).

and lungs, but which was used to write not only the word for 'lungs' but also the verb 'to unite', which possessed the same sequence of consonants. The word and its hieroglyph were the key components whenever the theme of the unification of the kingdom was presented. On top of this emblematic sign for 'unity' rests the oval cartouche containing one of the names of the king. Around the sign two plants are being tied in a reef-knot: on the left a clump of papyrus stalks, the heraldic plant of Lower Egypt; on the right a clump of reeds similarly characteristic of Upper Egypt. The act of tying is being performed by two gods: on the left the hawk-headed Horus, and on the right Seth, whose animal was a mythological creature.[20] The hieroglyphs above each god refer to two localities. Seth is 'The Ombite', i.e. from the city of Ombos (Nubt, near the modern village of Nagada) in Upper Egypt. Horus is 'Lord of Mesen', a town name used for places in both Upper and Lower Egypt (for reasons explained shortly), but here meaning one in Lower Egypt. On some of the throne bases Seth is called 'Lord of

Su', a place lying just within the northern border of Upper Egypt, whilst Horus is several times called 'The Behdetite', i.e. the one from Behdet, another toponym used for more than one place, but here clearly referring to somewhere in the north.

The artists who carved these statue bases were masters of elegant variation. Other dualistic themes were also woven into the same basic design. On five of the bases Horus and Seth were replaced by figures of plump Nile gods identified by symbols as Upper and Lower Egypt, whilst the hieroglyphic captions at the top refer to the 'Greater' and 'Lesser Ennead' (Company of Nine Gods), 'offerings', and ideas of fertility using paired synonyms in both cases. There is also another variation of the Horus-Seth theme. In this case the pairing is between, on the one side, 'The united portion of the two lords', with a little picture of Horus and Seth to identify who the two lords were, and on the other, 'The thrones of Geb', an earth-god who, in longer texts on the theme, presided over the reconciliation of Horus and Seth. The dualism could thus be extended beyond the pairing of two contrasting entities to the pairing of synonyms, each one of which contained a reference to some aspect of the balanced pairs.

Within this rearrangement of entities to illustrate the concept of harmony through the balancing of pairs we can glimpse a simple example of one form of the Egyptians' thought processes: the manipulation of words, especially names, as if they were discrete units of knowledge. Ancient knowledge, when not of a practical nature (such as how to build a pyramid and how to behave at table), was essentially the accumulation of names of things, beings, and places, together with their associations. 'Research' lay in extending the range of associations in areas which we would now term 'theology'. Meaning or significance was left in the mind and remained largely unformulated. Mythological scenes such as this one provided a kind of cross-tabulation of concepts.

The esteem in which names of things were held is nicely brought out by a class of text which scholars call 'onomastica'.[21] The best known, compiled in the late New Kingdom (c. 1100 BC) by a 'Scribe of sacred books' named Amenemope, and much copied in ancient schools, has the promising heading: 'Beginning of the teaching for clearing the mind, for the instruction of the ignorant, and for learning all things that exist.' But without a single word of commentary or explanation it runs on as a list of names of things: the elements of the universe, types of human beings, the towns and villages of Egypt in great detail, parts of an ox, and so on. To the modern mind this form of learning appears like the most stifling kind of pedagogy. But to the ancients knowing the name of a thing made it familiar, gave it a place in one's mind, reduced it to something that was manageable and could be fitted into one's mental universe. We can, in fact, still recognize some validity in this: the study of the natural world, whether bird watching or classifying plants, begins with knowing names, and with arranging the names in groups (the science of taxonomy), just as was done intuitively in the onomastica, which served as memory aids for the range of knowledge which was absorbed simply as a result of being a reasonably well-educated Egyptian.

This view of names led to a prominent characteristic of Egyptian religion. The names of gods became the building-blocks for expanded definitions of divinity. Thus in one version of the Book of the Dead, Osiris is defined as: 'Lord of eternity, Wenen-nefer, Horus of the Horizon, with many forms and manifestations, Ptah-Sokar, Atum in Heliopolis, Lord of the Mysterious Region'. The names of no less than five 'gods' are used here to enrich the imagery by which Osiris is to be understood.[22] A very explicit revelation of this phenomenon is contained in a short speech by the sun-god: 'I am Khepri in the morning, Ra at mid-day, Atum in the evening'.[23] Fascination with the 'names of god' produced Chapter 142 of the Book of the Dead, which carries the heading 'Knowing the Names of Osiris in his every seat where he wishes to be', and which is an extensive list of geographically local versions of Osiris, as well as of versions of several other divinities finally summarized as 'the gods and goddesses in the sky in all their names'.[24]

An appreciation of the Egyptian mode of thinking is essential to the correct evaluation of texts which may seem to have a more direct bearing on the real, material world; texts which can become sources for history. Place names were just as open to manipulation, giving rise to a form of symbolic geography. It was a kind of word game which sought an idealized and symmetrical layout of places which were handled primarily as place names given mythological associations. Often, perhaps always, there was something there on the ground, a town or a nondescript little locality. But although symbolic geography articulated a myth of territorial supremacy on the part of the state, it is a mistake to take the geographical references in religious sources as guides to ancient real geography. To do that is to miss the abstracting powers of the Egyptian mind which created an ordered and harmonious myth-world from common and often probably rather humble experience. The result was full of familiar names yet belonged to a higher plane. It hovered tantalizingly between reality and abstraction.

It also, however, sets a trap for the unwary. Modern scholarship inclines towards the approach of lawyers: documented facts are assembled, they are discussed point by point, and a verdict is reached which satisfies modern logic and the 'weight of the evidence'. But ancient texts and scenes reflect an intellectual aesthetic. They were composed from within the minds of their creators, and reflected an inner world which was not a straightforward projection of the material world, the world which, for example, archaeology uncovers. Symbolic geography was a product of an imaginative people. We should not think of using it as a straightforward basis for historical reconstruction.

We are now in a slightly better position to pursue the imagery on the throne bases of Senusret I. A written version of the myth occurs as part of a longer text known as the Memphite Theology, or the Shabaka Stone, after the king of the 25th Dynasty in whose reign it was copied down.[25] Outwardly it has narrative form:

> [Geb, lord of gods, commanded] that the Ennead gather to him. He judged between Horus and Seth; he ended their quarrel. He made Seth king of Upper Egypt in the land of Upper Egypt, up to the place where he was born, which is Su. And Geb made Horus king of Lower Egypt in the land of Lower Egypt, up to the place where his father (Osiris) was drowned, which is 'Division of the Two Lands' (a mythical place name). Thus Horus stood over one region, and Seth stood over one region. They made peace over the Two Lands at Ayan. That was the division of the Two Lands. . . . Then it seemed wrong to Geb that the portion of Horus was like the portion of Seth. So Geb gave to Horus his inheritance, for he is the son of his firstborn son. Geb's words to the Ennead: 'I have appointed Horus, the firstborn'. . . . He is Horus who arose as King of Upper and Lower Egypt, who united the Two

Lands in the Nome of the Wall (i.e. Memphis), the place in which the Two Lands were united. Reed and papyrus were placed on the double door of the House of Ptah (the temple of Ptah at Memphis). That means Horus and Seth, pacified and united. They fraternized so as to cease quarrelling in whatever place they might be, being united in the House of Ptah, the 'Balance of the Two Lands' in which Upper and Lower Egypt had been weighed.'

On the Lisht thrones Horus and Seth are representatives of Upper and Lower Egypt of equal status. On the Shabaka Stone Seth's place is diminished: from an initial equality with Horus he is subsequently disinherited, though acquiescing in his new role. This text, and a mass of further ancient allusions on the same theme spread over a good part of Pharaonic history, poses a fundamental question. Does the myth mask a formative phase in the history of the Egyptian state? Or was it devised as a piece of intellectual aesthetic to provide a philosophical basis for the Egyptian state which had, in fact, developed along a different historical path? Is this part of the Shabaka Stone an aetiological myth?

Past generations of scholars were frequently attracted to the first of these hypotheses, that the myth masked a formative historical phase. Before the 1st Dynasty they saw two kingdoms, each with a 'national god': Lower Egypt under Horus, Upper Egypt under Seth. A turning-point had come when Lower Egypt defeated the south and established a unified kingship, even though this might have been short-lived in view of other evidence which suggested that the 1st Dynasty began with unification imposed from the south. That there is an alternative explanation owes much to archaeology. Indeed, the synthesis of sources, of archaeology with ancient myth, provides a case history of how ideology is created.[26]

The formation of the state: a model for early Egypt

Ideology emerges with the state: a body of thought to complement a political entity. How states arose in the first place has been the object of much study by archaeologists and anthropologists in recent years. Individual cases vary a great deal in their particular circumstances, and we should not look for a check-list of universally valid causes. Egypt is particularly interesting because, apart from being one of the earliest examples, state formation seems to have taken place in the absence of some of the more obvious factors. It is hard to imagine, for example, that in a land where population was relatively small and natural resources so abundant competition for resources from sheer necessity was a factor. It also strains the evidence needlessly to promote trade into a major force. Nor was there an external military threat, and the conflicts that developed within the Nile Valley in the period leading up to the 1st Dynasty seem to have been amongst communities already well advanced along the path to statehood. Some evidence points to long-distance external connections in the Nagada II Period, reaching as far as southern Mesopotamia and Elam, and these were once thought to have marked the route along which ideas basic to civilization – especially knowledge of writing – reached Egypt from the more developed society of ancient Sumer.[27] But these connections are far more likely to be signs of local success than to be pointers to a determining influence in local affairs.

The dynamic for the growth of the state seems in many instances to lie inherent within the very fact of settled agriculture. To this extent it is as justifiable to look for 'causes' which slowed down the process in some parts of the world as it is to search for those which allowed it a rapid passage in others, such as Egypt. The essential factor is psychological. Permanent occupation and working of the same tract of land give rise to a powerful sense of territorial rights which come to be expressed in mystic, symbolic terms which in turn create a peculiar sense of self-confidence within the community concerned. The legacy of this in the modern world is the magic word 'sovereignty'. It awakens in some a competitive urge, and they see the possibility of obtaining an agricultural surplus, and thus a more satisfactory life, not through extra agricultural work on their own part, but by purchasing it or coercing it from others. The combination of ambition and mystic sense of identity put individuals and communities into potential competition with one another. It wrought a once-and-for-all-times change in the nature of society. From essentially leaderless aggregations of farmers, communities arose in which a few were leaders, and the majority were led.

The course which this competition took in a landscape of almost unlimited agricultural potential, of the kind supplied by ancient Egypt, we can envisage through the analogy of game playing (Figure 7). We can begin simply by imagining a board game of the 'Monopoly' kind. At the start we have a number of players of roughly equal potential. They compete (to some extent unconsciously) by exchanges of different commodities, and later more openly by conflict. The game proceeds by means of a combination of chances (e.g. environmental or locational factors) and personal decisions. The game unfolds slowly at first, in an egalitarian atmosphere and with the element of competition only latent, the advantage swinging first to one player and then to another. But although hypothetically each player's loss could later be exactly balanced by his gains, the essence of gaming, both as personal experience and in theoretical consideration, is that the initial equality amongst the players does not last indefinitely. An advantage which at the time may escape notice upsets the equilibrium enough to distort the whole subsequent progress of the game. It has a 'knock-on' effect out of all proportion to its original importance. Thus the game inexorably follows a trajectory towards a critical point where one player has accumulated sufficient assets to outweigh the threats posed by the other players and so becomes unstoppable. It becomes only a matter of time before he wins by monopolizing the assets of all, although the inevitability of his win belongs only to a late stage in the game.

Imagining a game of this kind concentrates attention on the essence of a basic process at work in history. We can move closer to historical reality by imagining thousands of games proceeding simultaneously, with winners promoted to join a progression of increasingly select games, where they dress in strange costumes and perform the acts of play with exaggerated formal gestures, the successful amongst them playing for ever higher stakes. We need also to correct the time-scale, our view of who the 'players'

Figure 7 Model landscape of Upper Egypt in the late Predynastic Period showing the likely environmental factors and local pattern of territorial and political expansion during the crucial phase of state formation.

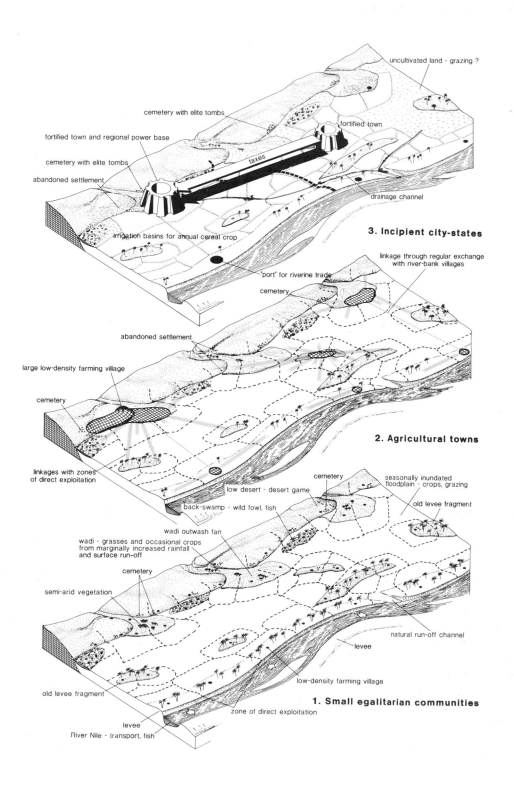

3. Incipient city-states

uncultivated land - grazing ?

cemetery with elite tombs

fortified town

fortified town and regional power base

cemetery with elite tombs

abandoned settlement

taxes

drainage channel

irrigation basins for annual cereal crop

"port" for riverine trade

linkage through regular exchange
with river-bank villages

cemetery

2. Agricultural towns

abandoned settlement

large low-density farming village

cemetery

linkages with zones
of direct exploitation

seasonally inundated
floodplain - crops, grazing

cemetery

old levee fragment

low desert - desert game

back-swamp - wild fowl, fish

wadi outwash fan

wadi - grasses and occasional crops
from marginally increased rainfall
and surface run-off

cemetery

semi-arid vegetation

natural run-off channel

levee

low-density farming village

1. Small egalitarian communities

old levee fragment

levee

zone of direct exploitation

River Nile - transport, fish

34   Ancient Egypt

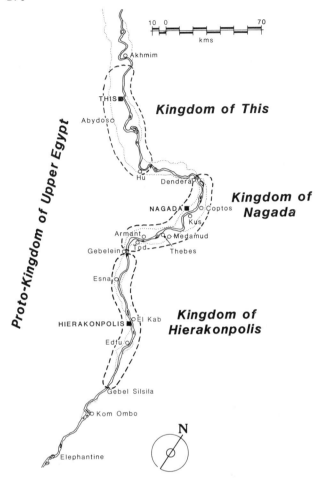

Figure 8 State formation: hypothetical map of the most important proto-states of Upper Egypt as they developed in the late Predynastic Period (cf. Figure 13, p. 45).

really are. So few significant changes of circumstance occur in any one real lifetime that each player is actually many generations treated as a unity. And in real life the games continue beyond the point of winning. Processes of decay and fission set in and the games go on with different likely outcomes.

The significance of this model lies in the implication that all parts of Egypt where settled farming communities were early established should have advanced some way along the trajectory of play before its final and more theatrical stages, simply as a result of local internal processes (Figure 8). There was thus a receptive background to the last phase of political unification. The final expansion of the winning kingdom (centred at Hierakonpolis) was into a social and economic landscape in which the processes of state formation were already under way, although at different rates.

Game theory helps us to understand the process of massive social and structural change which lay behind the appearance of the first states, the mechanics of a progressive decay of social and economic equality. It leaves untouched the question of why the game started in the first place. Modern people, living in societies marked by great inequalities, take for granted the urge to compete. Primitive people, on the other hand, existing for tens of thousands of years in tiny, isolated, egalitarian groups, were under no such pressure. The propensity to compete (not always knowingly or in the direct manner to which we ourselves are accustomed)[28] and thereby to disturb the equilibrium appears to be inherent within those societies which settle and create an agricultural base. Permanent and intimate association with a tract of land affects the mind: not only in the obvious wish to remain in secure ownership, but in stimulating the creation of a body of territorial myth. Primitive societies tend to live in an uncompetitive, egalitarian state of existence. By the time that the process of state formation has advanced to the point where it is readily visible to the archaeologist and historian a powerful urge to dominate will have come to the fore. Two factors therefore determine how far and how fast along this path particular communities journey. The first lies outside people and is the natural resource base, the potential for accumulating pockets of surplus commodities which form the basis of power. This is not difficult for us to assess and for the remarkably fertile land of Egypt we must give it a particularly high rating. The second lies within the human mind: the creative power of the imagination to fashion a distinctive ideology which through a wealth of symbol and ritual commands widespread respect. The Egyptians early showed a genius for this.

Foundations of ideology (1): local tradition

It is very difficult to penetrate in a specific way the minds and the dealings of people at this early period, before writing had appeared. But archaeology gives us two signals to inform us when the process of state formation was under way. One is the physical drawing together of communities into larger settlements which become towns, a process which increases the scope for interaction amongst individuals in whom the great psychological change is taking place. This is the process of urbanization. The other is the appearance of the rewards of successful competitive interaction in the form of evidence for conspicuous consumption and display. In Egypt this means more richly equipped tombs for a minority, and signs of an emerging ideology of power. Two sites in Upper Egypt, Nagada and Hierakonpolis, exemplify both aspects.

The modern village of Nagada, 26 km downstream from Luxor, on the west bank, has given its name to a site more properly known as Ombos (Nubt).[29] In Pharaonic times this was an important centre for the cult of Seth. Excavation and survey have revealed that a town had stood here from the Nagada II phase of Predynastic culture (from c. 3600 BC, thus around 700 years before the beginning of the 1st Dynasty), and that from the 18th Dynasty or earlier it had possessed a small stone temple dedicated to Seth. The extent and importance of the town in historical times seem to have been far less than during the Predynastic Period. For the Predynastic Period Nagada is, in fact, one of the largest known sites in the Nile Valley (Figure 9). This applies both to the area covered by a deposit of Predynastic settlement debris, which included part of a walled town (the South Town) built of brick, and to a series of cemeteries. One of them, cemetery T, small and lying on a ridge just behind the town site, has the hallmarks of a rulers'

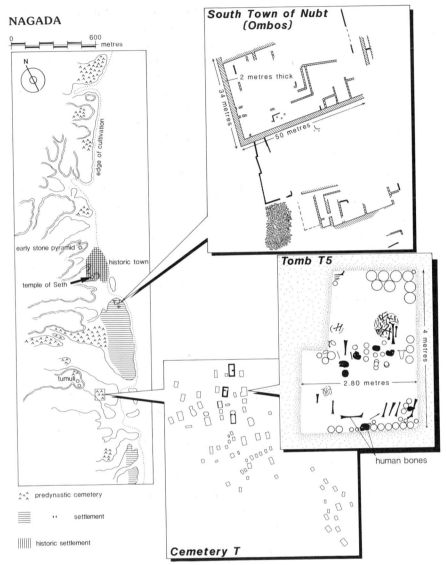

Figure 9 Nagada: centre of one of the first proto-states in the Nile Valley. Note the extent of the Predynastic town, with its substantial mud brick enclosure and other buildings at the northern end. The town of the historic period occupied much less space, but probably made up for this in increased density of occupation. The temple of Seth, however, remained a building of modest size throughout ancient times. The huge Predynastic cemetery behind the Predynastic town is the largest to have survived from this period. Cemetery T, although small, contained unusually well-constructed tombs for rich burials, probably those for a ruling house of Nagada. The basic map is after W. Kaiser, 'Bericht über eine archäologisch-geologische Felduntersuchung in Ober- und Mittelägypten', *Mitteilungen des Deutschen Archäologischen Instituts, Abteilung Kairo* 17 (1961), 16, Abb. 3 (cf. W.M.F. Petrie and J.E. Quibell, *Naqada and Ballas*, London, 1896, Plate IA); the inset map of the South Town is after Petrie and Quibell, op. cit., Plate LXXXV, and that of tomb T5, ibid., Plate LXXXII; the inset map of cemetery T itself is after B.J. Kemp, 'Photographs of the Decorated Tomb at Hierakonpolis', *Journal of Egyptian Archaeology* 59 (1973), 39, Fig. 1, itself after Petrie and Quibell, op. cit., Plate LXXXVI.

cemetery. Some of the graves had been unusually large and well furnished and, most unusually for the Predynastic Period, had been lined with brick. If we combine the archaeological picture of Nagada with the later position of Seth, we have a reasonably firm basis for claiming that at some time in the later Predynastic Period Nagada had been the capital of a chiefdom or small state.

The historical background to the cult of Horus is more complex. Aside from his connection with kingship, Horus (and to a lesser extent his female counterpart Hathor) was, in historic times, a god of widespread immanence who could be recognized in specific local forms. We find local forms of Horus (and Hathor) both within Egypt and in certain foreign territories under Egyptian control. We have met two of these on the Lisht throne bases: Horus, Lord of Mesen, and Horus, the Behdetite.[30] The place name Mesen was used both for a locality on the eastern frontier of the Delta and for the town of Edfu in Upper Egypt. The same was true for the place Behdet: the name was applied both to a Lower Egyptian town and to Edfu in the south. Now, since on the Lisht thrones, and in many other similar contexts, Horus as Lord of Mesen and as the Behdetite stands for Lower Egypt, we should conclude that in these particular contexts the Lower Egyptian places of these names are meant. However, because of the Egyptian interest in symbolic geography, we are not justified in drawing the conclusion that the Lower Egyptian places were the original ones, later transferred to the south, and that there had been in very early times an important centre for Horus in the north. All the unambiguous textual references are no earlier than the late Old Kingdom. Some 500 years separate this time from the period of state formation in Egypt, and it was during this interval that the basic shape of Pharaonic court culture was formalized. The process was a dynamic one, involving a systematizing of myth, which surfaces eventually in the Pyramid Texts, collections of short theological statements carved inside the burial chambers of pyramids from the end of the 5th Dynasty onwards, and the first surviving religious texts of any significant length. This effectively shuts us off from earlier forms of myth and symbolic expression.

The elusive geographical background to the cult of Horus may owe something to a phenomenon that is more difficult for us to control. All the evidence at our disposal points to the fact that the same ancient Egyptian language was spoken from Elephantine to the Mediterranean for as far back as we can trace. This probably applies to the Predynastic Period, despite the differences in material culture between Upper and Lower Egypt. The name Horus – which means 'The One on High' – may have had widespread currency within religious experience throughout Predynastic Egypt. Nevertheless, certain places gave this cult more emphasis than others.

If we turn to archaeology we can find a limited amount of evidence for kingly associations with Horus in the earlier periods. Although this material is largely mute in terms of the precise way that contemporaries would have read it, it does amount to a suggestive statement in its own right. Horus is one deity whose figure appears unambiguously in association with Early Dynastic kings. The figure of the falcon is not qualified by any written attribute, such as 'the Behdetite': it stands alone above a heraldic device containing the principal name of the king (Figure 10).[31]

At this time one of the most important places in Egypt was Hierakonpolis, now an extensive archaeological site in the most southerly region of Upper Egypt (Figure 11).[32] Its importance is apparent from the sheer size of the area over which settlement debris

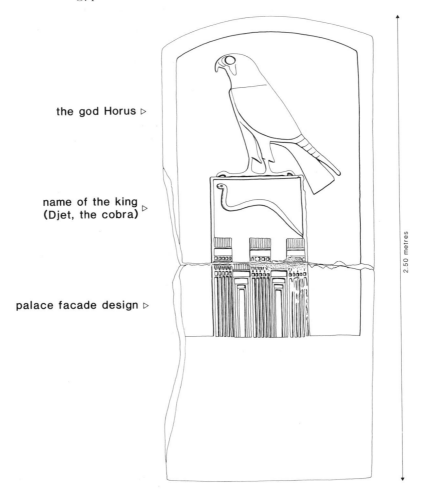

the god Horus ▷

name of the king
(Djet, the cobra) ▷

palace facade design ▷

2.50 metres

Figure 10   The substance of early monarchy. The name of King Djet of the 1st Dynasty (*c.* 2900 BC), written with the hieroglyphic sign of the cobra, appears above a stylized rendering of the distinctive architecture of the royal palace (cf. Figures 12, p. 42, 17, p. 51, 18, p. 56). Standing above is a figure of the falcon-god Horus, of whom each king was an embodiment. Funerary stele of King Djet, from his tomb at Abydos. After A. Vigneau, *Encylopédie photographique de l'art: Les antiquités égyptiennes du Musée du Louvre*, Paris, 1935, p. 4.

of the Predynastic Period occurs, as well as from a number of unusually rich and well-constructed tombs. One of them, no. 100, lined with mud brick and painted with a series of scenes, must have been the tomb of a late Predynastic king.[33] Although in style the painting appears alien in comparison with the formalized art of the dynastic period, we can recognize at least two motifs which survived into historic times: the victor smiting bound enemies with an upraised mace (Figure 16, p. 50), and the ruler standing beneath a simple awning, reminiscent of later scenes of the king seated during the jubilee or *Sed*-festival (Figure 11, p. 40, and see p. 59).

In its general aspect Hierakonpolis resembles Nagada. Both sites also exhibit a pronounced shrinkage towards the end of the Predynastic Period. This marks a fundamental change in the nature of settlement, bound up with the appearance of true urbanism in Egypt: the shift from sprawling low-density settlements to walled brick-built towns of far higher population density.

The city on the floodplain into which the low-density occupation of Hierakonpolis eventually coalesced has fared much better than Nagada. Destruction has been less intense, and much of the archaeological digging has been reasonably careful. Fragments of various parts of the Early Dynastic town have been discovered. One is a length of mud-brick wall pierced by a monumental gateway, the whole decorated in an elaborate panelled style that seems to have been a symbol of rule (the 'heraldic device' used as a frame around the king's Horus name is derived from it). We can recognize in it the gateway to an Early Dynastic palace, the only example of real palace architecture to have survived in Egypt from this early period. Another part is the earliest temple foundations, within which priests of later centuries had piously buried deposits of votive offerings from the late Predynastic/Early Dynastic Periods. Once more, the royal associations are plain. The deposits include statues, stone vases, and other fragmentary inscribed pieces of one or more kings of the late 2nd Dynasty, and, above all, the Narmer Palette (Figure 12). This remarkable object, carved in low relief on both sides of a palette of schist or slate, commemorates a victory over a northern enemy by a King Narmer from the very beginning of the 1st Dynasty. He wears the crowns of Upper and of Lower Egypt, and is faced on one side by a figure of the god Horus. The whole is decorated according to the full artistic canon of Pharaonic Egypt, displays certain of the key distinguishing marks of kings in its depictions of Narmer, and contains small groups of hieroglyphs. The Narmer Palette encapsulates certain of the essential elements of Pharaonic culture, and announces their presence at the very beginning of the dynastic sequence.

In later times Hierakonpolis was the seat of one form of the god Horus: simply Horus of Nekhen (Hierakonpolis). This form is one of the very few geographical forms of Horus recognized in the Pyramid Texts (which ignore Horus the Behdetite, as well as Horus Lord of Mesen). In so far as one can be sure of any cult identification for the Early Dynastic/late Predynastic periods, Hierakonpolis was the home of an important cult of Horus even then. We are thus left with two major Predynastic centres in Upper Egypt (Nagada and Hierakonpolis) which bear marks of having been capitals of chiefdoms or small states, and which, as part of the evidence, claim association with the very two gods which were to become symbols of united kingship.

The evidence for the two sites is not wholly symmetrical: we have to explain why other forms of Horus came to have precedence over the Horus of Hierakonpolis. Since we are dealing as much with the products of a form of rationalizing as with the consequences of political development, we have to be cautious in offering any kind of explanation. But one historical fact should be noted. Hierakonpolis remained important into the early part of the Old Kingdom, becoming a walled town of densely packed buildings (see Figure 48, p. 140). Thereafter it seems to have declined as a centre of settlement, although its temple remained important and was rebuilt in both the Middle and New Kingdoms. Its place as a major focus of urban life on the west bank in this part of Egypt was taken by Edfu, 15 km upstream. The archaeological record here reveals a place of negligible significance in the early periods.[34] Only with the Old

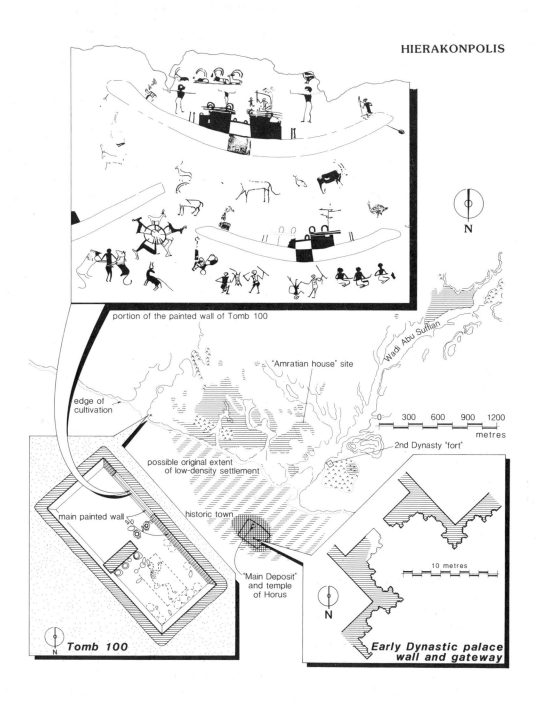

HIERAKONPOLIS

portion of the painted wall of Tomb 100

Wadi Abu Suffian

"Amratian house" site

edge of cultivation

N

0   300   600   900   1200
metres

possible original extent of low-density settlement

2nd Dynasty "fort"

main painted wall

historic town

"Main Deposit" and temple of Horus

Tomb 100

N

10 metres

N

Early Dynastic palace wall and gateway

Kingdom, perhaps the 4th Dynasty, does a walled town seem to have appeared, which then grew, reaching a maximum extent in the 1st Intermediate Period. The rise of Edfu as a regional centre at the expense of Hierakonpolis led to one of several outbreaks of local internal warfare in the early part of the 1st Intermediate Period. In the course of this, Edfu was for a time taken over by the governor of Hierakonpolis, a man named Ankhtifiy. By the early Middle Kingdom a Horus cult at Edfu had become prominent, remaining so until Roman times. The eventual use of the names Behdet and Mesen as synonyms for Edfu reflect this. Thus the mythical tradition was complicated by an episode of local history, the background to which is not fully understood, although it must have been socio-economic in nature.

What of the place Behdet? We are so much at the mercy of the Egyptians' play with words, including place names, that the close study of the evidence is unlikely to lead us back to the correct origin. We need not even assume that it began as a real place of importance on the ground. The Egyptian mind was very creative in this area. But two points can be made. The first time that 'Horus of Behdet' appears, on a carved stone panel beneath the Step Pyramid (c. 2700 BC), the symbolic connections are with Upper Egypt.[35] The second point is that, although Behdet did indeed become the name of a place in Lower Egypt, it appears to have been located close to the Mediterranean, in an area which, in early times, was a lagoonal marsh, probably without significant population at all. There is actually a well-documented parallel for the general process of cultic shift provided by the cult of Seth. Although we have no grounds for doubting that Seth was originally the local god of Ombos (Nubt/Nagada), during historic times a cult of Seth was also established in the eastern Delta. In the 19th Dynasty this eastern Delta cult had eclipsed that of Ombos, so that whereas the Ramesside kings built a major new temple for Seth in their eastern Delta capital of Per-Rameses, the New Kingdom temple of Seth at Ombos remained a modest affair. Because this process happened later than the equivalent one for Horus it is better documented, and thus more transparent.

Parallel to the symbolic geography of Horus and Seth is that for another pair of

Figure 11 Hierakonpolis: cradle of Egyptian kingship. The base map shows the areas of low-density Predynastic settlement together with the cemeteries on the low desert, and the possible continuation of settlement beneath the present floodplain, on an ancient wadi outwash fan now buried beneath alluvium. In the midst of the latter area stands the walled town of Hierakonpolis of the Dynastic Period (cf. Figures 25, p. 76, 48, p. 140) which represents, as at Nagada, a smaller but much denser settlement than its Predynastic predecessor. The map is after W. Kaiser, 'Bericht über eine archäologisch-geologisch Felduntersuchung in Ober- und Middelägypten', *Mitteilungen des Deutschen Archäologischen Instituts, Abteilung Kairo* 17 (1961) 6, Abb. 1 and M. Hoffman, *The Predynastic of Hierakonpolis*, Giza and Macomb, Ill., end map. Towards the beginning of the developmental sequence of kingship is tomb 100 (the 'Decorated Tomb'), probably the tomb of an early king of Hierakonpolis of the Nagada II Period (c. 3400/3300 BC); at the other end is the fragment of Early Dynastic Palace wall (c. 3000/2900 BC) and the huge mud-brick 'fort' of the end of the 2nd Dynasty, both monuments of the aristocratic family which continued to occupy Hierakonpolis for several generations after the beginning of the 1st Dynasty. The Early Dynastic Palace gateway and wall is after K. Weeks, 'Preliminary report on the first two seasons at Hierakonpolis. Part II. The Early Dynastic Palace', *Journal of the American Research Center in Egypt* 9 (1971–2), unnumbered figure. The 'Main Deposit' is an anciently buried cache of temple votive equipment of the late Predynastic/Early Dynastic Period and somewhat later, found in the early temple enclosure of Horus. A detailed plan of the temple remains is given in Figure 25, p. 76. Amongst the material in the deposit were the Narmer Palette (Figure 12, p. 42) and Smaller Hierakonpolis (or Two-dog) Palette illustrated in Figure 14, p. 48.

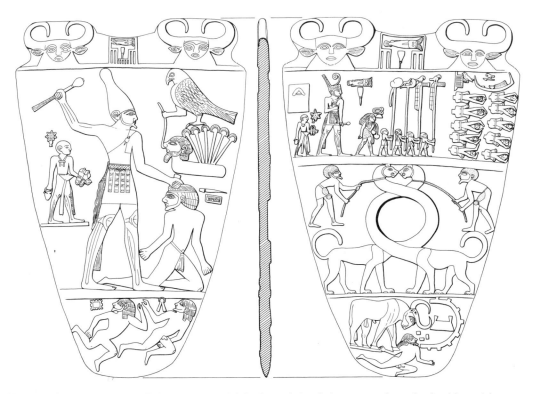

Figure 12 The Narmer Palette, 63 cm high, is a slab of slate carved on both sides with scenes commemorating the reign of a king with the Horus name of Narmer (written at the top in the 'palace façade' rectangles), who must have lived immediately prior to the beginning of the 1st Dynasty and may well have been the last and greatest of the kings of Dynasty 0 of Hierakonpolis. On the *left side*, Narmer, wearing the white crown of Upper Egypt and other insignia of early monarchy, stands with upraised mace about to smite a kneeling captive. Beside the captive's head a group of hieroglyphs gives his name as Wash. The design above probably conveys the supplementary message that the Horus-king (the falcon) has won a victory over an enemy based in the Delta, of whom Wash was presumably the ruler. Behind Narmer is a high-ranking figure who carries the king's sandals. On the *right side* the images of conquest in the top and bottom registers are balanced by the central design which expresses harmony, in the form of the intertwined and captive mythical animals. In the top register Narmer, now wearing the red crown of Lower Egypt and accompanied by two men of high and distinctive rank, walks to inspect two rows of bound and decapitated enemies. The party is preceded by four bearers of standards of distinctive shape. These standards were later called the 'Followers of Horus', or 'The gods who follow Horus'. Whatever their origin, by the time of Narmer they were clearly part of the array of symbols which contributed to the unique aura of kingship. The symbols above the decapitated enemies cannot be interpreted with confidence. In the lowest register the conquering power of the king, symbolized by a bull, is directed against a walled and fortified town. The drawings of the palette are after J.E. Quibell, 'Slate palette from Hieraconpolis', *Zeitschrift für Ägyptische Sprache* 36 (1898), Taf. XII, XIII; J.E. Quibell, *Hierakonpolis* I, London, 1900, Plate XXIX; W.M.F. Petrie, *Ceremonial Slate Palettes and Corpus of Proto-dynastic Pottery*, London, 1953, Plates J, K. For the Followers of Horus see W. Helck and E. Otto, *Lexikon der Ägyptologie*, Wiesbaden, 1975–86, III, 52–3.

deities who stood for the duality of kingship. They are the cobra-goddess Wadjit of the Delta city of Buto, and the vulture-goddess Nekhbet of El-Kab. Little is known about early Buto.[36] It was, like the later Behdet, located close to the Mediterranean coast, and was already settled in the later Predynastic Period, though how extensively is not yet known. El-Kab, however, lay across the river from Hierakonpolis. Its archaeological record appears to be that of a Predynastic settlement of only modest size, growing to a walled town during the Old Kingdom.[37] It is not a counterpart to Nagada and Hierakonpolis. The inclusion of its goddess within the basic symbols of kingship must reflect some local interest on the part of the late Predynastic kingdom of Hierakonpolis not apparent from the general archaeological picture. The necessity for a partner brought in Wadjit, for whose antecedents we have no early evidence.

Behdet and Buto lead us to the difficult topic of the early archaeology of the Nile Delta.

The two classic phases of Predynastic culture – Amratian and Gerzean, or Nagada I and Nagada II, depending on one's preference in terminology – are richly represented in the southern part of Upper Egypt, and in a few isolated enclaves further north, as far as the entrance to the Fayum. No settlement sites of any size are known north of Nagada, but this may well be a consequence of a much greater lateral spreading of Nile alluvium in Middle Egypt since ancient times. Modern fields have buried the key desert-edge sites which contribute so much to our knowledge of Predynastic culture further south.

Once we reach the delta, our chances of finding sites with which to make a fair comparison with the south become very slim indeed. In the south, the narrowness of the valley means that there is a good chance that what survives on the desert edge is a representative reflection of what once existed on the floodplain. The shape of the delta, however, reduces the chances of a proper assessment from equivalent evidence. Most ancient sites in the delta were, obviously, a long way from the desert margins. To date, no excavation or survey on the delta floodplain proper has made significant exposures of prehistoric material, although it is now proving possible to locate them by drilling. We therefore have to rely on desert-edge sites, knowing that they may have been far from the most dynamic communities, and thus not fully representative.

One of the most important sites is the Neolithic village of Merimda Beni Salama on the south-western edge of the delta.[38] Over a long period a succession of communities lived here, mixing areas of settlement with areas of burial, and exemplifying the kind of low-density occupation of ground which explains the huge areas also covered by Nagada and Hierakonpolis in their earlier phases. Both graves and huts were small and poor, displaying little if any sign of social ranking. The villagers farmed, and manufactured a limited range of artefacts. In comparison with their Upper Egyptian equivalents, their pottery and other products appear crude and unsophisticated. The only other sites which we can include loosely in a northern or Lower Egyptian Predynastic cultural zone are a group from around the edges of the modern city of Cairo, and a scatter from the northern perimeter of the Fayum depression. The latter, forming the Fayum Neolithic, belong to a mixed farming-fishing culture which is geographically even more marginal to the Nile valley and delta than Merimda. The Cairo-area cultures, however, even though they, too, are not really of the delta, do lie in a zone of utmost strategic importance politically. It is no accident that both the ancient capital city, Memphis, and the modern capital of Egypt, Cairo, occupy ground close to the junction between the Nile valley and delta.

We know most about the site of Maadi, now close to a southern suburb of Cairo of this name.[39] It was an extensive settlement with a history which spans at least part of the period equivalent to the Nagada I and II cultures of Upper Egypt. It contained houses built more substantially than those at Merimda. Yet, even so, neither by structures nor by artefacts can we detect any significant accumulation of wealth or prestige. Copper was present, not only as the material for a limited number of objects, but also as a poor-quality ore, and this may possibly point to an important factor in the economy of Maadi: it was conveniently placed for access to Sinai where copper was presumably available through trade with Palestinian copper workers, who are known to have been present in south Sinai at this period. But any wealth that Maadi drew in is not reflected on the ground. There is growing evidence that the culture of Maadi was representative for other regions of the Nile Delta proper. The term 'Maadi culture' is coming into use. Recent material discovered at Buto is said to resemble it, for example.[40]

In making a general assessment of Egyptian prehistory we have to allow for the extreme paucity of evidence from the delta. But this does not provide grounds for postulating a lost culture equivalent in its variety and distinctiveness to that in the south. The passage of time brought cultural change, but the most significant element here is the growing presence of material in the Upper Egyptian Nagada tradition, from the Nagada II period, through phase III to the beginning of the 1st Dynasty. This material is known from chance finds and from excavations, including a recent one in a cemetery on the eastern edge at Minshat Abu Omar.[41]

It is naïve to equate material culture and its 'level' with social and political complexity. We must accept that some degree of political and social centrality had developed in the Delta by late Predynastic times, and that the people of the north, like people everywhere irrespective of their lifestyle in material terms, had a well-developed body of myth and social tradition bound up with territorial claims. This is where the gaming model is useful. The settled farming way of life seems to have developed in the north at least as early as it did in the south. The same competitive processes must have begun to come into play there as well, losing out only in the later stages of disequilibrium. For the archaeological evidence points strongly to a marked disparity in the rate of development towards centrality in the closing stages of prehistory. A state, or more likely a group of states built around a large settlement in each case (an incipient city), developed from local expansion in the south (Figure 13); conflict ensued amongst them, further expansion of both political rule and material culture followed until, before the beginning of the 1st Dynasty, some degree of unity had arisen over north and south (see Figure 8, p. 34). In the last phase of the process, which involved internal warfare commemorated on various carved objects including the Narmer Palette, it is very clear that the centre of this activity – the capital of the most prominent of these incipient city-states – was Hierakonpolis. In cultural terms this period is Nagada III. Politically the term Dynasty 0 has sometimes been applied to it. This is a useful term as long as it is realized that it comprised not a single ruling line but numerous local rulers of the incipient city states only a few of whose names have come down to us.

In the principal king lists (Sakkara excepted) the earliest name is Menes.[42] Where

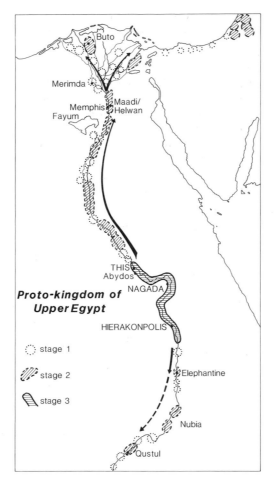

Figure 13 State formation: hypothetical map of Egypt on the eve of the formation of a unified state in the early 1st Dynasty. The processes of centralization are at work throughout the area but at different rates, so that different stages of development (arbitrarily reduced to three) had been reached by the time that the politically most developed centre, a Proto-kingdom of Upper Egypt based at Hierakonpolis (see Figure 8, p. 34), embarked on a military expansion (marked by arrows) which engulfed the whole of Egypt. Early in the 1st Dynasty the expansion continued into Nubia.

should we fit him? For the Early Dynastic kings, the later lists used alternative names to the Horus names familiar to us from Early Dynastic sources, and there remains a technical problem in equating the two sets for the very first group of kings. Menes may have been the alternative name for Narmer, or for his immediate successor, whose Horus name was Aha. It scarcely matters. As first king of the lists Menes has tended to attract more attention in modern times than he did anciently. For there appears to have been no special body of legend attached to him. In the Ramesseum (the mortuary temple of Rameses II) a short list of all the kings of the New Kingdom down to Rameses II is prefaced first by King Menthuhetep II of the 11th Dynasty, victor of the civil war of the First Intermediate Period, and before him by Menes. But we cannot be sure if this reflects any special knowlege of Menes as the first unifier, or is a deduction from the simple fact that his was the first name in other lists. The Sakkara king list actually omits him, starting its enumeration a few reigns further on. This is particularly surprising in view of the fact that Herodotus records a story that Min (as he calls him) founded the city of Memphis, to which Sakkara belonged as the principal cemetery. Manetho has nothing special to say at all. The entry for Menes reads: 'He made a foreign expedition and won renown, but was carried off by a hippopotamus.'[43]

Menes belongs to the final stage in state formation. One new aspect of the dynastic state was the keeping of written annals: brief hieroglyphic notes on the most significant events in a royal year. The Palermo Stone was compiled from such documents. Specifically these records commenced with what we call the 1st Dynasty (the earliest belonging to the reign of Aha, Narmer's successor). This may have been sufficient reason for later generations to start their lists with Menes (Narmer or Aha). He was the first of the kings to have a reign properly documented by annals.

We have mentioned that the Turin king list ventured beyond Menes, with groups of unnamed 'spirits' placed between him and the gods. The Palermo Stone provides us with a clue as to their origin. Along the very top of the stone ran a line of little rectangular boxes which contained not the events of the passing years but simply names plus little pictures of seated kings. On the main fragment they wear the crown which, in historic times, had come to signify the kingship of Lower Egypt. On another, in the Cairo Museum, they wear the double crown. These names must belong to prehistoric kings about whom nothing more was known by the 5th Dynasty. Grouped as 'spirits' they made a suitable transition between gods and real kings with recorded reigns. For us they must be the kings of Dynasty 0, in charge of several territories – the incipient city-states – throughout Egypt. The noteworthy fact that on the Cairo fragment some of these little figures wear the double crown means also that the Egyptians themselves did not, at least in earlier times, see Menes as the very first unifier. If it is a reliable tradition, it fits in with a more protracted political history of formation of a unified state, such as the archaeological and artistic record implies.[44]

Foundations of ideology (2): the containment of unrule

Conflict is one of the themes of a range of delicately carved low relief scenes in soft stone and ivory which must have originated from the courts or elite households of Upper Egypt.[45] They contain their own symbolism. Some elements survived into the iconography of historic times, but we cannot be sure if the values and meaning were modified in the course of transmission. More serious for our chances of correct understanding is the complete absence of many of the most distinctive features of the iconography of historic times. Thus almost the whole of the later iconography of kingship is missing, at least until the very end of the sequence of the objects in question. The end is represented by the Narmer Palette and a few related objects (most notably the Scorpion macehead, also from Hierakonpolis). As objects – commemorative slate palettes and stone maceheads – they belong to the world of the late Predynastic. But in their content and style the last pieces are the products of a great codifying of traditions that took place immediately prior to the beginning of the 1st Dynasty. At this time, and building on the work of the creators of earlier commemorative pieces, creative individuals thought out a remarkably homogeneous intellectual system. It embraced hieroglyphic writing, formal commemorative art of the kind that became one of the hallmarks of Pharaonic Egypt, and a basic iconography of kingship and rule. It was, in total, not quite the Egyptian culture of later centuries. Particularly in formal architecture and its meaning the Early Dynastic Period acquired a tradition of its own which was subsequently, during the early Old Kingdom, subject to a second major recodification of form and meaning. But despite later reworkings the meaning of Early Dynastic culture is to some extent accessible to us because of the wealth of later material in the same style. This is far less true of Predynastic material. The process of conscious, academic codification which laid down the initial rules by which we now interpret Egyptian culture also acts as a barrier to our understanding of the material which had been produced by previous generations, during the late Predynastic. Nevertheless, we can attempt to interpret certain motifs at an intuitive level.

One of the most prominent aspects is the use of animals, both real and imagined, as an allegory of the forces of life (Figure 14). Sometimes they occur alone, sometimes they share a scene with human figures. They engage in violence, the predatory strong attacking the weak, or are at rest. Prominent is a harmonious pairing and balancing of particularly fierce beasts – wild dogs, lions, and long-necked mythological creatures. They are always quadrupeds, and in no respect do they show a resemblance to the figures of Horus and Seth. One example occurs on the Narmer Palette, and here the context implies that the paired beasts stand for a political harmony. The theme generally conveys powerfully the intention on the part of the artist to depict an ultimate, attainable harmonious framework to a turbulent world, the framework in the form of reconciled opposites, portrayed in allegorical form. An alternative depiction of order, again using animals to symbolize raw, natural life-forms, was by peaceful processions of animals, arranged in orderly horizontal rows one above another. Sometimes the orderliness was emphasized by using parallel horizontal base lines on which the animals stand. In these cases we can see the beginnings of the register system which was to become such a distinctive feature of Pharaonic art. The use of animals as an allegory of untamed chaotic life-force survived into the religious art of historic times, most notably in scenes of king and gods capturing wild birds (and in the Graeco-Roman period animals as well) in a huge clap-net, where texts and context make clear the symbolism of containment of disorder (Figure 15).[46]

The wall painting in tomb 100 at Hierakonpolis is amenable to the same interpretation. It portrays a symbolic universe in which the central element is the line of boats: unassailable points of order and authority, which also conveyed the image of motion through time. One of them, with its depiction of a ruler seated beneath an awning and protected by female guardian figures, is specifically associated with rule. On all sides are the threats from manifestations of raw life-force, some in the form of desert animals and others in human form. The threats are countered by vignettes of capture or defeat. The same elemental struggle waged during a perpetual voyage through time lies behind some of the much later scenes painted in the tombs of New Kingdom Pharaohs at Thebes. But by this time fifteen centuries or more of intellectual and artistic development had transformed the simple real landscape of chaos into an imagined otherworld of dangers occupied by invented demons (see Figure 15).

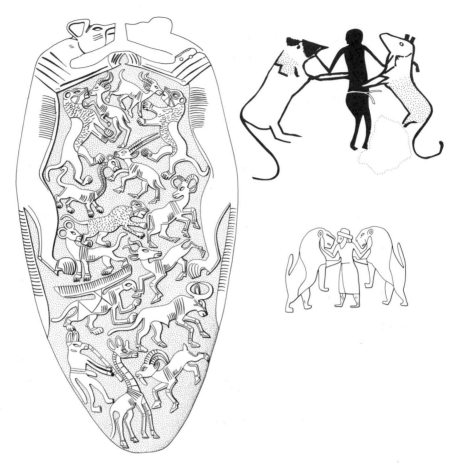

Figure 14 The containment of unrule in the universe. *Left*. The smaller Hierakonpolis (or Two-dog) Palette, reverse side. It portrays life allegorically as an unequal conflict between the strong and the weak, seemingly animated by the flute-playing presence of the Seth-like figure in the bottom left corner. The pre-eminent predators are the facing lions at the top who are, however, not far from a point of equilibrium in which their powers are mutually balancing. This ultimate point of harmony is hinted at by the framing figures of the fierce hunting dogs. *Right*. The actual point of arrested conflict is shown as having been achieved in two other scenes in which the facing lions are now held apart by a male human figure, perhaps a king. The upper example is from the Decorated Tomb at Hierakonpolis (cf. Figure 11, p. 40); the lower is on the Gebel el-Arak knife handle. Photographs of the palette are in W.M.F. Petrie, *Ceremonial Slate Palettes and Corpus of Proto-dynastic Pottery*, London, 1953, Plate F; J.E. Quibell and F.W. Green, *Hierakonpolis* II, London, 1902, Plate XXVIII; M.J. Mellink and J. Filip, *Frühe Stufen der Kunst* (Propyläen Kunstgeschichte, 13), Berlin, 1974, Taf. 208. For the Gebel el-Arak knife handle, see Mellink and Filip, op. cit., Taf. 210; W.M.F. Petrie, 'Egypt and Mesopotamia', *Ancient Egypt* 1917, 29, Fig. 4.

Figure 15 *Above.* The theme (containment of unrule) transferred to a cosmic plane of cyclic rebirth in which the triumphant voyager is the sun-god, here passing in his barque through one of the hours of the night. In the upper register are three beheaded figures identified as 'the enemies of Osiris', and three prostrate figures labelled 'the rebels'. In the lower register the demon of evil, the giant serpent Apopis, is butchered. Part of the Seventh Division of the 'Book of What is in the Otherworld' as painted on the walls of the tomb of King Tuthmosis III in the Valley of Kings at Thebes (*c.* 1430 BC). The cursive hieroglyphic text has been omitted. After A. Piankoff, *The Tomb of Ramesses VI* I, New York, 1954, Fig. 80. Coloured photographs are in J. Romer, *Romer's Egypt*, London, 1982, pp. 170, 173. *Below.* The same theme illustrated by simple allegory from nature. Disorder is symbolized by wild fowl of the papyrus marshes. They are trapped and therefore constrained by a fowler's clap-net operated by King Rameses II and the gods Horus (*left*) and Khnum (*right*). Great Hypostyle Hall at Karnak, inner face of the south wall. Cf. H. Frankfort, *Kingship and the Gods*, Chicago, 1948, Fig. 14.

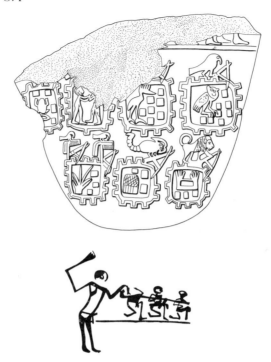

Figure 16 *Above*. One side of the Tjehenu Palette. The main scene, probably of battle, has been lost. The remaining bottom part shows seven fortified towns being attacked by animals symbolizing the monarchy and wielding hoes. The palette presumably celebrated a series of victories in the northward expansion of the kingdom of Hierakonpolis. After W.M.F. Petrie, *Ceremonial Slate Palettes and Corpus of Proto-dynastic Pottery*, London, 1953, Plate G; M.J. Mellink and J. Filip, *Frühe Stufen der Kunst* (Propyläen Kunstgeschichte, 13), Berlin, 1974 Taf. 214b. *Below*. The scene of a warrior brandishing a mace over a line of bound captives is taken from the Decorated Tomb at Hierakonpolis (see Figure 11, p. 40), and probably depicts a Predynastic king in his role of victor in battle.

We are entitled to ask: what was the source of the disorder that made itself felt at this time? It is a common sensation for the people of a settled society to feel surrounded and threatened by a turbulent and hostile outside world (compare Figures 78 and 79, pp. 226 and 227). For the small political units of late Predynastic Egypt the settings were parochial: the alien deserts and neighbouring communities not too far away along the Nile. But the more successful of these communities, the incipient city-states, had become engaged in more organized conflicts over territory, the conflicts which were to lead to the birth of the Egyptian state. The urgent reality of conflict involving attacks on walled settlements and the horrors of the battlefield were sometimes translated into pictorial scenes of actual combat (Figure 16), although the essence of conflict, of disequilibrium, was still viewed in generalized allegorical terms. From the experience of disorder and struggle, the shattering of an earlier equilibrium, arose the perception of a world in conflict, real or potential, between chaos and order. This was to remain a theme of intellectual concern for the rest of Egyptian history, as did the notion that containment (though not ultimate defeat) of disorder and unrule was possible through the rule of kings and the benign presence of a supreme divine force manifested in the

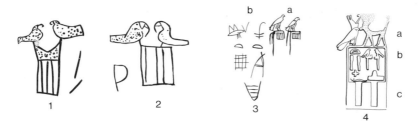

Figure 17 The theme of duality in early royal monograms and names. Nos 1 and 2 (transition to 1st Dynasty) are monograms which represent in a simple way a section of royal palace façade, without adding the king's name (compare Figure 10, p. 38), surmounted in each case by two Horus figures. After J. Clédat, 'Les vases de El-Béda', *Annales du Service des Antiquités de l'Egypte* 13 (1914), Plate XIII; H. Junker, *Turah*, Vienna, 1912, p. 47, Abb. 57. In no. 3 the same two Horus figures (a) accompany the name of King (Adjib) Mer-pu-bia (b) of the 1st Dynasty (after W.M.F. Petrie, *Royal Tombs* I, London, 1900, Plate V.12). No. 4 is a writing of the name of King Khasekhemui of the 2nd Dynasty in which one of the Horus figures has been replaced by a figure of Seth (compare Figure 6, p. 28). After J. Capart, *Memphis à l'ombre des pyramides*, Brussels, 1930, p. 119, Fig. 116.

power of the sun. The intellectual view of the nature of the universe coincided with the structure of political power.

The paired animals are always identical. Even the pair on the Narmer Palette has no distinguishing marks to suggest a wish to identify each one in a distinctive way with one part of the country or a separate kingdom. Political harmony must be there in the meaning, but only as an urgent aspect of the ideal of general harmony in the world that the Egyptians knew.

The paired animals on late Predynastic ceremonial palettes are, none the less, the forerunners of the paired figures of Horus and Seth. The former are the symbols of a general statement; the latter represent a more specific application of the concept and its depiction to the new political circumstances of dynastic Egypt. There is an interesting transitional phase to recognize, too. The earliest depictions of paired figures standing explicitly for the unity of two kingdoms are not figures of Horus and Seth, but two facing figures of Horus, in an archaic form which particularly resembles the specific form of Horus of Hierakonpolis (Figure 17).[47] This is a straightforward adaptation of the paired identical figures on the slate palettes. It recurs occasionally in historical periods, when the two kingdoms can both be represented as an inheritance from Horus.[48]

The cosmic balancing act was not, by itself, enough. Egyptian society of the dynastic period was strongly hierarchical. Harmony within the state flowed down from a single source, the king, through loyal officials to the people. The king's role of maintainer of order was paramount. It covered not only responsibility for justice and piety but also the conquest of unrule. The philosophical texts of the Middle Kingdom depict unrule not only in terms of social upheaval, but also natural and cosmic catastrophe. The final guarantee of harmony in society and in the natural order was not a balancing of opposites. One force had to be superior. We can glimpse this already in one of the vignettes of the Hierakonpolis Decorated Tomb (see Figure 14. Right p. 48). Here the two paired and facing animals (lions in this case) are held apart and balanced by the central figure of a ruler. The introduction of Seth enabled this to be reflected in the eternal verities of theology, and to understand this we must remember that each king was also a particular embodiment of Horus.

Seth becomes the loser, and the antagonist to Horus. He becomes the antagonist to order on a grand scale: celestial disturbance in the form of storms, the hostile nature of the surrounding deserts, the exotic character of foreign gods, even red-headed people – these were expressions of Seth. Yet, as the Shabaka Stone tells us, Seth also acquiesces in the divine judgement against him. He retains the power to be a reconciled force in the ideal balance of harmony.

The myth of Horus and Seth is not a reflection of how the Egyptian state emerged politically. The details of the period of internal warfare among the incipient city-states of the Nile Valley are unlikely ever to be known, but we can safely assume that it was not a simple epic struggle between two protagonists. The myth of the state in historic times was a clever adaptation of an earlier, more generalized statement of an ideal world originating in Upper Egypt. It combined the old concept of an ultimate harmony through balanced opposites with the newly perceived need for a single superior force. It was created as part of the great codification of court culture. It drew upon local mythology, which in the case of both Horus and Seth was centred in Upper Egypt. It became part of the long active interest which the Egyptians maintained in symbolic geography; in effect, a process of internal colonization at an intellectual level.

One further observation needs to be made. The 1st Dynasty began as a state which was territorially as large as most which were to occupy the lower Nile Valley until modern times. There was no long process of growth from a spread of city states, a common early political form which had a thriving history in, for example, Mesopotamia. We have already used the term 'incipient city-state' for territories in southern Upper Egypt centred on Hierakonpolis and Nagada. 'Incipient' seems an appropriate word since they cannot have matched the complexity of contemporary city states in other parts of the Near East. We can be fairly sure of two, and we can suspect that there were others either already in existence (e.g. one based on Thinis) or still at an even earlier stage of formation (perhaps at Maadi and Buto in the Delta, Abadiya in Upper Egypt, and Qustul in Lower Nubia).[49] The internal warfare pursued most vigorously from the south terminated this polycentric period of political growth, but as states everywhere discover sooner or later, regional assertion remains a powerful force even when its centres are submerged within a larger polity. The game goes on. The Pharaonic state was remarkably successful, through the mechanism of symbolic geography, in creating an ideology with numerous provincial ramifications. We can speak of a national framework of myth. Yet submerged local identities remained. The one we see most clearly in the later historic periods (from the 6th Dynasty onwards) is a submerged city-state of Thebes. More will be said on Thebes in Chapter 5. But there were others, in Middle Egypt and the Delta, which in times of weak dynastic rule (basically the three Intermediate Periods) revealed themselves. Sometimes a period of local transcendence left behind it a local aristocracy, able for a while to display the trappings of great authority. Aristocratic tombs and other large buildings in the general areas of Nagada, Hierakonpolis, and Abydos dating to periods later than the political heyday of each one belong to this terminal phase in a common trajectory of local history. It would, all the same, be wrong to try to reconstruct the late Predynastic political landscape from later regionalism, for far too many local changes took place after the beginning of the 1st Dynasty. The rise of Thebes at the expense of Nagada, and of Edfu at the expense of Hierakonpolis, are only particularly striking examples.

Foundations of ideology (3): architecture as political statement

The unification myth was but one aspect of what emerges with the 1st Dynasty as the principal focus of effort, both intellectual and organizational: the projection of kingship as the symbol of power supreme over all others. On the late Predynastic slate palettes conquering figures occur in the form of animals (a lion, a bull, a scorpion, a falcon, see Figure 16, p. 50), which we can take to be symbols of human power, perhaps of a king. But it is only with the Narmer Palette (and Scorpion macehead) that we find figures of human kings to which detailed treatment has been given in order to convey some of their symbolic attributes. When we turn to architecture we find an equivalent process but on a far grander scale. The royal tomb became the principal public statement on the nature of kingship. Changes in royal tomb architecture are thus our most important single guide to the evolution of ancient perceptions of monarchy.

Nagada and Hierakonpolis have provided us with tombs which, by their size, brick linings and, in the case of Hierakonpolis tomb 100, wall paintings, imply royal ownership. They are, none the less, very modest constructions, and it is unlikely that they ever possessed an elaborate superstructure. The 1st Dynasty brought a dramatic change. Against a background of enormously increased tomb size throughout the country, reflecting the greatly increased wealth and organization of the Early Dynastic state, we find the builders of the royal tomb taking the first steps towards monumental scale and distinctive architectural symbolism.

We must now focus our attention on another site: Abydos, a desert cemetery in a district which contained the city (Thinis, probably the modern Girga) which later tradition made the home of the kings of the 1st Dynasty. The kings of the 1st Dynasty, and the last two of the 2nd, were buried in an isolated part, now known as the Umm el-Qa'ab.[50] Their tombs consisted of brick chambers constructed in large pits dug in the desert, covered by a simple superstructure in the form of a plain square enclosure filled to the top with sand and gravel. This was a straightforward evolution from the brick 'royal' tombs at Nagada and Hierakonpolis. Their royal ownership was proclaimed by pairs of free-standing stone stelae bearing the Horus name of the king in question (see Figure 10, p. 38). Each tomb also possessed a second element, a separate building located closer to the edge of the floodplain, and just behind the site of the ancient town of Abydos. The best preserved are the pair from the end of the 2nd Dynasty, especially the last one, the Shunet ez-Zebib, belonging to King Khasekhemui (Plate 2).[51]

The Shunet ez-Zebib is an enclosure measuring 54 by 113 metres internally and 122 by 65 metres externally, surrounded by a double wall of mud brick, pierced by doorways. The inner wall, still standing in places to a height of 11 metres, is a massive 5.5 metres thick. On its outer surfaces it was decorated with niches to give a panelled effect. The panelled facade on the long side facing the cultivation was emphasized by the insertion at regular intervals of an inner, deeper niche. As for the interior of the enclosure, it appears to have been empty except for a free-standing building near the east corner. This contained a nest of rooms in some of which pottery storage jars had

Plate 2   Early royal architecture: the Shunet ez-Zebib at Abydos, mud brick funerary palace of King Khasekhemui of the 2nd Dynasty (*c.* 2640 BC), looking south-east.

been stowed. The outer faces of this building had been decorated in the same panelled style as the great enclosure wall (Figure 18).

Two paths lead us towards the meaning of this building and its companions. One concerns the panelled effect on the outer walls. The most striking examples occur on the façades of large tombs of the Early Dynastic Period (Figure 18B), mostly in the Memphite area (although one famous example is at Nagada).[52] Some examples preserve the lower part of elaborate painted decoration, which reproduces in great detail a way of further decorating the walls: by draping the narrow surfaces between the niches with long strips of brightly coloured matting lashed to horizontal poles. As a standard feature, the panelled surfaces were broken by deep recesses with similarly panelled sides. At the back of each recess stood a broader niche, painted red, apparently to signify the wooden leaf of a door. The whole design of panels, recesses, and applied matting patterns became a fixed scheme of decoration on later sarcophagi and offering-places in tomb chapels, and these supply us with the details missing from the upper parts of the Early Dynastic tombs.

The design occurs in another context, too. A narrow section of it formed the basis for the heraldic device in which the Horus name (the principal name) of Early Dynastic kings was written (see Figure 10, p. 38). From this it was long ago deduced that the architectural style belonged specifically to the royal palace. Scholars coined the term 'palace façade' for the architectural style. It was only in 1969, however, that an actual stretch of wall decorated in this style was found which was not part of a tomb. It lay in the centre of the Early Dynastic town of Hierakonpolis, and surrounded a gateway (see Figure 11, p. 40). Although nothing of the inner building has been found, and the size of the whole enclosure is not known, the identification of this wall as part of a real Early Dynastic palace enclosure seems inescapable.

The Hierakonpolis wall, the Shunet ez-Zebib, and the frame around the king's Horus name reveal that the Early Dynastic kings adopted the niched and decorated façade as a symbol of power. It denoted by itself the idea of 'palace' as a ruling entity, and for those who were part of the court – the palace elite surrounding the king and administering his power – it was permissible to use a scaled-down version to decorate their own tombs. By its distinctive and imposing style early monumental architecture in Egypt set up a barrier between king and people.

For the second path we must turn to a monument which in time is only a generation later than the Shunet ez-Zebib, but which belongs to another plane of architectural achievement: the Step Pyramid at Sakkara, tomb of Djoser, the first (or second) king of the 3rd Dynasty (c. 2695 BC).[53] It is the first building of truly monumental scale in Egypt, constructed throughout of stone. In its detailing it also contains many of the basic decorative motifs of Pharaonic architecture. It represents, in architecture, a major act of codification of forms such as had occurred in art around the beginning of the 1st Dynasty.

The Step Pyramid confronts us with a major problem of interpretation. It has many distinctive parts, each of which must have held a particular meaning. However, very little of it bore any figured or written decoration to declare its meaning explicitly. For much of it we have to rely upon interpretations derived from far later sources, principally the Pyramid Texts. By this time, however, pyramid layouts had changed radically, and so, too, must have the meanings of the various parts. There is thus, for example, no obvious and agreed answer to the basic question: why a stepped pyramid? By the time of the Pyramid Texts the true pyramid had long replaced it, and so, presumably, had a different symbolism which made a strong link with the cult of the sun centred at Heliopolis. A similar blank answer honestly attends the question: why is there a second, miniaturized tomb built within the southern enclosure wall of the Stepped Pyramid, the so-called Southern Tomb?

Fortunately not all of this amazing monument is mute. Djoser's Step Pyramid stands at the centre of a rectangular enclosure, 278 by 545 metres (Figure 19). It was

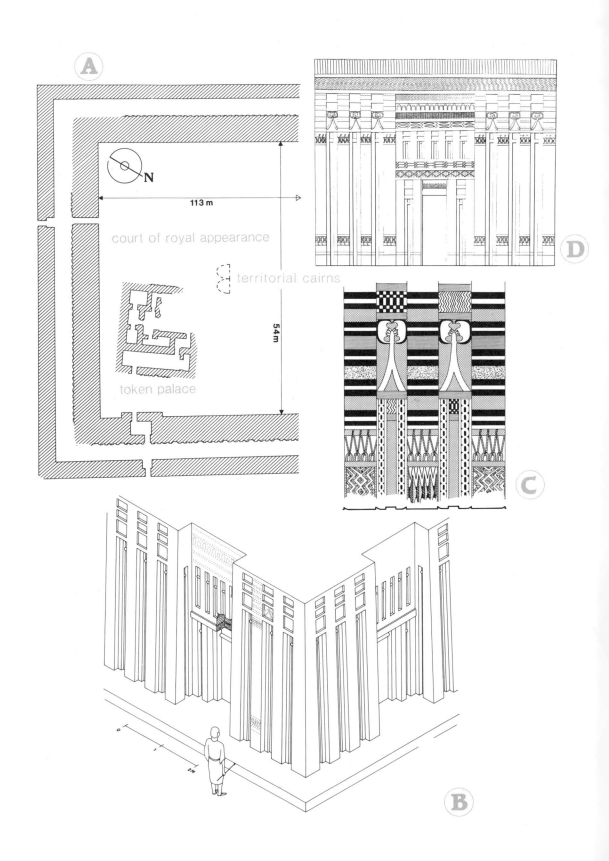

court of royal appearance

territorial cairns

113 m

54 m

token palace

N

surrounded by a thick stone wall with external towers, the façade carved with a simpler and modified version of the palace façade style. The one true entrance is at the south-east corner, and in the general design of the whole complex we can still recognize the basic shape of the Shunet ez-Zebib at Abydos. Across the centre of the enclosure extends a huge open inner space, a rectangle measuring 108 by 187 metres, faced by panelled walls. At each end stood originally a pair of stone horse-shoe-shaped cairns, and immediately in front of the pyramid a stone platform reached by steps faced down along the alignment of the cairns. This arrangement of cairns and stepped platform is known from Early Dynastic scenes. In one of them, on a macehead of the reign of Narmer (Figure 20), we can see that the setting appears to be in use for reviewing the livestock and prisoners captured in a battle. In another, a label of the reign of the 1st Dynasty King Den, the king appears twice: once on the stepped throne beneath an awning, and once actually on the arena running or striding between the groups of cairns. This latter element is one of two subjects of scenes actually carved within the Step Pyramid complex itself. Two groups of three carved panels occur at the backs of imitation doorways in underground corridors beneath the Southern Tomb and the Step Pyramid proper.[54] Some of the panels show Djoser performing this very ceremony of striding or running between the cairns, accompanied by other symbols. The shape of the cairns can be clarified by later references, as can one of the prominent groups of symbols. They are markers of territorial limits.[55] Later sources also tell us that the arena itself was called simply 'the field', and that the ceremony was termed either 'encompassing the field', or 'presenting the field', with the emphasis then on the dedication of the arena to a god, although this element is not apparent from the early depictions.

One of the general needs of monarchy (and of other forms of state leadership) is a formal setting for the display of the leader in person, either to the public at large or to the select representatives who compose the court. In later times the Egyptian sources make much of the 'appearance of the king', and we should anticipate that each age sought a dramatic setting for this great moment, built around certain basic elements: a large open space, an elevated place where the king could be seen within a formal framing, and a token palace where robing and resting could comfortably and privately take place. In Chapters 5 and 7 the elaborate devices adopted by the New Kingdom Pharaohs for displaying themselves will be described and we shall find settings of just this kind. The early sources, both pictorial and architectural, also combine to satisfy

Figure 18   The royal style of architecture in the Early Dynastic Period. (A) South-east sector of the Shunet ez-Zebib at Abydos (Plate 2, p. 54; reign of Khasekhemui, late 2nd Dynasty, c. 2640 BC). The position of the territorial cairns is hypothetical. After E.R. Ayrton, C.T. Currelly, and A.E.P. Weigall, *Abydos* III, London, 1904, Plate VI. Note the simplified 'palace façade' niched style of brickwork on external surfaces. For a section of real (as distinct from funerary) palace wall see Figure 11, p. 40, from Hierakonpolis, also Figure 10, p. 38. (B) Reconstruction of part of the façade of a 1st Dynasty court tomb, reproducing in miniature the 'palace façade' architecture of court buildings. (C) The reconstruction of the elaborate designs – largely painted – on the upper parts is based on later reproductions on sarcophagi and tomb chapel offering-places. This example derives from the 5th Dynasty tomb of Tepemankh at Abusir, after J. Capart, *L'Art égyptien I: L'architecture*, Brussels and Paris, 1922, Plate 46, itself derived from L. Borchardt, *Das Grabdenkmal des Königs Ne-user-re*, Leipzig, 1907, Blatt 24. (D) A further example, a carved 4th Dynasty sarcophagus from Giza, tomb of Fefi, after S. Hassan, *Excavations at Gîza (1929–1930)*, Oxford, 1932, Plate LXV.

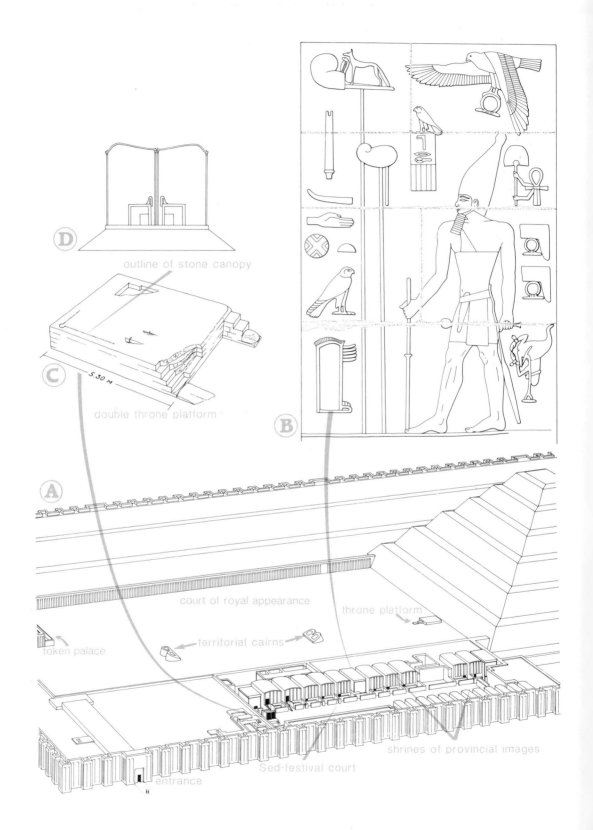

D

outline of stone canopy

C

5.30 M

double throne platform

B

A

court of royal appearance

throne platform

token palace

territorial cairns

shrines of provincial images

Sed-festival court

entrance

this demand exactly. We have to imagine that an important part of an Early Dynastic king's palace was a huge enclosed arena or plaza, equipped with cairns which symbolized territorial limits and with an elevated throne dais shaded by a canopy of distinctive shape (this latter element present already in one of the boats in Hierakonpolis tomb 100) at one end, and a token palace at the other. It was used as the setting for major royal occasions, such as the reception of tribute, and for a particular ceremony in which the king laid claim to his territory by striding forcefully around its limits. The Shunet ez-Zebib at Abydos and the great plaza in front of the Step Pyramid are full-scale replicas which provided the king with the necessary setting for his own pageantry for the eternity of death.

This is not, however, the end of the story. There is another element to the essential ritual of early kingship, a periodic celebration which the Egyptians termed the *Sed*-festival.[56] Sources from early times onwards make the *Sed*-festival a great jubilee celebration of the king's earthly rule over a period which was ideally thirty years, although second and third celebrations could subsequently take place at shorter intervals. The way that the festival was conducted changed over time, and so, probably, did the meaning. It is tempting with Egyptian religion to combine sources from all periods in order to create a comprehensive explanation for a particular ritual or belief because the pictorial forms tended to remain constant. But continuity of forms masked changes in meaning and practice. Inventing traditions was something that the Egyptians were very good at. For each period the sources should be interpreted within the spirit and for the illumination of that age alone.[57] Two aspects seem more than any other to have characterized the *Sed*-festival. The king, often wearing a distinctive robe, sits on a special dais provided with two thrones for an appearance as King of Upper Egypt and of Lower Egypt. The thrones are normally shown back to back, but this may be an artistic device for rendering a pair which were actually side by side.[58] More elaborate scenes, later than the Early Dynastic Period, give as the setting for this ceremony a series of shrines pictured as constructions of wood and matting. The origin and meaning of this style of architecture will be explored in the next chapter: basically this form of shrine originated as a type of temporary building, and in this context represented another pair of dual symbols, with one design for Lower Egypt and one for Upper Egypt. Sometimes they were specifically for the cobra-goddess Wadjit of the Delta town of Buto, and the vulture-goddess Nekhbet of el-Kab. But they were for other deities as well. This gathering of provincial images of deities in a series of

Figure 19 Political architecture. (A) Reconstruction of the southern part of the Step Pyramid of King Djoser at Sakkara, eternal plaza of royal display and setting for the *Sed*-festival (cf. Plate 4, p. 71), after J.-Ph. Lauer, *La pyramide à degrés*, Cairo, 1936, Plate IV. (B) Scene of King Djoser proceeding to visit the temporary shrine of Horus of Behdet. The column of hieroglyphs in front of the king reads: 'Halting (at) the shrine of Horus of Behdet.' The last sign is actually a picture of a temporary shrine of the kind modelled in stone around the *Sed*-festival court at the Step Pyramid. Northern stele beneath the Step Pyramid at Sakkara, after C. M. Firth and J.E. Quibell, *The Step Pyramid* II, Cairo, 1935, Plate 17, and A.H. Gardiner, 'Horus the Behdetite', *Journal of Egyptian Archaeology* 30 (1944), Plate III.4. (C) Stone platform with double staircase as found at the southern end of the *Sed*-festival court in the Step Pyramid (cf. Plate 4, p. 71), after Lauer, op. cit., Plate LVI.1 and p. 145, Fig. 146. (D) Ancient representation of the double throne dais with canopy as used at the *Sed*-festival, based on a carved lintel of King Senusret III (12th Dynasty), as reproduced in K. Lange and M. Hirmer, *Egypt: Architecture, Sculpture, Painting in Three Thousand Years*, third edn, London, 1961, pp. 102–4.

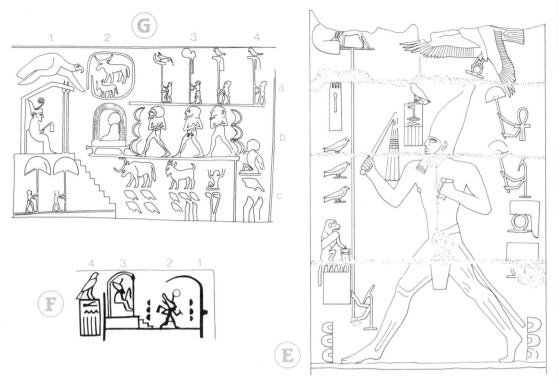

Figure 20 Ritual of territorial claim. (E) Scene of King Djoser running (or striding) across the ceremonial arena between the two sets of territorial marker cairns. In front of the king is the standard of the god Wepwawet, and a vertical column of hieroglyphs, the meaning of which is somewhat obscure. The literal translation is 'The Great White Ones', a plural reference to a baboon god whose picture forms part of the last hieroglyph. The first element in the name, however, is also a word for a shrine, evidently a 'White Shrine'. It has been suggested that the baboons in question are images of ancestral spirits, though this is only a hypothesis. See W. Helck and E. Otto, *Lexikon* II, pp. 1078–80; A. Erman and H. Grapow, *Wörterbuch der aegyptischen Sprache*, Leipzig, 1926–31, III, 209.6; H.W. Fairman, 'Notes on the alphabetic signs employed in the hieroglyphic inscriptions of the Temple of Edfu', *Annales du Service des Antiquités de l'Egypte* 43 (1943), 260–61; A.J. Spencer, *Catalogue of Egyptian Antiquities in the British Museum V, Early Dynastic Objects*, London, 1980, pp. 13, 16, no. 16, Plates 8, 9; G. Dreyer, *Elephantine VIII. Der Tempel der Satet. Die Funde der Frühzeit und des Alten Reiches*, Mainz, 1986, p. 69. Behind the king is a pair of symbols used to write a word (*mdnbw*) meaning 'limits'. Central stele beneath the Step Pyramid at Sakkara, after C. M. Firth and J.E. Quibell, *The Step Pyramid* II, Cairo, 1935, Plate 16. (F) Part of a wooden label of King Den of the 1st Dynasty from his tomb at Abydos, to be read from right to left: 1) the sign for 'regnal year' (cf. Figure 5, p. 23); 2) the king running between the territorial cairns; 3) the king appearing seated beneath a canopy upon a stepped throne dais; 4) Horus name of King Den. After W.M.F. Petrie, *Royal Tombs* I, London, 1900, Plates XI.14, XV.16. (G) Part of a scene from a ceremonial macehead of King Narmer, 1st Dynasty, from Hierakonpolis. It depicts a ceremonial appearance of the king on the stepped and canopied throne dais (1), accompanied by bearers of the 'Followers of Horus' standards (3a, 4a, cf. Figure 12, p. 42). The occasion is evidently the review of prisoners (2b-4b, 4c) and animals (2a, 3c, 4c) captured in battle. The many small signs in line 'c' are numerals. Note the seated figure (divine image?; 2b) in a portable carrying chair with curved canopy (cf. Figure 33, p. 93). A particularly significant element is the way that the human captives are paraded between the territorial cairns. After J.E. Quibell, *Hierakonpolis* I, Plate XXVI.B.

Plate 3 Provincial tradition: Preformal mud-brick temple at Elephantine in its late Old Kingdom phase, looking south-west. From G. Dreyer, *Elephantine VIII. Der Tempel der Satet*, Mainz, 1986, Taf. 2a. By courtesy Philipp von Zabern.

temporary shrines beside the double throne of the king was a gesture of provincial homage to the person of the king. The other element specifically associated with the festival after the 3rd Dynasty is the ceremony of laying claim to the 'field' by striding around the cairns. At some time, therefore, this separate and presumably more frequent ceremony was absorbed into the pageantry of the *Sed*-festival.

Again the Step Pyramid clarifies the picture. Beside the great arena with cairns is another but quite separate part of the complex. This runs along the east side of the main enclosure and consists of a series of mostly solid, dummy buildings arranged along both sides of a court (Plate 4). They have a very distinctive appearance: a series of small rectangular structures, with exterior detailing which creates in solid, full-scale, three-dimensional architecture the shapes of the temporary shrines which were envisaged as constructed of timber and matting. They are, in fact, representations of the very kind of buildings which later scenes show gathered for the *Sed*-festival. This seems to be their meaning at the Step Pyramid, too. For at one end of the court is a square throne dais with two flights of steps, originally covered with a little stone building. It is hard to escape the conclusion that this was a rendering in stone for eternity of the double-throne dais covered with a special canopy, and that this part of the Step Pyramid complex gave King Djoser the eternal setting for the periodic *Sed*-festival. Scenes of the king visiting the various shrines form the other subject of the carved panels in the underground galleries (see Figure 19, p. 58).

We can now better appreciate the meaning of the architecture of early royal tombs, of which the Step Pyramid is the most complete and elaborate. They provided an arena for the eternal pageantry of kingship as it was experienced on earth – the king as supreme territorial claimant: protected within its distinctive palace enclosure, the focus of rituals centred on his actual person.

With the 4th Dynasty the form of the royal tomb changed dramatically. The stepped pyramid became a true pyramid, and instead of occupying the middle ground of a great complex of other buildings, it towered at the end of a linear architectural sequence which stretched down to the edge of the alluvial plain (Figure 21). The great enclosed arena or plaza of the royal appearance and the special *Sed*-festival architecture all vanish. In their place comes a temple intended primarily for an offering-cult for the king's spirit via an offering-place on the east side of the pyramid, and via a group of statues. These elements had been present in Djoser's complex, but now they were dominant. *Sed*-festival scenes occur on walls, but alongside other themes. The true pyramid was a symbol of the sun (another aspect of the great codification discussed in the next chapter), and there is other evidence from the 4th and especially the 5th Dynasties to show that serious intellectual consideration – theology – was paying more attention to the power of the sun as the supreme force. The prominent title of kings, 'Son of Ra', appears first at this time.

The 4th Dynasty and later pyramids convey a new image of kingship. Gone is the raw power of a supreme territorial ruler. The king is now sublimated into a manifestation of the sun-god. Architecture conveyed this fundamental reappraisal to the greatest possible effect.

The social and economic climate in which the early Egyptian state arose still remains sketchily documented. We can recognize as a general background a relatively egalitarian farming society settled in low-density villages and larger settlement areas spread through the Nile Valley and Delta during the fourth millennium BC. Local identities and community leaders emerged, but at a pace and on a scale which varied from place to place. Inherent in the nature of the process was that local variations which were initially quite small were amplified on an ever-increasing scale. This became an exponential rate of growth for the most successful, which culminated in a single state by the end of the Predynastic Period. Those involved in this final phase of dynamic growth and terminal competition already perceived the consequences of power on a grand scale and codified its expression in distinctive intellectual form. This cleverly fused together a generalized concept – the superiority of a locally derived order over a universal chaos – and the position of a single king whose power as earthly territorial ruler was expressed in monumental architecture, in ritual, and in symbolic art. As a set of ideas and ideals for legitimizing the rule of a king over his subjects it was to survive

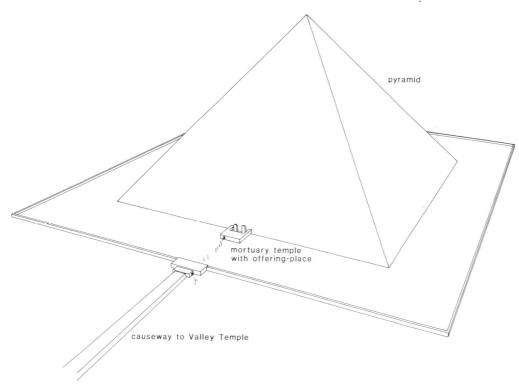

pyramid

mortuary temple
with offering-place

causeway to Valley Temple

Figure 21   The apotheosis of kingship. The pyramid of Medum (reign of King Huni, end of the 3rd Dynasty, *c.* 2575 BC) was the first of the new generation of pyramid tombs which conveyed a radically different view of the nature of the monarchy. In place of a tomb which celebrated the king as supreme territorial claimant and perpetuated his earthly pageantry (Figure 19, p. 58), the new-style pyramids proclaimed his absorption into the mystic symbol of the sun. The tiny offering-temple was the principal gesture to his human aspect. Later pyramid complexes softened this stark contrast in scale between pyramid and temples.

the ups and downs of political history for 3,000 years. It also left the Egyptians incapable of visualizing the polycentric pattern of their own early political growth. Whenever political fragmentation reappeared it seemed to be a fall from the original ideal but (as we can now see) quite mythical state of things. And as the next chapter will show, a parallel erection of a myth world shut the Egyptians off from their cultural beginnings.

2
The dynamics of culture

If I visit the pyramids of Giza or the decorated temples and tombs at Luxor I am aware immediately of facing a distinctive creation of mankind. I will feel the same when in the presence of a medieval mosque in Cairo or a castle or cathedral in Europe. All are products of great and distinctive traditions of culture. They leave conveniently different images in the mind. When, on the other hand, as an archaeologist I excavate amidst the dwellings of one of ancient Egypt's poorer communities, the distinctiveness is much less. The men from the local village whom I employ to do the digging will see the outlines of human life not too different from their own: here the kitchen, there the cattle byres. The ordinariness and predictability can be discouraging. I have to remind myself that culture and environment are never the same from place to place and from time to time, and that the search for variation within the broad regularities of human life is an essential part of understanding the complete spectrum of human behaviour.

'Great culture', which in time becomes tourist culture, was not the spontaneous creation of the common man. It is no accident that we meet its manifestations in large religious buildings, in palaces, mansions, and castles. Great culture, which requires patronage and the direction of labour, originates in courts. The wealth, size, splendour, craft standards, and intellectual novelties are part of the instruments of rule. When well established, a great tradition may have an influence which is felt throughout society. But to reach this stage it has to expand at the expense of other traditions. It has to colonize the minds of the nation. Whatever does not succumb becomes 'folk culture'.

Ancient Egypt is amongst the earliest of the world's great cultural traditions. We are fortunate in being able to observe, through a relative abundance of material, the great codification of tradition by which it started at the time of transition to the 1st Dynasty. It had, however, a very restricted scope in the beginning. The objects were themselves small in size, and were probably very limited in numbers. They expressed the pretensions of a new generation of rulers, and the beginnings of an attempt to systematize religion. But should we assume that, from this moment on, all cultural expression in material form took its cue from this source? Did the 1st Dynasty kings throw a cultural switch which instantly lit up the whole country? Was there the will, or the means, or even the interest to convert the whole country to this intellectual outlook?

To answer these questions we must investigate how court culture expanded at the expense of other local traditions, and consider not only early works of art, but also the general archaeological record in which we might find traces of 'folk culture'.

Conventionally the art historian ignores this issue. He selects the best pieces and finds that his material, drawn mainly from cemeteries of the elite, provides him with a record of continuous development in which geographical homogeneity is also prominent. From this perspective, which focuses on national achievement and takes a close interest in changes of style in the most accomplished art and architecture of the age, this material does provide a generally most satisfactory basis for writing a history of Egyptian 'high' culture. From prehistoric times, a single line of progress can be followed from the late Predynastic cultures of Upper Egypt, through the Early Dynastic Period, to the full flowering of Pharaonic culture in the Old Kingdom. Late Predynastic artistic achievement comes to us as a series of isolated objects, small in scale, individual in expression. Its culminating product is the Narmer Palette from the very beginning of the 1st Dynasty (c. 3100 BC). From this phase of great creativity emerged an academic visual art which successfully moulded the form of Pharaonic culture to the very end, and just as successfully has influenced modern appreciations of ancient Egypt. Hieroglyphic writing, statuary, and two-dimensional art became aspects of a single, rigidly studied mode of visual expression. Religious iconography was an integral part of this process, in which many of the gods were reduced to variants of a single image. This was the achievement of the Early Dynastic Period. Subsequently the Egyptian impetus for innovation turned to monumental architecture, culminating in the pyramids and their temples. In the eyes of the art historian the lights were indeed switched on in the Early Dynastic Period. Later dynasties added to their number and luminosity.

Early shrines as autonomous centres of culture

The simple unilinear model of a national cultural transformation from the tentative products of prehistory to the achievements of a Great Tradition serves the art historian well. Its weakness is that it fails to incorporate adequately the archaeological record of a group of significant sites. They are concentrated in Upper Egypt, but this may be coincidence. All are early temple sites. They introduce features which do not fit comfortably into a simple unilinear scheme. They suggest that, in the provinces, the great transformation was a matter of fitful court patronage applied to a scene that was changing only very slowly from the patterns of late prehistoric times. In local religion – in art as well as in architecture – old parochial traditions, more diverse, more informal, more intuitive and personal, and generally, to our own eyes, far less sophisticated, continued to remain strong. One by one they became subject to court initiatives, and these replaced local diversity with uniformity in the style that we are most familiar with from Egypt. But this process was a slow one, and had not been completed by the beginning of the Middle Kingdom (c. 2040 BC).

For an evaluation of the varying rate of change, the existing nomenclature is something of a hindrance. It is tied strictly to the course of Egyptian dynastic history, transferring to art and archaeology the major division between prehistory and history

(Predynastic *vis-à-vis* Early Dynastic or Archaic), and then the further divisions of political historians. The material in question, however, lacks the sensitive stylistic points which we can perceive in court art, and so fails to acquire the labels of precise dates. It consequently fails to find its proper place in a historical account of early Egyptian culture. If it is to escape from this limbo and find a status of its own, a new term is required which places this material in the cultural sequence of Egypt, without subordinating it to the inflexible progression of kings and dynasties. The term used here is 'Preformal'. It covers the products of the Predynastic Period, together with later material still in this tradition which runs well into the historic period. Some of the material is artistic, some is architectural, and both had their centres in local temples. It should also be noted that Preformal shrines were not replaced immediately by temples in the familiar architectural style of ancient Egypt. Evidence has been slowly accumulating for some time that the 'typical' stone temple of the New Kingdom so favoured by modern textbooks had been preceded by an earlier phase of local temple building, smaller in scale, often employing limited stonework set into an architectural framework of mud brick, and on the whole much simpler in form. The term used here for this phase is 'Early Formal'. With the New Kingdom came the 'Mature Formal' temple, and finally the 'Late Formal' temple absorbed much energy in the period between the 30th Dynasty and the earlier part of the Roman occupation of Egypt.

Having set out a scheme, a group of sites from Upper Egypt will be examined according to its terms.

Medamud

We will begin with Medamud. Here we can find, from the superimposed layers of architectural foundations, the four main periods of temple building. Furthermore, the first building period immediately challenges our preconceived images of Pharaonic culture. Medamud was a provincial town with a temple lying 5 km north-east of Karnak at Thebes. In historic times it was the cult centre for the falcon-god Menthu. The 18th Dynasty saw the erection of a new all-stone temple in the Mature Formal style. In the Graeco-Roman period a broad courtyard in stone in Late Formal style was added to the front, with a double colonnade. A stone wall had extended back from this to embrace the whole sacred precinct. Beneath this stonework and on the south side of the enclosure, excavations in the 1930s revealed a layer of mud brick foundations. No final report on the last and most vital seasons, those of 1938 and 1939, has been published, but one preliminary report does contain a general plan (Figure 22).[1] It represents a rectangular enclosure with external dimensions of 95.5 by 60 metres. The girdle wall was 5.5 metres thick. One entrance lay through the middle of the east side. The interior was densely built up with rectangular units, carefully pre-planned in the formally rigid style of the Middle Kingdom (see Chapter 4). Only the foundations have been preserved, below threshold level, so that the positions of doorways have been lost. Thus whilst we can distinguish individual units we cannot tell how their individual rooms communicated with one another. In general they seem to be surrounded by a more or less continuous street running along the base of the wall, as in the Middle Kingdom fortresses constructed in Lower Nubia (see Chapter 4). On the south a perpendicular street separates two individual blocks. A third, to the north, covers the full width. The streets were provided with limestone drains running along the centre line.

The space to the north is unfortunately the part where the later temple building was concentrated, destroying most of the brickwork of this level. The Middle Kingdom temple at Medamud had evidently stood in this location, but we have no direct evidence for its plan. Many stone architectural elements of this date, reused in later constructions, had been discovered during earlier seasons of excavation. These included columns, Osirid royal statues, door elements, and statues. Many blocks came from two huge portals which may have stood in the brick enclosure wall. As far as one can tell from the reports, however, there is insufficient masonry to account for a Middle Kingdom temple whose walls were of stone block construction. The walls would have been mostly of mud brick. The excavators produced a reconstructed plan of the complex, which includes a ground plan of the temple, and this has passed into textbooks. It seems to contain, however, a great deal of personal interpretation, and in Figure 22 (p. 68) the plan of actual remains has been preferred. The excavators recognized, none the less, that the southern part must have consisted of storerooms and houses for the temple community. They also drew attention to its fortress-like appearance, and, indeed, the Nubian forts do supply the closest parallel. We seem to have at Medamud the application to a temple of the powerful bureaucratic building machine of the Middle Kingdom. It is a fine example of the Early Formal phase of temple layout.

This Middle Kingdom intervention had left behind in the underlying ground traces of a yet earlier temple enclosure. This was excavated in 1939, and again is the subject of only a preliminary report.[2] A brick wall had enclosed an irregular, polygonal plot of ground, 83 metres at its widest point. The wall and its associated buildings stood on alluvial soil which had evidently not been built on before, although it contained a few prehistoric implements. The wall had enclosed a grove of trees, which had left burnt remains behind. Within the grove two oval structures had stood, inferred from negative traces on the ground. It was thought they had been simply mounds of soil. A winding corridor of brick passed to a chamber in the centre of each mound, the floors covered with fine sand. The corridors led from a courtyard by means of a vestibule in each case. Pottery supports for offering-basins or incense-burners stood in these vestibules. The courtyard was closed by a wall containing an entrance flanked by two small brick towers, and there is a strong temptation to restore the towers as pylons, so making them the earliest examples from the Nile Valley. Subsequently an outer court was added and the towers were replaced by a new pair further to the north. The emplacements for one flag-pole were in front of each of the new towers, in one case represented by a circular stone support. This outer court contained two rectangular brick pedestals, covered with ashes. We have to consider the possibility that they are equivalents to the podium in the forecourt of the Elephantine shrine (see pp. 94–5).

No inscriptions were found relating to this curious building, but pottery seems to date it to the latter part of the Old Kingdom. There has to be, therefore, the strong presumption that some kind of shrine had stood here even earlier, and that the surviving Preformal temple represents an act of architectural renewal within the dynastic period, made with little reference to court traditions.

This early temple seems to have been built around the architectural symbol of the

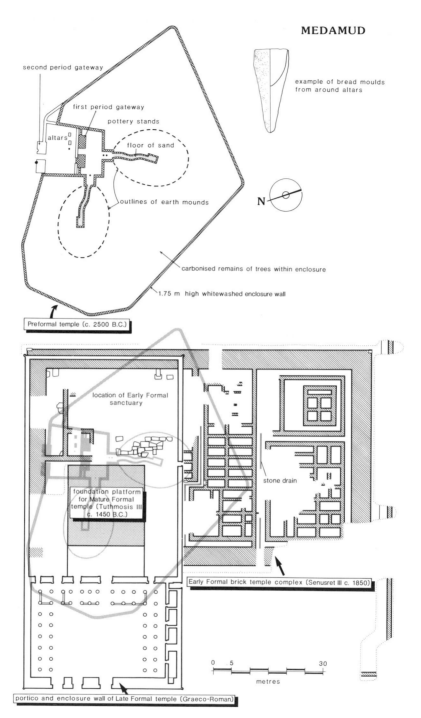

MEDAMUD

example of bread moulds from around altars

second period gateway

first period gateway

pottery stands

altars

floor of sand

outlines of earth mounds

N

carbonised remains of trees within enclosure

1.75 m high whitewashed enclosure wall

Preformal temple (c. 2500 B.C.)

location of Early Formal sanctuary

stone drain

foundation platform for Mature Formal temple (Tuthmosis III c. 1450 B.C.)

Early Formal brick temple complex (Senusret III c. 1850)

0   5   30

metres

portico and enclosure wall of Late Formal temple (Graeco-Roman)

Figure 22 Two-and-a-half thousand years of temple worship: the temple site at Medamud, showing the superimposed layers of architecture. After C. Robichon and A. Varille, 'Médamoud. Fouilles du Musée du Louvre, 1938', *Chronique d'Egypte* 14, no. 27 (1939), 84, Fig. 2; C. Robichon and A. Varille, *Description sommaire du temple primitif de Médamoud*, Cairo, 1940, folding plan at end.

mound. It is possible to interpret this in terms of the unifying theology of later times, which took the concept of the primeval mound which had first appeared above the waters of chaos as a symbolic source of regenerative power, including new life beyond the grave. But no inscriptions link this particularly to Medamud, and, as always, we should be cautious in making interpretations using sources from much later times. It still remains the most striking example of Preformal architecture from Egypt. Its date, well within the historic period, is an important reference-point for other sites. It adds credibility to historic datings for the other material discussed here, and is particularly useful in interpreting the architectural remains at Hierakonpolis.

Elephantine

Recent German excavations at Elephantine have added significantly to our knowledge of this local tendency towards extreme cultural conservatism.[3] This small town site on the southern tip of Elephantine Island was built over a core of natural rounded granite boulders. Its development as a town seems to have occurred during the early Old Kingdom. In 1972–3 a shrine serving this early town was discovered (Figure 23, Plate 3). It lay on the north side, in amidst the boulders themselves. This particular setting has provided archaeology with a so far unique set of circumstances. At other temple sites, on flatter ground, the rebuilding and enlargement of temples in later periods inevitably did much damage, and sometimes wrought havoc, to the earliest shrines. Not so at Elephantine. The builders of later temples, in seeking to escape the space restrictions created by the boulders surrounding the early site, simply filled the site in, and then paved it over, so sealing the early shrine and its associated floors and artefacts. The resulting archaeological record gives us, for the first time, a fairly complete picture of what an early local shrine looked like, and helps to solve more than one problem.

The first sanctuary was set in a corner at the back of a squarish space occupying the natural niche between the boulders. What the object of veneration was is not known. Nor did the cult leave any marks on the actual rock faces, which seem to have been left in their natural state. But whatever the cult image was, it was protected by two small brick rooms. The space in front was enclosed by further brick walls to create a courtyard, or just possibly a roofed hall. The date of this earliest phase is within the Early Dynastic Period, although some of the pottery found is Predynastic.

The basic form of the shrine – a niche in the rock served by modest brick shelters – was kept throughout the Old Kingdom, and apparently on until the time of the reunification of Egypt in the 11th Dynasty (c. 2040 BC): a period of six centuries. Over this time the principal changes were to replace the small shrine with a partition wall across the whole rock niche, and to provide a larger forecourt or hall, increasing generally the thickness of the walls. In the centre of the forespace stood a square pedestal, 0.95 by 1.1 metres, constructed from layers of brick separated by layers of matting for extra strength. A wooden pole stood against each corner. As will be argued in a later section of this chapter, this could have been a canopied podium (facing north) to support a portable divine image (see Figure 33, p. 93). The whole little complex was then protected by an outer corridor and second wall.

In the 11th Dynasty an entirely new shrine was laid out, employing areas of decorated stone. From what little direct evidence survived, its plan seems to have been a

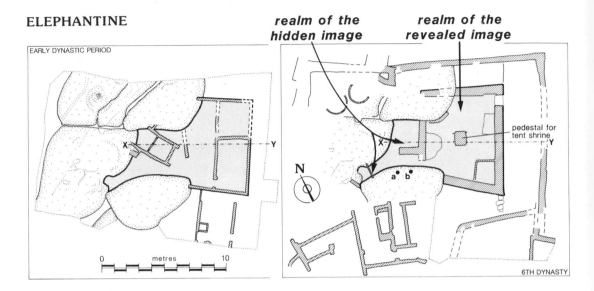

ELEPHANTINE

realm of the hidden image

realm of the revealed image

EARLY DYNASTIC PERIOD

pedestal for tent shrine

metres

6TH DYNASTY

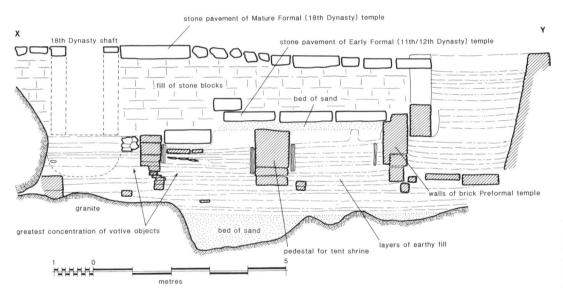

stone pavement of Mature Formal (18th Dynasty) temple

stone pavement of Early Formal (11th/12th Dynasty) temple

18th Dynasty shaft

fill of stone blocks

bed of sand

walls of brick Preformal temple

granite

greatest concentration of votive objects

bed of sand

pedestal for tent shrine

layers of earthy fill

metres

Figure 23 The early shrine at Elephantine, preserved beneath the pavement of the 18th Dynasty temple of the goddess Satis. The two plans at the top record two stages in the architectural evolution of the brick shrine. In the 6th Dynasty plan 'a' is a cartouche of Pepy II, 'b' is a short inscription of Merenra. Below is the section along the line X-Y. For a reconstruction of the pedestal for the portable image, see Figure 33, p. 93. After G. Dreyer, *Elephantine VIII. Der Tempel der Satet*, Mainz, 1986, Abb. 1, 4, 7.

Plate 4   The Step Pyramid of King Djoser, 3rd Dynasty, at Sakkara, looking north-west. In front of the pyramid are the renderings into stone of the tent shrines erected on pedestals, forming part of the *Sed*-festival court. Note the probable double-throne platform in the foreground.

continuation of the existing one. In turn this shrine was replaced at the beginning of the 12th Dynasty by another building using stone. However, to judge from the extent of stone pavement which is all that is left, even the 12th Dynasty temple kept to the same restricted limits as had developed during the Old Kingdom. The appearance of decorated stone blocks marks an application of court patronage, and probably the building of a small temple with mud-brick core in the Early Formal style.

In the 18th Dynasty the site took on a very different aspect. The existing stone shrine was pulled down, the ancient niche and court were filled with blocks of stone to build the level of the ground up to the top of the granite blocks. On this new higher and level surface, a larger stone temple was erected, in the reign of Tuthmosis III (*c*. 1450 BC). The Mature Formal phase had arrived. Yet even at this time the builders tried to maintain some contact with the original sacred ground which they had so thoroughly buried. The new sanctuary was sited over the old one, and direct communication was made by means of a stone-lined shaft which descended through the foundations to the floor of the early sanctuary.

If the simplicity of the early shrine is striking, corresponding to the great age of pyramid building in the north, so also is the relative crudeness of most of the votive objects recovered from the associated floor levels. These seem to relate to a stratum of religious belief and practice separate from the one to which we are accustomed in ancient Egypt. The 'formal' theology which decorates tomb and temple in Egypt does not prepare us for this material, which thus serves in its own right as the main evidence for an aspect of ancient religion. The votive objects were numbered in their hundreds (Figure 24). Many were found scattered in the various levels, but one particular concentration seems to have formed during the 5th Dynasty. Most were made from faience (the shiny blue/green glazed synthetic material which was anciently the equivalent to modern plastic), but pottery, ivory, limestone, and sandstone were used as well. They can be grouped as follows:

1 human figures: both adults and children, the most numerous group being children with fingers at their mouth; a unique figure is the lower part of a seated king, which bears a single sign interpreted as reading the name of the 1st Dynasty King Djer (although from a 6th Dynasty level)
2 baboons/apes, a few also with fingers to mouth
3 a small number of animals and birds, the former including frogs, crocodiles, lion, pig, hippopotamus, cat, and hedgehog
4 oval faience plaques bearing at one end the head of an animal, apparently a hedgehog (forty-one examples of this curious design)
5 faience tiles of the type otherwise used in wall inlays, many with an incised or painted sign on the back
6 faience objects of various forms, mainly large beads, necklace spacers, and model pots
7 natural flint pebbles of curious and bizarre shapes
8 flint knives

In addition to these groups a number of objects were found bearing the names of Kings Pepy I and II of the 6th Dynasty (*c*. 2250 BC). Some of them, perhaps all, were in celebration of the first *Sed*-festival (jubilee) of these kings. One was a vase in the form of a squatting ape holding its young. The remainder were faience plaques (mostly for Pepy I). The 6th Dynasty provided also the only inscriptions found in position: two graffiti of King Merenra and of King Pepy II scratched on one of the granite walls of the niche, the former commemorating a military campaign into Nubia.[4]

This material comes from a series of stratified layers which range through all of the first six dynasties. Yet vertical position does not automatically assign a date of manufacture to an individual piece; it merely shows when it was discarded, and some

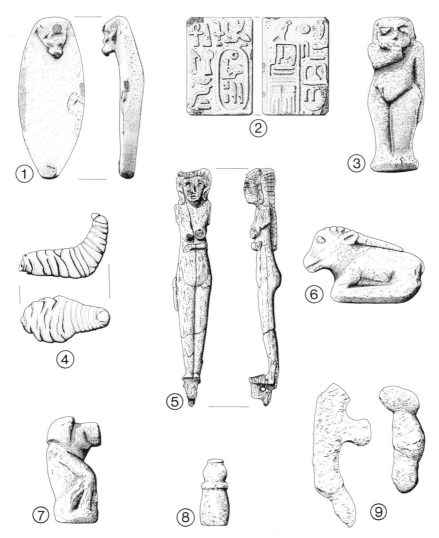

Figure 24 Selection of votive objects from the early temple deposits at Elephantine (*top row*), Hierakonpolis (*middle row*), and Abydos (*bottom row*). (1) Faience plaque with head of hedgehog, height 8.5 cm (after G. Dreyer, *Elephantine* VIII, *Der Tempel der Satet*, Mainz, 1986, Taf. 37.202). (2) Faience plaque commemorating the first *Sed*-festival of King Pepy I, 6th Dynasty, 6.4 by 4.5 by 1.5 cm (after ibid., Abb. 58, Taf. 56.440). (3) Faience figurine of a young girl, height 8.1 cm (after ibid., Taf. 17.42). (4) Faience scorpion with raised tail and sting, length 7.6 cm (after B. Adams, *Ancient Hierakonpolis*, Warminster, 1974, Plate 13.98). (5) Ivory figurine of woman, height 20.4 cm (ibid., Plate 44.360). (6) Faience figurine of kneeling ibex, length 9.4 cm (after J.E. Quibell, *Hierakonpolis* I, London, 1900, Plate XXII.17). (7) Faience baboon, height 18.9 cm (after W.M.F. Petrie *Abydos* II, London, 1903, Plate VI.51). (8) Faience model of pot on a stand, height 6.8 cm (after ibid., Plate XI.244). (9) Two natural flint nodules in suggestive shapes, heights 87.6 and 64.8 cm (after ibid., Plate IX.195, 196). For other early votive objects see Figures 12 (p. 42), 14 (p. 48), 32 (d)–(f) (p. 91), 33 (4) (p. 93).

pieces may have been very old when finally buried in the floor of the shrine. The traditions involved clearly began in the Early Dynastic Period, and set a tone which lasted for a long time. The detailed study of the material piece by piece,[5] however, shows that whilst the Early Dynastic Period is the date for the origination of the style and repertoire of forms, it is not necessarily the date for the manufacture of every piece. The tradition ran on through the Old Kingdom, and at the end the faience plaques bearing the names of 6th Dynasty kings were being produced in the same crude way. A small group of craftsmen attached to the shrine must have met a demand for temple votive objects, retaining forms and techniques over a long period of time, the entire first six dynasties in fact.

One other conspicuous feature of this group of objects, which applies also to similar groups from Hierakonpolis and Abydos, is the absence of representations which can be associated with the local cult deity or deities. Indeed, if we take all the Early Dynastic Period and Old Kingdom material from the Elephantine shrine on its own, it does not tell us to which deity the temple was dedicated at all. The stone blocks from the 11th and 12th Dynasty shrines mention the three local deities which henceforth were the principal ones at Elephantine: Khnum, Satis, and Anukis.[6] Their forms were distinctive: Khnum was a ram, and the others were ladies with unusual head-dresses. Nothing relating to these forms occurs amongst the votive material. The explanation probably involves two factors. One is that Early Dynastic Period formal religion had a range of emphases somewhat different from later times, although the early images themselves were preserved by later tradition, sometimes with changed identifications. The cults of baboons and scorpions are two examples.[7] The other is that whilst the shrine came at some time (presumably in the Old Kingdom) to have a formal dedication recognized by priests and kings, for the local population it served as the focal point for beliefs which had an independent origin and existence of their own. The most likely explanation for the figurines of children, for example, is that they mark an approach to the shrine by a local person before, or after, or in the hopes of, successful childbirth. Beliefs of this kind found no expression in formal theological texts. They are one aspect of the hidden dimension of life and society in ancient Egypt.

Hierakonpolis

During the Old Kingdom a walled town developed over the site of the final nucleus into which the sprawling low-density Predynastic settlement had shrunk (see Figure 11, p. 40). The southern corner of this town was occupied by a rectangular temple enclosure bounded by a mud brick girdle wall (Figure 25). Several periods are represented in a compressed stratigraphy that remains ambiguous.[8] The contents of the enclosure fall into roughly three parts. That on the north-west is largely blank, because the ground had been denuded down to below the main building levels. That in the middle is occupied by part of a dense arrangement of brick walls laid out on a strict rectangular plan, and overlying an artificial mound of sand kept in place by a rough sandstone revetment. That on the south contains fewer remains, but amongst them are most of the pieces that derive from a stone temple of the New Kingdom initially built by Tuthmosis III. It includes the remains of a pair of pylons from an entrance, the brick foundations for columns, and a scatter of foundation deposits. This southern part is the easier of the two archaeological areas to understand. A stone temple had been built here, and the pylons show that it faced north-eastwards, towards the river. As was usually the case, the New Kingdom builders levelled the walls of earlier constructions to make way for their own building. The brick walls of the middle part are at the same level as the 18th Dynasty temple. Are they of the same period? Although their overlap with the 18th Dynasty temple is slight, it does occur, and seems to bear no relationship to it. The whole sequence fits well our general knowledge of temple development if we regard the brick walls of the central part as being the remains of a pre-planned Middle Kingdom layout of temple and all ancillary buildings. This would be, for Hierakonpolis, its Early Formal phase, replaced in the reign of King Tuthmosis III by the Mature Formal stone temple. The developmental sequence is very similar to that at Medamud which, being more reliably dated, helps us to date the various parts at Hierakonpolis.

The centre of the brick complex may well be the actual Middle Kingdom shrine, broader than it is deep. Middle Kingdom parallels can be cited for its characteristics.[9] In the central chamber a brick-lined pit lay in the floor, covered with a basalt slab. The pit contained a complete divine image: a hawk of thin copper plate, with head and plumes of gold (Figure 26).[10] A second deposit was found beneath the floor of the end chamber to the north. This contained two copper statues of Pepy I and of another king of the 6th Dynasty, one of the schist statues of King Khasekhemui of the 2nd, and a fine pottery lion probably of the Early Dynastic Period. These pieces are all in the formal, 'classic' Pharaonic style.

Lying not far away in the ground beneath the walls, but in an ill-defined heap instead of in a pit, was the 'Main Deposit'. Part of it consisted of important artistic material: slate palettes (including the Narmer and Two-dog Palettes (see Figure 12, p. 42 and Figure 14, p. 48), carved maceheads, ivory statuettes, and other ivories carved with designs in relief, a fragmentary limestone statue of King Khasekhemui of the 2nd Dynasty, and stone bowls of the same reign. But numerically preponderant were small objects, often crude in execution. The commonest were maceheads, little shallow alabaster bowls, other vessels in stone and faience including model vessels on tall stands, and animal figurines in various materials: monkeys, including one hugging its young, birds, frogs, hippopotamuses, dogs, a boar, gazelle or ibex, and numerous scorpions or scorpion tails. These latter add a distinctive element to the collection. The parallel with Abydos and Elephantine is very close, and again, the material hardly corresponds with the known divine attribution of the temple, to the falcon-god Horus of Nekhen, the embodiment of early kingship.

The Main Deposit lay beneath the walls of part of the Early Formal temple. Beneath another part of it lay the greater portion of an earlier structure: a circular mound of clean desert sand encased within a sloping wall of rough sandstone blocks. Stratigraphic evidence implies that it was built between a date late in the Predynastic Period and the 2nd or 3rd Dynasty (say 2700 or 2600 BC). Old Kingdom houses had been built around it, but had not encroached upon it, so that it may well have stood in use for a part of the Old Kingdom at least. The universal interpretation of its function is that it was the base for the early temple at Hierakonpolis. Certain pieces of stone found in the vicinity may well have derived from the temple built on the mound and subsequently destroyed to make way for the Early Formal temple. These blocks included a granite door jamb of King Khasekhemui on which was carved a scene of the temple foundation ceremony,[11]

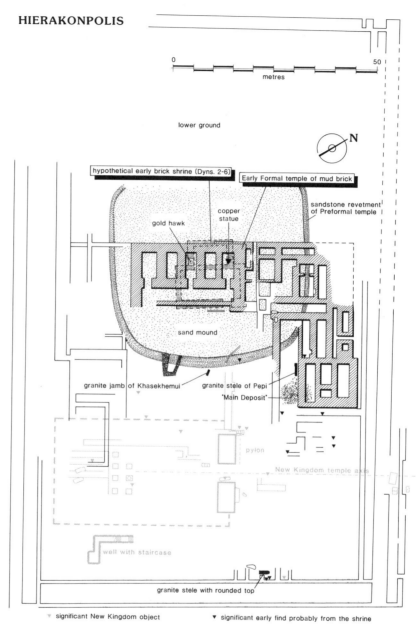

Figure 25 The temple remains at Hierakonpolis (cf. Figures 11, p. 40, and 48, p. 140). The scant remains of the Mature Formal temple (18th Dynasty and later) are in grey. After J.E. Quibell and F.W. Green, *Hierakonpolis* II, London, 1902, Plate LXXII.

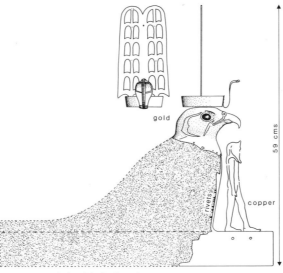

Figure 26 An early divine image: the falcon-god Horus of Hierakonpolis protecting the figure of a king. Originally of wood (now perished), sheathed in copper and with a gold head. Found buried in a pit in the sanctuary of the Early Formal Temple at Hierakonpolis (Figure 25, p. 76). After J.E. Quibell and F.W. Green, *Hierakonpolis* II, London, 1902, Plate XLVII; J.E. Quibell, *Catalogue général des antiquités égyptiennes du Musée du Caire: Archaic objects*, Cairo, 1904–5, Plate 65.

and a column or stele of one of the Kings Pepy of the 6th Dynasty.[12] An unusual piece was a plain, round-topped granite stele, 2.6 metres high, similar to the free-standing stelae which stood in open courts in the mortuary temples attached to certain of the Old Kingdom pyramids (see Figure 30 (3), p. 87, and cf. Figure 21, p. 63).[13] We can have no idea as to the shape of the building which stood on the mound, though it was probably constructed of mud brick and must have been quite small. But the circular mound immediately supplies for it a character alien to our expectations of Egyptian temple architecture. The contents of the temple are similarly alien. We know what they were from the Main Deposit and other buried material just described: a small number of recognizable 'classic' pieces, and a very large number of pieces in the Preformal tradition. Many may have been made in the late Predynastic Period, as were some of the slate palettes, but it is unlikely that all were, especially in view of the new Elephantine evidence.

Abydos[14]

The provincial town of Abydos probably came into existence close to the beginning of the 1st Dynasty. Late in the Old Kingdom the temple site which lay adjacent to the town mound passed through a major phase of rebuilding which represented a step towards formality, though the temple building itself remained a modest one of mud brick (Figure 27). The main emphasis was on creating a new enclosure with girdle wall. On the north-east side, towards the north corner, lay a stone-lined gateway bearing

ABYDOS

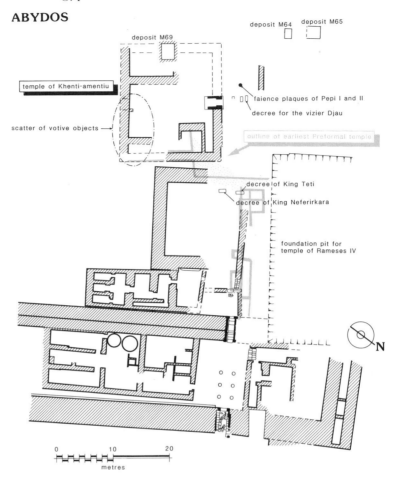

Figure 27 Remains of the early temple of the god Khenti-amentiu at Abydos. The temple stood close to the corner of a heavily walled enclosure, surrounded by storerooms and other buildings. After W.M.F. Petrie, *Abydos* II, London, 1903, Plates L–LIV.

traces of the cartouche of one of the Kings Pepy of the 6th Dynasty. The temple itself was a rectangular building, 18 by 21 metres, with internal subdivisions. It had been built of brick, but its doorway had been lined with stone. Inside it Petrie found a range of votive objects, including faience tablets and alabaster vases bearing the names of Pepy I and II. At a depth of 50 cm beneath the floor was a large deposit of ash and burnt earth containing 'hundreds of little twists of burnt clay'. Similar objects were later found in an apparently Early Dynastic deposit beneath the New Kingdom temple at Armant.[15] The structural remains that could be traced beneath the floor of the Old Kingdom temple consisted of only patches of sand and lengths of thin brick walls that do not join up to form a single coherent building. One part seems to consist of a rectangular courtyard from which a narrow, brick-lined corridor leads off, recalling in a general way the basic ground plan of the Preformal temple at Medamud.[16] A building without heavy construction and very formal design is very much what we should expect.

During these excavations Petrie also discovered several groups of votive figurines. Some had been buried in pits, one of them actually beneath the line of the wall of this late Old Kingdom temple. They consisted of human figurines, made mostly of ivory and faience, a large group of animal figurines mostly of faience, limestone, and ivory, and models of pots, boats, portable shrines, fruits and flowers, practically all of faience (see Figure 24, p. 73). One of the human figurines was a beautiful ivory statuette of a king in jubilee-festival robe.[17] This material shares the same dating problem with the deposits from Hierakonpolis: it was deliberately separated from its context anciently when the temple was rebuilt, and its Preformal style creates an impression of extreme age. It has, however, a close parallel with the material from Elephantine. Some is undoubtedly Early Dynastic, but other pieces probably extend the range into the Old Kingdom. By the time that the temple came to be rebuilt late in the Old Kingdom they were no longer actively required in the temple, so they were carefully buried in the foundations. In the late 11th Dynasty and the reign of Senusret I the temple was rebuilt, employing limited amounts of stonework, presumably set in a mud brick frame. All trace of this building had been destroyed in the rebuilding of the New Kingdom.

One consequence of court patronage and the involvement of the formalizing approach at Abydos was the change in the identity of the god to whom the temple was principally dedicated in the Old Kingdom: from Khenti-amentiu, a local jackal god, to Osiris, whose cult was to take on national significance. This aspect of the cult at Abydos, which exemplifies the recodification of tradition, will be taken up a little later. However, as at Elephantine and Hierakonpolis, the range of votive figures in no way reflects either of these deities who, according to the formal sources of the later Old Kingdom, were principally associated with the temple. One model of a portable divine image shows a figure without any of the characteristics of either Khenti-amentiu or Osiris (see Figure 33(4), p. 93).

It is possible that, in addition to the figurines from Elephantine, Hierakonpolis, and Abydos, a group can be identified from a fourth shrine. It is dispersed amongst several collections of antiquities and derives from an illicit find evidently made in the late 1940s or 1950s.[18] Although the core of the collection has been confidently ascribed to Abydos, other evidence has led to doubts being expressed, and other sites, such as Nagada, remain a strong possibility. This uncertainty, which may never be resolved, illustrates the general character of all of this material: on its own it provides few if any points of reference to local cults as they are known from later sources. Some of the pieces are particularly interesting, being models of tent shrines and, in one case, of a portable divine image (see p. 94 and Figure 33(4), p. 93).

Coptos

The final site of our Preformal group is Coptos, 38 km north-east of Thebes. Again the main source is an early excavation report by Flinders Petrie who dug out the temple area in 1894.[19] Most of the temple masonry had already gone. But the remaining traces suggest a familiar combination: a Ptolemaic portico on the front of a stone temple of Tuthmosis III of the 18th Dynasty – thus 'Late Formal' added to 'Mature Formal'. Unfortunately no earlier architecture was encountered at all. But in the soil beneath and around the temple Petrie uncovered a range of figurines, in stone and in poorly baked clay. They must be seen as products of another local Preformal tradition of votive offerings, and therefore equivalent to the material from Elephantine, Abydos, and Hierakonpolis. Faience was not part of this tradition. In view of the circumstances of finding no clear date can be given, although Petrie claims that Old Kingdom pottery lay in the vicinity. The clay figurines included humans, some of them carefully modelled statues, others 'roughly pinched into form with the fingers, and have details marked with scored lines.'[20] Crocodiles were also modelled. A distinctive class was ring-stands with relief designs. On one the design included hunting dogs and a pair of lotus flowers tied together. In stone were a bird and three lions.[21] The most remarkable objects found were pieces of three colossal statues of a male fertility god or gods, holding a wooden staff or similar object (now missing) in one hand, and an erect penis (carved separately in stone and now also missing) in the other.[22] One of the figures is illustrated in Figure 28, with an attempt at restoring the original appearance, using the battered head which Petrie also found. This restoration gives an original height of 4.1 metres, implying a weight of nearly two tons. The figures wear a broad girdle, and down the right side of each a series of symbols has been carved in relief on a slightly raised panel. They cover a curious range of subjects: a stag's head, *pteroceras* shells, the 'thunderbolt' emblem of the god Min on a pole, an elephant, a hyena, and a bull with feet resting on hills.

If we use Pharaonic art as the yardstick against which to assess these statues they appear strange and primitive in the extreme. The heavily bearded yet bald head and the broad pleated girdle belong to a different tradition from the Pharaonic. The proportions look wrong as the statue has the overall shape of a slightly flattened cylinder. Even the range of signs carved on the sides belongs to a vocabulary of symbols for the most part different from that which surfaces in hieroglyphic writing and court art. The technique of manufacture employed little secondary dressing to smooth away the irregularities of the process of hammering used to make them, although the decay of their surfaces makes them look much cruder than they originally did. Yet the statues communicate powerfully in their own way, and represented to their creators and admirers an emotional and aesthetic satisfaction very different from that of their counterparts and successors at the court.

Petrie found no evidence for the shape of the early temple to which the colossi belonged. But the general view that we have of early local temples makes it highly unlikely that they stood within a roofed building. More likely they were in a courtyard surrounded by a low wall, perhaps on an artificial mound, although substantial foundations would then have been required to hold the ground firm beneath their weight.

The date or dates of this collection of material, including the statues, is difficult to fix within any close or even medium limits. Indeed, the differences may indicate that the group covers a long period (see also p. 347). The lions have been studied in detail and dated on stylistic grounds of some weight to most probably the early 1st Dynasty.[23] But other material hangs in the art-historical limbo that has gathered around so much of it.

The case of the colossal statues illustrates the way in which scholarly arguments are often self-cancelling. Approached from an art history perspective, they are hard to place later than the early 1st Dynasty, simply because the sequence of pieces of sculpture that can be dated as later than this are properly within the Pharaonic style. One specific stylistic point can also be noted: the schematic way of rendering the structure of the kneecaps has a parallel on the Narmer Palette (see Figure 12, p. 42), although

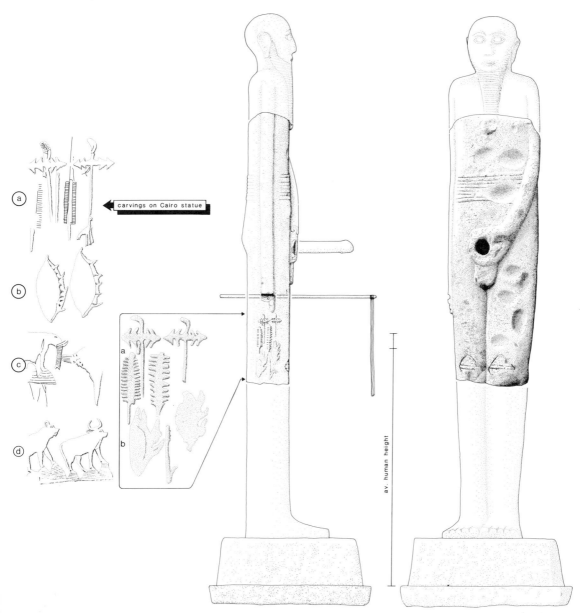

Figure 28 Preformal art on colossal scale: one of the three limestone colossal statues of a fertility god from Coptos. The part consisting of torso and upper legs is in the Ashmolean Museum, Oxford. Its height is 1.9 metres. The head and lower legs with pedestal are restored, although the general form of the head and beard is based on the very battered head from Coptos also in the Ashmolean Museum. The restored height (not including the rough lowest part of the pedestal) is 4.1 metres. The carved signs on the right side are after W.M.F. Petrie, *Koptos*, London, 1896, Plates III, IV. The carvings are identified as follows: a) a pair of standards topped with a 'thunderbolt' emblem and feather alternating with a pair of saw-bones from the Red Sea saw-fish (a small ostrich has been added on the Cairo statue); b) a pair of *pteroceras* shells (a Red Sea mussel, separated by a harpoon on the Ashmolean statue); c) an elephant, its feet resting on conical hills, and a bird (rear part only preserved); d) a hyena and a bull, their feet resting on conical hills.

emphasis of leg and knee musculature is still found in, for example, the 3rd Dynasty panels of King Djoser from the Step Pyramid (see Figures 19, p. 58 and 20, p. 60). However, the Coptos statues are not only pieces of artwork. They are large masses of stone brought from some considerable distance.[24] But if we approach them from the point of view of the history of stone technology in Egypt, we receive a rather different answer. For the quarrying and working of stone on this scale we will otherwise have to wait until the end of the 2nd Dynasty to find parallels. We can counter this argument by pointing to the well-studied case of the colossi on Easter Island in the Pacific Ocean, quarried and erected by people with a technology and organization probably not much different from that of the later Predynastic Period in Egypt. The vital element is the will to do the work: simple technology and communal effort do the rest. Just as the Coptos colossi are exceptional objects for us, so they could have been exceptional to their creators and thus not typical of the general level of stone usage of their day.

Even if we tentatively place their creation towards the beginning of the Early Dynastic Period we will have dealt only partially with their date. We need also to know for how long they were accepted as objects of veneration. The conservative atmosphere of local temples in Upper Egypt, to judge from the archaeological record, could have accommodated them until a royal edict came ordering their replacement, which could have been at almost any time in the Old Kingdom. Furthermore, even after they had been formally abandoned they probably remained a source of power to local people. They bear on their bodies a number of smooth rounded depressions probably from people grinding away to obtain magically efficacious dust. This can only have been done whilst the statues were lying on the ground.

Since their discovery the statues have seemed a particularly alien product of the Nile Valley. Yet that is because we ourselves see them with hindsight, our aesthetics moulded by what, in the end, became the sole significant tradition in art. To those who made and honoured them they must have represented a unique achievement of preferred local traditions.

Much of the Preformal artistic material has been known since the turn of the century (Elephantine excepted). Its discovery made a considerable initial impact, and provoked a book which is still a useful introductory study: J. Capart's *Primitive Art in Egypt*, published in 1905.[25] In Capart's view the stylistic contrast was to be explained by the widespread survival amongst the population at large of an indigenous 'primitive art', alongside a developing 'official art, the art of the masters', introduced by the small group of invading Pharaonic Egyptians who, it was then thought, brought in with them the essential ideas of ancient Egyptian civilization. Although its invasion aspect is no longer acceptable as a historical explanation, Capart's model did at least give to this material a weight that it has since lost. If we replace a superior invading group by an innovative but indigenous court circle then Capart's presentation becomes a reasonable one, although he, too, may have unnecessarily confined too much of the temple votive material to the prehistoric period.

The unilinear model of early cultural development in Egypt – the art history approach – oversimplifies, and in so doing discards evidence that does not fit. The strictly formal approach to design which we identify as quintessentially Pharaonic, and which replaced the more intuitive and less disciplined creations of the Predynastic

Period, was slow in coming to certain provincial corners of dynastic Egypt. The academic court art created during the Early Dynastic Period was not used in a wholesale programme of replacement throughout the country. In provincial temples, buildings and objects either inherited from the past or created in styles of the past continued to hold interest for a long time. The reasons for the slow and piecemeal progress of transformation may well have included limitations in court resources. For a long time they were concentrated on pyramid building and court cemetery construction. Furthermore, the creation ('birth') of a new divine image was an act imbued with great importance, so much so that individual examples were solemnly recorded in early annals as one of the few significant acts of a given year of a king's reign.[26] Yet the main reason must have remained individual preference for the old.

The time-scale is no mean one. The dynastic period must have begun around 3100 BC. The Old Kingdom ended around 2160 BC. Something like a millennium is involved at some of these sites. It means that for about a third of its history, Pharaonic Egypt was a country of two cultures.

The roots of culture

The key to understanding formal Egyptian visual culture – architecture as well as art – and its remarkable homogeneity through 3,000 years lies in the concept of the ideal type. This is a universal characteristic of the mind. We all have an image in terms of our own cultural experience of what, for example, a traditional king should look like, or a desirable residence, or a proper place of worship. Modernism in art and architecture has been directed at breaking ideal types and showing that within the imagination there need be no stereotypes. A different attempt to break stereotypes is found in Islam. God is to have no visual image at all, and is to be encountered through a multiplicity of names. The Egyptians were at the other extreme. The ideal type, the image of what constituted a proper form, was elevated to the pinnacle of intellectual and aesthetic desirability. Because it was centred in the art of the court, the prime source of patronage, it was a self-perpetuating ideal, automatically selecting and promoting those artists with a natural aptitude for absorbing the range of ideal types into their artistic consciousness and skilled in the translation of these types into the precise graphic style that was so preferred. It was a combination of mental aptitude and skill that in the modern world holds a premium in commercial art.

The history of writing in Egypt aptly illustrates the power which visual archetypes had.[27] The first short groups of hieroglyphs used as writing occur at the transition to the 1st Dynasty. The signs are pictures of objects which conform in style to the developing canon of formal art. Properly drawn hieroglyphs were not, however, very suited to the rapid writing that is needed for letters or administrative documents. By the 4th Dynasty, or perhaps before, the Egyptians had developed a more rapid form of writing which we call hieratic (see Figure 39, p. 115, and Figure 41, p. 119, for examples). Individual hieroglyphs were reduced to a few easy strokes of the reed pen, and sometimes run together into groups. Hieratic changed its style over the generations, so that modern scholars can date texts to within certain limits by handwriting. Some good scribes, particularly in the later New Kingdom, developed elegant flourishes in their handwriting. But in no case can we honestly claim that this represents calligraphic art as developed, say, by traditional Islamic or Japanese culture. The reason is simple: the writing which demanded care and attention was hieroglyphic writing. Although more signs were added from time to time the ideal type never changed. It was the accurately delineated natural form as pioneered in the late Predynastic. The artist who wished to lavish his talents on hieroglyphs did so by working harder at the internal details of outlines which it would have been unnatural and improper to change.

The Pharaonic art style is relatively easy to describe,[28] and to judge from the scale of the ancient output, it was relatively easy to pick up, given that there was every incentive to do so. A good artist was amongst the official, scribal class, as the sculptors' workshops in the New Kingdom city of el-Amarna show (see Chapter 7). We can select three essential elements. Whole compositions were given a markedly linear format through subdivision by horizontal lines from which individual figures spring. The resulting bands, or registers, of figures portray themes, but the sequence of registers could contain a more general element of order: of space progressing away from the viewer although no thought was given to diminishing the size of figures with distance; or of time, in a sequence running vertically upwards. The second element, which also relates to overall composition, is the intimate connection between figures and accompanying hieroglyphic writing. Because hieroglyphs retained their original natural forms and were drawn to the same conventions as other elements in a picture, texts and pictures combined harmoniously into a single channel of communication. This is most apparent when signs are worked emblematically into the actions of the scene, as illustrated by the Lisht throne bases (see Figure 6, p. 28). In the Early Dynastic Period hieroglyphs and pictorial groups tended to mingle more equally than later when the balance changed and hieroglyphs became more of a commentary on a dominant pictorial scene.

The third element concerns the conventions of the individual figures, be they humans, animals, or pieces of furniture. Each figure or each major component part of a figure is reduced to a characteristic profile and, if necessary, recombined to produce a composite image which does not offend common sense too much. For an ox the reduction was into three parts: side profile of the body, front profile of the eye, and front profile of the horns. The human body was similarly treated. For birds the shape of tail feathers was profiled as if seen from above.

Because of the limited subject matter and format of Egyptian art, both wall scenes and statues, the reproduction of ideal types was a straightforward affair. Indeed, for certain elements, primarily the proportions of the human figure, a specific canon of proportions was devised which, from the Middle Kingdom onwards, related the parts of the body to a grid consisting of eighteen squares from the soles of the feet to the hairline.

The aim of the artist was to render the elements of his pictures truthfully and informatively. The subject matter itself, however, portrayed reality only within frames of reference taken from a world of myth and ideals. In the case of religious scenes this is self-evident. But Egyptian tomb art also sought to record an eternal environment for the deceased tomb owner. The scenes that were selected created a world of banquets with friends, of hunting parties, and of overseeing the affairs of a country estate which included busy craftsmen. It is easy to conclude from tomb pictures that most ancient Egyptians of all ranks lived in the country, in a society without towns and cities. Yet the archaeological record shows that this was not the case.[29] By the latter part of the Old Kingdom densely settled walled towns had grown up in places which suggest that a mature urban framework existed, and that for most educated Egyptians the town provided the basic experience of living. But this had no part in dreams of an ideal world, which was that of a peaceful agrarian existence.

Egyptian art (and, as we shall see, architecture also) was a carefully and deliberately constructed style. It was not, however, built upon an empty cultural landscape, but over a pre-existing culture (the Preformal) which, if Pharaonic Egypt had advanced no further, we would recognize and study as a viable tradition in its own right. The creation of Pharaonic art and its gradual expansion as a medium of religious communication involved a complex interplay with the Preformal tradition, selecting some elements and rejecting others. Two examples will illustrate this. The first concerns the religious iconography of the god Min.[30]

In formal Pharaonic religion the god Min had a prominent place as a god of fertility, with an important centre at Coptos. In the classic iconography he is depicted as a swathed standing male figure, holding a flail aloft in one hand and grasping the root of his erect penis in the other (Figure 29). His head-dress is a pair of tall plumes. Other distinguishing attributes are a strange tall version of the primitive tent shrine, and a bed of growing lettuces, the milky sap of which was apparently interpreted as the god's semen.[31] He was also given an emblem on a carrying-pole, an object still not positively identified but called conveniently a 'thunderbolt'.

This stock set of images had been codified by the late Old Kingdom.[32] Indeed, the basic image of the god Min himself appears as early as the late 2nd Dynasty.[33] Now with Min, the Preformal colossal statues also found at Coptos provide us with some of the raw material from which the classic stereotyped image was fashioned. We can see how the court intellectual systematizers went to work. The basic pose was retained, but details and overall style were remodelled to produce a variant of the single standard image of a god which the court style of religious art dictated. A number of emblems were associated with the original cult, carved on the sides of the colossi. The religious systematizers from the court circle chose one, the 'thunderbolt', and ignored the rest. The overall result of their work was a collection of attributes pinned, as it were, on to the stock all-purpose model of a god. In this state he became amenable to theological language/image-game. The combination Min-Amun appeared, in which a degree of merging took place with the god Amun from the nearby town of Thebes. At Abydos, in the Middle Kingdom, a cult of 'Min-Horus the Victorious', which brought the cult of Min into association with the cult of Osiris, achieved some popularity.

The second example is the sacred *benben*-stone.[34] It seems to have stood in a shrine at Heliopolis, and was presumably an example of the widespread ancient cult of individual stones thought to have peculiar properties. The original is now lost, but pictorial evidence suggests that it was an upright stone with a rounded top (Figure 30). The stone became the prototype for a range of architectural symbols, and as such reappears sporadically through Egyptian history in its primitive shape. King Akhenaten, for example, set up a round-topped *benben*-stone in one of his sun temples at el-Amarna.[35] An earlier elongated version was erected in the Fayum, at the site of Abgig, by King Senusret III of the 12th Dynasty.[36] But the rounded shape more frequently jarred on the aesthetics of the Egyptians. It lacked geometric purity. They preferred to convert

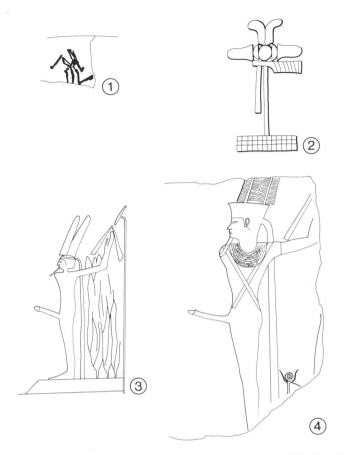

Figure 29   The formalized images of the god Min. Nos. 3 and 4 exemplify the classic image of Min as fertility god, adding to the ideal anthropomorphic image of god the elements of erect penis and brandished flail derived from the Coptos colossi. The tall plumed crown is also common to the image of the god Amun from nearby Thebes. Behind Min in no. 3 is a stylized bed of tall lettuces, their white sap regarded as a symbol of semen; behind no. 4 was originally a depiction of a tent shrine peculiar to the Min cult: a tall cylindrical tent linked by a rope to a staff topped with bovine horns. No. 3 is from a decree from the Coptos temple of the reign of Pepy I of the 6th Dynasty (*c.* 2250 BC), after R. Weill, *Les décrets royaux de l'ancien empire égyptien*, Paris, 1912, Plate VII; no. 4 is from the same place, but of the reign of Senusret I of the 12th Dynasty (*c.* 1950 BC), after W.M.F. Petrie, *Koptos*, London, 1896, Plate IX; H.M. Stewart, *Egyptian Stelae, Reliefs and Paintings from the Petrie Collection* II, Warminster, 1979, Plate 39. The earliest recognizable image of Min in the formalized tradition is no. 1, an ink drawing on a sherd from a stone bowl from the tomb of King Khasekhemui of the 2nd Dynasty (*c.* 2640 BC) at Abydos, after W.M.F. Petrie, *Abydos* I, London, 1902, 4, Plate III.48. No. 2 is the 'thunderbolt' symbol of Min also used for the name of the Coptos nome. It was the only one of the symbols carved on the Coptos colossi (see Figure 28, p. 81) which was taken into the formal canon of images used for Min. This example is from the Valley Temple of Sneferu at Dahshur (*c.* 2575 BC), after A. Fakhry, *The Monuments of Sneferu at Dahshur* II.1, Cairo, 1961, p. 20, Fig. 9.

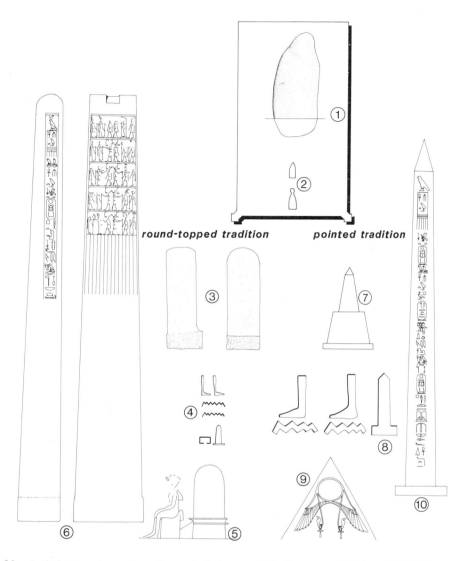

round-topped tradition   **pointed tradition**

Figure 30   Artistic transformation of a symbol: the sacred *benben*-stone of Heliopolis. (1) Hypothetical original sacred stone. (2) Early depictions as hieroglyphs in the Pyramid Texts (Pyr 1652b, 2069a). Artists preferred to give it a symmetrical, geometric shape, creating two traditions, one of flattened rectangular section with a rounded top (3-6), and another of square section and with a pointed top (7-10). (3) Round-topped stele from Hierakonpolis temple, height 6 metres, after J.E. Quibell and F.W. Green, *Hierakonpolis* II, London, 1902, Plate LXVII. (4) Writing of *benben*-stone in the tomb of Meryra at Amarna, 18th Dynasty, after LD III, 97e. (5) Depiction of a *benben*-stone erected in a temple at Amarna (see Chapter 7), tomb of Meryra, after N. de G. Davies, *Rock tombs of El Amarna* I, London, 1903, Plate XXXIII. (6) Granite standing stone at Abgig, Fayum, erected by Senusret I, 12th Dynasty, height 12.62 metres, after K.R. Lepsius (ed.) *Denkmaeler aus Aegypten und Aethiopen*, Berlin, 1849–58, II, Bl 119. (7) Profile, partially restored from ancient depictions, of the central feature of the 5th Dynasty sun temples at Abu Ghurab; (8) Writing of *benben*-stone on an inscription from Amarna, after J.D.S. Pendlebury, *The City of Akhenaten* III, London 1951, Plate CIII.48. (9) Top of a pyramidion from the top of the pyramid of King Khendjer of the 13th Dynasty at Sakkara. On it is carved the winged disk of the sun. After G. Jéquier, *Deux pyramides du moyen empire*, Cairo, 1933, Fig. 17. (10) Granite obelisk of Senusret I at Heliopolis itself, height 20.4 metres, after Lepsius, op. cit., II, Bl 118h.

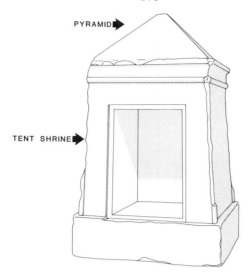

PYRAMID

TENT SHRINE

Figure 31 Combining unrelated symbols. A naos (or inner shrine for a divine image) in the form of a tent shrine with a pyramid placed on top, something structurally incongruous, but aesthetically satisfactory as a combination of symbols. 30th Dynasty, after G. Roeder, *Catalogue général des antiquités égyptiennes du Musée du Caire: Naos*, Leipzig, 1914, Taf. 16b.

the rounded top into a purer geometric shape, a pyramid, and the complete stone into a truncated obelisk. Monumental versions in this form were built as the focal point of solar temples associated with the pyramids of 5th Dynasty kings near the site of Abu Sir, and the pointed tops of pyramids and obelisks were called by a feminine form of the name: *benbent*. They could even be added (incongruously from our point of view) to the tops of replicas of tent shrines (Figure 31, and see p. 100).

But why the solar connection? Theologians took up the similarity in consonantal sequence between *benben* and the verb *weben*, 'to shine', 'to rise' (of the sun). Verbal similarity supplied a logical linkage. From the practice of theological language-game the *benben*-stone became a symbol of sunrise and the renewal of life. For the same reason, the heron ('phoenix'), which in ancient Egyptian was called *benu*, was brought into association with the cult of this stone, whilst the temple at Heliopolis could be called 'The Mansion of the Phoenix'. The statement which linked them all together and implied that a cogent meaning was there ran as follows: 'O Atum-Kheprer (god of creation), you became elevated on the height, you rose up (*weben*) as the *benben*-stone in the Mansion of the "Phoenix" (*benu*) in Heliopolis'.[37] By this kind of rationalization, which aroused no further curiosity in the Egyptian mind, order was imposed on a small part of the Egyptians' inheritance from prehistory. Language-game replaced some sacred meaning which that particular stone had once held and is probably permanently lost to us. The ideal type was recast in both shape and meaning. In this instance, as with the history of the god Min, we are witnessing the invention of tradition, something that the Egyptians enthusiastically pursued until the end of their civilization.

We can recall a further example. By the early Middle Kingdom Abydos had become the centre for the cult of Osiris.[38] The theologians who tried to systematize and rationalize the diverse local traditions concerning holy things in Egypt had already, for reasons that we shall probably never know, made a connection between Osiris and Abydos during the late Old Kingdom. We know this from statements in the Pyramid Texts. Yet on the ground, in the temple which actually stood in the town of Abydos, the first known reference to Osiris dates only to the 11th Dynasty. In the Old Kingdom the temple belonged to a local jackal-god associated with the great cemetery nearby, called Khenti-amentiu, 'Foremost amongst the Westerners', a reference to the blessed dead. From the Middle Kingdom onwards this name becomes principally an epithet for Osiris, as 'Osiris, Foremost amongst the Westerners'. For the earliest period of the Abydos shrine's existence there seems to have been a similar complex relationship between Khenti-amentiu (assuming that his cult was of this antiquity) and popular practice as revealed by the votive objects. They contain no image of this god, although a model shrine depicts a human-headed deity to which we are unable to give a name.

From the range of evidence available it is all too apparent that intellectual intervention shaped Egyptian religion over a long period, stirring the cauldron of tradition and adding new ingredients. The problem for modern scholarship in too ready an acceptance of this, namely a powerful dynamic element in ancient religion, is that it undermines the principal method of our research: that of carefully following the sources backwards in time from the better understood later ones to the more fragmentary and elusive earlier ones, and assuming that the meaning always remained the same. We tend to work by trying to identify fossils of early beliefs embedded within later sources. Yet if we take this easy course we run the risk of substituting for ancient language-game a modern scholarly game.

Folk culture?

The urge for purity of form and consistency of style came to have a generally debilitating effect on spontaneity. The modern world recognizes that cultural expression appears at more than one level. Whilst great or high culture originates from centres of established patronage and inevitably makes the greatest general impact, popular culture, which is 'folk culture' when of the past or of agrarian roots, though less intellectual, has a vigour and originality of its own and is a legitimate aspect of the whole culture of a people. We should be prepared in studying ancient societies to encounter the same plurality of expression.

The problems that arise for the distant past are, however, peculiarly large. Popular culture uses music, oral tale, and dance as much as figurative arts. These are lost to archaeology except when caught in rare ancient pictures which cannot, in any case, convey more than the briefest programme note. This is true for ancient Egypt. Tomb pictures and occasionally temple scenes show dances and acrobatics, and singers and musicians performing. But we cannot reconstruct living shows from them. In local shrines the serious business of religion kept local tradition alive. But outside these cultural enclaves the success of court art and the tendency towards mass stereotyped production of artefacts sapped local creativity.

We can apply a simple test. Pottery has survived abundantly from all periods of ancient Egypt and had common use in the households of rich and poor alike.[39] It has also become in other cultures a vehicle for folk art expression. Predynastic Egyptian pottery contains the beginnings of just such a tradition. A class of Nagada II (Gerzean) pottery, actually called 'Decorated Ware' by early archaeologists, combines a distinctive shape with a range of simple painted designs which belong to the same tradition that created the scenes in the Hierakonpolis Painted Tomb. It is easy to imagine that this type of decorated pottery could have become the archaic phase of a long history of decorated ceramics in which the characteristics of the medium produced distinctive derivatives from the Pharaonic art style with a life of their own, matched in modern times by detailed analysis by art historians. This did not happen. The development, in the late Nagada II period, of the low relief carvings which represent the beginnings of court art and the codification of ideas seems to have sapped any further interest in ceramic art. The decoration on pottery declines into simple squiggles and then vanishes altogether. Henceforth pottery decoration was a rarity, except for a brief interlude in the mid-New Kingdom. Pottery became a utilitarian product. It is sometimes well made, notably in the case of fine orange-burnished bowls produced in the Old Kingdom, but nevertheless still falls short of an artistic tradition offering individual expression. And the fine quality served refined court tastes. There was an element of regionalism in pottery styles. But none of this amounts to a tradition of ceramic folk art. The Early Dynastic and Old Kingdom pottery types of the provincial towns which possessed the local shrine cultures outlined above are regional variants of utilitarian objects ranging from the coarse to the bland.

If we look carefully, however, we can find exceptions. One concerns the art of carving seals. The cylinder seal was a foreign idea early brought to Egypt.[40] The first ones occur in the late Nagada II and are either imports from, or copies of imports from, the contemporary cultures of western Asia. From the 1st Dynasty the Egyptians began to carve hieroglyphs on them and to use them as instruments of administration, sealing letters, jars, doors, boxes, and so on with a distinctive official design. Carved cylinders continued to be, however, objects of interest in their own right, with a value that was not straightforwardly administrative. Numerous private seals are known from the Early Dynastic Period bearing designs which use both hieroglyphs and other design elements in a somewhat surreal manner, displaying an interest in developing designs away from the natural models which normally so entranced the Egyptians (Figure 32).[41] By the latter part of the Old Kingdom they had become a minor art form, occurring occasionally in court cemeteries and sometimes utilizing normal hieroglyphic inscriptions. They then passed through a sudden transformation, abandoning the cylinder shape for a flat disk with a shank, or a prism shape, becoming stamp seals bearing designs in the same non-formal tradition on their bases.[42] The centre of this industry seems to have been Middle Egypt. Further steps in design development can be observed through the 1st Intermediate Period, and by the end the characteristic Egyptian scarab-shaped seal had been born. Moreover, it had also been taken up by the administrative class as a more convenient way of applying seals, and so the scarab replaced the cylinder seals altogether. With official recognition came the application of proper formal designs, and the snuffing out of this minor provincial art tradition.

This particular case illustrates how court culture could continue to take on board new designs of provincial origin. It was part of the success of the Egyptian state that it managed to build local traditions into a national framework of myth and design. The process took time and, as discussed in the first part of this chapter, in provincial shrines local tradition continued to thrive until well into the Old Kingdom. In later periods when new elements appear, such as the popularity of the domestic god Bes from the New Kingdom onwards, or the huge interest of the Late Period in sacred animal burial, we are entitled to suspect a derivation from within popular consciousness and

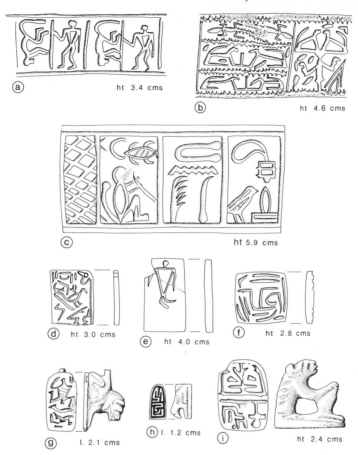

Figure 32   The makings of an alternative art-style which failed to develop, revealed by small carvings on Old Kingdom objects. (a)–(c) seals, from Abusir, Staatliche Museen, Berlin, 15600; Cairo Museum, JdE 72610; Staatliche Museen, Berlin, 16433. After H.G. Fischer, *Metropolitan Museum J* 6 (1972), 5–16, Figs 4, 18, 21; (d)–(f) faience votive plaques from the temple at Elephantine, after G. Dreyer, *Elephantine VIII. Der Tempel der Satet*, Mainz, 1986, p. 151, Abb. 60, Taf. 57; (g)–(i) button seals from Middle Egypt, after G. Brunton, *Qau and Badari* I, London, 1927, Plate XXXIII.118, 121, 112.

behaviour: folk culture surfacing only when taken up by official patronage and made explicit and visible in sources that we can understand.

Ideal types in architecture

Architectural ideal types were less amenable to mechanical reproduction, and had a more complex evolution. They had a very real existence in the minds of the Egyptians, but gave rise to broader scope in their realization as structures and buildings. Even more than with art, Pharaonic architecture reveals how tradition was invented.

By the Early Dynastic Period the normal material in use for building was mud brick.

Men used it for houses, for town walls, for the linings of tomb pits, and for the memorials and offering-places built above them. The potential of brick for creating interesting patterns in the method of laying was realized for palaces, and for court tombs, in the palace façade style of architecture (see Figure 18, p. 56). Its most important monumental survivor, copied in stone, is the great plaza and token palace in front of the Step Pyramid at Sakkara (see Figure 19, p. 58). It seems not, however, to have been used for temples. It appears suddenly, its details fully realized, at the beginning of the 1st Dynasty. This has led to a theory that it derives from the temple architecture of Mesopotamia where the style was deeply rooted with a long history of evolution behind it. This is not so far-fetched as it might seem at first, for there is other specific evidence for contacts with southern Mesopotamia during the later Nagada II period, although their nature and significance are now hard to judge.

Alongside the palace façade style of brick architecture, however, we have to recognize the existence of a second architectural tradition that was to have, in the end, the determining influence on Egyptian stone architecture to the end of Pharaonic Egypt. This was the architecture of temporary structures built of wooden frames covered partially or wholly with plain wooden panels or with sheets of woven matting or bound reeds. To appreciate the technology we can turn to early artistic representations which are inevitably ambiguous in communicating to us their details, but better still, actual examples have survived from the Old Kingdom. The two most famous are the cabins on the funerary boat of Khufu (Cheops) at Giza,[43] and the tent of Queen Hetep-heres, Khufu's mother, from her tomb also at Giza.[44] The various sources agree as to structural form: slender wooden supports often with papyrus-bud finials, wooden roofing-ties to join them together, being equally slender and either flat, or evenly though only gently curving upwards, or curving asymmetrically. At the front these formal tents could be completely open, or only partially so through the use of a screen covering the lower part. The ancient word for such a structure was *seh*, and one of the hieroglyphic signs used to write it was a simplified picture of the structure itself.

The Hetep-heres tent was made for temporary use and to be portable. The whole structure could be taken apart, packed up in a box, and transported. This fact probably explains the widespread use of this type of structure. It was suitable for royal occasions outside the brick palace; for funerals, where the burial equipment could be laid out for display and possibly even for the preparation of the body prior to burial; and for the comfort of the official class when visiting the countryside (Figure 34(3), p. 96).[45] Their use in private funerals has a striking analogy in modern Egypt, where large portable tents consisting of decorated coverings laid over a rectangular framework of poles can be hired to accommodate mourners paying their last respects and listening to a religious oration. Some representations of what seem to be portable tents mounted on carrying-frames provided with a seat are also known from the Early Dynastic Period, as in the scene on the Narmer macehead (see Figure 20 (G), p. 60) and some votive models (Figure 33).

By the 1st Dynasty brick architecture was well established in Egypt, and from the material reviewed in the first part of this chapter it seems fairly clear that built temples of various kinds made early appearances in provincial towns. It seems unlikely, therefore, that the image of the tent-shrine reflected the common appearance of provincial temples. Yet some early representations of what appear to be shrines are of

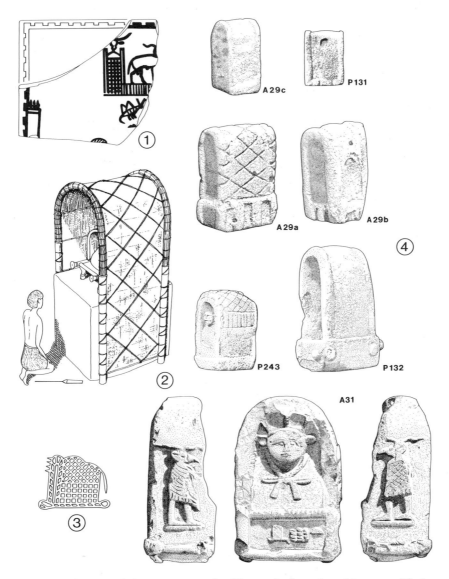

Figure 33 The early tent shrine: prototype for Pharaonic formal architecture. (1) An early tent shrine for the cult of a ram statue, set within a panelled brick enclosure. Ivory tablet from the tomb of King Den at Abydos, 1st Dynasty. After W.M.F. Petrie, *The Royal Tombs of the Earliest Dynasties* II, London, 1901, p. 25, Plate VII.8. (2) Reconstruction of a tent shrine for the revealed image of god, based on the brick dais in the Old Kingdom temple at Elephantine, see Figure 23, p. 70, and Plate 3, p. 61. (3) Ancient depiction of tent shrine with the profile of an animal, perhaps on a carrying frame and thus portable. Part of the design on a mud-seal impression from the tomb of the reign of King Hor-aha, early 1st Dynasty, after W.B. Emery, *Hor-aha*, Cairo, 1939, p. 27, Fig. 23. (4) Models of early tent shrines, P131, P132 and P243 in faience from early deposits at Abydos (after W.M.F. Petrie, *Abydos* II, London, 1903, Plates VII.131, 132, XI.243); A29a-c in faience and A31 in limestone from an uncertain source, possibly also Abydos (after H.W. Müller, *Ägyptische Kunstwerke, Kleinfunde und Glas in der Sammlung E. und M. Kofler-Truniger, Luzern*, Berlin, 1964). They vary in size between 4 and 10 cm.

tent form (Figure 33(1)).[46] One class seems to have been made to look like a horned animal (Figure 33(3)). How are we to explain this contradictory evidence?

The answer is provided by some of the votive objects from early shrine deposits.[47] They actually depict little tent shrines with curving tops, in three cases (P243, A29a on the outside, A31 on the inside) showing the criss-cross pattern on the cover which appears also in the early depictions and is probably a pattern or method of binding in the matting used as covering material. Three examples (P132, P243, A31) seem to rest on frames with legs (A31) or projections representing carrying handles which made them portable. Two of them, however, (A29a and b) rest on pedestals with sides decorated with panelling, making it likely that they are of solid, mud brick construction.[48] Two of them (P243, A31) contain a human-like figure, in the latter case with a face very similar to those which top the Narmer Palette. It is labelled with the hieroglyphic word *Repit*. Whether this is a proper name for a goddess, or a term for a type of image or essence of a divinity, is now impossible to decide, for, as so often, later references cannot be relied on to exclude considerable reinterpretation.[49] Occasional hieroglyphic writings of this word use a sign depicting the same small portable shrine, and in so doing imply that portability was of its essence.

Institutions which are basically irrational thrive on an interaction between a hidden and a revealed element. The carefully staged drama of formal appearances of the king illustrates this. In New Kingdom and later times, when the nature and rhythm of temple life are much better known, we can see it reflected in religious architecture and ceremonial. The hidden aspect of divinity required a sanctuary, in which resided the most sacred images, as cut off as possible from contact with normal human life. Revelation was achieved by careful theatrical management which brought a tangible symbol of the divine presence into the public, or semi-public, domain, yet still behind barriers, both physical and psychological. By the New Kingdom the means of public manifestation was by portable boats borne on carrying poles and supporting, in place of a cabin, a small and partly enclosed shrine (see Plate 5, p. 186, Figure 66, p. 188).[50] The word used for this shrine on a boat was *kariy*. It is reassuring to find that the earliest known writing of the word, in the Pyramid Texts of the late Old Kingdom, uses as its hieroglyphic determinative a picture of a portable tent shrine of the Early Dynastic type; reassuring because the two are functionally the same.[51] Wherever the later portable images were rested, a special platform or a complete building was constructed. In the New Kingdom they, too, could be called a 'tent of the god', though built of stone. Within them the actual resting-place was marked by a more or less cubical pedestal of stone with ornamental top on which the portable boat shrine was placed.

We can therefore look to earlier periods for functional equivalents, and if we do this, some of the key pieces of evidence fall into place. Portable holy images were already widespread, but carried not in boat shrines but in carrying-chairs of the kind used by the nobility, sheltered by a canopy of matting on a curved wooden frame. Wherever they were set down, a pedestal was needed, often built of brick either with plain or panelled sides. This could have its own canopy similarly constructed. The one complete early shrine that we possess, at Elephantine, can be interpreted along these lines (Figure 23, p. 70). Here, in a simple and modest way, is visible the duality of domain that belongs to a religion in which sacred images play a major part. At the rear, between the granite boulders, we find the enclosed sanctuary for the hidden images; in the courtyard in front is the pedestal for the portable image, complete with poles for the canopy support.[52]

The portability of the revealed images (called generically *Repit*)[53] took them not only on very localized journeys, but also from time to time to the royal court for the *Sed*-festival, where they were likewise housed inside tent shrines erected on larger brick pedestals. Although the design of these tent shrines was basically a common one, they were sometimes given a distinctive appearance by varying the shape slightly, or by adding details, including pairs of vertical poles.

It has generally been thought that in the tent shrine we have an image of what local temples in the Early Dynastic Period looked like, despite the evidence that mud brick, which lends itself to a different kind of architecture, had been in widespread use for some time. The interpretation offered here, which utilizes the one actual early shrine to have been found and recorded in any degree of completeness (Elephantine), puts the architecture of wood and matting into a very specific setting. It had been abandoned as a way of making a complete shrine. It survived only as a shelter for the revealed image, but at the same time its antiquity and distinctiveness made it an ideal basis for an easily recognizable symbol for shrines and holy places in general.

The originality of the Step Pyramid lies in the way that the architect created a style of permanent stone architecture from this vestige of traditional architecture. The vocabulary of forms now rendered into stone became henceforth the ideal type of religious building to which later temple architects almost invariably looked. We can recognize three versions at the Step Pyramid. The most common, with more than twenty examples, depicts a rectangular wooden framed tent with curved roof standing on a pedestal (see Figure 19, p. 58, and Plate 4, p. 71). Some are small and with plain fronts; the fronts of the larger ones, however, display carved poles supporting the roof, implying that they are really depicting tents which are open at the front. From this we can guess that the smaller ones were thought to have open fronts as well. In two cases at least, a flight of narrow steps ran up to the top of the pedestal or platform on which the tent stands.

In examining the Step Pyramid architecture we must not forget that we are seeing the fruits of modern reconstruction. When excavated, the all-important façades of the buildings inside the complex were found reduced to the lowest courses of stonework. We are fortunate in that the study and partial reconstruction of these buildings have been carried out by a gifted architect, Jean-Philippe Lauer, who based his results on a close examination of loose blocks found in the rubble as well as on ancient depictions of traditional shrines. The honesty of his work has made this particular group of shrines look very similar. But from the evidence of ancient pictures we must hold in our minds the possibility that some or all of them bore some distinguishing mark to make them look individual, since they probably represent the temporary festival shrines to house divine images assembled from provincial towns.

The second type is a larger variant, and directly on the ground instead of on a pedestal. There are two examples, the so-called North and South Houses. Again they depict an open-fronted building displaying the outer row of slender carved roof supports. But privacy of the interior is provided by a screen running between the roof supports and broken only by a doorway (Figure 34). The screen was thought of as made from reeds, a message conveyed by carving in stylized form the knots tied in the loose

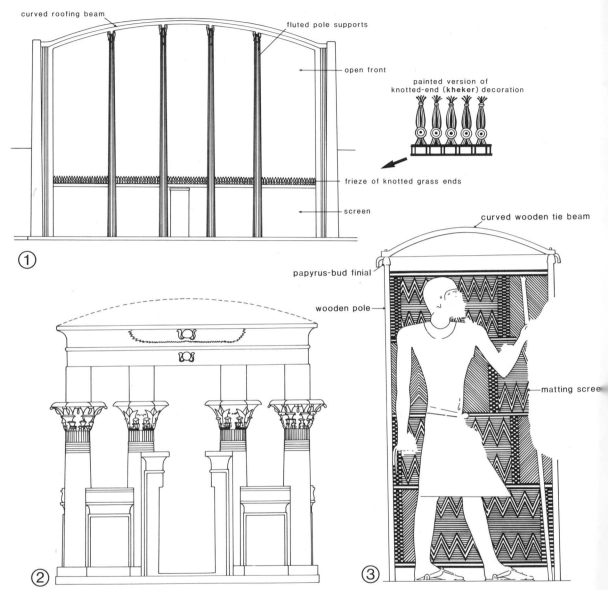

Figure 34 Ideal types in architecture: the open-fronted tent shrine (cf. Plate 4, p. 71). (1) Rendered into stone at the Step Pyramid of Djoser at Sakkara, after L. Borchardt, *Ägyptische Tempel mit Umgang*, Cairo, 1938, Blatt 10. (2) Likewise, but in a more developed form, at the Roman kiosk at Philae, the broken roof line representing a now perished curved wooden roof, ibid., Blatt 5. (3) The same architecture retained for convenience as a portable framed tent for visits to the countryside, from the tomb of Werirni, 5th Dynasty, at Sheikh Said, after N. de G. Davies, *Rock Tombs of Sheikh Saïd*, London, 1901, Plate XV.

top ends. This general design was a potent one, particularly in the use of the screen wall linking columns, and in the row of stylized knots which, as the *kheker*-frieze, passed into general use as a decorative motif.

The third version of the temporary wooden structure had perhaps four examples. One of them, 'Temple T', is of particular significance since it is one of the very few 'real' buildings of the Step Pyramid, having a complete interior of rooms and corridors. The exterior of Temple T is a severe version of the wood and matting style (Figure 35(1)). All four exterior walls look the same: plain rectangular surfaces, topped by a narrow horizontal rolled binding and above this the loose tops of reeds reduced to a plain frieze. All four corners of the building were protected by further bound rolls of reeds. The interior, however, is incompatible with a building of these materials. Its complex internal plan resembles the funerary palaces at Abydos constructed of mud brick. Although pilasters have been added, decorated after the style of bundles of reeds, it is the plan of a building of solid materials, an impression reinforced by the ceilings, which were carved in imitation of closely set logs of wood. This is a type of roof which, from its weight, demands solid walls of brick or stone. Light timber frames and matting screens are structurally unsuited.

Temple T, with its wrap-around application of tent architecture to a building of more solid form, set the style for centuries to come. Externally it shows the essence of the ideal type of later Egyptian temples. This is occasionally made explicit in temple scenes where, in a ceremony of purification of the temple building, the building itself is depicted hieroglyphically in this simple original form (Figure 35(3)). It was, however, primarily the model for temple exteriors. The severe rectangular wood and matting building became a façade, the proper wrapping for a building whose interior reflected the practical needs of the occasion.

Just how the reconciliation between form and function was achieved by later architects becomes, in effect, the remaining history of Egyptian temple architecture. Internal plans accommodated needs that changed from time to time and from place to place. In Chapter 5 we shall see how the New Kingdom fad for portable boat shrines, and various aspects of the royal funerary cult, created distinctive plans which were still kept uncompromisingly inside the old ideal type. For the moment this point will be illustrated by examples which show just how enduring the imagery created at the Step Pyramid was. The first is the almost intact temple tomb of the God's Wife Amenirdis I at Medinet Habu, which dates to the 25th Dynasty (c. 715 BC; Figure 35(2)). Essentially the building consists of two tent shrines nested one inside the other. The shrine which covers the entrance to the tomb of Amenirdis is a simple version, a single chamber which approximates to the original form in both interior and exterior. This is set within a larger building which includes a colonnaded courtyard, a favourite element in the design of temple interiors. For the final external impression the architect has returned to the tent shrine prototype, though emphasizing the front of the building by making the wall taller. This was also a favourite device, though on larger buildings the tall façade was normally, from the New Kingdom onwards, divided in the centre to create the characteristic pair of 'pylons', a limited gesture of reinterpretation of original form. It is particularly to the kind of inner shrine found here that the Egyptians gave the name 'tent of the god' (*seh-netjer*), although from the New Kingdom onwards it was also used more loosely as a synonym for 'temple' generally.[54] This was not an illogical move since

Figure 35 Ideal types in architecture: the enclosed tent shrine. (1) Temple T at the Step Pyramid of Djoser, after J.-Ph. Lauer, *La pyramide à degrés* I, and II, Cairo, 1936, Plate LV and Fig. 157. (2) The temple tomb of the God's Wife Amenirdis I at Medinet Habu (*c.* 715 BC), in which one tent shrine is nested within another, a common Egyptian architectural ploy. After U. Hölscher, *The Excavation of Medinet Habu V. Post-Ramessid Remains*, Chicago, 1954, Fig. 24. (3) Scene of King Tuthmosis III purifying the temple of Amada in Nubia by sprinkling natron over it, before the god Horakhty. The temple itself is symbolized by a picture of a tent shrine (marked by arrow). After H. Gauthier, *Les Temples immergés de la Nubie: le temple d'Amada*, Cairo, 1913, Plate XVII.

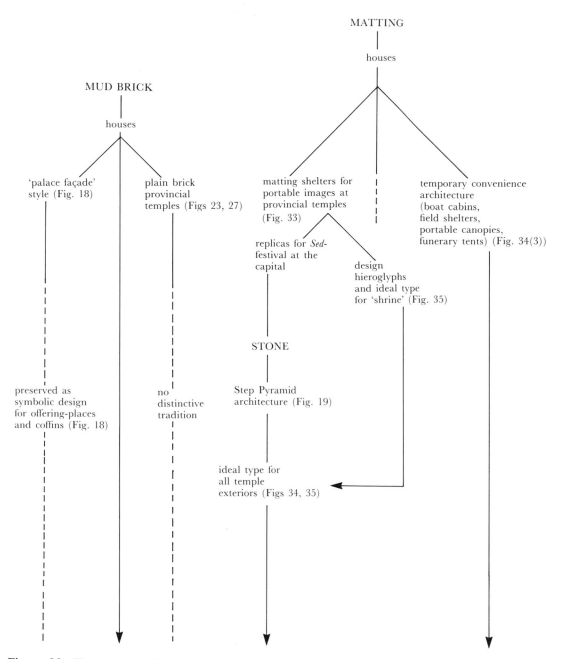

Figure 36 The sources of Egyptian architectural styles.

the whole exterior of the building was modelled on the same ideal type.

We can gain the most impressive idea of how strong was the hold of the ideal types from Egypt's beginnings by looking at buildings from the very end of ancient Egyptian civilization, when the country was ruled first by the Ptolemies, Greek-speaking inheritors of Alexander the Great's Egyptian province, and then by the Roman emperors following the death of the last of the Ptolemaic line, Queen Cleopatra VII. In the rural hinterland of the Nile Valley these alien rulers encouraged the building of traditional temples in which they themselves appeared in the guise of the divine Egyptian kings of old, featuring in similar scenes of divine birth as had occurred in New Kingdom temples.

The finest example of Ptolemaic temple architecture is the temple of the falcon-god Horus at Edfu (237–57 BC).[55] Outwardly the body of Edfu temple faithfully recalls the plain box-like form of the archetypal tent shrine, the front magnified into two pylons. Inside, the architectural vocabulary continually pays deference to this ideal, from the ornate screen wall and canopy in front of the main columned hall, to the shrine in the sanctuary carved from a single block of syenite which renders this form in miniature, although a pyramidal *benben*-stone has been carved on the top (very similar to the one in Figure 31, p. 88). The arrangement of the elements of the plan, however, is characteristic of the time and could not be mistaken for a temple of a much earlier period. Equally distinctive of the period is the *mammisi*, or birth-house, outside the front of the temple. Its purpose was to celebrate the divine birth of the king, and for its form the architects returned to the idea of the semi-open tent shrine with screen walls. Some buildings of this type even had curved wooden roofs in closer deference to the ideal type, something apparent from surviving holes for timber beams (see Figure 34(2), p. 96).

For the Egyptian priests this was a time of threat to traditional culture. The scenes and texts that cover the walls of Edfu as of other Ptolemaic temples reveal an enhanced awareness of their own rich inheritance of mythology and ritual. They are far more informative in these areas than are earlier temples. The texts on the walls are not, however, the complete originals. Rather they are extracts from or summaries of several longer 'books', often referred to by their names, which must have been held in the temple library. One set concerns the building itself.[56] These building texts are rich in language-game and symbolic geography, and incapable of resolution into a single scheme of modern logical form. They do reflect, however, a common viewpoint. This was that the new stone temple which was being built, although designed in the style of the times, embodied a range of ideal types whose existence could be counted on through the descriptions and allusions of the texts themselves. The texts, which actually contain the dimensions of the ideal buildings expressed in cubits, were capable, with the help of ritual, of holding the essence of these mythical constructions in place. At the same time their history was set in a mythical time-frame, 'The early primeval age of gods', and within a mythical geography wherein the temple site itself was the 'Seat of the First Occasion'. The term 'reign of Tanen', an earth-god, is also used, recalling the historical scheme of the Turin king list which began with a series of reigns by gods. The setting is devoid altogether of human life. In places it recalls instead the time of the creation of the world, which began with the appearance of a mound from the all-covering waters. The mound, or mounds, became the site or sites of the original shrines. One of these contained the perch of the falcon-god to whom the temple was dedicated, Horus the

Behdetite, which originated as a slip of reed planted in the primeval water. For the mythical shrines brief descriptions with dimensions are given (Figure 37). One of the terms used for the sanctuary (*seh*) is the common Egyptian word for the tent shrine, and helps to reinforce the view that these primeval buildings were seen as the timber and reed constructions of which the Ptolemaic Edfu temple was a reincarnation in stone.

It is, of course, tempting to take these accounts literally, particularly in view of the dimensions given, and to regard them as containing something of the real history of Edfu temple. It is, indeed, true that Edfu stood on a mound of natural sand and rock within the alluvial floodplain, and so became at inundation time an island. However, the archaeological record shows that until the Old Kingdom it was not a place of significant settlement. The archaeological record of early temples shows great variety in construction, but also the use of brick and of informal plans in the earliest ones that have survived. The earliest shrine at Edfu, therefore, is likely to have been of brick, and probably along the lines of the Elephantine shrine. The precedence of the tent shrine in the Ptolemaic texts as the exclusively correct and original temple design arose not from correctly recorded architectural history, but because it fitted exactly the myth-world of the primeval age of the gods.

As to where the measurements in cubits of the primeval temples came from, we just cannot tell. They could be records of buildings which had been erected on the site at various times since, say, the Middle Kingdom, or they could be the result of a symbolic numbers game carried out by the Ptolemaic priests themselves.

Egyptian visual culture strove consciously to create the impression of a direct transfer from nature. But it was far from being a spontaneous celebration of natural or inherited primitive forms. It involved a very deliberate process of selection and modification in order to create a set, a vocabulary, of ideal types possessing internal consistency. This latter aspect was sufficiently achieved to produce a degree of interchangeability which gave scope to an endless (and for us bewildering) recombination of elements which lay at the heart of the constant invention of tradition. From this we can expand our understanding of the language-game that underlay Egyptian religion: its vocabulary was also rich in elements of visual culture that could be manipulated just as words were.

Nor were the limits of recombination ever reached. The process is continued, unintentionally, by modern scholars as we try to 'explain' Egyptian religion and its art and architecture. For the relationship between modern study and ancient source is not quite what it appears to be at first sight. We like to think that the sources are inert, and ourselves objective observers. But the interplay is much more complex. Ancient thought is not dead: it lies dormant in the sources and within our own minds, and when we study the former the latter begins to move within us. One example will suffice to illustrate this. Excavations at western Thebes early in the present century led to the discovery of a combined tomb and temple of King Nebhepetra Menthuhetep of the 11th Dynasty (*c.* 2061–2010 BC) at the site called Deir el-Bahari (Figure 38). The centre-piece was a square mass of stone masonry standing on a huge podium and surrounded by a colonnade. The excavator, E. Naville, restored a pyramid on the top of the square base, and the reconstruction drawing passed into textbooks and for over half a century remained a very familiar element in Egypt's architectural history.[57] It fitted within the general line of architectural development, and could even be seen as echoing the

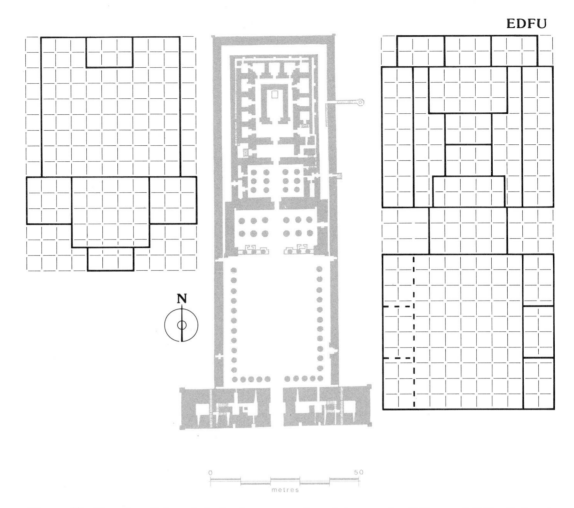

N

0   50
metres

Figure 37 Temples of the mind. In the centre, plan of the temple of Horus of Edfu, Ptolemaic Period, 237–57 BC. To left and right, outlines representing mythical temples invented through speculative processes by the priests, and expressed as written descriptions complete with dimensions in cubits. Each square equals 10 cubits. *Left*: The primitive temple of the sacred falcon (Horus). The opening text reads: 'Laying out the foundation made in the temple of "Uplifter of God" in the reign of (the god) Tanen, in the presence of Ra, according to what is in the book called "Specification of the Sacred Mounds of the Early Primeval Age".' *Right*: The temple of the sun-god. Although these temples (and others) are set in a mythical primeval age of gods before humankind existed, in their overall scale and proportions they reflect the architectural perspective of the Ptolemaic priests. They are unlikely to be records of early real buildings. After E.A.E. Reymond, *The Mythical Origin of the Egyptian Temple*, Manchester, 1969. Other Edfu texts which describe the foundation of the real temple provide a description, with cubit dimensions, which is fairly realistic, see S. Cauville and D. Devauchelle, 'Les mesures réelles du temple d'Edfou', *Bulletin de l'Institut Français d'Archeólogie Orientale* 84 (1984), 23–34.

landscape, for a natural pyramidal peak rises above the cliffs and was regarded as a holy place by the Egyptians themselves. The building was re-examined by a German expedition, under D. Arnold, in 1968–1970. Finding that there was no specific evidence for preferring a pyramid on top of the base, Arnold restored it as a flat-topped construction, and linked it, with ample scholarly reference, to the notion of the primeval mound.[58] More recently, in a general study on pyramids, R. Stadelmann has published a drawing which adds an actual tree-covered mound of earth on top.[59]

Whichever solution we adopt we can justify it by learned references to specific Egyptian sources. Thus, although only one (or none of them) must be technically correct, all are true to Egyptian cultural roots and potentially present in ancient times, even if they have had to wait 3,000 years before being realized.[60]

There is a parallel of sorts here in the classical revival of Renaissance Europe, and, limited more to architecture, the later Gothic and Egyptian revivals. Here artists strove to use the spirit and the visual vocabulary of a dead culture in pursuit of a living art, and thus realized the potential latent for further development within a past culture, though producing an overall effect that the ancients would never have thought of. The gifted forger of antique art is doing the same. And sometimes scholars unintentionally pursue the same path in constructing hypotheses to explain a very fragmentary past.

Egyptian temple architecture recalled a lost and largely mythical past of primitive simplicity. What we know, and the builders of Edfu temple did not, is the relatively late and to a degree artificial nature of the myth behind the ideal type of shrine. The Step Pyramid shows that it arose from the rejection of Early Dynastic brick architecture which had demonstrated, in the palace façade style, potential for proclaiming places of power. By the 3rd Dynasty this style had been in Egypt for at least three to four centuries and could well have remained the model for all formal architecture, including temples, as it did in Mesopotamia. Instead, after the Step Pyramid, it was retained only in token form in funerary architecture: in the offering-places of tomb chapels, as a way of decorating sarcophagi, and as decoration for a section of wall around the royal burial chamber. Henceforth, formal temple architecture looked for inspiration to what the Egyptians considered to be their roots, a world of tent shrines and no palaces, blotting out a distinctive aspect of the early state. Just as the political history of ancient Egypt was shaped by a mythical view of the past, so the history of Egyptian formal temple architecture is a record of deference to another myth.

The recodification of architectural form in the 3rd Dynasty did not, however, provide a model for religious architecture which all desired to follow at once. No general rebuilding programme followed in the provinces, as the first part of this chapter showed. The new style was an intellectual creation of the court. It was confined at first to the royal tomb, and was used as a guide elsewhere only in cases of fitful royal patronage of other temples. The form of the royal tomb itself underwent major recodification again at the end of the 3rd Dynasty, though this was as much a matter of function and meaning as of style. The eternal palace was replaced by a temple to the king's spirit and to the sun dominated by the true pyramid, a geometricized version of the *benben*-stone in deference to grand and more abstract theology. A further major recodification took place at the beginning of the 18th Dynasty, as will be explained in Chapter 5. But this further history of change in layout and meaning, which went far beyond the changes that took place in art, remained true in forms to the ideal types that we first meet as

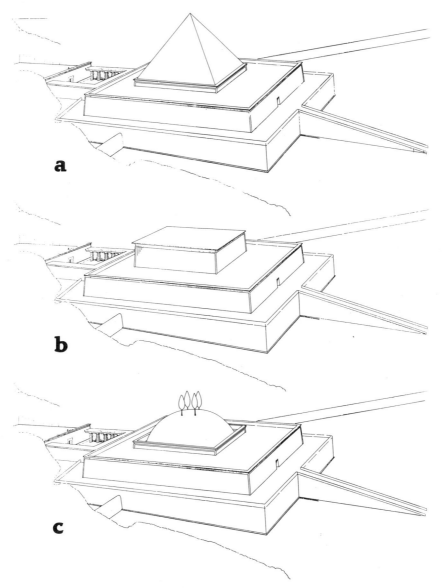

Figure 38 Religious language-game resumed: scholarly manipulation of Egyptian religious symbols for modern didactic ends. Three reconstructions of the mortuary temple of King Nebhepetra Menthuhetep at Deir el-Bahari, Thebes, 11th Dynasty. Each is 'true' to the spirit of Egyptian religion and can be supported by scholarly argument, and thus they continue the realization of the potential of ancient Egyptian thought. Whether any of them is 'true' in the sense that it was actually built at Deir el-Bahari we shall probably never know. (a) a true pyramid, after E. Naville, *The XIth Dynasty temple at Deir el-Bahari* II, London, 1910, Plate XXIV; (b) a flat-topped mound made of stone, proposed by D. Arnold, *Der Tempel des Königs Mentuhotep von Deir el-Bahari I. Architektur und Deutung*, Mainz, 1974, Frontis. (c) a mound of earth supporting trees, proposed by R. Stadelmann, *Die ägyptischen Pyramiden*, Mainz, 1985, p. 229, Abb. 74.

monumental architecture in the Step Pyramid. Religious architecture well illustrates the Egyptian genius for clothing change in traditional costume. Pharaonic culture provided a language of form and meaning which was able at one and the same time to accommodate new ideas and to give them the appearance of being true to antique models.

The role of individual initiative

The instrument of change was personal intervention. We have to think in terms of great artists and architects. But the ancient myth that whatever was new and admirable was in fact true to the past allowed no room for the recognition of individual genius. The initiative in art and architecture was articulated by royal decree. The process is documented in the Berlin Leather Roll.[61] This is a New Kingdom copy of a building text of King Senusret I of the early 12th Dynasty. It begins with a formal 'appearance' of the king in his palace, before his assembled courtiers. He opens with an oration on his own divinely appointed destiny, then announces his plan: the construction of a temple for the god Atum. The motive is not disinterested piety. Piety is mixed with the pragmatic observation that the best means of immortality is a building constructed in one's own name. 'A king who is evoked by his works is not doomed.' His courtiers offer deferential support for the scheme, emphasizing the personal benefit for the king himself: 'When your temple is built, it will provide for the altar. It will give service to your image. It will befriend your statues in all eternity.' Finally comes the action. The king appoints the architect:

> the royal seal-bearer, sole companion, overseer of the two gold-houses and the two silver-houses, and privy-councillor of the two diadems: It is your counsel that carries out all the works that my majesty desires to bring about. You are the one in charge of them, who will act according to my wish. . . . Order the workmen to do according to your design.

This is, for an Egyptian text, an unusually frank statement on royal delegation of creativity. But note who the architect was, or rather was not. No name is given, and the man's titles have no specific reference to building at all. We know of dozens of officials with titles of this kind from the Middle Kingdom, but if they were great artists or architects we cannot tell. The great architect's skill was perceived as admirable performance of a royal commission, on the same level as organizing a large and difficult quarrying expedition, or clearing navigable channels through the rocky barriers of the First Cataract at Aswan. It was not a deliberate anonymity. Some draughtsmen and builders who did little else with their lives used these callings as their official titles, and so we can identify them.[62] It reflects more the Egyptian lack of awareness of abstract divisions of knowledge. Art and architecture were parts of the stream of directed activity that emanated from the court. The process worked simply because an intuitive appreciation of what was really good ensured that good artists and imaginative architects were promoted at the expense of bad ones. But they were applauded for their success as good officials rather than as good artists or architects.

The case of the builder of the Step Pyramid provides another angle from which to view the question of who the real creators were. We have no ancient account of the building of the Step Pyramid, yet we instinctively recognize in it a work of architectural genius. This remote and poorly documented period has in fact provided us with the name of a great man of Djoser's court, Imhotep.[63] On the base of a statue of Djoser from the Step Pyramid Imhotep's name is carved, together with his titles: 'seal-bearer of the King of Lower Egypt, first one under the king, administrator of the Great Mansion, prince, chief of seers' (a religious title). On the wall of the unfinished step pyramid of Djoser's successor (King Sekhemkhet) his name occurs again, simply as 'Sealbearer of the King of Lower Egypt, Imhotep'. From the discovery of this material Egyptologists have made the not unreasonable assertion that Imhotep was the man behind the Step Pyramid. Now Imhotep was also one of the lucky few who achieved long posthumous fame in ancient Egypt. His name was honoured 1,500 years later in the New Kingdom, but not as an architect. He was famous as the author of a set of thoughtful sayings. 'I have heard the words of Imhotep and Hordedef, with whose discourses men speak so much', says one song, pairing him with another famous sage of old, one of the sons of King Khufu. Imhotep's fame did not stop here, however. By the 26th Dynasty he had become a minor god, son of the god Ptah of Memphis, and healing was to become his speciality so that the Greeks identified him with their god of healing, Asklepios. In some late texts he is given a set of titles, but they are creations of the day: 'vizier, overseer of works, mayor'. He was correctly placed in the reign of King Djoser, but the history of Djoser's reign was recast into more modern shape. A papyrus of the first or second century AD, for example, sends Djoser and his vizier, Imhotep, off on a campaign to Assyria.

We are probably still right to identify Imhotep as the Step Pyramid's architect. (Though having done that we have simply played the ancient game of elevating names into knowledge. It really tells us nothing about him.) Through this he achieved fame as a great official, and it was as a great official, with the inevitable attribute of being 'wise', that he was remembered. It was the fact of his success that counted, not the means – architectural genius – that gave it him. Indeed, it would have been contrary to the myth-world of his architecture if it had been given a historical point of origin.

This raises another conundrum for us. We must accept that from time to time the Egyptians produced figures of great intellectual ability responsible for major changes in traditions. Yet the Egyptians remained without the means to conceptualize this. Past innovators were remembered, but as 'wise men'. How, therefore, can we find out why these people were famous?

In the previous chapter the point was made that with the pyramid of Medum of the reign of King Huni we have the product of a major re-evaluation not only of architectural form but also of the meaning of kingship, amongst the most important intellectual concerns of the day. If we wish to credit the originality of the Step Pyramid to a single outstanding mind, we should be prepared to do the same with the Medum pyramid. By the Middle Kingdom the Egyptians possessed the testimony of a 'wise man' which they believed to belong to just this period, the reign of Huni. It is a set of instructions on good behaviour which urges an abstemious approach to life. The author was a vizier whose name is unfortunately lost (it may have been Kai-irisu, another famous sage). He addressed himself to his children, one of whom may well have been the vizier Kagemni whose name occurs at the end of the text. This vizier Kagemni is a known figure, for his tomb exists at Sakkara. But it dates to the reign of King Teti of the early 6th Dynasty, thus nearly three centuries after the time of Huni. Furthermore, a fair case can be made for dating the actual composition of the text later still. We can comprehend this inconsistent evidence if we see it as part of a more general phenomenon which runs through ancient Egypt (as through other cultures): the invention of tradition, which has in this case involved a process of compression. We have to imagine a sequence like this: a great rationalizer and organizer at the court of Huni responsible for the extraordinary Medum pyramid; the loss in subsequent generations of the reasons which made him famous, leaving him as a 'wise man'; eventual confusion with a vizier of the late 5th/early 6th Dynasty, famous for some other reason; final crediting of this person with a suitable wise teaching composed even later.[64]

Tradition is not wholly a mechanical repetition of ancient forms which thereby provide a key to past times. It is given meaning to a later age through modification, and sometimes through invention. Traditions can thus obscure the past as well as illuminate it. They answer current needs and are the products of ingenious minds.

When we look at Early Dynastic brick palace architecture and Preformal shrines and their associated objects it is possible to imagine that they could have formed the beginnings of a cultural and artistic tradition very different from the one that actually did develop. Or if, as with the Indus Valley civilization, Early Dynastic Egypt had advanced no further along a straightforward cultural trajectory and the early material was all that we had, our evaluation and interpretation of it would be rather different from the way it actually appears now: simply as a formative stage to something much richer and greater later on. This is another way of saying that Pharaonic culture was not a naturally evolved tradition. It was invented, but so successfully that it left the Egyptians (and to some extent ourselves) feeling that it was all somehow rooted in the country and in the psychology of the people in a most fundamental way.

At the heart of a cultural tradition is a trade-off between respect for past achievements and the accommodation of fertile and creative minds who look for something new. Ancient Egypt provides an early case history of the dynamics of the Great Tradition of culture: how it arose and was maintained as a living system, how it expanded at the expense of local traditions, and how it achieved this difficult balance between past and present. It also enlarges our understanding of the scope of myth in society. The first chapter was devoted to showing how the Egyptians wrapped history and political power in myth. This chapter has attempted to do the same with material culture. Myth is not only a narrative form of expression. Myth statements which do not require verbalization can be conveyed powerfully through art and architecture. They provide a distinctive dimension to the assault on the senses which lies at the heart of state ideologies.

Part II
The provider state

3
The bureaucratic mind

The material achievements of ancient states – pyramids, conspicuous wealth, palaces, temples, conquests – all depended on a particular skill: administration of resources. Although its basic purpose was to manipulate the economic environment for the benefit of the elite, in so doing benefit was incidentally spread to a significant sector of the population. This was achieved essentially through taxation to bring in resources and then through their redistribution as rations to an element of the population – probably a large one – engaged temporarily or permanently on work for the state. The first part of this classic resource cycle of early states – taxation – is best illustrated for Egypt by material from the New Kingdom, and this will be done in Chapters 5 and 6. This chapter is more about bureaucracy as a shaping force in society and the consequences of large-scale ration distribution on the relations between state and population.

A developed bureaucratic system reveals and actively promotes a specific human trait: a deep satisfaction in devising routines for measuring, inspecting, checking, and thus as far as possible controlling other people's activities. This is a passive and orderly exercise of power in contrast to direct coercion. It draws upon a particular aptitude, as distinctive and important for a society as the genius of its artists and architects, or the bravura of its military men. We call a member of this class a 'scribe'. It is a fair translation of an Egyptian word which means simply 'a writing man'. There is a tendency in modern societies where literacy is widespread to denigrate the junior official or clerical worker. But this is a luxury inappropriate to less developed societies. Where most are illiterate the writing man holds the key to the power that administration bestows. In Egypt scribes were not only amongst the elite, they knew it, and said so plainly. 'Be a scribe', ran the advice, 'it saves you from toil, it protects you from all manner of labour.' 'Be a scribe. Your limbs will be sleek, your hands will grow soft. You will go forth in white clothes, honoured, with courtiers saluting you.'[1] And many a senior figure in the state included 'scribe' amongst the accumulated titles of his curriculum vitae. The reader of this chapter should suppress any feeling of disdain associated with words like 'bureaucracy' and 'scribe'. In the Egyptian world both attracted a very different set of values.

Tidy minds

Large numbers of administrative sources have survived from ancient Egypt, which carry the history of bureaucracy back to the third millennium BC. We will begin with a set of early texts which reveal vividly the bureaucratic scribe's concern with system and detail. It is the papyrus archive from the pyramid temple of King Neferirkara of the 5th Dynasty at Abusir.[2] It dates mostly to the reign of King Isesi, thus to at least fifty years after the king's death (in c. 2427 BC).

By the beginning of the 4th Dynasty a standard royal tomb layout had developed. Burial was within or beneath a pyramid. The offering cult for the king's eternal well-being focused on a mortuary temple on the pyramid's east face. A causeway linked this temple with a separate one on the valley floor, the Valley Temple. Central to the cult was the presentation of food and drink offerings. Priests were needed for this, and for other ceremonies, and other staff were required to protect the building and its equipment. All were paid in kind, in commodities, which included a basic ration of bread, beer, and grain, and additional items such as meat and cloth. The receipt of income and distribution of rations set in motion its own little administrative cycle. Although the income could be supplied by the palace of the living king, a greater security of source was obtained by establishing a pious foundation in perpetuity. This consisted essentially of agricultural estates, the income of which was directed to the support of the staff maintaining cult and fabric at the pyramids.

The papyrus sheet illustrated in Figure 39 is a table of daily income written in an early style of hieratic which still maintained many of the outlines of the original hieroglyphic signs. We can recognize instantly a sensible tabular format, ruled in red and black ink. Each horizontal line is set aside for one day in a thirty-day month, and contains mainly numerical entries in vertical columns. Each column bears a concise two- or three-tier heading, covering the supplying institutions, the kind of foodstuffs involved, and (for the three right-hand columns) the status of the delivery.

The supporting foundation, composed of individual estates, was cleverly incorporated into the formal decorative schemes at pyramid temples, illustrating once again the Egyptian genius for deft symbolic presentation of humdrum reality. Few peoples have turned the collection of rents and gathering of taxes into subject matter for sacred art. Each funerary estate, or domain, appears as an offering-bearer, individually named. The most complete set comes from the Valley Temple of King Sneferu at Dahshur (Figure 40).[3] They formed a frieze running along the base of some of the internal walls. Each estate is personified as a woman bearing an offering-table. On the head is a sign-group reading: 'The town: Mansion of Sneferu'. In front of each is the name of the place, compounded from the name of Sneferu in a cartouche, with further signs to designate the nome. Altogether thirty-four estates belong to Upper Egypt, distributed amongst ten nomes (with the record of eight nomes missing). In Lower Egypt the record is fully preserved for only a single nome, and numbers four estates. This scattered pattern of landholding is typical for ancient Egypt. No details are given of the size of these holdings, but other and rather rarer statements on size vary from 2 arouras (16.4 hectares) to 110 arouras (905 hectares).

The temple staff was organized into groups for which the conventional modern term is 'phyle' (a Greek term meaning company, tribe). This was the common form of temple organization, with five phyles in the Old Kingdom, each one subdivided into two divisions, which apparently worked at different times. Each subdivision served only for one month in ten.[4] Presumably for the extended leave periods they reverted to agricultural or other work in their villages, so that the undoubted benefits of temple service – payments as well as prestige – were widely spread. Whatever ancient reasoning lay behind the system, the practical consequence was a massive sharing out of jobs by the state. The number of employees required was multiplied by many times, hugely increasing the numbers of people receiving partial support from the state. Because most of the jobs were only part-time the system itself was not clogged by the presence of unnecessary personnel.

In the course of duty, a complete inspection of the temple and its property was arranged. From the Neferirkara archive we know that the inspection included the seals on all doors and every item of temple equipment. The sheet illustrated in Figure 41 is an example of an inventory of this kind. Again a sensible tabular format meets the practical requirements. The items are not listed haphazardly. Far from it. They are arranged according to an overall scheme of classification which includes an element of progressive subdivision to create subclasses of a broader category, so displaying a basic grasp of taxonomy of the kind that underlies modern knowledge. By the time of this archive the temple equipment was becoming worn. Exact details of damage are listed underneath each item, together with the numbers present. The fragment of table illustrated also reflects some kind of double-entry procedure which is not properly understood, for the space for each set of inspections is itself subdivided by double lines ruled in red to accommodate two sets of observations if necessary.

One set of sheets covered an activity which the ancient Egyptians rated very highly: sealing. Instead of sealing-wax the Egyptians used a very fine grey clay which took the impression of a seal and then set very hard around a binding of cord. In the Old Kingdom the seals themselves were little stone cylinders bearing incised hieroglyphs which could be rolled across the clay. In the Middle Kingdom they were replaced by stamp seals carved in the shape of scarab beetles, the design or inscription scratched into the flat base. Seals were fixed to rolled-up letters and other documents, around the knobs on wooden chests to secure the lids, around the necks of sacks and jars, and over the wooden bolts which closed doors. The sheet from the Neferirkara archive deals with the seals on doorways of rooms in which sacred boats were stored.[5]

The physical barriers to theft in ancient Egypt were not very strong. No ingenuity was displayed in inventing locks. Breaking and entering would have been quite simple, and the long history of tomb robbery in ancient Egypt shows that some people were strongly motivated towards theft. The great fuss that was made over sealing, including the repeated inspection of seals, was a psychological ploy. It concentrated the minds of those responsible on a specific point of security, laid security open to bureaucratic control, and the link between sealings and the keeper of the seal became a bond of responsibility. The system was probably more effective than one might think at first. It created a little field of symbolic power around storeroom doors.

Much of the Neferirkara archive reflects methodical routines – inspections and duty rosters – where the units recorded were single and indivisible, namely human beings and manufactured objects. But many units of administration (land and commodities), in being divisible, required exact quantification as well. Many texts reveal how

name of the porter	through deliveries sent to the residence						name of the place of origin	brought from the palace *ida*-bread, *padj*-bread, *hetja*-bread, *pesen*-bread, beer		the altar of Ra — in the solar temple: consignments of *pat*-bread			in crates: good things		
	jars of *sekhpet*-drink	jars of beer	jars of flour	*beset*-bread	*pesen*-bread	*hetja*-bread				balance	delivered	amount due	balance	delivered	amount due
temple								18				14			
employees		3		1	1		estate of Kakai	18				14			
	1	1	1	1	1	1	Iu-Shedefwi	18	18		70	14			
								18	18	14		14			
Ni-Ankh-Kakai		3		1	1		estate of Kakai	18		14		14			
								18		14		14			
Ni-Tawi-Kakai, son of		3		1	1		estate of Kakai	18		14		14			
Hatu	1	1		1	1	1	Djed-Sneferu	18	36	14		14	10		10
								18		14		14	10		10
								18			14	14			
								18			14	14			
		3		1	1		estate of Kakai	18	36		14	14			
											14	14			
								18			14	14			
								18			14	14			
											14	14	10		10
Ni-Tawi-Kakai	2 haunches of beef	mixed 30	4 fowl		100	(?)	brought from the altar of Ra			(14)	14	14	(10)		(10)
										(14)		14	(10)		
brought by	mixed 30		mixed 30				solar temple			(14)	14	14			
boat					1						14	14			
	1	1	1	1	1	1	Iu-Shedefwi				14	14			
											14	14			
								18		14	14	14			

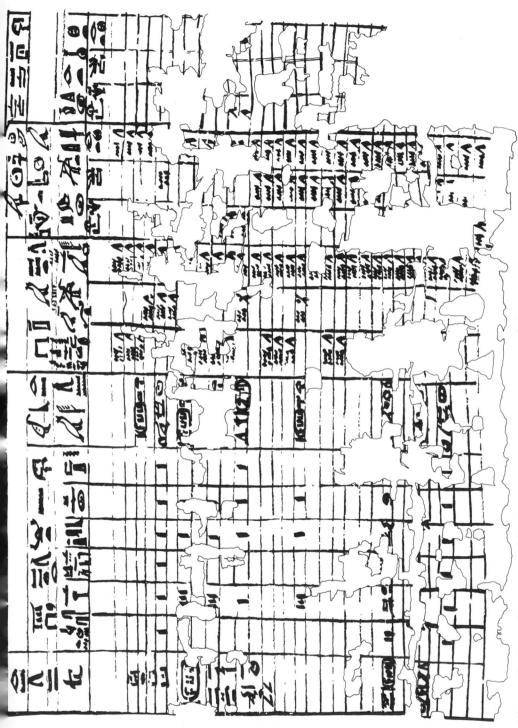

Figure 39 Sheet of accounts of daily income over the period of one month, from the administrative archive of an Old Kingdom pyramid, that of King Neferirkara at Abusir, cf. Figure 41, p. 119, for another part of the archive, and Figure 49, p. 142, for site plan. After P. Posener-Kriéger and J.L. de Cenival, *Hieratic Papyri in the British Museum. 5th series. The Abu Sir Papyri*, London, 1968, Plate XXXIV.

Figure 40   Part of a list of estates providing the income for the pyramid temple of King Sneferu of the 4th Dynasty at Dahshur. Each estate is personified as a female bearer carrying a tray of food offerings. The name of each estate is written over and in front of each figure, and they are grouped according to nomes (administrative districts). In front of the second figure from the left is the heading 'Oryx nome', the area of Beni Hasan. After A. Fakhry, *The Monuments of Sneferu at Dahshur* II, Cairo, 1963, Fig. 16; redrawn by B. Garfi.

arithmetical procedures were developed to facilitate this.[6] At the risk of deterring the general reader a few examples will be cited simply to convey the flavour of this kind of work, which occupied a significant number of those who ran the ancient Egyptian state. One feature of ancient Egyptian mathematics which is a major obstacle to modern readers should be noted at the outset: with the sole exception of $\frac{2}{3}$, no fraction was ever written which had a numerator greater than one. Thus the fraction $\frac{3}{4}$ was written by them as $\frac{1}{2} + \frac{1}{4}$; $\frac{6}{7}$ was written as $\frac{1}{2} + \frac{1}{4} + \frac{1}{14} + \frac{1}{28}$; and so on. Although we find it cumbersome because of its unfamiliarity, Egyptian scribes used the system fluently and to great practical effect. Furthermore, at moments of uncertainty they could refer to arithmetic manuals. These often deal with problems that are quite complex, but it reflects the basic Egyptian mentality that each problem is dealt with as a specific and individual case rather than as an application of general mathematical principles. Practised scribes must have developed a degree of mathematical intuition, but the idea of pursuing this as an end in itself – to create the subject of mathematics – did not occur to them.

Rationing

An important area of arithmetical administration was food supplies: rations. The word 'rations' has a special significance. No one had yet invented money. In the modern world money has become such a basic part of life that it is easy to conclude that a world without it would be a very simple place indeed. Where there is no money people have to barter rather than buy and sell, and the word 'barter' is itself stamped with a colonial image of beads and trinkets changing hands in savage lands. This is one of the comfortable myths by which modern people distance themselves from the past and regard their world as being not merely much better but a different kind of place altogether.

Money does, indeed, provide a wonderfully easy way of doing business at every kind of scale. Banks and credit cards take away the need even to carry notes and coins, let alone beads and trinkets. But non-money systems have, in the past, managed remarkably well. They exemplify a general characteristic of cultures: that systems tend to be adequate for the demands placed upon them. People cope. The ancient Egyptian economy supplies a good example. The Egyptians managed large economic operations over long periods of time with a moneyless system that was adequate. They were able to do this partly because in the ancient world in general people remained in far closer handling contact with real material wealth – commodities – than we do, and partly because they had developed an accounting system which was half-way towards the abstraction of 'money'. It was half-way in the sense that its language was that of commodities – loaves, jugs of beer, *hekat*s of wheat, and so on – but its procedures allowed for the manipulation of quantities which was not necessarily matched by the movement, or even existence, of the substances themselves. It was a typical ancient compromise: abstraction disguised by concrete terminology. We will meet it again in Chapter 6, in looking at the way that goods were priced, and bought and sold (cf. Figure 85, p. 250). It is also another lost world of the mind. For it is now very difficult to reconstruct the whole system in a way which pays suitable heed to the niceties of the ancient documents and satisfies modern common sense. This will become apparent in the next few paragraphs.

Rations administration lay at the heart of the system. In the absence of money people were paid in kind, in commodities. In effect this was a 'wage', but on account both of the commodity-based nature of the recompense and the modern connotations of personal economic freedom of the word 'wage', the term 'rations' is preferable. But the distinction is somewhat artificial.

The basic cereal food cycle from harvest to ration distribution involved a whole series of points of scribal intervention. The initial yield of grain was measured at the threshing-floor by means of wooden scoops of a given capacity, which gave quantity in terms of a *hekat*, about 4.78 litres. Transport, frequently by river, to the granary

haematite	crystalline stone				flint	iron		offering-tables	
bowl:	bowls		vases		ritual knife	blade	total of		
gold-plated	black	white	black	white			silver items	small	large
	⬓	⬓	🏺	🏺	ⵌ	▯		⊟	⊟
1	2	1	1	1	1	2	23	2	1
	(?)	various repairs to rim & base (x2) (x2) & to sides	repairs to rim & base	repairs to sides; holed (x2)	handle chipped; repaired	splinters missing, having been dropped		badly split; loose joints; corroded	badly split; loose joints; corroded
1	2	1	1	1	1	2	23	2	1
	(?)	ditto	ditto	ditto	handle & blade chipped	ditto		ditto	ditto
1	2	1	1	1	1	2	23	2	1
	ditto	ditto	ditto	ditto	ditto	ditto		ditto	ditto
1	2	1	1	1	1	2	23	2	1
	(?)	ditto	ditto	ditto	ditto	ditto		badly split; loose joints; holed	badly split; loose joints; holed
1	2	1	1	1	1	2	23	2	1
		(repairs) ditto	ditto	(chipped) ditto	ditto	ditto		ditto	ditto
1	2	1	1	1	1	2	23	2	1

18 cms

Figure 41 Sheet of equipment inventory, from the same source as Figure 39, p. 115. After P. Posener-Kriéger and J.L. de Cenival, *Hieratic Papyri in the Briiish Museum. 5th Series. The Abu Sir Papyri*, London, 1968, Plate XX.

involved scribal checking to ensure no theft took place *en route*. Another group of scribes receiving the delivery at the granary checked it again. They or their superiors would already know the maximum capacity of the individual silos, even if they were circular, by calculation:

A circular container of 10 by 10 cubits.
Take away $\frac{1}{9}$ of 10, thus $1\frac{1}{9}$; remainder $8\frac{2}{3} + \frac{1}{6} + \frac{1}{18}$
Multiply the $8\frac{2}{3} + \frac{1}{6} + \frac{1}{18}$ by $8\frac{2}{3} + \frac{1}{6} + \frac{1}{18}$ (i.e. square it); result: $79\frac{1}{108} + \frac{1}{324}$
Multiply the $79\frac{1}{108} + \frac{1}{324}$ by 10; it becomes $790\frac{1}{18} + \frac{1}{27} + \frac{1}{54}$
Add a half to it: it becomes 1185
Multiply the 1185 by $\frac{1}{20}$, giving $59\frac{1}{4}$. This is the amount that will go into it in quadruple-*hekats*, namely $59\frac{1}{4}$ hundreds of quadruple-*hekats* of grain.[7]

The interest of this model calculation is that the container is circular. The first two steps involve squaring $\frac{8}{9}$ of the diameter, which yields a very fair approximation to the correct answer that we would find by using a formula involving π.

The next points of scribal intervention were at the beginning and end of the milling, and at subsequent stages in the production of the staple elements of the Egyptian diet: bread and beer. Ancient beer, readers should note, was rather different from its modern watery counterpart. It was probably an opaque liquid looking like gruel or soup, not necessarily very alcoholic but highly nutritious. Its prominence in Egyptian diet reflects its food value as much as the mildly pleasurable sensation that went with drinking it. Baking and brewing came near the end of the whole cycle of cereal production. For the scribes who painstakingly followed the progress of cereals from fields to ration pay-outs the essentially messy and labour-intensive processes of baking and brewing presented a challenge, and it was met by a simple but ingenious solution.

For the background – the realities of brewing and baking – we are very well supplied with evidence, in the form of detailed wooden models and tomb paintings of the Middle Kingdom. The two activities had much in common, both starting with the making of dough, the barm (the yeasty froth that forms on the top of fermenting malt liquors) from the beer supplying the yeast necessary for leavened bread.

The model building illustrated (Figure 42, from the tomb of Meket-ra, a high official of the 11th Dynasty)[8] has two major parts, each with a subdivision. The outer door leads to a vestibule, to the right of which is the brewery. At the far end is a flat circular element which must represent a circular limestone mortar set into the floor, as is sometimes found in excavations. A man wielding a long wooden pestle crushes grain in it. This is an operation preliminary to grinding, which loosens the husks. Beside the mortar stand two grindstones set in quern emplacements. Excavated evidence shows that the normal grindstone was an oval piece of quartzite or granite, rough underneath but with a smooth and slightly curved upper surface. Each stone was set into a mud-brick construction, sometimes built against a wall and then having the plan of a letter 'B'. The stone was set into the top of one half, with sloping surface, and the coarse flour and husks fell into the little trough formed by the mud-brick curb of the other half of the 'B'.[9] The Meket-ra models lack the collecting trough, but are otherwise of this design. The miller stood behind the higher end and leant forwards over the stone,

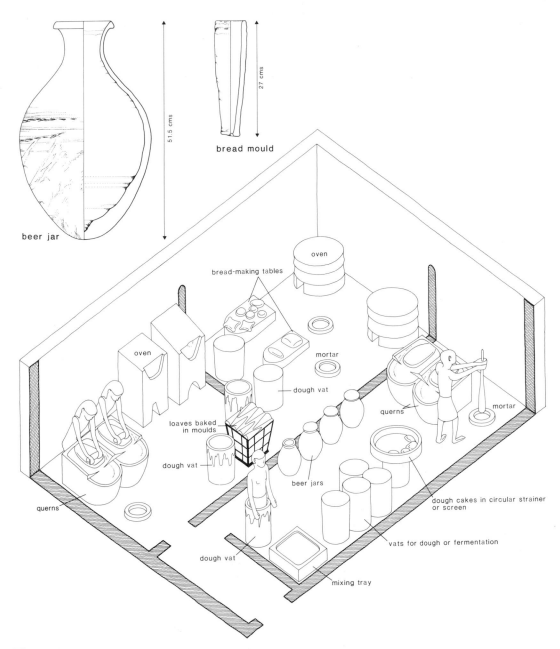

beer jar

51.5 cms

bread mould

27 cms

oven

bread-making tables

oven

mortar

dough vat

loaves baked
in moulds

querns

mortar

dough vat

querns

beer jars

dough cakes in circular strainer
or screen

dough vat

vats for dough or fermentation

mixing tray

Figure 42 Baking and brewing: the model bakery/brewery from the tomb of Meket-ra at Thebes, 11th Dynasty, after H.E. Winlock, *Models of Daily Life*, New York, 1955, Figs 22, 23, 64, 65. The two pots shown as insets are from the mortuary temple town of Amenemhat III at Dahshur, after Do. Arnold, 'Keramikbearbeitung in Dahschur 1976–1981', *Mitteilungen des Deutschen Archäologischen Instituts, Abteilung Kairo* 38 (1982), 29, Abb. 5, 31, Abb. 7.

using a smaller stone for the crushing. The millers were normally women. The ground product would not have been an evenly textured flour, but a crushed mixture of flour and husks which needed to be sieved. Analyses of ancient bread have also shown up the presence of much gritty material as well, although modern experiments in replicating the ancient technique show that grittiness was not an inevitable product.[10]

Just inside the door of the brewery-half of the model is a tall pottery vat. A man stands waist deep in it, holding on to its rim, as he mixes the dough by treading it with his feet. The dough next had to be made into little cakes, and at this stage dates could be added. The flat square tray beside the mixing vat probably served this purpose. The dough cakes were allowed to rise, but were evidently not baked for there is no oven in this part of the building. The risen dough cakes were next placed in a circular tray which was probably a fine screen, perhaps lined with linen. The tray was set over another pottery vat, and water poured in. As it drained through the screen someone would agitate the dough cakes so that they broke up and mixed with the water. Left to stand, the mixture fermented. The final act was to pour the fermented liquid into pottery beer jars, and to stopper them with mud. Some of the jars are shown stoppered in this way. In terms of the Middle Kingdom pottery repertoire, the beer jars must have been a well-known type, also illustrated in Figure 42, inset.

The adjacent room contained the bakery, subdivided into two by a low partition wall. The subdivision reflects two different methods of baking, one to produce flat loaves, the other to produce cylindrical loaves baked in pottery moulds. Two mortars stand in the floor of the inner compartment, and two quern emplacements and a mortar in the outer. In each compartment are also two large kneading vats. In the inner compartment they stand next to two low tables on which individual open loaves are made. Not all bread came in the form of hand-formed loaves, however. A common practice was to bake some bread in pottery moulds. During the Middle Kingdom these were characteristically long narrow tubes, hand-made, rough on the outside, but with a fine smooth inner surface (Figure 42, inset).[11] They occur in large numbers on Middle Kingdom sites, and the practice continued into the New Kingdom. The pottery moulds were used only once, and probably produced a finer quality of bread which, in the New Kingdom at least, was baked in the vicinity of shrines and temples. Beside the doorway which connects the two compartments stands a square basket filled with loaves of just this shape, which had presumably just been filled from the adjacent dough vats. Each compartment also contains two ovens, but of a different design in each. In the inner compartment they are of a standard cylindrical type with a hole at the bottom for inserting the fuel. The other two, however, are rectangular. Excavated evidence shows that these were used specifically either for baking the bread in pottery moulds or for the initial firing of the moulds themselves.[12]

Paintings in the tomb of Intef-iker (a vizier of the early 12th Dynasty)[13] complement the Meket-ra models (Figure 43). In the upper register mortar and pestle are wielded on the right, a woman grinds with a hand-quern to the left, assisted by a squatting woman who sieves the result to remove the coarsest components (a necessary activity which is omitted from the Meket-ra models). At the far left another pair of women fill pottery moulds from jars of dough, their companion at the left end apparently finishing off one of the hand-made moulds. In the very centre a man tends a rectangular oven filled with

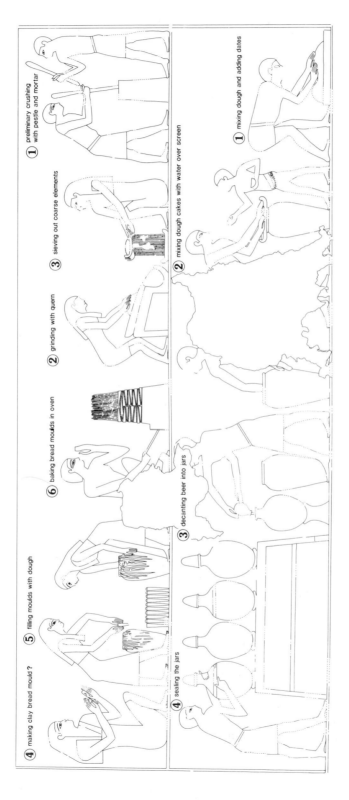

Figure 43 Baking and brewing, as portrayed in the tomb of Intef-iker at Thebes, after N. de G. Davies, *The Tomb of Antefoḳer*, London, 1920, Plates XI, XII.

the pottery bread moulds. Brewing is shown in the scene below (again without an oven being present): forming dough into cakes at the right, an accompanying inscription telling us that dates were added at this stage. Behind this man, after the rising of the dough cakes has taken place, another man agitates and presses the dough cakes through a sieve or screen into a large jar. The child carrying the bowl is saying in an accompanying inscription: 'Give me some ale, for I'm hungry'. The final act is the filling and sealing of the pottery beer jars at the left, which stand in wooden racks.

Baking and brewing contained elements which unavoidably thwarted a simple control of quantities as they passed from one stage to another. Water was added, dough rose, other elements such as dates were added as well, whilst a proportion of inedible matter was lost through milling and sieving. Loaves emerged in a variety of shapes. The scribes' approach was to treat the whole operation as a kind of 'black box': it was possible to measure what went in (either neat cereal grains or already milled flour) and what came out at the other end as quantities of loaves and vessels of beer. Ignoring what went on inside, input and output bore a simple relation to one another: the number of loaves and jugs of beer which derived from a given quantity of grain or meal. This scale of values the Egyptians called *pefsu*, which we can translate as 'baking value', and it represented a stage on the road towards mathematical abstraction. The *pefsu* scale was set for the number of loaves or jugs of beer that could be obtained from 1 *hekat* of grain.[14] The higher the value the smaller the loaves or the weaker the beer (or the smaller the jugs). *Pefsu* enabled the scribe to calculate equivalences between loaves and jugs of different sizes and strengths. '155 loaves of baking-value 20 are equivalent to how many loaves of baking-value 30? You express the 155 loaves of baking-value 20 in terms of meal: thus 7½ + ¼ *hekat*s. Multiply by 30: result 232½.'[15]

Many ration lists have survived. They tend to ignore *pefsu* values.[16] They assume standardized jugs of beer, and the various kinds of bread can be grossed together as 'mixed' loaves. This assumes standardization, a reasonable step in thinking in view of the scale and ubiquity of the operations, in which those involved, including potters making beer jugs, would tend naturally to produce standarized shapes from a lifetime's practice. We do actually have an opportunity to check for ourselves. Although very few actual loaves have survived, we have substitutes. The most common are the pottery moulds in which bread was baked. Thousands have been found on excavations. They went through an evolution over time. In the Old Kingdom they turned out loaves which were in the shape of a squat cone, characteristically about 16–20 cm across the base. By the Middle Kingdom the cones had evolved into tall thin cylinders (see Figure 42, p. 121, inset). Although so many have been discovered, they have never, oddly enough, been examined from the point of view of how the loaves they turned out compare with ancient accounting practices and dietary needs. Photographs of some large finds do give the impression of reasonably standardized capacity within that particular group, which could have been maintained if, as has been suggested, they were themselves formed over reusable moulds (perhaps of wood).[17] Nevertheless, examples from different sites and dates vary by quite a lot. There is no hint that they met a standard officially laid down. The scribe presumably performed his *pefsu* calculations periodically to test whole batches. This was not, however, the end of the story. Not all bread rations were in the form of mould-baked loaves. Soldiers at one of the Middle Kingdom Nubian fortresses (Uronarti) possessed wooden tallies in the shapes of their bread rations, with amounts

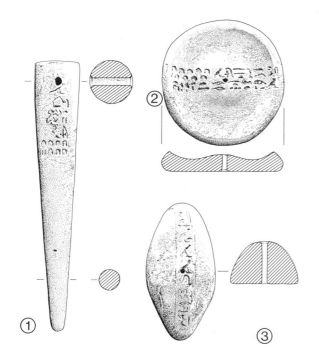

Figure 44 Soldiers' bread-ration tokens, made from wood, plastered over and painted. Each one is in the shape of a particular kind of loaf, and bears a short incised inscription, difficult to translate. No. 1: a cylindrical loaf of the kind baked in pottery moulds, height 24.7 cm; the hieroglyphs refer to seventy-five loaves for a soldier. No. 2: a round flat loaf with raised centre, diameter 12.8 cm; the hieroglyphs refer to ninety loaves from 1 *hekat* of wheat. No. 3: an oval loaf with flat base, length 12.7 cm; the hieroglyphs refer to $60\frac{2}{3}$ loaves. From the late 12th Dynasty fortress of Uronarti in Nubia. After D. Dunham, *Uronarti Shalfak Mirgissa*, Boston, 1967, Plates XXVII, XXVIII, and pp. 34–5.

of wheat and barley or numbers of loaves carved on them in hieroglyphs (Figure 44).[18] Some represent mould-baked loaves (of barley), but others flat round hand-made loaves (of wheat). These tallies look like the recipient's (a soldier's) own check on the value of his rations, calculated partly in terms of grain allocation behind them rather than on the actual number of loaves received. They could have formed the basis of a demand to the scribe to check the *pefsu* value of a batch of mixed loaves issued as rations.

Beer-jug capacity is more difficult for us to check. We know which was the common shape of Middle Kingdom beer jugs, and although most pottery from excavations is too broken to enable capacities to be calculated, many complete ones have been found. As with bread-moulds, however, it does not seem to have occurred to people to measure actual capacities with this question of standardization in mind. However, modern drawings of such vessels found in different tombs in a single cemetery certainly look as though they reflect a range of sizes and only roughly met a standard.

It is typical of the ancient lack of interest in the idea of efficiency that standardization does not seem to have been a conscious goal. Scribes and potters (and bakers) were worlds apart. The gulf of status kept the scribe from breaking out of the limits of his own art, that of procedure and calculation, and his procedures arose from an acceptance that a crucial part of the operation was virtually beyond his control.

Real ration lists show that the regular wage or ration was calculated in terms of so many loaves of bread and jugs of beer, with extras sometimes appearing, such as cakes or wine.[19] A standard basic wage consisted of ten loaves and a measure of beer that could fluctuate between a third of a jug to one or even two whole jugs. This basic ration was what was thought fit for an ordinary labourer. Ration lists also show that as one moved upwards through the ranks of officialdom the distributions increased by multiples of the basic ration. This was sometimes expressed by listing those of higher rank as if they were more than one person: perhaps five, ten, or even twenty men. The Rhind Mathematical Papyrus helped the scribe cope with the consequences.

> Method of distributing 100 loaves amongst 10 men, if the skipper, the crew-leader and the doorkeeper (receive) double.
> Its procedure: you add up the people to receive supplies: thus 13.
> Divide the 100 loaves by 13. That makes $7 + \frac{2}{3} + \frac{1}{39}$ (i.e. $7\frac{9}{13}$).
> Then you say: (this) is the consumption of the 7 men, (while) the skipper, the crew-leader and the doorkeeper receive double.[20]

Thus the ten men with unequal shares are converted into thirteen fictitious 'recipients' with equal shares. The seven 'one-man' shares are each $7\frac{9}{13}$; the three 'two-man' shares for the three officials amount to twice that quantity, i.e. $15\frac{5}{13}$.

The Rhind Mathematical Papyrus also, however, envisaged more complicated cases of distribution where the scaling by rank was not done in simple multiples of one basic ration. '100 loaves for 5 men. $\frac{1}{7}$ of the rations for the three superiors goes to the two inferiors. What is the difference in the shares?' To answer this question (Rhind Problem 40), the author provided tabular calculations which show that he was really asking for an arithmetic progression of shares for the five men, each one $\frac{1}{7}$ smaller than the next. The answer is correctly found: $38\frac{1}{3}$, $29\frac{1}{6}$, 20, $10\frac{2}{3} + \frac{1}{6}$, and $1\frac{1}{3}$. The difference between any two is $9\frac{1}{6}$.

Documents about rations create a problem which tells us that we are dealing not just with a pragmatic earthy business of feeding people, but with an economic system of more ambitious scope having a greater notional or abstract content than at first sight seems to be the case.

If a basic minimum daily ration consisted of ten loaves, a senior official could be credited with anything up to 500 per day. This would have exceeded the most gargantuan of appetites. Was the extra to support his staff? Some texts make separate reference to staff payments and so help to rule this out. In any case, some of the ration lists relate to expeditions sent to mines and quarries in uncomfortable desert locations, such as Sinai and the Wadi Hammamat. These were hardly suited to taking along one's family or household, or to bouts of high living. But then there are the fractions to consider. The Rhind Mathematical Papyrus is not alone in considering awkward fractions of loaves and jugs of beer. The same occur in real lists. Equally arresting is the accounting system of a provincial Middle Kingdom temple, that of the god Wepwawet at Asyut.[21] Some staff were paid according to the number of 'temple days' allotted to them. A text explains:

> As for a temple day, it is $\frac{1}{360}$ part of a year. Now, you shall divide everything which enters this temple – bread, beer and meat – by way of the daily rate. That is, it is going to be $\frac{1}{360}$ of the bread, of the beer, and of everything which enters this temple for (any) one of these temple days which I have given you.

Each staff member was entitled to two temple days, except for the chief priest, who got four. The real entitlement was thus $\frac{2}{360}$ (or $\frac{4}{360}$ in the case of the chief priest) of every loaf and jug of beer that the temple received by way of its income. Part of the income was meat. The archive of another temple (at Kahun) deals with fractions of cattle![22]

Common sense tells us that we are not dealing with a system that distributed breadcrumbs and minced meat in finely weighed portions, and piled up uneaten surpluses around high officials. The system must have combined a distribution of real and of notional rations, the latter being, in effect, credit, in which a paper accumulation of undistributed ration allocation was exchangeable for something else. The loaves and the jugs were measures of value, or units of account, as much as they stood for actual amounts of foodstuff in hand, waiting to be carried off and consumed. The *pefsu*-system allowed the interchangeability of bread and beer to be calculated, as well as the keeping of a record of just how much wheat or barley lay behind them. The implication, however, is that a wider range of equivalents in value would have been needed, where, for example, the grain or bread equivalent of linen cloth was expressed. But it is here that the documentation runs out. Neither the Rhind Mathematical Papyrus nor administrative documents cover this wider field of value exchanges. For the New Kingdom we have ample records of village barter transactions which display a wide range of values of commodities expressed in terms of *hekat*s of grain or weights of metal (mostly copper). A feeling for relative values seems from this material to have been part of the basic mental equipment for living which Egyptians possessed from an early age. But at an official level the gap in the texts remains. Either we are missing some key element in the system, or the 'cashing' of one's accumulated surplus of rations was done unofficially, by barter and out of the scope of normal record keeping.

The lack of standardized bread and beer strengths lets us down in another respect. We cannot jump immediately to the actual figures for the average wheat and barley allocations which lay behind the basic ration, and so answer the most essential question: how much cereal did the ancient Egyptians normally consume? How nutritious was the diet of those who dragged stones from quarries to pyramids? For convenience, rations were normally expressed in simple numerical form, leaving it to the *pefsu* system and the wooden tallies to satisfy any doubts or queries. There must, nevertheless, have been an average quantity that we can attempt to establish, or perhaps more realistically we can aim to set maximum and minumum figures.

One American scholar has used the short inscriptions carved into the Uronarti tallies as a source.[23] They are, unfortunately, cryptic and the results therefore somewhat tentative. They lead him to the figure of two-thirds of a *hekat* of barley, and one *hekat* of wheat per soldier as a ten-day ration. How feasible is this in reality?

Modern estimates of the size of the Egyptian *hekat* vary slightly. One reasonably reliable figure is 4.78 litres. One *hekat* of wheat is thus 0.00478 cu. metre. A cubic metre of wheat is reckoned to weigh 785 kg. One *hekat* of wheat should thus weigh around 3.75 kg. An equivalent amount of barley is reckoned to be lighter: 705 kg per cu. metre. Thus, two-thirds of a *hekat* of barley should amount to about 2.25 kg. When added together, 6 kg of grain per ten-day period is involved, or 0.6 kg per day.

By the standards calculated for the Roman world this seems a somewhat meagre portion. According to another scholar, figures given by the Greek author Polybius, writing around 140 BC, imply for an infantryman, whether legionary or auxiliary, 0.94 kg of grain per day, although Roman records from Pselchis (modern Dakka in Nubia) can be interpreted to produce the smaller figure of 0.8 kg. For both Egyptian and

Roman societies there is another unknown factor: the amount and variety of dietary supplement to a grain ration. In the case of Egypt this was probably fairly small. The impression derived from many sources is that bread and beer from wheat and barley were the staple diet.

The discussion can be taken at least one stage further by estimating caloric values.[24] One *hekat* of wheat represents about 8,100 calories, and barley about 9,720. One *hekat* of wheat and two-thirds of a *hekat* of barley thus would yield 14,580 calories for the ten-day period, or 1,458 per day. How realistic is this figure? Comparisons suggest that it is also low. For example, a report on prison diet in Egypt published in 1917 gave the following energy values required in daily diets: 1,800 calories for subsistence, 2,200 for no work, 2,800 for light labour, and 3,200 for hard labour.[25] These figures derived from the regime laid down for prisoners in the Egyptian army. We may thus take, with some confidence, the figures derived from the Uronarti tallies as being the very minimum, and set as our maximum a figure of 1 kg of grain per day. Indeed, if the Uronarti tallies stand only for the loaves that were issued we can understand better what seems to be a short ration: we have to add the grain content of the separately issued beer. The maximum is thus even more likely to be closer to the truth. But we still have to accept that the pyramids were built on a modest health-food diet.

Apart from a general interest in ancient diet this discussion also serves a more specific archaeological enquiry concerning the capacities of ancient granaries and the number of people dependent on them which will surface in the next chapter.

Cereal administration was not confined to human foodstuff. The obliging Rhind Mathematical Papyrus (Problem 82b) includes the following:

> Amount of what a fatted goose eats:
> ten geese $1\frac{1}{4}$ *hekat*s (of flour made into bread)
> in ten days $12\frac{1}{2}$
> in 40 days 50 *hekat*s
> which represents grain in double-*hekat*s: $23\frac{1}{2} + \frac{1}{4} + \frac{1}{8}$ *hekat*s, and $4\frac{1}{4} + \frac{1}{6}$ *ro*
> (1 *ro* $= \frac{1}{320}$ *hekat*).

The essence of this problem, somewhat cryptically laid out, is to calculate the volume difference between grain and flour. For this one-tenth of two-thirds is subtracted – presumably a rule-of-thumb ratio – and the result halved to reduce it to double-*hekat*s. The answer is not quite correct, although the scribe has aimed at great exactitude by using fractions of *hekat*s.

Management of labour

A similarly intense scrutiny was applied to building projects, another major goal of administration. All concerned, whether officials and architects in charge, or the army of workers and craftsmen, were employed directly, and their work and their reward measured and scrutinized. A typical task was the precise measurement of materials to be moved and used, whether cut blocks of stone, sun-dried mud bricks, straw and earth for making bricks, rubble, or sand. A conscientious scribe would measure (or write down the measurements called out by another) in the full standardized notation of

Egyptian linear measure: cubits (20.6 inches or 523 mm), palms, fingerbreadths, and fractions, as well as in halves, thirds, and quarters of a cubit. He would then calculate the volume of material. The multiplication of fractions and subdivisions of a cubit involved considerable calculating skill, and the scribe may have referred to ready-made tables. From the volume he could calculate the number of labour-units that would be required, using standard ratios. In one example the daily labour norm for one man was to transport 10 cubic cubits.[26] From these figures the scribe could estimate the rations that would be required and produce work figures which could later be compared with the actual work done.

In this way the supply of the three essentials for major building projects – materials, labour, and rations – could be constantly monitored. It was the scribe's pen as much as the overseer's lash or the engineer's ingenuity that built the pyramids.

By conscription the state temporarily cast its net over a larger labour force than was regularly available from the pool of those in part-time or full-time state employment. For its part, the state paid rations, so that those affected did not have their labour taken from them for nothing. But the tasks were typically arduous: the occasional army to serve abroad, or surges of activity at quarrying or construction sites. There were those who tried to escape, and then the state revealed its punitive side. A key document from the late Middle Kingdom, a prison register, opens for us a little window on the fate of those who chose not to co-operate.[27] One typical entry reads:

> The daughter of Sa-anhur, Teti, under the Scribe of the Fields of the city of This: a woman. An order was issued to the Great Prison in year 31, 3rd month of summer, day 9, to release her family from the courts, and at the same time to execute against her the law pertaining to one who runs away without performing his service. Present [check mark]. Statement by the Scribe of the Vizier, Deduamun: 'Carried out; case closed'.

This sounds very much as though her family had been held hostage until her arrest.

The mobilizing effects of bureaucracy when applied to a major project were impressive. Sadly we lack any part of the original documentation for major building works that have survived, such as the Giza pyramids. But our imagination is readily stimulated by records left scratched in the stone at ancient mines and quarries. For sheer scale we can turn to the same quarrying and mining records that have furnished us with detail on the method of payment. In the thirty-eighth regnal year of King Senusret I (1933 BC) an expedition went to the quarries in the Wadi Hammamat. It was under the leadership of a 'herald' called Ameni.[28] Under him were 80 officials, roughly 18,660 skilled and unskilled workers (who included 30 hunters and a contingent of soldiers), plus a train of millers, brewers, and bakers. Amongst the officials were 20 'mayors' of towns, presumably because it was their responsibility to supply most of the drafted or conscripted labour. Interestingly the whole enterprise was looked after by only 8 scribes.

For the intensity of the control and scrutiny that the Middle Kingdom observed we can do no better than refer to a group of papyri that relate to various activities being carried out in a provincial part of Egypt, in the vicinity of the city of This, near Abydos.[29] No pyramid-building or quarrying expedition of epic magnitude was involved. Part of the archive relates to a carpentry shop attached to a royal boatyard, where every minor movement of planks and goat-hides was listed, and which received written instructions on matters great and small directly from the vizier based in the vicinity of Memphis. Another part deals with construction on a provincial temple, evidently an example of the type revealed by excavation, where mud brick rather than stone was the most common material. It is this text which provides the most striking evidence for detailed measurements of volumes of materials moved and conversion to work-loads mentioned above. There is no reason to suppose that this provincial setting for so great an intensity of supervision was anything special. Rather it implies that this level was typical for the Middle Kingdom.

It is possible for an authority to order its people to do such-and-such a task and leave them to get on with much of it as best they can. Once you decide to take control of every detail of the operation, however, the burden of administration rapidly mounts and in the modern world easily gets out of hand. The Egyptians, with clear (if ambitious) goals and no dissenting philosophies to divert their energies, got away with it.

Bureaucracy is an attitude of mind, an aptitude which we encounter with most immediacy in original documents. It can easily appear to be a cosy self-contained world of order, particularly as the documents tend to be studied in isolation by experts in ancient language working in quiet studies or libraries and equipped with dictionaries and manuals of grammar. For the ancient scribe, however, the order belonged to his inner mental world. When he rested his pen and looked up from his sheet of papyrus the scenes that met his eyes may well have been a good deal less orderly. Indeed, the essence of the act of writing (and of drawing) is to reduce a complex and often chaotic reality to a comprehensible order.

Ancient documents lie at an interface of reality: the far side is available to us only through archaeology. This has already intruded in the description of baking and brewing. These messy and smoky processes were the reality behind the precision of the Rhind Mathematical Papyrus. They represent, however, only a token of the roughness and complexity of life which bureaucracy sought to tame.

Although we lack the original written documentation on the building of the Giza pyramids, through the window of archaeology we can gain some idea of the physical complexities of the operation which bureaucracy had somehow to control. To do this we have, so to speak, to stand back and not be overwhelmed by the pyramids themselves (Figure 45). We must try to see them in the context of their setting, the whole Giza plateau, as the outcome of a huge management operation, in which several interlocking lines of administration had to be pursued simultaneously, with the danger that a mistake in one could disrupt others and delay the whole gigantic project. To be successful this required a total managerial overview, the scope of which we can reconstruct using the range of archaeological observations from the site.[30]

The Giza plateau was not a blank page on which the architects had a free hand to design and to lay out the buildings of their choice. One basic constraint was provided by the site's geology. Much of the surface of the plateau is the top of a bed of limestone (the Mokattam Formation) which has a general slope down to the south-east. It seems to have been the desire of the pyramid builders to keep to more or less the same level for each of the three major pyramids (of Kings Khufu, Khafra, and Menkaura), and this could be met only by laying them out along a single line running perpendicular to the direction of the slope. The limestone of the Mokattam Formation was also suited to

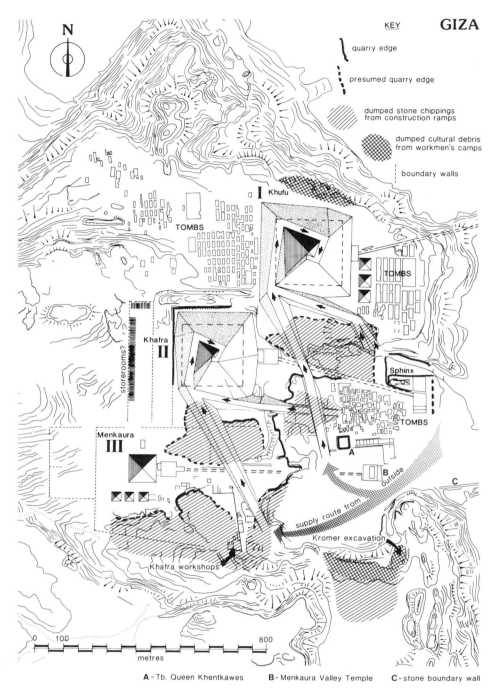

Figure 45 The archaeology of large-scale public works: the Giza pyramid plateau, showing quarries and construction debris, plus the hypothetical outlines of the partly 'spiral' construction ramps for the 1st and 2nd pyramids, after M. Lehner, 'A contextual approach to the Giza pyramids', *Archiv für Orientforschung* 32 (1985), 136–58. For the Khafra workshops see Figure 46, p. 134, for the Menkaura Valley Temple see Figure 51, p. 146; for the Khentkawes town see Figure 50, p. 144.

provide much of the stone for the cores of the pyramids, although it was not fine enough for the outer casings. For each pyramid a conveniently sited quarry was opened.

Convenience involved another major consideration. As the pyramid rose so the stones had to be taken to ever higher levels. Although scholars differ as to the details there is general agreement that much of the stone was raised by dragging it up huge ramps which had to be raised in phase with the construction work. Keeping the gradient to a minimum as well as minimizing its distance from the quarry was a further consideration of prime importance. Furthermore, the builders of the second and third pyramids had their limits of manoeuvre reduced by the works of their predecessors. Khufu had chosen an area at the far north-eastern end of the Mokattam Formation, immediately above a high escarpment, drawing stone from quarries on the south side, and filling up the ground to east and west with tombs for members of his court. His successors were obliged to move further to the south-west, so that no one was able to use the advantage of the natural slope of the ground by constructing ramps down its line. All the ramps to some extent must have run up the slope. There was probably, however, a good reason for preferring this arrangement of ramps. Not all of the stone was quarried locally. Originally the pyramids were encased in a layer of fine limestone from quarries across the river, at Turah, supplemented in the case of the pyramids of Khafra and Menkaura with granite from Aswan. The temples that accompanied the pyramids also required stone from outside, and there must have been, as well, a considerable demand for timber, which was, amongst other uses, laid across the tops of the ramps to provide a suitable surface for the sledges. Transport of heavy materials to the site must have been by boat on a canal or canals, requiring a docking area. The natural site for this is towards the south, where the dip of the plateau leaves a depression. If the zone for receiving deliveries of building materials and preparing them for their places on the site was here, the alignments of the construction ramps would need to take this into consideration as well. Site management employing the skills of co-ordination and anticipation was thus the real pinnacle of command in pyramid building, and it is not surprising to find that the task was performed by the most senior figures in the land, close to the king, to the extent of being, in the 4th Dynasty, normally a son of the king.[31]

The picture of managerial choices and constraints has two sources. One consists of direct observations. The location of several of the quarries is apparent from modern excavations, and certain pieces of evidence point to the existence of an ancient basin towards the south end of the site. The other is the result of putting oneself in the position of the builders and looking for an economical solution within the framework provided by the archaeology. The alignments of the ramps, huge constructions in their own right, can be deduced only in this way since when the pyramids were finished the ramps were all cleared away, leaving no direct traces. The need for clear forward thinking and the demarcation of zones of activity to prevent them from spreading too far may have been one reason behind a pattern of rough stone walls which divides the Giza plateau in the areas of the pyramids of Khafra and Menkaura into large zones. They were left as permanent features and, with some additions, would have continued to define the ground which properly belonged to each pyramid.

The construction ramps were, as noted, major projects in themselves. Each one may have equalled two-thirds of the volume of its pyramid. At the end of the day they had to be disposed of. What were the ramps made of? Some later sources show that ramps could be built up from compartments constructed of mud brick and filled with sand. There is no sign at Giza, however, of huge dumps of mud brick. Instead several parts of the Giza plateau, especially the quarries and the low area to the south, were buried in stone chippings and dust, in vast quantities sufficient probably to account for the ramps. This reveals another managerial responsibility: directing the quarrying and the necessary extra labour to put quarry debris and loose desert materials into the right position to create the appropriately graded ramp for the stage of pyramid construction reached, the ramp being a long and broadly based heap of loose material.

No one knows how many people were employed to build the Great Pyramid. Herodotus was told 100,000, but that may have been a guess on the part of his guide.[32] Clearly it was a great number, and this introduces a further question for the archaeologist to answer: where were they all housed? It is possible, of course, that the answer was: on the floodplain, and at a level now so deeply buried as to be inaccessible to archaeologists. But it is also possible that the camps or work villages were on the plateau itself. It is certainly something that archaeologists have to consider and look for.

In the search for the remains of the work-camps one site was proposed late last century. It lies to the west of the Pyramid of Khafra and really forms part of the pattern of rubble walls and alignments on the Giza plateau: a long narrow annexe built against the western enclosure wall of the pyramid. The wall outlines are visible today, but for a scientific examination of this site we are confined to an account given by Petrie in the report of his survey of the pyramids carried out in the 1880s. Petrie writes:

> Beyond the western peribolus wall there lie the large barracks of the workmen. These have been hitherto considered merely as lines of stone rubbish, or masons' waste heaps; and though Vyse cut through one part, he merely says that the ridges 'were found to be composed of stones and sand, and their origin was not discovered'. . . . But on looking closely at them I observed the sharply defined edges of walls; and as soon as these were begun to be cleared, the ruined tops of the walls were seen, the spaces being filled with blown sand.
>
> These galleries are built of rough pieces of limestone (somewhat like the W. peribolus wall), bedded in mud, and faced with hard mud, or mud and lime [Petrie must mean gypsum]; the floors of the galleries are also of hard mud. Their length was variable, about 90 feet; their width 113 inches, with entrances 85 inches wide. There are in all 91 galleries; which make an aggregate of over a mile and a half of gallery length, 9½ feet wide, and 7 feet high. Such a vast amount of accommodation seems only attributable to the workmen's barracks.[33]

Petrie went on to calculate that they could hold about 4,000 men.

At this time he was working on a very modest scale, and it is unlikely that his excavation involved anything more than a trial pit or two. However, since then this interpretation has been widely accepted. It does leave unexplained, however, the absence of an accumulation of domestic refuse that such a dense occupation would leave behind. Furthermore, the general plan resembles one of the blocks of storerooms which the Egyptians built at religious sites and which points, therefore, to an alternative hypothesis. Without fresh excavation we are in a poor position to evaluate this building.

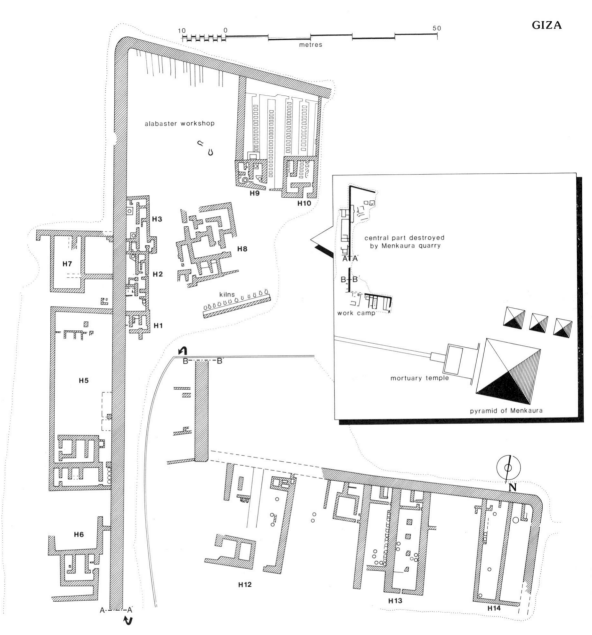

Figure 46   Part of the work-camp near the pyramid of Menkaura at Giza, but intended probably for the building of the pyramid of Khafra, see Figure 45, p. 131. After Abdel-Aziz Saleh, 'Excavations around Mycerinus pyramid complex', *Mitteilungen des Deutschen Archäologischen Instituts, Abteilung Kairo* 30 (1974), 132, Fig. 1, 142, Fig. 2.

Not all of the labour force may have been accommodated in separate and specially constructed barracks. Certain groups may simply have camped and lived on the construction sites. A part of one such area was excavated in 1971–2 to the south-east of the Pyramid of Menkaura (Figure 46).[34] It consists of a collection of structures built on either side of a rubble wall which makes a series of sharp changes of direction. The full extent of the site is not known, for it continues unexcavated beneath the desert on both east and west. The individual buildings, like the enclosure walls, were constructed of rough stone and mud mortar. On the north lies a group of three. The central one (H13) contained a hall, 15 by 5.5 metres, with square supports which may have been column bases. In the adjacent room and in the two other northern buildings, H12 and H14, the ground contained numerous circular pits. Along the east side of the main wall are three units, H5, H6, and H7. For want of a better term they may be called 'houses', but the real range of activities carried on in and around them remains uncertain. It should be noted, however, that in building H5, the central room in the northern part contained a low dais, of the kind which usually indicates a sleeping-room. Unlike later examples, however, this dais sloped from one side to the other, from a height of 20 cm down to 5 cm. This was true for others at this site. On the west side, at the southern end of the site, a large open area was cleared, revealing a mixture of constructions. Along the west side of the main wall clustered a row of very small houses. Building H1 contained a dais in an alcove in the centre chamber on the south. Buildings H2 and H3 contained ovens, and one probable pottery kiln. Along the north side of the cleared space ran a length of wall sheltering a row of twelve more pottery kilns. These imply local provision for part at least of the great demand for pottery vessels to which ancient societies were always prone. To the south lies a free-standing building, H8, probably a house or administrative building. Two rooms on the north possess alcoves each with a dais. Two more smaller buildings, H9 and H10, lie not far away. H9 contained two ovens. Over this open area were scattered a large number of rough blocks of alabaster, together with an unfinished alabaster column base. This helps to identify the site as belonging to a work-camp for pyramid construction. The same open space contained a group of structures which defy explanation. There are four of them: broad shallow trenches containing rows of closely set rectangular pedestals built from stone and mud plaster. The pedestals measure 95 to 110 cm by 57 to 65 cm. They number seventy-two in all. Whatever their purpose, it seems to have been short-lived, for buildings H9 and H10 were constructed over them.

This excavation adds another piece of evidence to the picture of Giza as a giant construction site. The reason why the work-camp was so well preserved is simply that it had been buried beneath a vast dump of the stone chippings which occur in various parts of the Giza plateau. Their late appearance on the scene – after the camp had been abandoned – is understandable if we see them as the remains of a pyramid construction ramp, removed after the end of building and dumped in the nearest convenient place.

Not all of the ancient dumps at Giza are of limestone chippings and archaeologically sterile. East and south of the Menkaura work-camp lies a large bay in the line of the rock escarpment largely filled up. Although at first sight the filling appears to be natural, archaeological soundings have suggested otherwise. Petrie was the first to note that this was no natural patch of desert: 'The whole surface is covered for many feet deep with broken stone-chips from quarrying.'[35] Then between 1971 and 1975 an

Austrian expedition (under K. Kromer) extensively probed the eastern edge, where it becomes the western slope of the prominent rock outcrop south of the Mendaura Valley Temple.[36] A substantial layered deposit of Old Kingdom domestic rubbish was revealed, which included pottery and other artefacts, but no structures. These two probings, and the record of Menkaura work-camp, are pointers to the possibility that the whole southern edge of the Giza plateau, which is its lowest part, is the site of a gigantic rubbish infilling consisting in part of ramp debris and in part of the dumped remains of building sites and work-camps. This would imply that many were camped in the vicinity, and thus close to the likely ends of the construction ramps and the docking area, a place where we might expect much work to have been concentrated.

These largely hidden aspects of pyramid building, creating and maintaining the construction sites and then clearing them away, are no mean ones. From an administrative point of view it hardly mattered if the operation in hand involved highly skilled sculpting and engineering or the transportation of mountains of rubbish. The size of the Giza pyramids has, since ancient times, been a marvel, and people have speculated on the numbers of labourers needed and their conditions. But whilst it would be an exaggeration to say that in organizational terms the pyramids that we see are only the tip of an iceberg, we nevertheless have to recognize that administratively the actual piling up of stones into pyramidal shape was only one of several major and pressing tasks. If we had some of the ancient texts they would document the devices by which the huge administrative needs were met. But even then we would be unlikely to have the full picture. Looking at the less spectacular aspects of the archaeology of Giza is essential for understanding the total scope of the necessary administration. The study of ancient texts reveals to us only one aspect of ancient administration, the technical devices by which it was accomplished. Archaeology supplies an equally important part of the picture. In this particular case it also provides us with an interesting problem of evidence: the archaeology of what is no longer there.

Bureaucracy in the ancient world was an instrument of prosperity of a kind that has surfaced in modern economic debates, revolving around the question: are public works entailing massive state employment a good thing? Modern debates mix economics and ideology inextricably, and involve a degree of abstract knowledge and an ability to manipulate economies that is unique to our day. Nevertheless, even if we reject public expenditure as a modern route to prosperity, we must recognize that part of the back-cloth of history is the fact that the central direction of resources committed to massive labour-intensive projects was in earlier times the great engine of growth, creating many of the world's civilizations. For the ancient Egyptians we can reconstruct the system in a quite specific way. We can see that huge numbers of people received a basic ration – a minimum wage – and a not insignificant number did better still. The number of jobs (with ration entitlement) was artificially inflated by an early work-sharing device: the phyle system in which people performed their duties for only a limited part of each year. The land and its farmers were obliged by the pressure of demand dictated from above to produce enough. The state had already become the great provider and it produced whatever it is that we wish to call Egyptian civilization. Welfare (as yet innocent of social ideology) arrived early in human history.

4
Model communities

Bureaucracy, although characteristically concerned with minutiae, cumulatively deals with large sections of society and to some degree shapes it. Nowadays this tends to be done in deliberate pursuit of social goals, and to be part of the processes of 'planning' and 'social engineering'. The modern landscape universally bears witness to this in the size, nature, and distribution of towns and villages, as well as in the appearance of individual buildings. We should also expect to find counterparts in the archaeological record of ancient states. Although the balance between what the natural environment and human stubbornness allowed and what government dictated was much more weighted towards the former in ancient times, nevertheless it was a balance. We err if we treat ancient societies as having been passively moulded by nature.

The creation of buildings and complete settlements is a supreme act of imposing order on the natural environment. From the way in which any society – ancient or modern – goes about it so it leaves its stamp, its signature on the ground. It is this which archaeologists most frequently encounter. The record that they make is inevitably shaped in the visual language of ground plans – a symbolic language of its own – frequently incapable of resolution into the terms of the builders' original intentions (even in well-documented societies such as that of ancient Egypt it remains extremely difficult to determine the specific purpose for which individual rooms and sometimes whole buildings were made). But still this remains the most widespread testimony of one particular facet of the creative element in society: its capacity to structure its own environment, and beyond this, its power to create visions of how human society should look. Where we live – shanty town or garden city – is a statement about our society. To see the shapes of towns, ancient and modern, as microcosms of society gives us the most consistent basis there is for comparing societies across space and time. For whereas the survival of written records is a chancy matter, and for some societies may amount to nothing at all, archaeology has a consistently good world-wide record for the recovery of plans and other material information about the places where communities once lived.

If, however, we admit that the evidence in a particular case points to a clear and

137

consistent underlying ideal, then we are tacitly admitting the existence of an ideology. Not necessarily a formally conceived and expressed ideology such as that which portrayed Egyptian kingship, but an implicit ideology of social ordering.

Our starting-point has to be the physical record supplied by the plans of ancient sites, but before we look at the spread of early Egyptian evidence we have to confront the difficult question of architectural aesthetics.

Modern architects create their buildings as drawings and models on a small scale. The hoped-for harmony of the end-product can be seen at a glance and discussed in comfort. We do not know if the Egyptians, even in the case of large temples, ever did more than make working sketches for use on the spot (Figure 47). What is likely to have been common is that planning and discussion were done directly on site at full scale. Ropes and pegs and simple sighting instruments took the place of scribal equipment, whilst the ground served instead of the papyrus sheet.[1] It may have been more laborious, but supply of labour was never a problem. The plan that first became really visible was the network of foundations in the ground.

In the process three elements came together. The first was the likely system of measuring over long distances, using a rope knotted at set intervals, as was used in land survey. When the ground was relatively flat and the buildings were intended to be rectangular a certain frequency of measurements tended to recur. The second element was the range of functions that each building was to house, expressed on the ground by a pattern of partition walls to create rooms and corridors. It was normal at this stage not to mark the position of doorways. The third element was everybody's natural sense of proportion and harmony which all of us have and use, for example in arranging furniture in our living-rooms. The result was often a plan which looks as though it were the result of a much greater degree of premeditated planning based on a mathematical knowledge of the harmonies of natural proportion than was actually the case. It is possible to take, for example, the plan of the Middle Kingdom town of Kahun (described on pp. 149–57 and see Figure 53, p. 150) and to analyse it to show two things: one, that a module of 8 cubits, further subdivided into squares of 10 cubits, seems to govern the layout; and two, that the overall town plan and the plans of the houses reflect the conscious application of a rule of proportion based upon an isosceles triangle where the ratio of base to height is 8:5, the classic 'golden' ratio or section of classical harmonics.[2] That these proportions are present at Kahun and in numerous other Egyptian buildings is easy to demonstrate. What is very doubtful indeed is that this is anything more than the consequence of combining the use of knotted ropes with an intuitive sense of harmony and proportion.

The norm for early town layouts

During the Old Kingdom (and sometimes before that) at many places towns came into existence. Commonly they were surrounded by a thick high brick wall, sometimes following a curving course, sometimes built in straight sections. The lack of conformity in what must have been the town's major building work – its enclosure wall – implies that these walls represent local initiatives rather than the result of royal decrees, but whether true or not perimeter walls played a significant part in shaping the internal

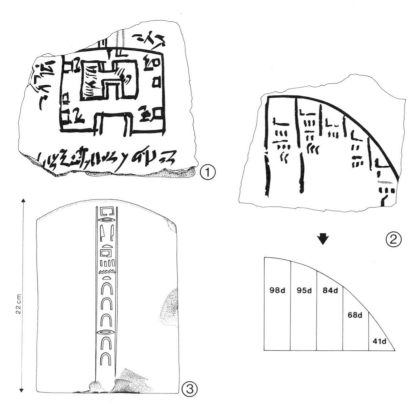

Figure 47 Practical scribal aids to building: (1) A quick sketch with overall dimensions may have been all that was necessary to start the builders off, marking out the ground and digging the foundations. In this case the sketch is on a piece of broken pottery, and dates to the late 18th or early 19th Dynasty. Brief annotations, including measurements, are written in hieratic. The building was evidently a cultic way-station open at each end, containing an inner chamber also open at both ends, and surrounded by a colonnade. The outside measurements were 27 cubits (about 14 metres) each way; the inner shrine was to be 14 by 6 cubits. Six columns are shown at the sides (labelled 'column' against four of them), but this may not have been the exact number intended. Details were probably worked out on the stonework as the building proceeded. Width 9.5 cm. British Museum 41228, from Deir el-Bahari. After S.R.K. Glanville, 'Working plan for a shrine', *Journal of Egyptian Archaeology* 16 (1930), 237–9. (2) A diagram sketched on a flake of limestone showing how to draw an even curve. At regular intervals (of 1 cubit each, though this is not stated explicitly) one should draw a perpendicular line of a stated length. The lengths are given in the cubit notation (here reduced for convenience to digits). When the points at the ends of the lines are joined a curve is produced. From Sakkara, perhaps 3rd Dynasty and used in the building of the curved top to the Southern Tomb. Width 17.8 cm. Cairo Museum JE 50036. After Somers Clarke and R. Engelbach, *Ancient Egyptian Masonry*, Oxford, 1930, pp. 52–3, Figs. 53, 54. (3) Limestone tablet from Kahun, perhaps used to mark out the position of an intended group of houses. The inscription reads something like: 'A four-house block – 30 x 20 (cubits)', i.e. about 15 x 10 metres. After G.A. Wainwright, 'Antiquities from Middle Egypt and the Fayûm', *Annales du Service des Antiquités de l'Egypte* 25 (1925), 144–5, and plate; also H.G. Fischer, 'Deux stèles villageoises du Moyen Empire', *Chronique d'Egypte* 55, no. 109-110 (1980), 13–16.

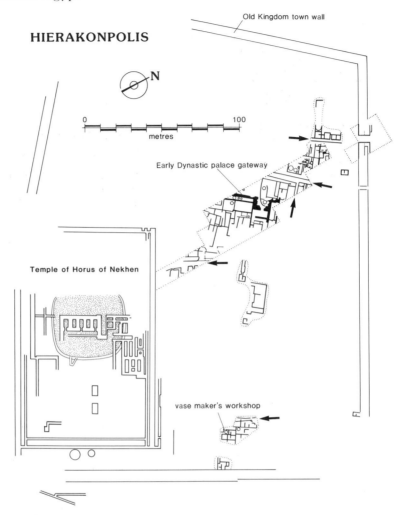

HIERAKONPOLIS

Old Kingdom town wall

N

0   100

metres

Early Dynastic palace gateway

Temple of Horus of Nekhen

vase maker's workshop

Figure 48   Urban layout with a degree of regularity dictated by a town wall: the Old Kingdom town of Hierakonpolis (cf. Figure 11, p. 40, Figure 25, p. 76). The arrows point to probable streets. After J.E. Quibell and F.W. Green, *Hierakonpolis* II, London, 1902, Plate LXXIII; W. Fairservis, K.R. Weeks and M. Hoffman, 'Preliminary report on the first two seasons at Hierakonpolis', *Journal of the American Research Center in Egypt* 9 (1971–1972), Figs 3, 9–15.

layouts of individual towns. Buildings close to the town wall tended to align themselves by it, perhaps actually using it to prop up the whole structure. The alignment of adjacent streets could be similarly influenced. If the town wall was built as a series of straight sections then the interior would tend naturally to contain a degree of internal regularity. The clearest early example is Hierakonpolis (Figure 48).[3] The Old Kingdom wall enclosed an irregular area, but by means of a series of straight lengths. A broad diagonal swathe of the town has been excavated, together with a few isolated patches. Within these exposures we can see an obvious tendency for walls and the narrow streets to follow similar directions for some distances. At the south end the direction is set by the southern stretch of the enclosure wall. In the central area, however, it was set by an existing but by then ruined wall of an earlier palace, which seems also to have been matched by the northern stretch of town wall. Similar house alignments taken from the nearest length of town wall can still be seen in exposed parts of the Old Kingdom-Middle Kingdom towns at Tell Edfu and Abydos.[4]

This is order arising from immediate convenience, and it is misleading to apply to it the term 'planning'. It differs, as we shall shortly see, from the products of true urban planning in several ways. The latter tend to pursue predetermined alignments which ignore topography, to maintain common alignments over very long distances, and to display repeated modular building units, and signs of planning involvement in the layouts of the interiors of buildings.

Pyramid towns in the Old Kingdom

The great uncertainty over who was responsible for initiatives in provincial town developments fogs the question of how far the Old Kingdom state had an interest in urban layout. Fortunately there is another set of examples which does provide a very revealing answer.

Organized life at pyramid sites did not end with the completion of the stone buildings and burial of the king. From Old Kingdom written sources we know of the existence of 'pyramid towns', looked after by a hierarchy of officials.[5] Altogether some forty-two different titles of officials have been recorded, though many are rare. Where these titles can be ranked, they tend to be headed by a senior priest, or by an 'overseer of the town'. The Neferirkara archive examined in the last chapter fills in the detail of how the pyramid towns were run. How were they represented on the ground?

The Neferirkara archive introduces us to a community busying itself in detailed daily bookkeeping exercises at one of the pyramids at Abusir. This is a good place to start looking. The most obvious traces of antiquity at Abusir were excavated by a German expedition between 1902 and 1908 (Figure 49).[6] There had been, as usual, a mortuary temple built against the eastern face of the pyramid. It had consisted of the normal grouping of cult chambers, storerooms, colonnaded forecourt, and entrance from the access causeway. It was a building finished cheaply, the forecourt and most of the storerooms being in brick with wooden columns. One unusual feature came to be added when the causeway was rerouted to serve the adjoining pyramid of King Neuserra: a formal columned entrance portico. This alteration coincided with the building of an inner enclosure wall of mud brick. The spaces between this wall and the stonework of the temple were filled with mud-brick buildings. Some of them appear to be houses. We can have little doubt that they belonged to the official community of priests and others looking after King Neferirkara's mortuary cult. We can recognize from the plan probably no more than nine separate 'houses'. They must be where the scribes and priests and others on duty resided whilst doing all the tasks so meticulously recorded in the papyri. It is the only sign of occupation around the Abusir pyramids found so far, but its small size and wholly unpretentious appearance match evidence from other sites. As an example of a model community it falls into the 'out of sight, out of mind' category. The sole element of order was provided by the enclosure wall which fitted in

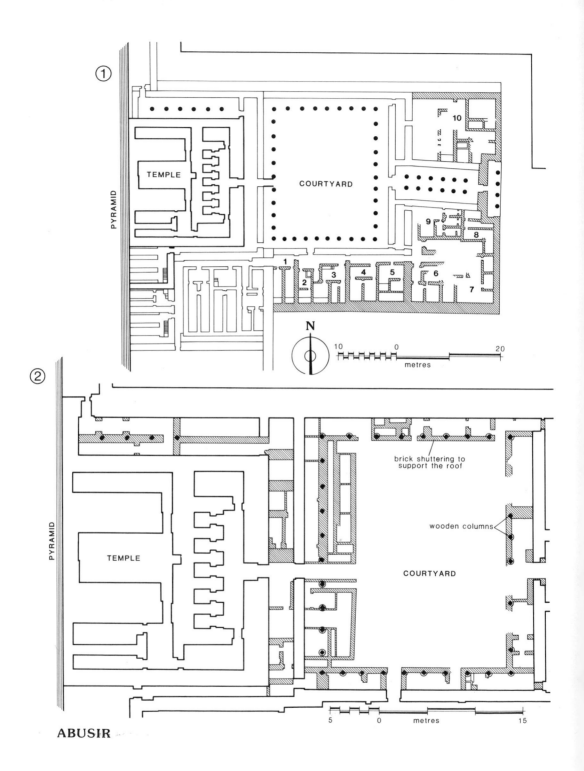

① TEMPLE

PYRAMID

COURTYARD

10

9

8

1

2

3

4

5

6

7

N

10   0   20

metres

② TEMPLE

PYRAMID

COURTYARD

brick shuttering to
support the roof

wooden columns

5   0   metres   15

ABUSIR

with the pyramid's monumental exterior, and hid from the outside world the huddle of houses on the inside.

This 'town' could have accommodated only a small community, fewer, one would guess, than those who appear in the lists of the Neferirkara archive. Yet it must be remembered that temple personnel put in a month's work only periodically. The permanent homes of these people may have been elsewhere. Where we lack direct evidence altogether is in whether their permanent homes were in nearby villages which had grown up piecemeal, or whether the state had provided a complete planned town for them all, now lost beneath the fields. The former is more likely to be true.

The same site also dramatizes a problem faced by all states which foster grandiose building: maintenance. By the end of the Old Kingdom Egypt possessed more than twenty pyramids with their associated temples, constructed with varying degrees of solidity (and not all of them finished). The Neferirkara temple was one of the less well-built examples. During the lifetime of its 'town' roofs became dangerous and the wooden columns weakened, no doubt from the attacks of termites which quickly turn their attention to woodwork in desert locations. The priests' response (Figure 49) was to shore up the threatened parts with brick walls and shuttering. It badly disfigured the building, completely obliterating the colonnade around the forecourt, but it presumably achieved its purpose.

From this, and from the even more cavalier treatment of Menkaura's Valley Temple by its priestly community to be described shortly, we may deduce that there was no general policy towards or means of funding the maintenance of the stock of historic buildings. At any one time a significant proportion of them would be derelict or shabby. We sometimes read of kings piously restoring particular temples, whilst Rameses II's eldest son, the priest Khaemwese, even took an interest in restoring a few of the ancient pyramid sites.[7] But this was a piecemeal process which cannot have kept pace with the decay. The principal improvement came with the New Kingdom, when a general policy was followed of replacing old temples in the towns with new stone-built ones. But still the unequal fight against time did not go unnoticed. A poet of the period wrote, with respect to the tombs of famous wise men remembered for their teachings:

> Their portals and mansions have crumbled,
> Their mortuary-priests have vanished;
> Their tombstones are covered with dirt,
> Their graves are forgotten.
> Yet their name is pronounced over their books,
> Which they composed whilst they had being.[8]

Figure 49   The decay of a monument and the archaeology of maintenance: the mortuary temple at the pyramid of King Neferirkara of the 5th Dynasty at Abusir. (1) Thicker lines of the temple represent stonework; the rest was built in brick. The hatched portion represents the pyramid 'town' built following the completion of the monument. Buildings 1 to 9 are presumably houses; the function of no. 10 is uncertain. (2) The same mortuary temple, a generation or more later. The hatched portions are brick supports and shutterings built by the priests to keep up the roof of the colonnade around the forecourt and the roofs of the eastern and northern corridors of the temple. The columns had been of wood, and there was evidently a danger of the whole front of the temple collapsing. The extra shelter provided by the support walls was utilized where convenient for cooking-fires. After L. Borchardt, *Das Grabdenkmal des Königs Nefer-ir-ke-re*, Leipzig, 1909, p. 56, Abb. 63, Blatt 10.

GIZA - tomb of Queen Khent-kawes

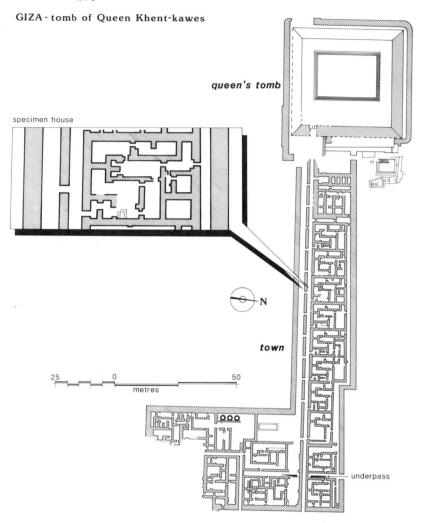

Figure 50   Early urban planning: the town intended to house the community supporting the cult of the deceased Queen Khentkawes at Giza, 4th Dynasty (cf. Figure 45, p. 131, for location). After S. Hassan, *Excavations at Giza IV (1932-33)*, Cairo, 1943, Fig. 1.

Returning to the Old Kingdom pyramid towns: with the 5th Dynasty pyramids at Abusir the peak of monumentality in pyramid building had already passed. Can we find more substantial traces at Giza?

The one part of the Giza necropolis where evidence for pyramid communities has been found by excavation lies to the east of the third pyramid of King Menkaura of the 4th Dynasty, towards the foot of the low desert plateau, where the cultivation begins to lap against it. As excavated, two separate parts seem to be involved, the one built into and around the Valley Temple of Menkaura's pyramid, the other adjoining the large tomb of Queen Khentkawes, one of the major figures of the 4th Dynasty. We will examine this latter one first (Figure 50).[9]

The tomb of Queen Khentkawes was fashioned around a sculpted cube of rock, which provided a free-standing, rectangular podium. This had been raised higher by means of a large masonry construction. Near the south-west corner lay the pit for a wooden funerary boat. The mortuary temple had been cut into the eastern face of the rock podium. From in front of the entrance to the mortuary temple there extended a long, narrow, mud brick compound, 150 metres from west to east. Along its south side ran a double street, and on the north a single one. A 2.5-metre-thick girdle wall marked the boundaries on these sides. To the east, an annexe ran southwards, measuring 80 by 40 metres, giving the whole complex an L-shaped plan. Several entrances are visible in the girdle walls. The street running south passed actually beneath the main east–west street by means of a tunnel using a staircase on the north and a ramp on the south. The long northern wing contains a row of eleven separate buildings, most of which are probably houses. In several cases the same plan is repeated with minor modifications, perhaps brought about by changes introduced by occupants. In the centre are six such unit houses of similar plan, each measuring 12 by 15 metres. The house plans show a certain resemblance to those at other sites of the Old Kingdom as well as of the Middle Kingdom. Within the interlocking rectangular rooms convenience of access seems often to be subordinated to privacy or security, leading to the use of corridors, ante-rooms and numerous turns, creating an involuted layout. In most of the houses a central room can be identifed, which gives access usually to three other rooms. No signs existed that any of the roofs had been supported on columns. In two houses there were circular grain bins: a single one in the third house from the west, four in the sixth house from the west. The central room at the back (or south) served as the kitchen, determined by the presence of ovens and ashes.

The southern wing of the Khentkawes settlement contains at least four separate buildings which might have been for residence or administration. On the north side of an open space in the middle lay a group of four circular grain silos. This space was reached by means of a staircase on the west, reflecting the slope down from the desert. To the north of this court lay another, containing only a rectangular basin cut into the rock. Further excavation in the south and south-east of the town was prevented by the existence of a modern cemetery, but deep soundings revealed the presence of brick walls over a considerable area, but at depths of up to 6 metres below the modern ground level.

The reason for the L-shaped plan is not really clear, although it must be remembered that, according to the reconstruction of the overall ancient layout of the Giza plateau discussed in the last chapter, the quays and basins of the reception zone for building materials probably lay close by and provided a limit to eastward building. But the effect was to bring the southern extension almost into contact with another related and quite remarkable site: the Valley Temple of King Menkaura (Figure 51).[10]

Menkaura's architects had planned that both his mortuary temple and valley temple would be built in the prevailing megalithic tradition. The king probably died prematurely, however, and the building was completed in mud brick. At the pyramid temple itself up on the plateau beside the pyramid no trace has been found of an accompanying settlement like that at Abusir, but the surrounding area has not been cleared to any great extent. We know that the mortuary temple was still in use late in the Old Kingdom from fragments of two inscriptions, probably decrees, bearing the name of King Merenra of the 6th Dynasty.

GIZA   Valley Temple of Menkaura

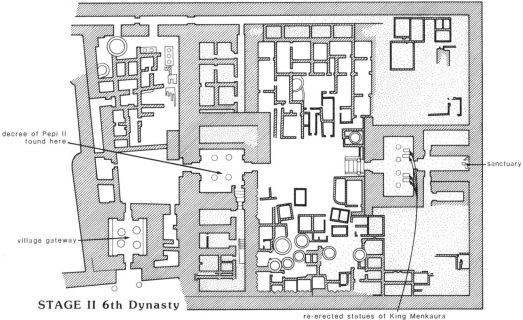

STAGE I 4th Dynasty

0   15
metres

decree of Pepi II
found here

sanctuary

village gateway

STAGE II 6th Dynasty

re-erected statues of King Menkaura

N

Figure 51   The 'villagization' of a monument: the Valley Temple of the Pyramid of King Menkaura (Mycerinus) at Giza (cf. Figure 45, p. 131, for location). *Above*. Plan of the temple as finished after Menkaura's death (*c*. 2471 BC). Note the palace-façade decoration of the sides of the main court. The whole is a good example of formal, monumental architecture in mud brick. *Below*. The same building about three centuries later, in the time of King Pepy II. The royal decree on a stone tablet found in the entrance hall shows that the building was still the officially designated pyramid-town of Menkaura. As time had passed the priestly community had moved in and built its houses and granaries (the circular constructions) partly inside and partly on top of the remains of the temple. Its thick enclosure wall and twin massive gates made it, in effect, a fortified village. After G.A. Reisner, *Mycerinus*, Cambridge, Mass., 1931 Chapter III, Plates VIII, IX.

The Valley Temple had been completed in mud brick, and included a central courtyard surrounded by a wall decorated with niches in the panelled palace façade style (Figure 51, Stage I). Outside the original front a formal addition in brick was made, which turned the entrance to the north, towards the space separating it from the town of Queen Khentkawes. It also faced a brick-paved roadway running in from the east. An entrance with two-columned portico led to a four-columned vestibule. This led in turn to a court crossed diagonally by a path of limestone slabs originally running into the Valley Temple building of Menkaura. Further corridors and spaces were laid out beyond, to the south. But over this area small dwellings were built, in places on accumulations of rubbish. Towards the south of these dwellings lay circular brick silos for storing grain.

Subsequent to the completion in brick of the Valley Temple proper, houses began to spread within the main courtyard. Circular granaries were constructed in some numbers, clustering towards the north side of the original court. From this point onwards most of the temple except for the sanctuary was allowed to decay. In places it was actually demolished to make further room for the expanding settlement, which gradually buried the lower parts of the temple. The plan shows walls constructed over the filled-in ruins, particularly on the south and south-west sides, where houses mounted the old enclosure wall. The excavators also found a good deal of temple equipment still in the original storerooms, buried in the dust and rubble. In this category were the slate triads of the king and other figures which represent some of the finest work of Old Kingdom sculptors. The process of decay had been hastened by a flood from a sudden storm which had broken into the rear of the building. An attempt at renovation followed, but only on top of the debris. This recognized the existence of the settlement, and surrounded it with a new wall. A new inner gatehouse and sanctuary were also built over the sites of the old ones. Anyone approaching the sanctuary, therefore, still had to walk from the gatehouse between two groups of huts and silos.

The new sanctuary had a vestibule with four columns. These had been of wood on limestone bases. On the mud floor, four beautiful life-size statues of Menkaura were set up, two on each side of the door to the inner chambers. The offering-place of the rebuilt sanctuary was found more or less intact. It consisted of an altar about 50 cm high, made from a worn slab of alabaster resting on two rough upright stones. A crude libation basin stood beside it. Nearby lay four unfinished diorite statuettes of the king, lying on their side. They may have actually stood on the altar and been the object of the offering cult in this last phase of the temple's existence.

The date and circumstances of this rough-and-ready cult being carried on in a dingy chamber at the back of a tightly packed mud village (within a girdle wall and gateway which made it virtually into a fortified village) are clear from two sources. One is the associated archaeological material, which seems not to extend beyond the end of the Old Kingdom. The other is a decree of King Pepy II of the 6th Dynasty, found in the floor debris of the inner gateway. The text of the decree exempts the pyramid town from certain obligations, and appoints an official to it. It demonstrates that this site was officially regarded as part of the pyramid town at a date very close to the end of the Old Kingdom. After this time the site appears to have been abandoned and the cult of King Menkaura to have ceased entirely.

The whole history of this settlement reveals how great could be the gap between

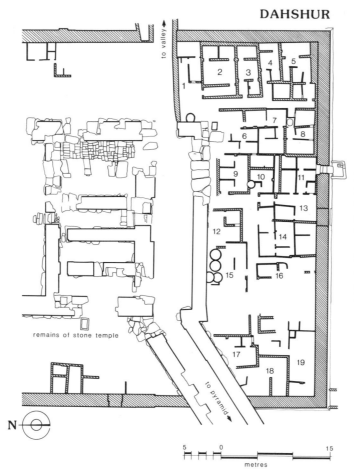

DAHSHUR

Figure 52 The Old Kingdom mortuary-cult 'town' attached to the Valley Temple of King Sneferu at Dahshur (cf. the reliefs, Figure 40, p. 116). Nos 1–11, 13, 14 and 16 are probably houses, no. 15 contains a set of four granaries. After A. Fakhry, *The Monuments of Sneferu at Dahshur* II.1, Cairo, 1961, Fig. 4.

intention and practice, between the products of superlative craftsmanship and the way they were treated, and between the inner world of bureaucratic order and the rough reality outside. This was an application of the 'out of sight, out of mind' philosophy with a vengeance. The Khentkawes part seems to have remained free from this muddle, but the reason is probably that it was occupied for only a fairly short time.

Menkaura was not an unusual case. The Valley Temple of King Sneferu of the 4th Dynasty at Dahshur provides a further illustration of the same philosophy (Figure 52).[11] Here we see the remains of a limestone temple with finely carved reliefs (including the personified offering-bearers of Figure 40, p. 116). It stood within a rectangular enclosure defined by a mud-brick wall, leaving a fateful space on the south side of the temple, 15 by 48 metres. This was filled up with the houses of the serving community, so creating another pyramid 'town'. Altogether some fifteen houses seem to have been present, offering accommodation for perhaps a hundred people if they were occupied by families.

Bureaucracy begins by imposing order on defined areas of activity. The scope of control can grow, however, and become the prime factor in a community's existence. If this is harnessed to a tradition of architectural planning, the 'model town' comes into being. The available evidence suggests that in the Old Kingdom this connection was still in its infancy. Two ingredients were there in the form of the planned royal cemetery and the creation of new towns, particularly at the pyramids themselves. But the Old Kingdom pyramid towns – classic examples of communities deliberately planted by the state – reveal that the potential was realized only to a limited degree, exemplified in the surviving evidence only by the short-lived town of Queen Khentkawes. It was left to the Middle Kingdom to integrate them fully.

Planning at its height: the Middle Kingdom town of Kahun

The name 'Kahun' was given in 1889 by Flinders Petrie, the British archaeologist, to a large Middle Kingdom settlement in the vicinity of the modern town of el-Lahun, which stands close to the entrance to the Fayum depression (Figure 53).[12] It lies on the rising edge of the desert, and part has been lost to the lateral spreading of the cultivation since ancient times. The nature and purpose of the town are evident from its context. Beside it lay a temple, reduced to a slight ruin even by Petrie's day, and this from its position was the Valley Temple to the pyramid of King Senusret II which stands 1,180 metres to the west. The town, following the same orientation as the pyramid, is clearly an unusually large example of a 'pyramid' town, housing the priests and lay personnel responsible for the perpetual cult of the deceased king. Papyri found in the town confirm this, for they include part of the administrative archive of the mortuary cult. They also give us the ancient name of the town: Hetep-Senusret ('King Senusret is at peace').

The size of Kahun is, however, far greater than that of other known pyramid towns, although it has to be admitted that the basis for comparison is small. But on the general scale of ancient urbanism, too, Kahun stands out as an important town in its own right. Its functions may therefore have gone much further than simply housing the workmen who built the pyramid, and the priests and others who kept up the cult of the dead King Senusret II. A good many administrative papyri have come from Kahun, but there has been a disappointing use of them by scholars for reconstructing the activities of the whole community. One good reason for this is that the papyri were found in two groups towards the end of the nineteenth century, and one of them still remains without a full publication.[13] The groups represent two quite separate archives with noticeably few points of contact. Only in part is this because they date from different periods within the Middle Kingdom. Much more is it because they reflect two different areas of organized life. One group derives from the temple of the royal cult and is concerned with temple organization and temple personnel; the other comes from within the town and covers the life and business of a broader community involved not only with the priestly foundation but also with many areas of interest unconnected with it. A few documents actually deal with work located outside Kahun altogether, on a construction project of King Amenemhat III – possibly part of his own pyramid complex. The dragging of stone by gangs of men is the subject of several papyri, as is the farming and measuring of land belonging to the priests and to the temple estates. Whether Kahun also contained people who followed their own agricultural pursuits is not known. But perhaps we are starting to think along the wrong lines: a pyramid town of full urban

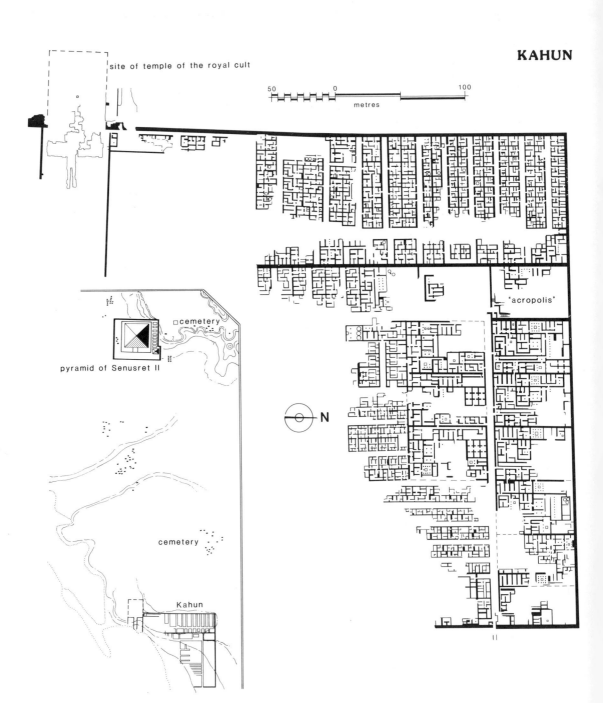

Figure 53 The type-site for orthogonal town planning in ancient Egypt: the Middle Kingdom town of Kahun, attached to the pyramid of Senusret II. After W.M.F. Petrie, *Illahun, Kahun and Gurob*, London, 1891, Plate XIV; W.M.F. Petrie, G. Brunton, and M.A. Murray, *Lahun* II, London, 1923, Plates II, XXXIII, XXXVIA.

dimensions and with a total inner administrative dependency may have fitted the king's pretensions.

The town was roughly square, its sides measuring 384 metres on the north and 335 metres on the west. The ground slopes gradually from the south-east corner up towards the north-west corner, the highest point being the so-called Acropolis. A thick wall divides the main part of the town from a separate strip on the west. The reason for this division is not known. The surrounding walls show no trace of fortification. Only one gateway is preserved, that towards the north-east. An isolated room just inside the gate may have housed a watchman, but no extra protection at the gateway is visible. If Petrie's plan is to be believed, this gateway measured 2 metres across.

Within the walls the town displays a strict grid-iron, or orthogonal, plan. The north side of the main east–west street is subdivided into seven main units, with three more on the south side. The westernmost unit stood on a natural eminence of rock which had been sculpted to form a platform with vertical sides rising above the town on east and south. Petrie called this the Acropolis. The scant traces of walls on the summit imply that it was not dissimilar to the other large units. It was reached, however, by an impressive staircase cut into the rock. The other units seem to have been large houses (Figure 54). Most of them measured 42 by 60 metres.

As is usual with Egyptian buildings the centre of interest for these large houses is focused almost exclusively on the interior. To judge from the plan, the exterior seems to have been a continuous blank façade of brickwork broken only by the door spaces. This would have created a stark effect if left entirely devoid of decoration of any kind. Fortunately we have another source of evidence for what large Middle Kingdom houses actually looked like. These are more or less contemporary models of houses buried in tombs, and particularly the ones from the tomb of Meket-ra at Thebes, which date to the 11th Dynasty, and provided the baking–brewing model illustrated in the last chapter.[14] The outsides of the two models of Meket-ra's house (Figure 54), as well as the inside wall facing the garden, have three rectangular panels. The central contains the main entrance to the house. It has two pivoting door leaves, braced with horizontal struts, and secured by a central bolt. Above it is an ornate design based on the *djed*-hieroglyph, a simplified tree trunk, used in the writing of the word 'stability', with two bunches of lotus flowers in the top centre. We cannot tell from the model if this upper part was a carved fanlight, or simply a painted moulding in the mud plaster of the façade. To the right of this on the outside wall is a side entrance, with single pivoting leaf and no surrounding decoration. To the left is another rectangular feature which seems to be a tall, latticed window with narrow openings which would admit air and a dim light, but could presumably be easily sealed during windy spells when much dust blows in the air. We can tentatively add these details to the sides of the Kahun main street and so enliven it a little.

The internal plan of the large Kahun houses is highly intricate. It displays a great interest on the part of the builder in adhering most rigidly to an unbroken rectangular outline, and to filling the interior with a dense and complex arrangement of interlocking rectangular spaces, often using the involuted solution to the problem of access. Rectangular modules are all-pervasive, and seem to fit the intensely structured and bureaucratic nature of the Middle Kingdom state as revealed from many sources.

From careful inspection of Petrie's plans we can recognize several basic subdivisions.

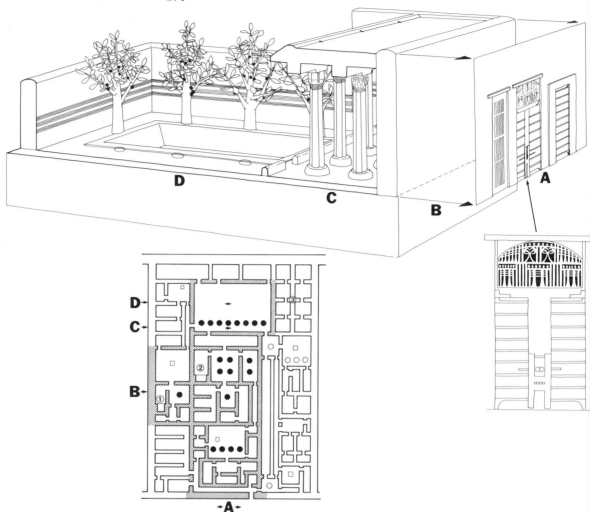

Figure 54   Large town houses: the plan is a composite derived from Kahun (Figure 53, p. 150). The core-house – the residential part – is cross-hatched. Two master bedrooms with bed alcoves can be recognized (nos 1 and 2, cf. Figure 98, p. 295). The remainder of the building must be given over to storage (including a granary, no. 3), and workshops. The perspective drawing is derived from the 11th Dynasty house models from the tomb of Meket-ra at Thebes. The parts A to D correspond to the similarly labelled parts on the plan. 'A' is the façade to the street, 'B' is the core-house (reduced to the thickness of the wooden end panel in the model), 'C' is the portico, 'D' is the garden. After H.E. Winlock, *Models of Daily Life in Ancient Egypt*, New York, 1955, Figs 9–12, 56–7.

The residential part – the house proper – seems to be the central core of rooms and courtyards. The unit as a whole is entered from the street. In the case of those on the north side of the street, however, the house proper was entered from the north, via a long passage which ran beside it, to a garden court on the north side. A colonnade shaded this northern, inner façade of the house. With the houses on the south side of the street this inner court seems to have been more in the centre of the building. If one extracts this core-house plus its garden court and colonnade one has essentially what is represented in the Meket-ra house models: a house with formal entrances at back and front (reduced in these models to a single thickness of wood), adjacent to a walled garden, the inner façade of the house shaded by a columned portico. The Meket-ra models add further details (see Figure 54, p. 152): a central pool surround by trees, and walls of the garden and portico painted with a broad black dado, above which is a frieze of blue, yellow, and white bands, topped by a wider white band. In the portico are two rows of four slender wooden columns, carved and painted, which rest on bases painted white to simulate limestone. The rear row of columns is carved in the form of a cluster of papyrus stalks, and the front row in the form of lotus buds bound together with gaily coloured bands of red and blue. The wooden architraves which they support are bespangled with stars, and the wooden ceiling between them is carved to represent palm trunks split in two, painted with stripes of green and red. The portico itself has a flat roof whose low front parapet is pierced by three rainspouts, painted white to indicate limestone.

Within the Kahun core-house a central reception room can be recognized, its roof supported on four columns. Beside it on the west is a small colonnaded court containing a stone tank set centrally in the floor. Petrie's plans also depict locations where the walls of a room were stepped back at the far end to create an alcove. Later evidence shows that alcoves like this were for beds in master bedrooms. If this holds true for Kahun, then one master bedroom was located within the central house core, but another was on the west, in what appears to be a residential annexe, with its own court. The possible purpose of this annexe will be discussed shortly.

On three sides, the core-house is surrounded by groups of chambers and little courts, comprising parts of an urban estate. For only one group can we identify directly from the plan the function that the building had. The group of square interconnecting rooms in the north-east with its courtyard in front is almost certainly a granary. Identical granaries occur in some of the Nubian forts dealt with later in this chapter. Their presence reflects the commodity-based nature of the Egyptian economy. The Meket-ra models, too, include a fine granary evidently designed along the lines of those at Kahun. In this the entrance leads to a long vestibule, accommodating models of one doorkeeper, four seated scribes with document boxes, an overseer and his assistant, and three labourers who measure loose grain with a *hekat* measure before filling sacks. A door from the side of the vestibule leads to a room containing a staircase rising to a broad walk along the tops of three square interconnecting chambers where the grain is stored.

The combined capacity of the granaries in the large Kahun houses is very considerable. It is easy, from Petrie's plans, to measure the areas of the various storage chambers. For the height, some of the Nubian forts provide direct evidence: 3.4 metres. The Nubian granaries were, however, somewhat larger, so that for Kahun a reduced figure for a filled height of 2.5 metres can be assumed. How much grain could they hold? Even more important: how many people could they support on the average rations calculated in the last chapter?

Table 4.1 summarizes the estimated capacities of the Kahun granaries. These seem to show that all the Kahun granaries together could hold sufficient grain for a population of 5,000 on maximum rations, and 9000 on minimum rations, assuming five houses only on the north side with granaries. The latter figure of 9,000 is of the same order of

Table 1   The numbers of annual ration units storable in the granaries using minimum and maximum estimates of ration size

Site	Capacity of granary (in cubic metres)	Minimum annual ration units	Maximum annual ration units
Kahun: N. house	337.50	1,164	675
Kahun: S. house	316.40	1,091	633
Kahun: all large houses	2,636.70	9,092	5,273

magnitude as the total population for Kahun that has been postulated on other grounds, namely between 8,500 and 10,000. Even the lower figure implies that a significant proportion of the Kahun population was dependent on the large houses for rations. Moreover, as will be argued shortly, these population figures may themselves be considerably too large.

The Kahun granaries are a key piece of evidence for regarding Kahun as a town not only created by administration but also maintained by administration, with much of the population dependent upon rations held in store by the chief officials. But why several large granaries instead of a single central one? The answer must lie in the social structure of Kahun, which will be looked into shortly.

What of the other parts within the Kahun large houses? The plans themselves and Petrie's notes have little more to tell us directly. But the range of activities which an important Middle Kingdom official might wish to see accommodated around him is provided again by some of the sets of tomb models. Here the Meket-ra group is particularly rewarding. We have already considered three so far: two almost identical ones of the main house, and the granary. There are five more building models. One of these is a cattle shed, a second is a butchery, a third is a combined bakery and brewery described in the last chapter (see Figure 42, p. 121). The remaining models are a weaving shop and a carpentry shed.

Are all of these models together parts of a large house of the Kahun type? Here we need to jump forward in time, and in terms of the arrangement of chapters in this book, and bring in for comparison a typical dwelling for a high official from the New Kingdom city of el-Amarna (see Figures 97, 98, pp. 293, 295). Here we can recognize the various parts more easily. The dwelling consists not only of a residence but also of a granary, separate kitchen which might have an adjacent bakery-brewery, cattle-shed, other outbuildings which we know in some cases were used for craft production, and frequently also a subsidiary house. Who lived in the latter is less certain. As an educated guess we might see it as intended for the eldest son who would gradually be taking over his father's responsibilities, but it must be admitted that other types of occupant can also be proposed: servants or a steward. We know, too, from excavated evidence that the spinning and weaving of linen were practised in these households. All of these parts were arranged informally and rather loosely within a walled compound, with the house usually towards the centre. At Amarna, the hand of the planner was given only limited scope. In particular, it did not extend to laying out the residential areas, which seem to be the relaxed product of individual preferences within prescribed limits. However, if we try to imagine the ancient planner, faced with the task of laying out a compound containing the Amarna elements, we would find him quite likely producing a tightly organized scheme of interlocking rectangular rooms and spaces: the very kind we find at Kahun. The large Kahun houses are best understood as planned and geometrically more elegant versions of the Amarna estates, containing a series of units which the Meket-ra models represent, for convenience, as single structures.

The contrast between Amarna and Kahun large houses tells us something important about the two different societies. At Amarna, household and services have been separately perceived, the services belonging to the perimeter of an enclosure in which the house stands as a central isolated feature. The variety of layout and size of compounds also reflects a society with a broad range of personal wealth and status. At Kahun, household and services have been indivisibly regarded as parts of a formally constituted unit. Nor is there much of a social gradient. As a model community it recognizes two main groups of people: owners of very big houses and owners of very small houses. The whole reflects the prevailing mentality of the Middle Kingdom, which tended towards an extreme structured view of society, apparent both in an inclination to devise arithmetic calculations for every facet of economic life, and in the attempt to control human behaviour and property by means of a strict bureaucratic framework. Amarna reflects a graded society, Kahun a society of distinct levels.

A good part of the remainder of the interior of Kahun is occupied by small houses built in rows, frequently back to back. Somewhere in the region of 220 are present on Petrie's plan, a ratio of 20:1 with the large houses. Petrie's plan gives the impression that much more of the missing space in Kahun would have been filled by small rather than large houses, and to this unknown extent the ratio must be increased. The number of houses offers the safest guide to estimating the original population. Even if we assume that only half of the original houses are included in Petrie's plan, and allow six persons per house (see p. 157), we reach a total population of just short of 3,000, well below the figure of up to 10,000 suggested on other grounds. The effect of this, of course, is to increase the impression of dependency of the population as a whole on the granaries in the large houses.

The interior arrangements of rooms in the small houses vary considerably. To some extent this may reflect changes brought about by occupants in response to individual circumstances. They also show the same complex inner articulation of rooms as is present in the larger Kahun houses. Characteristically an entrance passage leads to a room, which whilst not conspicuously large nevertheless acted as a pivotal point within the house, in that several doorways lead from it, frequently to ante-rooms rather than to terminal chambers. Ante-rooms sometimes deliberately lengthen journeys, placing security or privacy above convenience. In a few cases it looks as though two or more houses have been knocked together to form a larger house, and columns have been inserted. Examples lie in the west sector, eighth block from the north. In several houses circles are marked on Petrie's small-scale plan. Smaller ones seem usually to be column bases, which according to Petrie supported octagonal wooden columns about 25 cm in diameter. In his brief published notes on the architecture Petrie himself describes granaries, circular brick structures measuring between 1.7 and 1.93 metres across, plastered inside and out. They seem mostly to have occurred singly, but one pair is present. In the western block, from a total of about 150 houses, thirteen contain circles large enough to have been granaries. These would have augmented the grain storage capacity of the town, but their relative infrequency amongst the smaller houses points to significant differences in the wealth of the inhabitants of Kahun.

One further building inside Kahun deserves notice. It lies immediately south of the 'Acropolis'. It looks as though it stood in an open space. It may have been an administrative and storage building, but a temple is another possibility. We know from many references in papyri from Kahun that the town possessed its own temple, different from the mortuary temple of the pyramid. It was dedicated to the star-god 'Sepdu, Lord of the East', and possessed its own priesthood. To the south of this building is another which does not resemble either the large or small residences and may, for this reason, have been administrative, whilst across the street to the east lay a court containing three medium-sized circular granaries.

Papyri found at Kahun deal with many aspects of the town's organization, but await a full modern study. One important contribution they make is to supply information on who, or rather what classes of people, lived in Kahun, the people whom we must put into the large and small houses if we wish to convert an archaeologist's plan into a reflection of an ancient reality.

We can, without difficulty, identify a small number of important officials. The town had a 'mayor' (*haty‘a*), the normal head of an ancient Egyptian town. It also possessed an 'office of the vizier', where legal proceedings took place and oaths were made, and where the vizier himself was sometimes present. We must exclude him as a permanent resident, however. He was a peripatetic figure, based at the capital. An office of the administrative subdivision called the 'area of the northern district' (*wa‘ret*) was located somewhere, as also was an office for another senior government official, the 'reporter' (*wehemu*). In the latter, trials could take place, and the town possessed a prison. One valuable text is a census-like household list which deals with a priest of the official mortuary cult of King Senusret II. His name was Khakaura-Sneferu. Of his own family one son and one daughter are listed. But they are followed by groups of 'serfs' from various sources. These included the ones which evidently came with the office of priest, and numbered thirteen; a group of three given him by another official, and a group of unknown number (but a minimum of five) evidently inherited from the sister of his father. The most striking fact about these serfs is that most are female, and many are children of serfs. Just how extensive this list was is not known because the end of the papyrus is lost. But a document from the same period dealing with the serfs of an official at Thebes listed originally ninety-five of them.[15] Over half seem to have been Asiatics, and women outnumber men by about 2:1. The men bear titles like 'domestic servant', 'field labourer', 'brewer', 'cook', 'tutor' or 'guardian', and 'sandal-maker'. Most of the women whose profession is listed are clothmakers, but a 'hairdresser' and 'gardener' are also included. It can be inferred that the Kahun list belonged to one of the wealthiest of the Kahun inhabitants, one of those who lived in the large residences in the north of the town. If we convert the Meket-ra models into the units of one of these residences, the 'serf' list presumably covers the figures who fill many of the models with industrious labour, though they need not have actually lived on the premises.

The dependence of many people upon the large residences is also to be read into the enormous provision for storing grain within each of them. A significant proportion of Kahun's population belonged to redistributive sub-centres in the shape of the large residences. This in turn reflects a basic modular organization of society. Instead of all being dependent upon a single large granary with a single administration of rations, the population was broken down in this respect into several distinct groups. This team- or gang-organization of dependent population seems to have been common in ancient Egypt. The temple *phyle*-groups encountered in the Neferirkara archive are one example.

The range of occupation and status of the Kahun population is glimpsed from the papyri found there. Apart from 'serfs' there were soldiers and their scribes, and temple personnel including doorkeepers and foreign singers and dancers of both sexes. Three more census lists have survived, found rolled up together. They list the members of the household of two soldiers, father (Hori) and son (Sneferu) over an unstated period of time (Figure 55).[16] The father's household consisted initially of himself, a wife, and son (Sneferu); later they are joined by his mother, and five female relatives, who seem to be the householder's sisters, bringing the total to nine. When the son inherited, the final list was drawn up, and the household then consisted of just himself, his mother, his paternal grandmother, and three of his father's sisters. It is tempting to regard this as the household of an occupant of one of the small houses. It reveals a second tier of dependence, within the small households, a tier which changed with individual family histories: early decease of wife, marriage of sister, and so on. The fluctuation in the size of the household is also notable: from three to nine to six. It is a tiny base from which to generalize, but the average of six persons is within the range often used to calculate ancient populations. Other papyri document the legal affairs of the Kahun inhabitants, as they disposed of property 'in town and country' and wrestled with problems of debt, in all cases revealing that their dependence upon the state was only partial.

The variety apparent in Kahun society points to the central problem of all planning: matching reality to an abstract model of society. Kahun was laid out by someone who saw only two social levels: top bureaucrats and others. In reality the latter was a diverse category with varied needs and expectations, exemplified by the changing size of the Hori-Sneferu household (Figure 55). The simple twofold division represented a social myth held by the elite. It made no serious attempt to cope with the social and economic differentials within the numerous body of people with an 'official' capacity of one lesser kind or another. After the Middle Kingdom the state gave up the idea of planning for communities other than small groups of workmen. The city of Amarna (Chapter 7) illustrates this vividly.

Planning in other Middle Kingdom settlements: an instrument of urban renewal and internal and external colonization

Kahun provides a classic example of the application of bureaucracy to community creation on the scale of a complete town of no mean size by ancient standards. Although the rest of the evidence from Middle Kingdom Egypt is very patchy, it is sufficient to suggest that Kahun illustrates a general preference for rigid large-scale layout of residential and administrative quarters. Furthermore, from the spread of examples we can begin to conclude that the Middle Kingdom state embarked upon an extensive programme of remodelling communities in this strictly regimented fashion. One example – of an integrated temple, storage, administrative and probably residential unit of the Middle Kingdom at Medamud – was briefly illustrated in the previous chapter

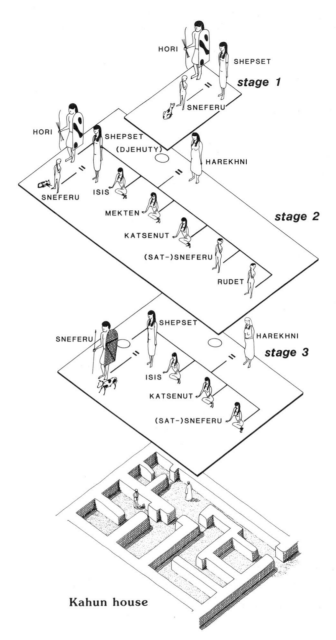

Figure 55 The changing size of a Kahun household, belonging to a soldier and his family. From a papyrus archive from the site. The time-span is not known but is probably fairly short. It is presumed that they lived in one of the ordinary houses, as illustrated.

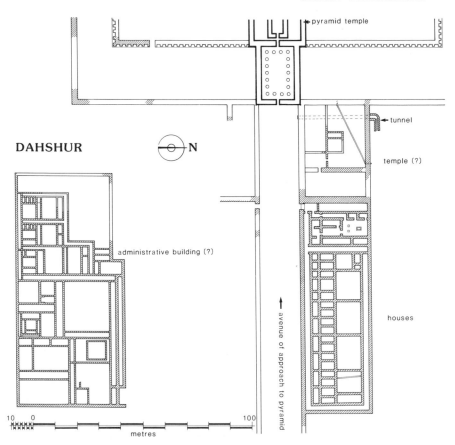

Figure 56 Foundations of the houses and ancillary buildings of the 'town' of the pyramid of Amenemhat III at Dahshur, showing orthogonal planning without a surrounding enclosure wall. After D. Arnold, *Der Pyramidenbezirk des Königs Amenemhet III. in Dahschur, I. Die Pyramide*, Mainz, 1987, Taf. 36.

(see Figure 22, p. 68), with the implication that another similar one can be identified at Hierakonpolis. More sites will now be chosen to spread the picture further.

The first belongs to the Middle Kingdom mud-brick pyramid of King Amenemhat III at Dahshur (Figure 56).[17] In function it must be comparable to Kahun, though the scale is smaller. Little more than the foundations have survived, frequently only up to a level below door thresholds, so that door positions are then not known. The buildings are aligned exactly with the pyramid, thus with the compass points as well, but unlike Kahun the group as a whole dispenses with an enclosure wall. Two main parts exist, on either side of the pyramid causeway. That on the south stands back from the causeway, and represents a building measuring about 50 by 100 metres. It displays the same nesting of rooms and larger units within a rectangular exterior as is present at Kahun, necessitating, as there, the use of long corridors. Note that one of the rooms in the central part displays the same thickening of walls towards the back (or south) as occurs at Kahun and in later times when it is taken as a sign of a major bedroom. The excavators also concluded from the pottery that the life of the building had been fairly short, perhaps no more than the reign of Amenemhat III himself. The amount of interior but evidently open space is much greater than usual in settlements of this kind. Again the excavators have suggested, though very tentatively, a temporary centre for the organization of the pyramid construction work, and perhaps places where masons worked. If this were true it would offer an interesting contrast with the *laissez-faire* construction site of the Old Kingdom at Giza, described in the last chapter.

Running beside the causeway on the north lay another block. It measures 33 by 137 metres, and seems to consist of a building with adjacent courtyard (both of uncertain purpose) at the west end, and then of several neighbouring houses with a room arrangement very similar to Kahun houses in its complex articulation. In size they fall mid-way between Kahun large and small houses.

The second example is potentially the most important: Thebes, the new *de facto* capital of a province consisting of the southern part of Upper Egypt. The location of Thebes in the Middle Kingdom has emerged only from work carried out since the 1970s. The most ancient city mound is nothing less than the ground on which the Karnak temple complex of the New Kingdom stands (see Figure 71, p. 203). Indeed, it seems to have spread well beyond the limits of the later Karnak enclosure wall.

To date there are five such excavations:

1. the most important was made in 1970–1 to the east of the Sacred Lake, behind the modern seating tiers for the Sound and Light Show at Karnak (Figure 57).[18] The edge of the lake is on the west. The wall with towers which divides the excavation is part of the 18th Dynasty temple enclosure wall. The walls to the east, however, are at a lower level, and run on beneath the wall and buildings on the west. They have a somewhat different orientation. Although only a fragment of plan is visible, it belongs to a settlement with buildings of markedly different degrees of solidity of construction. All, however, conform rigidly to a single grid plan. A 5-metre-thick enclosure wall crosses the site from west to east almost in the middle. On its south, and separated by a street, is a fragment of what seems to be another example of a large, rectangular, intricately planned building, with columns, to which the term 'palace' is probably not inappropriate. The edge of another smaller one lies at the northern edge of the excavation. If this section is at all typical, Middle Kingdom Thebes may have resembled a larger and internally more varied version of Kahun.
2. on the east side of the courtyard separating the ninth and tenth pylons, and immediately in front of the Jubilee Hall of Amenhetep II, a shallower excavation has brought to light house walls, circular grain silos, and small storerooms, with pottery of the Middle Kingdom and Second Intermediate Period.[19]
3. to the east of the Karnak enclosure and actually outside the 30th Dynasty enclosure wall, probes beneath the floor level of a badly damaged temple of Akhenaten have revealed town debris again of the Middle Kingdom and Second Intermediate Period. The evidence includes a length of 6-metre-wide enclosure wall running true north–south (with this thickness we can conclude that it was probably the main city wall), and many surface sherds of a kind of coarse domestic pottery with incised linear patterns characteristic of Upper Egyptian town levels of the late Middle Kingdom and Second Intermediate Period.[20]

4. again outside the 30th Dynasty wall, but this time on the north, the foundations of a stone building have been excavated which is aligned not to the main New Kingdom temple but to the general trend of the earlier walls exposed to the east of the sacred lake. The building itself is identified as a 'Treasury' of Tuthmosis I of the 18th Dynasty.[21] But probes beneath the floor have encountered walls and pottery of the Second Intermediate Period, whilst outside the building similar earlier material occurs at a level higher than the 'Treasury' floor. This is a particularly interesting site, for it suggests that the New Kingdom Treasury was built in a slight pit in the debris of the abandoned older city, but that the sides of the pit preserved the outlines of a plot of ground defined by the old city's general street alignment.

5. Middle Kingdom and Second Intermediate Period houses have been recovered beneath the New Kingdom ground level in the enclosure of the temple of the goddess Mut.[22]

These exposures derive from a city at least 1 km in length. Only exposure no. 1 gives us an intelligible plan of any size, so that we cannot judge whether the whole of Thebes at this time was turned into a giant version of Kahun, or only a part of it. We can suspect, however, that in the manner of some medieval European cities which retained outlines of the street-plans of their classical predecessors, some of the New Kingdom and later alignments at Karnak reflect those of earlier times. Some of these are marked on Figure 57, but the true extent of this will only come from future excavations. We are already entitled, however, to consider Thebes as a major example of a Middle Kingdom planned city.

The urge and the means to create the fully planned town enabled the Middle Kingdom state to spread urbanism, and bureaucratic control, into parts of the country hitherto thinly settled. Two examples will illustrate this, from opposite sides of the Nile Delta.

Abu Ghalib lies on the desert edge of the Nile Delta, 40 km north-west of Cairo.[23] Three seasons of survey and excavation were carried out between 1932 and 1934 by a Swedish expedition, devoted partly to test exposures of a Middle Kingdom town. From surface indications it was estimated that it covered an area measuring about 600 metres by 700 metres. If so it would mean a town about twice the size of Kahun. The site was thickly covered by aeolian sediments, and the area revealed by excavation remains very limited. Sufficient was exposed, however, to show that buildings had been laid out in rectangular units, following an underlying grid (Figure 58, left), which instead of being aligned to natural topographic features, was oriented by the compass points, another characteristic of some Middle Kingdom planned buildings and settlements. The reason for locating a new town here at all is not known. Perhaps, located beside one of the Nile branches, it was involved in the trans-shipment of commodities between the Delta and Upper Egypt, but this is pure speculation. Two of the buildings, on either side of a street about 2 metres wide, look as though they were quite large. The cross street leading to an open area is wider, being 3.5 metres across. The interiors of the main buildings are somewhat less intricately subdivided than those at Kahun. Many bread-ovens and fireplaces were found. The most remarkable discovery, however, was thousands of flint tools, many of them microliths, apparently used in a substantial stone-bead-making industry. Their contemporaneity with the Middle Kingdom town cannot

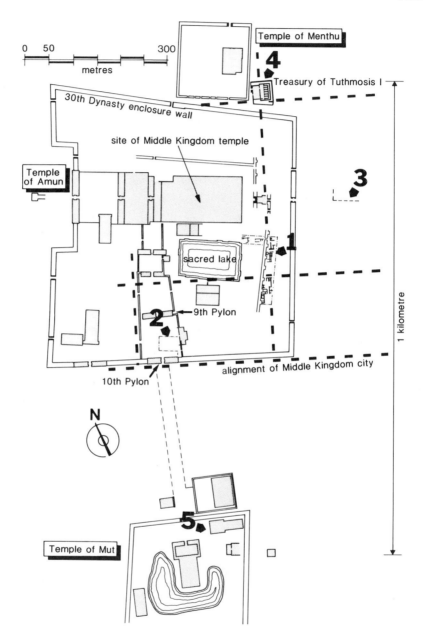

Figure 57 The ancient city of Thebes. *Left.* Outline plan of the New Kingdom temple complex showing principal exposures of the pre-New Kingdom city (nos 1–5, see text for explanation). *Right.* Detail of exposure no. 1, part of the orthogonally planned Middle Kingdom city, after *Karnak V (1970–2)*, 26, Fig. 13.

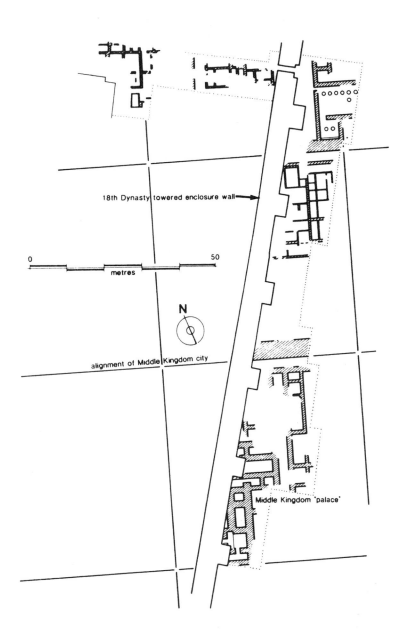

18th Dynasty towered enclosure wall ➤

0   50
metres

N

alignment of Middle Kingdom city

Middle Kingdom 'palace'

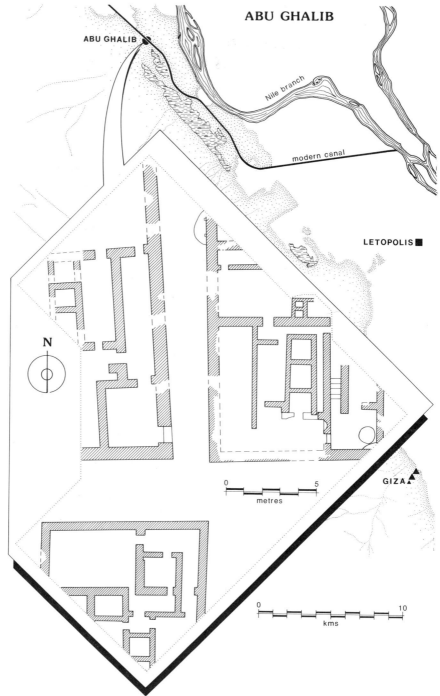

Figure 58 Internal colonization in the Middle Kingdom through the building of new towns. Both examples are in the Nile Delta. *Left*. The site of Abu Ghalib, perhaps originally beside the river and an internal port. Note the rigid northwards orientation, in conflict with the natural trend of the site. After H. Larsen, 'Vorbericht über die schwedischen Grabungen in Abu Ghâlib 1932–1934', *Mitteilungen des*

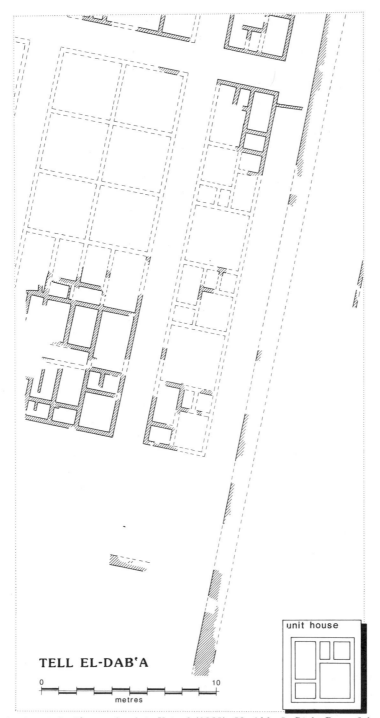

TELL EL-DAB'A

0   10

metres

unit house

Deutschen Instituts für Agyptische Altertumskunde in Kairo 6 (1935), 52, Abb. 5. *Right*. Part of the earliest level at the north-eastern Delta site of Tell el-Dab'a, dating to the 1st Intermediate Period/early Middle Kingdom, and perhaps a military colony. After M. Bietak, 'Tell el-Dab'a', *Archiv für Orientforschung* 32 (1985), 132–3.

be disputed, despite the fact that when viewed out of their context they have the appearance of being prehistoric. They provide an important lesson in the conservatism of ancient technology, and the slender correspondence between technology and finished product, for despite the primitive nature of the tools used Middle Kingdom stone bead jewellery was often of very fine quality.

Tell el-Dabʿa in the eastern Delta is important primarily for its contribution to the history and archaeology of the Second Intermediate Period, being the site of the Hyksos capital of Avaris. Since 1966 it has been the object of careful stratigraphic excavation by an Austrian expedition. Although the Hyksos Period strata form the main focus of interest, the history of Tell el-Dabʿa extends at least as far back as the First Intermediate Period. A survey of the adjacent fields has revealed a vast settlement from the time of the Middle Kingdom onwards, covering an area of 1.5 if not 2 sq. km. In 1979 and 1980 excavations were begun in agricultural land about 400 metres west of Tell el-Dabʿa itself. These have revealed, beneath an imposing Middle Kingdom palace, a large, planned, orthogonal settlement of the First Intermediate Period.[24] The limited area so far exposed contains small unit houses, apparently beside a length of straight enclosure wall (Figure 58, right). The historical dating to the First Intermediate Period is particularly interesting, for literary texts of the time demonstrate a concern by kings for the security of the eastern Delta in the face of migratory pressure from southern Palestine. We can read into the creation of a planned town at Tell el-Dabʿa the foundation of what was, in effect, a state colony to provide a better base for control and administration.

The limits which the drive for planning reached are represented by a particularly isolated site, at Kasr es-Sagha on the north-western edge of the Fayum. Here a rectangular brick settlement was constructed, its sides carefully aligned to the compass points (Figure 59). For once the context offers an explanation for its existence: it lay close to the end of a long paved road which led to basalt quarries in distant hills, and was probably close also to the then shoreline of the lake which, for a time in the Middle Kingdom, filled the Fayum depression. It must have been there to supervise the quarry work. The care and order shown in its layout contrasts with the Old Kingdom quarry settlement at Umm es-Sawan (see Figure 83, p. 247).

This use of settlement creation (and the administration which would, in the Middle Kingdom, inevitably accompany it) as a means of asserting political control of land provides a suitable introduction to the major example of this from ancient Egypt: the Middle Kingdom in Nubia.

The Nubian forts

The experience gained in building pyramids, creating towns, and dispatching quarry expeditions to distant regions found a new outlet in the Middle Kingdom: logistics for conquest. This demonstrates that important lessons had been learned. Valour, savagery, and successful tactics on the battlefield were less certain if soldiers and commanders were not adequately provided for, and victory had little point if it could not be backed up by permanent control. And so fighting in Nubia became only the sharp tip of a huge bureaucratic thrust. Empire-building now involved two very different sets of people, scribes and soldiers. As the New Kingdom evidence shows

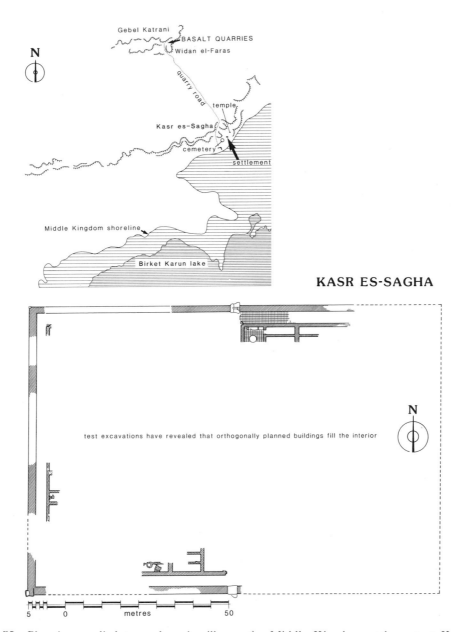

Figure 59 Planning applied to workmen's villages: the Middle Kingdom settlement at Kasr es-Sagha, serving the basalt quarries of the Gebel Katrani, northern Fayum. Still only partially excavated. Contrast it with the Old Kingdom village at Umm es-Sawan, Figure 83, p. 247. After J. Śliwa, 'Die Siedlung des Mittleren Reiches bei Qasr el-Sagha. Grabungsbericht 1983 und 1985', *Mitteilungen des Deutschen Archäologischen Instituts, Abteilung Kairo* 42 (1986), 170, Abb. 2; also D. and Do. Arnold, *Der Tempel Qasr el-Sagha*, Mainz, 1979, p. 26, Abb. 14; B. Ginter, W. Heflik, J.K. Kozłowski, and J. Śliwa, 'Excavations in the region of Qasr el-Sagha, 1979. Contributions to the Holocene geology, the Predynastic and Dynastic settlements in the northern Fayum desert', *Mitteilungen des Deutschen Archäologischen Instituts, Abteilung Kairo* 36 (1980), 119, Fig. 7. The inset map, which also shows the greatly increased size of the Birket Karun lake in the Middle Kingdom, is after Arnold and Arnold, op. cit., p. 24, Abb. 13.

(Chapter 5), the two groups were well aware of the differences in their attitudes.

The Egyptian conquest of Nubia had begun in the 1st Dynasty.[25] In the Old Kingdom the Egyptians took the first steps towards settlement in Nubia. This reflected the attitude that was to become much more marked in later periods, that Nubia was a quasi-province of the Egyptian state. A fragment of an Old Kingdom town at Buhen North is the only site of this earliest phase known from excavation, but a few Old Kingdom sherds from Kubban further north may be a sign that Buhen was not alone at this time.[26]

Following the civil war of the First Intermediate Period, the reconquest of Lower Nubia seems to have got under way rapidly, in the reign of the victor of the civil war, King Nebhepetra Menthuhetep II. A further campaign of conquest in year 29 of King Amenemhat I, first king of the 12th Dynasty, is recorded in a graffito actually within the heartland of Lower Nubia. The building policy which was well advanced in the reign of his successor, King Senusret I, is itself evidence of a massive kind that Lower Nubia had been thoroughly subdued. The powerfully bureaucratic attitude which seems to characterize the Middle Kingdom was now directed towards Lower Nubia, and to a renewed phase of settlement creation. This had produced, by the end of the 12th Dynasty, a line of forts and of fortified towns, regularly spaced along the 400 km between the First Cataract and Semna at the head of the Second Cataract. Although these constructions reflect specialized local considerations, they also have much to tell us about the scale of Middle Kingdom administration and its determination to create a desired environment in the face of considerable difficulties.

The Nubian forts fall roughly into two groups, representing partly two different types of terrain and partly two major building phases.[27] At some sites, moreover, forts built in the first phase saw several major modifications and enlargements, representing probably the initiatives of the local communities active during a period of more than two centuries.

The first group of forts may be termed the 'plains type'. They were constructed on the flat or shelving banks of the Nile north of the Second Cataract. They were the largest forts built in Nubia, and with their citadels and the even larger areas within an outer perimeter wall they could have accommodated many activities and housed a numerous population of men and animals. The fort of Buhen towards the southern limit of this zone provides the type site (Figure 60).[28] Inscriptions show that it was in existence by year 5 of King Senusret I (1967 BC). It lay on a gently shelving plateau adjoining the river directly, without significant cultivation in the vicinity. The indigenous population of both ancient and modern times was concentrated on the opposite and far more fertile river bank. Two ancient fortification lines enclosed an inner citadel and an outer area.

The citadel measured approximately 150 by 138 metres, and lay adjacent to the river. It was defined by a mud-brick enclosure wall 5 metres thick, with external towers. From one standing fragment of the wall an original height of between 8 and 9 metres can be estimated. The river frontage was given added protection through two spur walls which prolonged the eastern wall to north and south. These walls were also provided with towers. Two gates gave access to the waterfront. Beneath the northern one ran a stone-lined passage intended to ensure a safe water supply in time of siege. A single massive gateway on the west provided access to the desert side. This latter gateway was protected by two projecting parallel walls also provided with towers. No direct traces were found of how the upper parts of the wall were shielded, but contemporary pictures of forts in the tombs at Beni Hasan show that crenellations were normal.

The base of the wall was protected not only by a ditch, but also by a narrow, brick-paved rampart with its own parapet wall (Figure 61). The parapet was a narrower brick wall pierced by loopholes in groups of three, intended for the use of archers. At intervals, and at the corners, the rampart and lower parapet widened to form semicircular towers, provided with a second set of loopholes. The preserved loopholes on the west pointed down into the ditch, but on the northern and perhaps other sides, an upper row pointed directly forwards. North and south sides differed also in that a special kneeling step running along the base of the wall for archers was added as well. As for the ditch, it was dry, cut into the rock, and had average dimensions of 7.3 metres in width, and 3.1 metres in depth. A counterscarp had been built up on the outer lip of the ditch to support a glacis.

The interior of the citadel seems to have been largely occupied by rectangular brick buildings arranged around a rectilinear or orthogonal grid of streets. All buildings, except the one of the north-west corner and some towards the north-east corner, were separated from the main wall by a continuous street. The buildings on the west and north had been relatively well preserved. But over the remainder destruction and erosion had reduced them to broken lengths of foundation walls. The excavator's plan of this part, in joining up many of these fragments into continuous lengths, creates an odd impression which is to a degree illusory. They were far more fragmentary than this.

The building in the north-west corner seems to have been the garrison headquarters. It was built directly against the main wall, and had its own staircase leading to the top. The building itself had possessed at least two storeys. At ground level it had contained pillared halls, and a colonnaded court with stone floor. A square stone tank was sunk into the floor of the main hall. This is a common feature of large Middle Kingdom buildings, and was noted in the large houses at Kahun. The pillars in these rooms had been of wood, octagonal and red-painted, standing on circular stone bases. Doorways had been framed with wooden jambs and lintels. Adjacent to this on the east stood a group of long columned halls which the excavator W. B. Emery conjectured was a barrack-block. This would, however, imply official provision for communal living, whereas on comparable sites small modular houses seem to have been the norm. These halls may thus have served another purpose, perhaps storage. Further to the east lay a building which was identified as a temple. Its plan suggests this, and it lay beneath the later 18th Dynasty temple of Queen Hatshepsut. However, no artefacts were found to bear this out, and we know that during the Second Intermediate Period the building was reused for domestic purposes, despite inscriptional evidence that building work on a temple of Horus was carried out. Along the inside of the west wall of the citadel lay several buildings with layouts of interlocking rooms which exemplify Middle Kingdom domestic architectural practice. Over large parts of the remainder of the site a strict grid of walls was laid out. Much of this grid most likely served as foundations for houses or workshops composed of even units of modular rooms. Some of the Second Cataract forts supply smaller examples of back-to-back modular houses of a few rooms each. One dense group of rectangular chambers lay in the north-east corner, touching the girdle wall directly. The preserved height here was sufficient to show that many must have been cellars entered from above, and some may have been for storing grain.

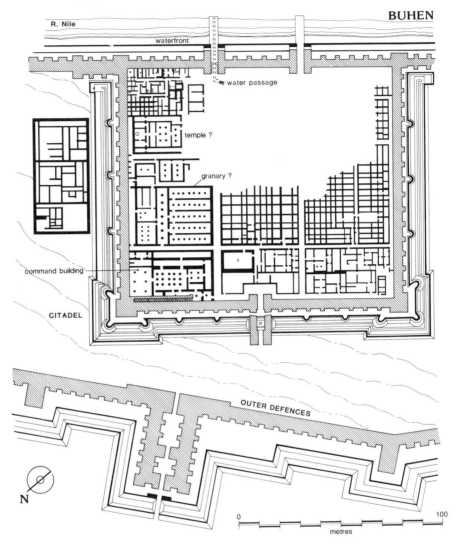

Figure 60   Urban planning in the service of the military: the Middle Kingdom fortress of Buhen in Nubia. The cellular pattern represents foundations; at ground level there would have been more doorways. After W.B. Emery, H.S. Smith, and A. Millard, *The Fortress of Buhen; the Archaeological Report*, London, 1979, Plate 3.

The outer line of fortifications enclosed an area measuring roughly 420 by 150 metres. It contained the citadel. The outer defences ran as a series of rectangular salients, backed by a brick wall 5 to 5.5 metres thick, set with rectangular towers on the outside. The rock-cut ditch had an outer rampart with uninterrupted parapet, and was crossed by a rock causeway opposite the enormous gateway on the west side. This gateway had the form of twin parallel walls with towers on the inside and outside. The outer defences in this particular form may have been a creation of the late Middle Kingdom, for in places it was found that beneath them lay the remains of a much more lightly

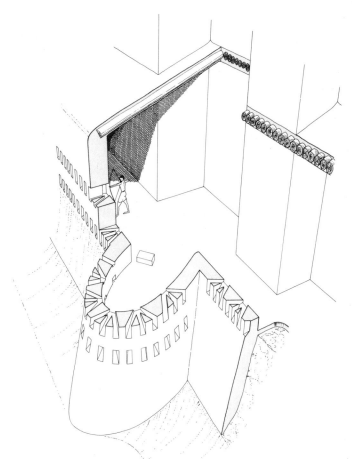

Figure 61 The ingenious mind of the military architect (doubtless a 'scribe'). Reconstruction of the fortifications of the citadel at Buhen, see Figure 60.

constructed brick parapet with rounded towers, perhaps a product of the early Middle Kingdom.

The space between the citadel and outer fortifications has never been fully examined, but it seems highly unlikely that it was ever built up to any great density. On the west side, the outer fortifications ran along a 2-metre-high escarpment. During the Middle Kingdom (probably the late Middle Kingdom) this had been utilized as a cemetery, running almost the full length of the enclosed ground. No traces of housing were found during the excavation of this part. The implication is that the entire western side of the outer enclosure remained free of buildings, except for the tombs. For the area south of the citadel we have very little information. But on the north an important construction was found almost immediately against the north wall of the citadel. It was so close, in fact, as to mask and render ineffective the whole northern side of the citadel fortifications. Only the foundations of this building survived, but they belong to a massive block, measuring 64.25 by 31.25 metres. Although some of the walls were preserved to a height of up to 1.5 metres, they showed no doorways, suggesting a basement or platform to support chambers at some height above the ground. In the early New Kingdom (or possibly during the Second Intermediate Period) this block was partly demolished, and the small temple of Horus built over. The internal divisions of this building make it a characteristic large pre-planned block of the Middle Kingdom.

The style and strength of the Buhen fortifications seem designed to thwart a fairly sophisticated type of siege. We know from pictorial evidence that by the beginning of the 12th Dynasty siege warfare using siege engines was known in Egypt, as is shown in a scene from the tomb of the seal-bearer and general Intef of the late 11th Dynasty at Thebes, where a wheeled siege tower is in use.[29] This poses the interesting question: does the Buhen citadel represent a form of urban fortification developed in Egypt during the civil wars of the First Intermediate Period, which was transferred to Nubia as an administrative act? Is the architecture itself, therefore, the product of a bureaucratic decision rather than of a local strategic assessment?

In the same general area of Lower Nubia lies also the fort of Serra, on the east bank of the Nile.[30] The unusual feature here is the river basin enclosed within the fortified perimeter. It provides an important pointer to one of the purposes of these forts, which was to safeguard the passage of Egyptian shipping in Lower Nubia. Serra possessed a dry ditch, but no outer rampart or parapet. The north side was protected, however, by a projecting ditch which looks as though it was intended to surround a projecting wall with end tower. In this it possesses a point of resemblance to the Second Cataract Forts. To accommodate the internal buildings to the slope of the ground, they were constructed on artificial terraces. Enough survives of the upper terrace to reveal buildings on an uncompromising grid plan, separated from the perimeter wall by a narrow street.

The Second Cataract forts

The second group of forts resulted from an Egyptian annexation of the entire Second Cataract area in the reign of Senusret III. Despite its name, the Second Cataract is not a single precipitous fall of water but a series of lesser obstructions in two groups, separated by about 35 km of reasonably clear water. The northern end is marked by a dense group of rocky islands treacherous for navigation, the southern, at Semna, by a narrow rocky barrier through which the river gushes in several torrents. In both cases sailing was hazardous when the river was low, but at full flood the obstacles were sufficiently submerged to allow safe passage to careful sailors. In the rugged and broken terrain each of the new forts took the form of an irregular polygonal figure designed to fit over an irregular natural prominence. Narrow ridges which ran up to the site were covered with spur walls to render them safe, and in most places the steep natural slopes rendered a ditch unnecessary. They show that, when occasion demanded, the rigidities of grid-iron planning could be sensibly abandoned.

A good example of this type of fort is Shalfak, on the west bank, on the edge of an escarpment overlooking the Nile (Figure 62).[31] The fortified area is relatively small, measuring 80 by 49 metres at the widest point. It was surrounded by a 5-metre-thick brick wall with external towers. The defended ground was, however, greatly increased by spur walls, that on the north running for 115 metres. On the north a small gateway led round the walls to a staircase descending the cliff to the water's edge. The main gateway was defended by a pair of projecting walls. The interior was completely built up except for narrow streets, which ran around the base of the main wall, and divided

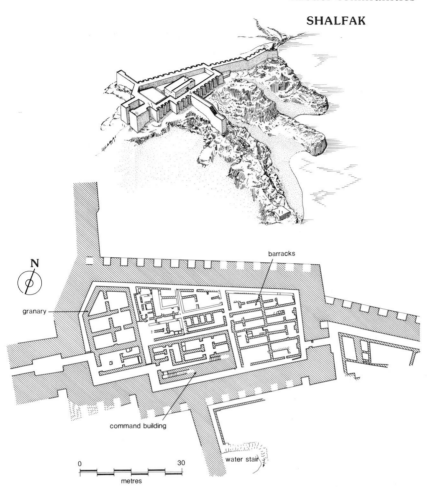

SHALFAK

Figure 62 Imaginative adaptation of architecture to topography: the fortress of Shalfak in the 2nd Cataract area of Nubia, built by Senusret III of the 12th Dynasty on a high rocky outcrop above the river. Plan after G.A. Reisner, N.F. Wheeler, and D. Dunham, *Second Cataract Forts II. Uronarti Shalfak Mirgissa*, Boston, 1967, Map X.

the principal blocks. Opposite the gateway lay the granary, well preserved and with a plan like those at Kahun, its grain chambers showing no sign of an external doorway. They must have been reached by ladder and roof entrances. Beside the east wall the command post can be recognized by its thick walls, which could have supported sufficient masonry to turn it into a tower. The other buildings are presumably for the garrison's occupation.

Shalfak was one of a group of forts built by King Senusret III which cluster around the southern part of the Second Cataract and form an obvious defensive grouping across the narrow Semna Gorge. An inscription of Senusret III from Semna confirms that this was indeed intended as a true frontier.

Year 16, 3rd month of winter: His Majesty made the southern boundary at Heh. 'I have made my boundary, having sailed further south than my fathers. I have increased what was bequeathed to me.'

As for any son of mine who shall maintain this boundary which My Majesty has made, he is a son of mine who was born to My Majesty. . . . But as for whoever shall abandon it, and who will not fight for it, he is no son of mine, and was not born to me.

My Majesty has had a statue of My Majesty set up on this boundary which My Majesty has made so that you might be inspired by it, and fight on behalf of it.[32]

More will be said about this statue later.

At Semna a barrier of crystalline rocks crossed the Nile, leaving a gap of about 400 metres across. On a rocky eminence at either end Senusret III sited a fortress: Semna, the larger, on the west, and Kumma on the east (Figure 63). Semna fort took an L-shaped plan, the western wing covering a piece of relatively flat ground.[33] The principal dimensions are about 130 metres from north to south, and the same from west to east. The girdle wall on the landward sides was protected by regularly spaced small towers, strengthened at greater intervals by larger projecting towers. The ground surrounding the wall was flattish, but still no outer rampart or parapet was thought necessary. Instead it was cleared for a distance of up to 29 metres, and beyond this, material was heaped up and covered with a stone pavement to form a glacis and counterscarp. At either end of the eastern wing the girdle wall was pierced by fortified gateways which allowed a road to pass entirely through the fort, crossing to the glacis by means of causeways. A narrow gate in the east wall gave access to a stairway running down to the water's edge. This was protected by means of a massive tunnel of dry-stone masonry.

The narrow streets within Semna were paved with irregular slabs of stone. They ran around the base of the girdle wall, and divided the interior into blocks. Unfortunately, we do not have the full plan of the inside. A certain amount had been lost or obscured by the 18th Dynasty stone temple built in the middle of the east wing, and a good part of the remainder has never been excavated. In the west wing the ground rose towards the west, and at the highest point in the fort a substantial building stood which was perhaps the command post. The walls were preserved to sufficient height to show the tell-tale marks of the ends of timber beams supporting the floor of an upper storey. Other buildings show the use of an initial modular layout and seem to have been houses, of two or three rooms. No granary has been identified.

The boundary inscription of Senusret III refers to a statue of the king present in the fort to inspire posterity to defend the frontier. The original statue has not been found. But in the reign of Tuthmosis III of the 18th Dynasty a small sandstone temple was built in the middle of the eastern wing. One of the statue cults within it was of King Senusret III, the founder of Semna. On the walls of the sanctuary were carved figures of the statue itself seated inside a portable boat shrine of standard New Kingdom form.[34]

Across the river from Semna lay Kumma, much smaller, and built over a steep rocky outcrop.[35] So steep were its sides that the walls had in some places to be built on stone

SEMNA

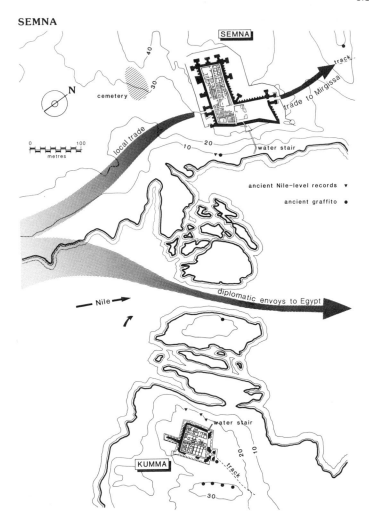

Figure 63 The southern frontier of Egyptian territory in the late Middle Kingdom. The fortress system at Semna not only provided military protection, it also regulated trade and diplomatic traffic northwards.

embankments. The fort has an irregular quadrilateral outline, with projecting spur walls to cover lesser ridges. A water-gate with stairs lay at the northern corner. Inside was the usual arrangement of narrow streets, like those at Semna paved with irregular stone slabs. Amongst the individual buildings a granary is easily recognized.

The Semna defences included a third fort 1,500 metres to the south of Semna fort.[36] It lay in modern times on the southern edge of a plain of alluvium, but in ancient times it must have lain on the far side of a bay in the river bank. It was small and square, measuring about 52 metres along each side. It possessed a main wall 9 metres wide at the base, and strengthened with corner towers, then a ditch, and an outer wall above a glacis. The interior of the fort seems to have been open. A tunnel lined with granite slabs passed beneath walls and ditch, intended to secure a fresh water supply. It is this feature, found buried beneath the modern alluvial plain, which shows that originally the fort stood at the river bank. The smallness of Semna South implies that it was a dependency of Semna, either a forward observation post, or check point for traffic coming in from the south.

A further defensive work at Semna was discovered in 1965–6.[37] It was a 2.5-metre-thick mud-brick wall, fortified by towers on high points and running beside the roadway which, on leaving the north gate at Semna, followed the river through the Second Cataract area. It was traced for a distance of 4.5 km, and had actually begun to the south of Semna, skirting round the fort to the west to create a large protected zone. Possibly Semna South marked its real beginning. This wall brings home the seriousness of the threat felt by the Egyptians in the area, and the fact that land traffic played an important role in their strategy. It is also an early example of a linear territorial defensive work (of the Hadrian's Wall type), which has a probably contemporaneous counterpart at Aswan, protecting the land route around the First Cataract.[38]

The Second Cataract forts are striking examples of military architecture anywhere and illustrate an extension of the urban planning already encountered at Kahun and elsewhere. But in two further respects as well they illustrate Egyptian bureaucracy: the forts stood as centres for administered activity over an extensive open hinterland, and they provide a particularly vivid witness to the scale and importance of making provision for rations.

The Egyptian strategy in Nubia was not confined to static defence behind massive walls. A number of look-out posts were manned in the Second Cataract area. These are mostly known from groups of graffiti left at suitable points by Middle Kingdom persons.[39] It has also been suggested that look-out posts and forts in the Second Cataract were in mutual contact by means of signalling, presumably by smoke column. More explicitly a group of documents from a tomb at Thebes and dated to the reign of King Amenemhat III shows that the forts maintained contact with each other and with their base, probably Thebes itself, by means of regular written reports. These documents are known as the Semna Despatches.[40] They reveal also that an active policy of desert surveillance was maintained. This was done by sending out patrols to look for tracks and to bring in any wanderers for questioning. For this the Egyptians used Nubian desert men, named Medjay. The policy produced reports such as this: 'The patrol which set out to patrol the desert-edge . . . has returned and reported to me as follows: "We have found a track of 32 men and 3 donkeys".' Other dispatches deal with trading with Nubians at the frontier fort of Semna itself. The fine detail that occurs in these letters, evidently to be scrutinized at Thebes, is characteristic of the Egyptian urge to record happenings that might be of interest to a superior official, and nicely illustrate the bureaucratic framework of the Egyptian presence in Nubia.

The network of total control which the Egyptians threw over the region extended to regulating contacts with the Nubian communities lying to the south, beyond the limits of direct Egyptian control. Semna has provided another formal inscription of Senusret III:

> The southern boundary which was created in the 8th year under the Majesty of King Senusret III to prevent any Nubian from passing it when faring northwards, whether on foot or by boat, as well as any cattle of the Nubians. An exception is a Nubian who shall come to barter at Iken, or one with an official message.[41]

Trade and diplomacy with the enemy were to be recognized and properly regulated.

For many years the location of Iken was disputed. It was settled by discoveries in the 1960s, which showed that Iken was the ancient name for the great fortress site of Mirgissa, lying well behind the fortified frontier area, at the northern end of the Second Cataract.[42] Unfortunately, nothing found at the site adds to our knowledge of its function as a trading centre, although it provides yet another fine example of fortification and planned living.

Many of the forts mentioned so far, including Mirgissa, possessed large, well-built granaries. Since we can identify the granary buildings and measure them – and even find out what their original height was in some cases – we can also take the same tentative steps as at Kahun towards calculating how much grain they might have held, and what this tells us about the Nubian operation in general. Although there are many uncertainties in doing so we must bear in mind the Egyptian passion for measuring and calculating. No granary would have been built without it.[43]

Table 2 lays out the capacities and, applying the minimum and maximum figures used for Kahun, sets gross population figures. Even taking the lower figures the resulting populations are hugely excessive when compared to the size of garrison that has been postulated in the past. One excavator, G.A. Reisner, on intuitive grounds, estimated for Kumma a garrison of between 50 and 100 men, for Semna one of between 150 and 300, and for Uronarti one of between 100 and 200.

The activities of the Nubian forts are still only sketchily documented. In addition to their function as static points of defence we know from the Semna Despatches that a desert surveillance system was operated from them, using Medjay-people from the deserts who were presumably paid in grain; some grain may have been needed for the donkeys who must have formed an important element in transport; we also know that some of the forts engaged in trade in which bread and beer were given out by the Egyptians. If this last factor was a significant one, however, we might have expected the largest granary to have been at Mirgissa, which we know from inscriptional evidence to have been the officially designated trading post for Nubians from the south, the place called Iken. This is not so.

The Nubian forts around the Second Cataract south of Mirgissa were built by Senusret III to defend a frontier newly established by him. However, the military measures

Table 2 The numbers of annual ration units storable in the granaries using minimum and maximum estimates of ration size

Site	Capacity of granary (in cubic metres)	Minimum annual ration units	Maximum annual ration units
Shalfak	389.28	1,342	779
Uronarti (block VI only)	444.34	1,532	889
Uronarti (VI plus IV)	770.37	2,656	1,541
Mirgissa	1,063.69	3,668	2,127
Kumma	574.31	1,980	1,149
Askut	1,632.18	5,628	3,264
Semna	[1,000?]	[3,448?]	[2,000?]

undertaken at this time also involved campaigns into areas lying yet further to the south. Armies need rations, and although there would doubtless have been hopes of seizing defeated Nubians' grain stores, the Middle Kingdom administrative machine was not one to leave supplies and rations to chance. From the texts mentioned in Chapter 3 we can well imagine the preparations: calculating the numbers of men, the length of time, the size of rations, and thus the maximum size of the stores. We can only understand the size and location of the Second Cataract granaries if we see them as part of an integrated military strategy of defence and attack. The granaries belong to a carefully planned chain of supply. Their importance in military thinking is amply demonstrated by the island fortress of Askut, located well back from the Semna frontier and therefore the most secure of the group. The granary occupies so much of the interior space as to suggest that the whole fortress was really a fortified grain store acting as an emergency or rear supply depot.[44]

The care taken with all preparations is evident from two other excavated sites, where the 'ghosts' of two temporary Middle Kingdom palaces have been discovered. One is the 'Administrative Building' at Kor,[45] the other is the 'Palace' on Uronarti island (Figure 64).[46] Both were occupied for only a brief period and were laid out with a ritual care for northerly orientation, ignoring the lie of the land (as is apparent also at Abu Ghalib and Kasr es-Sagha, see Figures 58 and 59, pp. 164 and 167). They make sense only if we interpret them as temporary residences thrown up for the king during his leadership of campaigns into the regions lying beyond the frontiers.

The archaeological evidence from Middle Kingdom Nubia projects into this military frontier region a massive application of Middle Kingdom administration. Behind the forts must lie a hidden mountain of scribal effort. We can only marvel at the excess of zeal and energy that the whole operation reveals.

The prescriptive society

The history of town planning offers a paradox in value judgements. Today we regard planning as a basic responsibility of civilized government; thus, a good thing. We are therefore inclined to applaud it when it makes its appearance in antiquity. However, ancient planning inclined towards a form – the grid-iron or orthogonal layout – that we have come to regard as the very worst kind of planning, and much to be avoided. Modern planners have returned to the roots of pre-modern community life and have attempted to distil principles from unpremeditated 'organic' communities, such as medieval Italian hill villages. This being the case, should we not regard early grid-iron plans as bureaucratic impositions and question whether they are really a civilized virtue? The question is very much to the fore in considering the greatest city that has survived from ancient Egypt: el-Amarna of the New Kingdom, the subject of Chapter 7. Most of this city was built around a rejection of, or an indifference to, a social prescription and a geometric aesthetic. The organic harmonies and discords of personal decision-making prevail instead, and reflect a mentality very different indeed from that behind Kahun.

The paradox mirrors something more fundamental still. In the texts considered in the last chapter and in the archaeological sites considered in this one, the Middle Kingdom

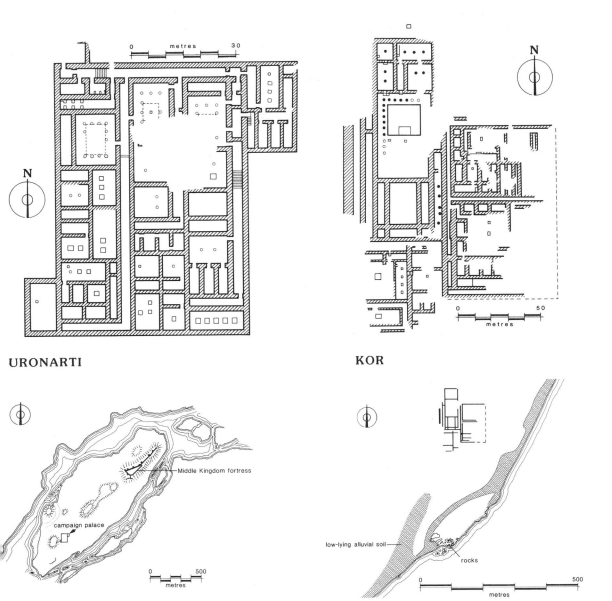

URONARTI

KOR

Figure 64 Two short-lived buildings in Nubia, carefully aligned to true north (cf. Figure 59, p. 167) against the natural trend of the ground, at Uronarti and Kor. Were they the king's temporary headquarters during major campaigns? After G.A. Reisner, N.F. Wheeler, and D. Dunham, *Second Cataract Forts II. Uronarti Shalfak Mirgissa*, Boston, 1967, Maps II, VI, and J. Vercoutter, 'Kor est-il Iken? Rapport préliminaire sur les fouilles françaises de Kor (Bouhen sud), Sudan, en 1954', *Kush* 3 (1955), Plan D, Plate VI.

takes on a distinctive character: it was motivated by a vision – fragmentary and incomplete perhaps – of a bureaucratic Utopia, an unformulated ideology which acted as a pattern in the making of decisions. We find it in an inclination to formulate arithmetic devices for calculating a range of aspects of economic life, we see it in documents attempting a centralized control and direction of work and property, it lives at Kahun in a prescription for how a complete city should be arranged. It may seem crude in many respects, but it could have had a future. Better systems are built by improvements to older ones. But the resources of the state, and by this we mean in the end its human resources, proved unequal to the task. As the remaining chapters will show, the bureaucratic tendency of the Middle Kingdom made no further headway. The New Kingdom state, although successful for nearly five centuries in creating and distributing wealth and honours, was a less rigid system holding temporarily in check a great many individualistic ambitions.

Why did ancient Egypt decline and its civilization fail? The same answer applies as to all civilizations: too great and too prolonged a rejection of systematized life in favour of freedom of manoeuvre. If the work of Middle Kingdom Egypt – and of equivalent periods of bureaucratic dominance in ancient China, the Indus Valley, Mesopotamia and pre-Columbian Central and South America – had been pursued as a peaceful continuum, converting all who encountered it to enthusiastic support for order and the beauty of logical systems of government, then by now a Utopian world order might well have been achieved. But anarchic love of disorder and the rejection of authority are equally part of the human personality. History is a record of the struggle between the two polarities of the mind – order and disorder, acceptance and rebellion (as the ancient Egyptians themselves perceived). Both the rise and the fall of civilization are present in each one of us.

Part III
Intimations of our future

5
New Kingdom Egypt: the mature state

I switch on my television set, and the news bulletins bring into my home scenes of presidential motorcades on thronged boulevards, excited crowds cheering a leader at the balcony of a palace built in antique style, public acts of worship and homage performed in strange costumes. I watch, in other words, re-enactments of the lives of Bronze Age rulers. Nor need I remain passively at home. I can, as a member of one of Britain's ancient universities, participate myself in minor manifestations of ancient ceremonial. Or I can go to church. Why do we need such things now (for a real need there certainly is)? Why do we find comfort in weird legacies from a very ancient past? History is a subversive subject. It undermines our claim to live in an age of reason and progress. Technology streaks ahead into the Atomic Age, but institutional man (and sometimes thinking man, as well) still struggles to escape from the Bronze Age.

Early bureaucratic states failed to provide the basis for peaceful evolution towards a rational harmonious society. The failure has left us these strange legacies. We can argue that to maintain unity and stability early societies, lacking a rational philosophical basis for government, needed a divine leader, his position defined by theology, and his person treated with the reverence and ceremonial of a god. The theological underpinning and the presentational devices had a real point. The divine ruler's authority was unique, beyond question, the threat of subdivision or duplication arising only in times of civil war. But mankind has moved on since the days of the Pharaohs. Between ourselves and ancient Egypt stretches a long and complex history of developing political thought and varieties of forms of government, in part based on philosophies that do not derive from religion. Yet as the host society has changed, so the forms and trappings of rule by a divine leader have shown remarkable capacity to adapt and to live on, often much loved. Rationality lures, atavism rules.

With the New Kingdom – the five centuries or so (c. 1540 to 1070 BC) of the 18th to 20th Dynasties – we can see that Egypt was already well advanced along the path of complex accommodation between political reality and the myths of the state. We will find no evidence that people seriously considered alternative forms of government to direct rule by a divine king. What we can observe is, on the one hand, the evolution of a more pluralist society which destroyed the possibility of the state ever fully developing into a single hierarchy in which each person knew and accepted his place; and, on the other, the adaptation of divine monarchy to the changing circumstances in ways that have proved to be indestructible. It is the purpose of this chapter (and parts of Chapter 7) to delineate the massive apparatus which articulated state myth and yet had the flexibility to accommodate a form of rule which was essentially political. All readers of this book will live under a similar compromise.

Outwardly the style of the New Kingdom was still firmly in the tradition created in the earlier periods. It was, nevertheless, a different society from the one which had seen the building of the pyramids. The bureaucratic tendency advanced no further. Kings still wallowed in the exercise of personal power, but their state had to allow for a changed balance of internal forces, which had arisen principally through the emergence of institutions with a greater professional coherence. From their earliest stages states require the services of loyal agents who will offer advice and carry out the king's wishes, defend and even enlarge the realm by armed force, and look after the all-important practical aspects of ideology. Ministers, soldiers, priests: these three fundamental instruments of the state are identifiable in Egypt in the Old Kingdom. The first and the last also looked to a distinctive and prominent physical setting for their lives – palace and temple. The palace must early have become an institution, and by the 4th Dynasty so had the larger royal mortuary temples at the pyramids. But whereas in earlier periods the different sides to government appear to be facets of a single system, with the New Kingdom we can recognize their thoroughgoing institutionalization. To this we must add Egypt's unprecedented international position as an imperial power. And overall there were developing a polish and style that make the New Kingdom more like the states that have come and gone in the world ever since, down to recent times. We must reckon, too, with another force quietly and almost invisibly eating away at the prescriptive society: personal economic emancipation. This will form the basis of the next chapter. Ancient Egypt has a modern reputation for extreme cultural conservatism. But the New Kingdom demonstrates that this is itself something of a myth, brought about by a confusion between form and substance. Circumstances had changed, and basic ideology and practices were adapting to them.

History is one of several branches of the humanities which are essentially verbal. Yet to those who actually lived in any particular period their experiences were powerfully (if largely unconsciously) shaped by the natural and the built environment. The archaeologist dealing with the more ancient past is inevitably bound to focus more on the record of physical surroundings simply because that is often all, or most, of the evidence to hand. But this is not necessarily a defeat. It is a reminder that history that is written and that arises only from ancient written sources takes for granted the material evidence that helped to shape the experiences of its subjects. Indeed, evidence of material culture provides an unintended diagrammatic statement about the society that produced it in a way and with a symbolic power that written evidence cannot match. Our picture of the prescriptive society of the Middle Kingdom is drawn not only by the administrative texts but also by the planned towns that it produced. In a more complex and varied way the same is true for the New Kingdom.

Temples and priesthood

Ideology needs architecture for its fullest expression. By its potential for a dwarfing scale architecture compels respect in the individual and becomes the dominating horizon for crowds. Together with its style and detailing it creates a mood. We will begin our survey of the New Kingdom with the temples, which now and in later periods also brought a kind of corporatism to Egypt.[1]

In the Old and Middle Kingdoms, as far as we can tell, monumental architecture in the shape of the pyramids and their temples was kept to the periphery of the visible world: the edge of the western desert between the entrance to the Fayum and Abu Rawash, to the north of Giza. Local temples, built largely of mud brick, were scaled to fit within the dense vistas of modest brick-built towns. As an institution the local temple was an adjunct to the office of the head of the local community, so that the title 'superintendent of priests' was frequently held by the local 'mayor'. In the New Kingdom the monumental scale and the preference for building in stone were brought into towns. This was the age of the Mature Formal Temple, as outlined in Chapter 2. People in general began to live in the shadow of giant stone constructions which proclaimed the gentlemen's agreement between king and gods that power was exclusively theirs. New Kingdom Thebes epitomizes this, as will be illustrated later in this chapter.

For a fuller appreciation of the New Kingdom style in temples two particular factors need to be pointed out. The first arose from the structural dualism of temple worship, accommodating a hidden and a revealed aspect (Chapter 2). The New Kingdom saw great attention given to the latter, the portable religious image, of which the most familiar was the portable boat shrine. Sacred boats were not new. They seem from early times to have had an important symbolic and ritual role.[2] What the New Kingdom did was to lavish great attention on certain of them (especially the barge of Amun of Karnak called Userhat-Amun, 'Mighty of prow is Amun'), and to develop the smaller, portable version. One 'Superintendent of Carpenters and Chief of Goldsmiths' called Nakht-djehuty, who lived in the reign of Rameses II and evidently specialized in making them, was repeatedly commissioned to make new ones for a variety of temples, probably up to a total of twenty-six.[3] Both the riverine and the portable boats were put at the centre of temple design and temple celebrations. The portable boat shrines were made of wood, but ornately gilded and decorated and equipped with a closed cabin (sometimes called a *seh-netjer*, 'Tent shrine of the god') in which the image of the deity sat (Figure 66, and Plate 5). Long carrying-poles on each side or set laterally and up to five in number bore the shrine along on the shoulders of priests.[4] The resting-places of boat shrines have a distinctive plan: an oblong chamber with a doorway at each end and a central square stone pedestal on which the shrine rested (cf. Figure 68, p. 192). We should recall here the pedestals in early temples on which portable images were set, sheltered by a curved canopy of matting (see Chapter 2 and Figure 33, p. 93). Most New Kingdom temples were in fact built around the shrine of the sacred boat, and the plans of their interiors and the layouts of their exterior sacred precincts began from the desire to parade the boat shrine to the most dramatic advantage (Figure 65). Temples continued to contain fixed images of gods, but these now had second place. The elevation of the boat shrine to a position of eminence in temple religion matched the

Plate 5 Large temples were places of constant activity. Here priests carry boat shrines, as part of the procession of the festival of Amun. From the temple of Medinet Habu, reign of Rameses III, north-east wall of the second court.

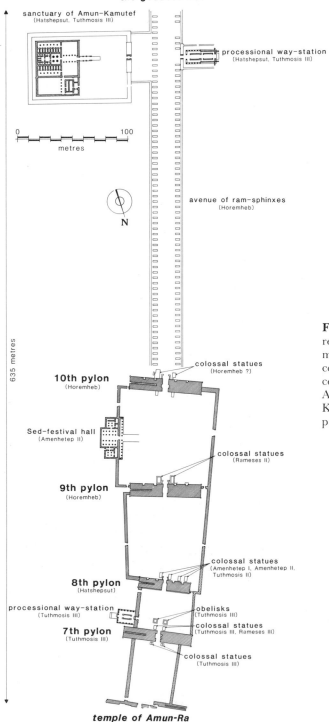

**temple of
the goddess Mut**

sanctuary of Amun-Kamutef
(Hatshepsut, Tuthmosis III)

processional way-station
(Hatshepsut, Tuthmosis III)

0   100

metres

N

avenue of ram-sphinxes
(Horemheb)

635 metres

colossal statues
(Horemheb ?)

10th pylon
(Horemheb)

Sed-festival hall
(Amenhetep II)

colossal statues
(Rameses II)

9th pylon
(Horemheb)

colossal statues
(Amenhetep I, Amenhetep II,
Tuthmosis II)

8th pylon
(Hatshepsut)

processional way-station
(Tuthmosis III)

obelisks
(Tuthmosis III)

7th pylon
(Tuthmosis III)

colossal statues
(Tuthmosis III, Rameses III)

colossal statues
(Tuthmosis III)

temple of Amun-Ra

Figure 65 The grand setting for religious processions provided by monumental architecture and colossal sculpture. The processional route linking the temple of Amun-Ra and the goddess Mut at Karnak, Thebes, cf. Figures 57, p. 162, 71, p. 203.

Figure 66   Religious processions in the New Kingdom centred on portable sacred barques (also Plate 5, p. 186). In this scene the barque is the major one for the image of Amun, having its own name 'Userhat'. It is shown at the mortuary temple of Seti I at west Thebes during the 'Beautiful Festival of the Valley'. The pylon of Seti's temple (identified faintly by painted cartouches, not shown in this drawing) is at the left side. The barque is carried by priests and accompanied by officials. (1) and (2) priests; (3) chief priests; (4) Ipiuy, a sculptor from Deir el-Medina; (5) the vizier Paser; (6) the scribe of Deir el-Medina, Amenemipet. From a sculpted block from Deir el-Medina, reign of Rameses II, in Cairo Museum, 43591. After G. Foucart, 'Etudes thébaines. La Belle Fête de la Vallée', *Bulletin de l'Institut Français d'Archéologie Orientale* 24 (1924), Plate XI (omitting texts); K.A. Kitchen, *Ramesside Inscriptions: Historical and Biographical* I, fasc. 7 & 8, Oxford, 1975, p. 403.

new monumental scale of local temples. Not only did they dominate the city physically, the processions of the boat shrines along prepared avenues brought a greatly enhanced degree of religious spectacle to the life of the city. The scale and professionalism of New Kingdom temple religion now held the populace more in thrall, replacing some of the older bureaucratic control with greater and more overt psychological manipulation. Then, as now, people loved festive processions put on by the state and, after one of these, felt more amicably disposed towards their rulers.

For the second factor we must turn to the external architecture of temples, how they looked to the world outside, a world which, for the most part, was excluded for ever from passing through the temple doors. The stone walls bearing scenes painted in hard, bright colours on dazzling white backgrounds did not rise directly from streets or public spaces. Between the temple and the outside world lay a precinct filled with brick service buildings and perhaps lesser shrines, all surrounded by a massive wall of mud brick. It was by this wall that the temple made its most public statement. In the New Kingdom the enclosure walls of the larger temples were made to look like fortresses, with towers and battlements.[5] Part of the evidence comes from excavation. At Karnak the same excavation to the east of the sacred lake which revealed the planned Middle Kingdom town beneath (see Chapter 4 and Figure 57, p. 162) also uncovered a 200-metre-long stretch of the 18th Dynasty enclosure wall with square towers set at roughly 17-metre intervals. Other more complete examples are known from other sites. There is also, however, contemporary representational evidence. This is important because it depicts what the tops of the walls looked like, something which the excavation of foundations

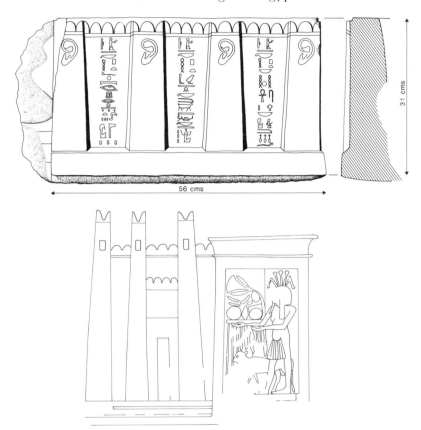

Figure 67   The forbidding appearance of large New Kingdom temples, surrounded by walls built to resemble fortresses. *Above*. Ancient model of the walls surrounding the temple of Ptah at Memphis, originally carved in the form of an offering-basin being presented by a kneeling statue. After J. Jacquet, 'Un bassin de libation du Nouvel Empire dédié à Ptah. Première partie. L'architecture', *Mitteilungen des Deutschen Archäologischen Instituts, Abteilung Kairo* 16 (1958), 164, Fig. 1. *Below*. Portrayal of a temple wall and portal at Karnak, from a scene inside the temple of Khonsu at Karnak, reign of Herihor, transition to the 21st Dynasty, after The Epigraphic Survey, *The Temple of Khonsu I. Scenes of King Herihor in the Court*, Chicago, 1979 Plate 53.

can never reveal. The most explicit source is a limestone libation tank of the 19th Dynasty from Memphis, which is modelled to show a wall with regularly spaced towers along all four sides and protecting the corners, and with a line of battlement crenellations running all the way round the top (Figure 67).[6] The sides are inscribed with prayers to the god Ptah of Memphis, one of them reading: 'Praise to thee at the great rampart; it is the place where prayer is heard.' To emphasize this a human ear has been carved at the top of each tower. There can be little doubt that this castellated structure represents the main enclosure wall of the New Kingdom temple of Ptah at Memphis, into the interior of which the public was not admitted. To the citizen of Memphis who made the model as part of a votive statue the temple was not a wondrous stone house of god, it was a citadel before which he could only stand and, in a small shrine beside or between the towers, appeal to the power of god to pass through the massive barriers that his fellow men had erected. The eastern temple at Karnak, mentioned on p. 202, is probably a more grandiose example of the same phenomenon.[7]

The castellated appearance of these temple walls must have been, in the New Kingdom, largely symbolic. In cases where the front pylon of the temple interrupted the wall and bore, as it normally did, giant scenes of the king vanquishing his foes in the presence of the gods, the towers and battlements on either side continued the mood. In scale, style, and detailing the temple wall had, in a world now more militarily conscious than it had been, taken over the bluntest image of temporal power.

Thus did the temple present to its community two contrasting faces: one in the image of temporal might, the other, on feast days, of release through communal celebration. This did not prevent people from trying to establish a more personal contact with the great deity who dwelt within, as the Memphis shrine at the ramparts reveals.

So much that has survived from ancient Egypt is to do with religion that we might conclude that the state then was sacerdotal. If we were unable to read hieroglyphs we might well deduce that Egypt was ruled by a high priest in view of the frequent occurrence of pictures of the king performing acts of piety towards figures of gods. We would not, in fact, be far wrong as long as we remember that modern English words like 'king' and 'priest' are not coloured in quite the way that they were in ancient times. But we would be wrong if we interpreted this as demonstrating that the state rested upon a greater degree of spirituality. Religion was the language in which weighty and important matters were couched.

Somewhere amidst the ranks of the priests whose names we know were the theologians responsible, for example, for the elaborate texts and scenes which appear in the royal tombs, and who carefully copied and studied old texts and read into them new interpretations. They are the ones, with an interest in theology, who would most resemble our image of a 'priest'. But they are hard to identify. As they appear in the sources that have survived people with priestly titles look very much like the officials in other branches of the administration. Indeed, they might well possess a string of titles that cover a priestly role as well as others quite unconnected. The modern term 'priesthood', although convenient, misleads if it implies the existence of a class of people leading a particularly distinctive life. Much of the work in temples was either routine performance of well-established rituals or pure administration of commodities and personnel. The temples as institutions are of interest in a study of the New Kingdom state as much for their economic role as for their spiritual contribution, and their part in bolstering the monarchy.

Egyptian temples were conceived, with some literalness, as a shelter for the divine images and a house for the gods who dwelt within them. The spiritual essence of gods (and of statues of kings and indeed of any person) required the sustenance that could be derived from food offerings placed regularly before them. These offerings derived from productive sources owned by the temple. But this was not the only function of temple property. It also bestowed on the gods a status which corresponded to power and importance on a strictly material scale. The gods were given the status of landed nobility, which suited some of the Egyptians' concrete conceptions of divinity. Furthermore, we find the material enrichment of divine property a major theme in texts dealing with the duties of kingship.

The riches bestowed on the gods seem to have been drawn from the full diversity of Egyptian financial resources, both durable forms of wealth (precious substances as well as sacred vessels in valuable materials), and permanent sources of revenue. Foremost amongst the latter was cultivable grain land, not necessarily in the vicinity of the temple itself, but possibly 320 km (200 miles) away, or even in the conquered territories of Nubia.[8] Although New Kingdom temples possessed their own labourers, often prisoners of war, much temple land seems to have been farmed on a complex rented basis, with up to 30 per cent of the crop paid to the temple in rent.[9] One document late in the period, the Wilbour Papyrus, reveals a picture of temple land subdivided into an elaborate tapestry of holdings, some cultivated by temple agents, and others by people who cover almost the entire spectrum of Egyptian society, from small farmers cultivating on their own behalf, through priests and soldiers, to the vizier himself, these latter groups being clearly landlords employing labourers and so introducing a third party into the division of produce.[10] The implications of this for our understanding of the basis of middle-class life will be pursued in the next chapters. In another document, the Amiens Papyrus, we meet a fleet of twenty-one barges cruising slowly up the Nile and making repeated landings to collect the rents from smallholdings of this nature for transportation to temple granaries at Thebes (cf. Figure 69).[11]

Other forms of agricultural holding donated to temples included animal herds, fishing and fowling rights, flax fields to provide the raw material from which linen garments were manufactured in temple workshops, vegetable beds, vineyards, and beehives. Animals, like crops grown from seed, multiply if tended properly, and it seems that, as with the land, it was common in the New Kingdom for people to look after livestock under a leasing arrangement with a temple. So a royal butler named Nefer-peret, who had fought in one of Tuthmosis III's Palestinian campaigns, was by a special decree of the king put in charge of four Palestinian cows, two Egyptian cows, one bull, and a bronze bucket (presumably for carrying the milk).[12] His brother was to look after them and his son was to carry the bucket. The cattle were, however, to be 'offered' to the mortuary temple of Tuthmosis III, i.e. this temple was their real owner (the word 'offering' is not always to be taken literally). The decree made the arrangement heritable, so that Nefer-peret's heirs would go on looking after this little collection of livestock. It was also specifically excluded from the authority of the Overseer of Cattle, a mini-example of a well-documented area of ancient Egyptian law: protection from institutional poaching (which will be examined in the next chapter). Thus Nefer-peret would go on tending his little herd, obliged to deliver to the king's mortuary temple a quota of offspring and of milk (which his son had to carry), and allowed to keep the rest for himself, secure in his legal protection from the official who was normally in charge of such arrangements.

Temples could also be granted access to mineral resources. Thus the temple of Seti I at Abydos was granted rights at the gold mines in the eastern desert, a gang of workmen to bring the gold back to the temple, and a settlement with a well at the mines themselves.[13] The temple of Amun at Karnak seems to have had a similar arrangement for gold mining in this area, and another for acquiring galena, used for eye pigment and as a medicament, also from the eastern desert.[14] Direct gifts of precious stones and metals also appear as a regular expression of royal piety. It was to the temples also that the king turned to dispose of surplus or unwanted booty from foreign campaigns. The

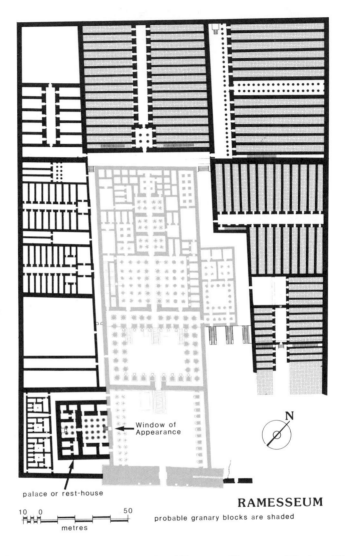

RAMESSEUM

probable granary blocks are shaded

Window of
Appearance

palace or rest-house

10 0   50

metres

N

Figure 68 The Ramesseum, mortuary temple of Rameses II at west Thebes. The stone temple is rendered in grey; the surrounding brickwork (see Plate 6, p. 196) in black. The latter includes a small palace or rest-house with a Window of Appearance (cf. Figure 73, p. 212), and a huge set of granary chambers (shaded). It has been assumed that all those blocks with staircases were granaries, the staircases enabling them to be filled through roof apertures. The total floor area is about 8,261 sq. metres. The storechambers were tall and vaulted (Plate 6) and it is reasonable to assume that grain was stored (perhaps in compartments) to a depth of 2 metres. This would give a total capacity of 16,522 cu. metres, or 16,522,000 litres, equivalent to about 226,328 *khar*. On an average annual ration for a working family of 66 *khar* of emmer and barley combined, the Ramesseum granary would have supported about 3,400 families, easily the population of a medium-sized city. After U. Hölscher, *The Mortuary Temple of Ramses III*, Part I, Chicago, 1941, Plate 10, opp. p. 74.

temples offered secure storage and administration and, perhaps even more important, a receipt in the form of texts and scenes displayed in the temple which recorded the gift as a great deed of pious generosity.

All of these various types of wealth, from beehives to boats, were designated by a common word for 'offerings'. What was actually presented to the god during the offering ceremonies must have been regarded merely as tokens.

In considering the economic role of temples we are faced with a classic example of the general problem which one culture (our own) has in categorizing another. Temple records were written as if each temple were an independent institution, and this can create the impression that they were independent sources of wealth and power. But if we take a more structuralist stance we can see that, shorn of theological nuance, temples comprised a major sector of 'the state' as we would see it, working in a symbiotic relationship with the palace. Thus a separate section of the Wilbour Papyrus is devoted to a special category of agricultural land, called *khato*-land, which belonged to Pharaoh but was administered by temples.

The absence of demarcation between temples and other areas of administration becomes very prominent when we consider the example of the payment of the necropolis workers of Deir el-Medina at Thebes whose job it was to prepare the royal tomb in the Valley of Kings.[15] They were essentially employees of the king, and so it seems natural to find that their wages sometimes come from the 'Treasury of Pharaoh' and its overseers. However, late in the 20th Dynasty, apparently a time of economic difficulty at Thebes, we find grain from tax assessments on various temples, and from *khato*-land administered by them, taken to western Thebes for the necropolis workmen and stored in granaries under the charge of the mayor of western Thebes (another interesting use of mayors).[16] A little earlier we find another mayor of western Thebes blamed for not having paid these workmen from the 'offerings' of the century-old mortuary temple of Rameses II (the Ramesseum), and the demonstration by these men outside others of these temples suggests that they, too, regarded them as potential sources of payment, something largely confirmed by a few surviving pay records.[17] At other times these men were paid from the temple of Maat at Karnak, across the river.[18] And when things went wrong, the ultimate court of appeal was the vizier. The independence of temples as owners of wealth was probably very much a matter of theological nuance.

A second channel of expenditure was the temple overheads, principally the payment of staff in kind. By the 'Reversion of offerings' the offerings actually presented to the god were first taken before any statues of lesser cults, and then finally divided amongst the priests and temple staff. By the same or by a different channel temple resources reached others with entitlement as well, such as the Theban necropolis workmen from Deir el-Medina. For the largest temples the flow of daily 'offerings' was considerable. At Medinet Habu it totalled 5,500 loaves, 54 cakes, 34 dishes of sweets, 204 jars of beer, and an extensive array of other foods.[19] How far temples paid for their own aggrandizement and fabric maintenance is unknown. The building and enlargement of temples were also traditional duties of kings, but since temple income was initially bestowed by the king, its further use to pay for improvements would have remained within the spirit of the original bequest, and, in any case, his authority was presumably necessary for any major alteration in the disposal of temple income. The system had an element of elasticity, too, so that apart from a degree of *ad hoc* requisitioning by one

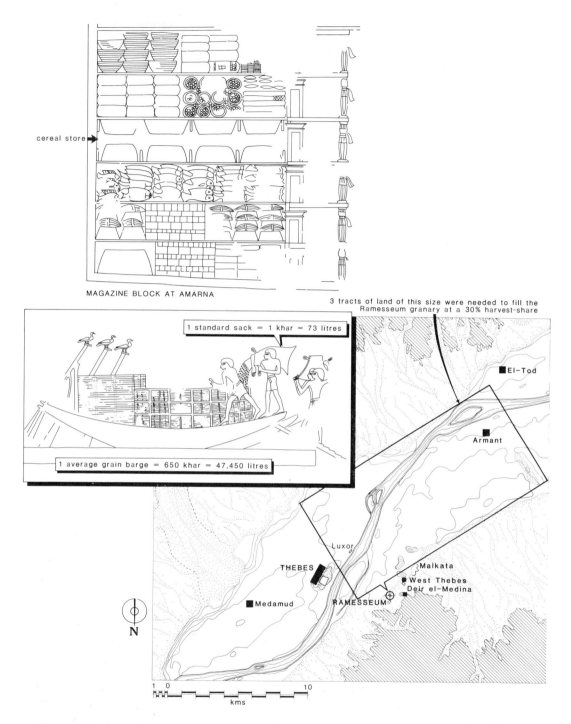

cereal store →

MAGAZINE BLOCK AT AMARNA

1 standard sack = 1 khar = 73 litres

1 average grain barge = 650 khar = 47,450 litres

3 tracts of land of this size were needed to fill the
Ramesseum granary at a 30% harvest-share

El-Tod

Armant

Luxor

THEBES

Malkata

West Thebes
Deir el-Medina

Medamud

RAMESSEUM

N

1 0   10
├┼┼┼┼┼─┼──┼──┼──┼──┤
kms

Figure 69 The key to economic stability: buffer-stocks of grain. The long narrow storerooms –
'magazines' – in large temples such as the Ramesseum at west Thebes (Figure 68, p. 192) were used to
store a wide variety of commodities, as illustrated by the Amarna tomb scene (top, tomb of Merira),
which depicts part of a magazine block at Amarna. However, it is highly likely that in any large
magazine block most of the capacity was used to store cereal grain, as at the Ramesseum (Figure 68,

institution from another (see Chapter 6), it was possible for one temple to rent lands from another temple.

It seems clear from ancient written testimony as well as from the logic of the situation that temple economies produced a surplus of income over requirements. Some years were good to farmers, some years were bad. Temples expected in general to build up substantial reserves or buffer-stocks of grain and other commodities which they stored in massive warehouse-blocks (or magazines) within the temple enclosure. Several relatively complete layouts have survived, and these are supplemented by detailed contemporary pictures.[20] The best preserved archaeologically is the set of magazines attached to the Ramesseum, the mortuary temple of Rameses II (Figure 68 and Plate 6).[21]

To give the reader some idea of the immense concentration of cereal wealth that a major temple could store, the total capacity of the chambers most likely to have stored grain has been calculated, and is given in the caption to Figure 68. When converted to ancient Egyptian measures it amounts to 226,328 *khar* (or 'sacks'). On an average ration for a workman's family of 66 *khar* per year of emmer and barley (attested in New Kingdom records from Deir el-Medina), the Ramesseum granaries, if ever filled to capacity, would have supported about 3,400 families for a year, i.e. 17,000 to 20,000 people, the population of a medium-sized ancient city, and a considerably greater population than the Memphis palace of Seti I discussed later in this chapter (pp. 222–3). We can draw two general conclusions from this exercise: it is unlikely that at any one time the granary of more than one mortuary temple was fully in use; and, like the granaries at the Nubian forts discussed in the last chapter, storage capacity reflects much more than the needs of an immediately resident and dependent population. The Pharaonic economy in times of internal stability operated at a level much higher than that of subsistence. Grain was wealth, and great stores of it were there for shipping around the country and even abroad for the realization of grandiose royal schemes. Major temples were the reserve banks of the time.

The ideal was excessive abundance, with granaries overflowing. There is no mention in ancient texts of a 'profit', but in practice that was what good harvests brought. For the larger temples also possessed their own merchant ships, not only in Egypt but also abroad. The temple of Seti I at Abydos, for example, was given a sea-going ship for foreign trade equipped with 'traders' by Rameses II.[22] 'Traders' seem to have been a regular component of temple staffs and presumably bore the responsibility for exchanging surplus produce – not only grain but other things such as linen – for goods

---

p. 192, Plate 6, p. 196). We know (from the Amiens Papyrus) that the average capacity of a grain barge was 650 standard sacks, or *khar*. It would have taken about 350 boatloads of grain to fill the Ramesseum granary. Cereal yields varied according the quality of the land, between about 5 and 10 *khar* per aroura (2,735 sq. metres). At the low but common yield of 5 *khar* from land which paid to the temple a 30 per cent harvest-rent, the Ramesseum would have been drawing on a tract of land equivalent to about 412 square km. To give readers some idea of what is involved a piece of land about one-third of this is marked on a map of the Theban area. In practice temple landholdings were split into large numbers of widely spaced fields. If one considers an extrapolation from the diagram to include the numerous lesser provincial temples it is easy to envisage just how much farmland was tied in some way to temple ownership or management. Amarna magazines after N. de G. Davies, *The Rock Tombs of El Amarna* I, London, 1903, Plate XXXI; the boat-loading scene after B. Landström, *Ships of the Pharaohs*, London, 1970, p. 134, Fig. 393.

Plate 6 Institutional wealth: some of the mud-brick granary chambers in the magazine-blocks attached to the Ramesseum, mortuary temple of Rameses II at western Thebes, looking north-east. The arched roofs belong to the original building.

for which the temple had a demand, which might be sesame oil or papyrus rolls.[23] Since everything in Egypt was exchangeable, a gradual accumulation of non-perishable goods, particularly metals, in the temple stores increased the temple's permanent reserves. The consequences of this are difficult to penetrate. But the institutional dominance of the country's economy and the capacity to build up massive reserves must have had a markedly steadying influence on the general economy, balancing out, for example, the effects of good and bad harvests and so keeping prices reasonably stable through the year and from year to year. When we come to consider the private sector in the next chapter this will emerge as a significant factor in the little evidence we have available.

The wealth of the large temples and the authority of their gods leads to a key question. Did the managers – the priests – perceive the extent of their power? In particular, were the priests of Amun at Thebes a political threat to kings? To answer this we have to consider two further aspects of New Kingdom society: the interrelationship between the monarchy and the cult of Amun, and the power of other institutions, the palace and more particularly the army.

Monarchy and the cult of Amun

The demands on kings were now considerable. They stood at the head of a large administration which, in the case of the temples, now included substantial institutions of a semi-independent nature; theirs was the responsibility for leading armies into battle against the well-equipped forces of western Asia; and in them resided the dignity of an imperial state with far-reaching diplomatic ties. Respect for kings was essential if they were to hold the edifice of state together. Monarchy on its own, however, does not guarantee respect. Too much hangs on accidents of birth. It requires the backing of myth and the regular reinforcement of ceremony to put into perspective the shortcomings of individual kings. By myth and ceremony a king is not left to stand entirely by his own merits. The respect of his people focuses on the office. The New Kingdom put much effort into this, and nowhere more than in the mutual absorption of king and Amun.

During the Old Kingdom the dogma strongly emerged that the king was the son of Ra, the sun-god. From the mid-4th Dynasty onwards one of the king's two cartouche-names described his manifestation as just this: 'The Son of Ra, N.' (where N. was the personalized Ra-name of the king), e.g. 'Enduring are the souls of Ra' (Ra-name of King Menkaura, builder of the third pyramid at Giza). The importance of the royal dependence on the sun was proclaimed in stone in the form of the pyramids and, in the 5th Dynasty, by large solar temples attached to the pyramids. The Egyptians sometimes used the word 'son' metaphorically, to refer to a loyal and loving son-like status which a person, including a king, might hold *vis-à-vis* someone else. However, the 'son of Ra' claim was taken more literally. A late Middle Kingdom tale (Papyrus Westcar), set in past time at the court of King Khufu, contains an account of how the future ultra-pious kings of the 5th Dynasty were born from a sexual union between Ra and the wife of a priest of Ra.[24] The tale is not a solemn piece of theology and may not be evidence that a literal myth of the divine origin of the king was standard serious theology in earlier periods. But in the New Kingdom it was.

Having the sun as a supreme deity creates a difficulty. It is the most visible and obvious of sources of superhuman power. Yet its very visibility and fixed shape make it more difficult to comprehend in personalized terms. A religion which has hymns, prayers, and offerings assumes a human-like capacity on the part of the deity to receive them. The Egyptians instinctively appreciated this, and at an early date gave to most of the gods and goddesses of Egypt the form of a human body, though sometimes retaining as an emblem an animal head. One form of the sun-god, Ra-Horus of the Horizon (Ra-Horakhty), was a man with the falcon head of the god Horus. But in other contexts the sun's disk was left as a detached element, perhaps symbolically conveyed forwards by a scarab-beetle, itself a symbol of creation as the god Kheprer, or journeying in a solar barge above the head of a ram-headed god. When it came to the direct worship of the sun by hymns and the presentation of food-offerings, the air of mystery that is needed to cloak a somewhat artificial act was difficult to sustain. Sun temples were open to the sky, and the hymns were chanted and offerings presented from the top of an open platform. The sun provided a good poetic image for the king, but was far less suitable a model for his divine counterpart.

New Kingdom theologians overcame this. The supreme god who fathered the king and remained the ultimate basis of royal respect was given the form of a man. This was the god Amun. It was not an arbitrary choice, for Amun was an ancient god of Thebes, the home of the kings of the 18th Dynasty. The early history of Amun is not well documented, but it is clear that his New Kingdom pre-eminence was a result of deliberate theological emphasis.[25] Two characteristics, at least as old as the Middle Kingdom, gave Amun a particularly powerful image. With no modification of his human form he had become the sun-god, Amun-Ra, and was now the recipient (even under the simpler name Amun) of hymns addressed to the sun. He was also depicted as the source of nature's fecundity, to be seen most forcefully in the cult of Min of Coptos, whose ithyphallic image he took over. In the New Kingdom his position was well expressed by a common epithet: 'Amun-Ra, King of the Gods'. At Thebes especially he was shown in the temples as the divine father-figure who looked after the king and presided over his victories, and this role extended to the mortuary cult now centred in new-style mortuary temples on the west bank of Thebes.

Amun also took over the myth of the divine birth of the king, which now joined the repertoire of scenes on temple walls. Two complete examples have survived – in Queen Hatshepsut's mortuary temple at Deir el-Bahari, and in Amenhetep III's temple at Luxor – but fragments of others are known.[26] The crucial episode of the whole sequence is handled with great delicacy (Figure 70). The reigning monarch's mother is shown seated opposite the god Amun, who with one hand touches one of her hands and with the other offers her the emblematic hieroglyph for 'life'. The protective goddesses Neith and Selket sit below on the marriage-bed, holding the couple aloft. The accompanying text is more explicit:

> Words spoken by Amun-Ra, Lord of Karnak, pre-eminent in his harem, when he had assumed the form of this her husband, King Menkheperura (Tuthmosis IV), given life. He found her as she slept within the innermost part of her palace. She awoke on account of the divine fragrance, and turned towards His Majesty. He went straightway to her, he was aroused by her. He allowed her to see him in his divine form, after he had come before her, so that she rejoiced at seeing his perfection. His love, it entered her body. The palace was flooded with the divine fragrance, and all his odours were those of the land of Punt.

After a brief speech of joy by the queen he declares: 'Amenhetep, prince of Thebes, is

Figure 70 An immaculate conception: the god Amun (*upper right*) impregnates Queen Mutemwia (*upper left*), wife of Tuthmosis IV and mother of the future god-king Amenhetep III. Beneath them sit the goddesses Selket (*left*) and Neith (*right*). A scene from the divine birth cycle at Luxor temple (cf. Figure 72, p. 207). After H. Brunner, *Die Geburt des Gottkönigs*, Wiesbaden, 1964, Taf. 4; E. Otto, *Egyptian Art and the Cults of Osiris and Amon*, London, 1968, Plate 30 (redrawn by B. Garfi).

the name of this child which I have placed in your womb.' Subsequent scenes portray
the fashioning of the child and his spirit (*ka*) on a potter's wheel by the ram-headed
creator-god Khnum, and the birth itself in the presence of numerous protector spirits.

Queen Hatshepsut's version goes on to illustrate how the power and authority of well-
tailored mythical portrayals can replace reality. Historically she was the daughter of
Tuthmosis I and wife of the next king Tuthmosis II, whom she outlived by more than
twenty years. For the first few years of her widowhood she acted as regent for the young
successor, her nephew Tuthmosis III, but then had herself proclaimed king, and ruled
as the dominant partner. In her mortuary temple at Deir el-Bahari, western Thebes, she
appears throughout as the rightful king, depicted and frequently referred to in texts as
being of male gender. In this latter respect the conventions of kingship offered no
choice. A fine set of scenes at Deir el-Bahari records the story of her origins. Early on
occurs the divine birth sequence, in which she is from the beginning designated as king
of Egypt. As the story unfolds it shifts gradually and subtly to the mortal world. She
visits Lower Egypt with her real father, Tuthmosis I, and is taken in hand by all the
gods of Egypt, who crown her and draw up her titulary. Now merging more closely with
the material world her father presents her to the court and appoints her as his successor
and co-regent:

> This is my daughter, Khnemet-Amun Hatshepsut, may she live. I designate
> her as my successor. She it is who shall be on this throne. Assuredly, it is she
> who shall sit on this heavenly throne. She shall issue decrees to the people
> from all departments of the palace. Assuredly, it is she who shall guide you.
> Obey her word, assemble you at her command. . . . For she is your god, the
> daughter of a god.[27]

The people react with delirious joy, the lector-priests compose her titulary, her name is
set on buildings and on official seals, and finally her coronation takes place on New
Year's Day. Other records of this situation – that Hatshepsut was the heir and successor
of Tuthmosis I with no reference to either Tuthmosis II or III – have survived at
Karnak. All of them describe on a monumental scale events which are specific and
detailed, but, as far as we can see, wholly fictitious. Even the New Year's Day
coronation date referred back to an ancient custom now obsolete.[28] Had accident
deprived us of all sources for the period other than these, their detail and consistency
would oblige us to accept their record as authentic history.

This presentation of Hatshepsut's reign takes us back to Chapter 1 and to the basic
myth of the state: the uninterrupted sequence of legitimate kings ruling in a single line
of succession descended from the gods. Hatshepsut's reign was simply made to conform
to the ideal image. To dismiss the sources as propaganda misses the point, particularly
if it is implied that they differ in purpose from documents of other reigns. The temples
recorded for eternity and provided only a single formula for kingship into which earthly
events had to be fitted with whatever degree of transformation was necessary. The
record of Hatshepsut's reign was made consistent with an ancient, established pattern,
and this was all that mattered.

Thebes: the ceremonial city

Thebes was not really, in the New Kingdom, Egypt's capital city in the sense that the court and the highest tiers of administration were centred there. This was the role of Memphis and, in the later New Kingdom, the eastern delta city of Per-Rameses (near the modern town of Khatana). The family of the 18th Dynasty kings had come from Thebes, and during the New Kingdom the Theban god Amun was given extraordinary prominence. This left the city with a special role in the state, that of a sacred city given over to religious festivals in which the cult of divine monarchy took a major role. Poetry celebrated its symbolic primacy:

> Thebes is the pattern for every city. Both water and earth were within her from the beginning of time. There came the sands to furnish land, to create her ground as a mound when the earth came into being. And so mankind also came into being within her, with the purpose of founding every city in her proper name. For all are called 'City' after the example of Thebes.[29]

Two comments are required: the basic image is that of the first primeval mound emerging from the waters of chaos and on which the act of creation was first performed. Here the mound is identified as the site of Thebes. The second point is linguistic: Thebes was frequently called simply 'The City'.

The monumental heart of New Kingdom Thebes was the temple of Amun at Karnak.[30] This now stands within a huge enclosure surrounded by a massive brick wall of the 30th Dynasty. In places, particularly in the south, this wall must follow the line of the New Kingdom enclosure wall, but in the east it takes a course somewhat outside. Even so, in the New Kingdom the enclosure must have covered an area of at least 400 by 400 metres.

For more than 100 years engineers and scholars have worked to preserve and to record the Karnak temples. It is, however, only in relatively recent years that serious attention has been paid to what lies underneath them. Several excavations (summarized in Chapter 4, cf. Figure 57, p. 162) have now revealed dramatically just how great was the impact of the New Kingdom temple builders on the old city: they completely destroyed it. The city of Thebes of pre-New Kingdom periods had grown by the late Middle Kingdom into an extensive city mound covering an area at least 1,000 by 500 metres and possibly a lot more. This puts it into a category of places that were quite large by ancient standards. A good part of it had been laid out to conform to a rigid grid plan, and within it lay palaces (known also from texts). During the 18th Dynasty the whole city was evacuated and levelled to provide a foundation platform for the new, dominating stone temples. This probably occurred on a piecemeal basis, with some parts of the site, notably the 'Treasury' of Tuthmosis I and the southern part of the southward processional avenue (between pylons 8 and 10), aligned according to the dominant street and plot pattern of the old city (see Figure 57, p. 162), whilst the rest of the temple took on an alignment perpendicular to the river which, apparently, the old Middle Kingdom temple had followed as well.

The residential part of Thebes must have been built anew, on fresh ground involving a fresh allocation of plot ownership. Being on new ground meant that it was at a lower level than the new temple now perched on the levelled top of the old city mound. This new city is probably now beneath the general level of the ground-water. Certainly no modern excavations have yet encountered it. The location of one neighbourhood is given by an inscription on a giant obelisk quarried in the reign of Tuthmosis III and finally erected by Tuthmosis IV in a curious chapel built against the back, i.e. eastern, wall of the main Karnak temple building. This chapel was intended for people who had no right of access to the main temple. It was a 'place of the ear' for the god Amun, where the god could hear the prayers of the townspeople. It seems also to have contained a statue of 'Rameses who hears prayer', a revealing glimpse of the reality behind the cult of divine kings.[31] The obelisk inscription states that it was set up in 'The Upper Gateway of Karnak, opposite Thebes'.[32] The clear implication is that it faced towards the city lying over to the east. We should imagine, however, a city covering a much larger area than before, reflecting the more expansive atmosphere of the New Kingdom (Figure 71). The short-lived city of Amarna spread its main built-up part over an area about 5 km long by 1 km wide.

There is evidence at other sites to show that what happened to Thebes in the New Kingdom was not unusual. The period seems to have been characterized by urban renewal. For the Middle Kingdom we can speak of urbanization as a policy of the state, achieved by laying out pre-planned settlements which in their rigid grid-plans reflected an intense bureaucratic control of society. Urban renewal in the New Kingdom displays far less of this, and may have arisen as a consequence of the redevelopment of key sites within towns as temple precincts. Provincial temple building on a grand scale became a priority of state expenditure in the New Kingdom for the first time; the rebuilding of towns and cities, in a more open style which reflected the changed nature of Egyptian society, was a by-product which became generally desirable in itself.

The main part of the temple of Karnak was constructed during the 18th Dynasty, surrounding on four sides the old Middle Kingdom temple which had an alignment at variance with the main axis of the planned Middle Kingdom quarter of the city and faced directly towards the river. Egyptian temples of the 18th Dynasty display considerable variation and originality in design, and this is particularly true at Karnak. The layout is unique, both in its internal complexity and in the small allocation of open space. The central element was a shrine, open at both ends, which contained the portable barque by which the image of Amun could be carried outside the temple on important festivals. The present granite shrine is a very late replacement, by the Macedonian King Philip Arrhidaeus, of the New Kingdom original. In the reign of Tuthmosis III the main temple building was enlarged by about 50 per cent through the addition at the rear of a stone building which has come to be known as the 'Festival Hall' of Tuthmosis III.[33] Its entrance was flanked by a pair of statues of the king in the form of Osiris, which may have immediately announced that kingship was a particular concern of the building. Inside, the most striking architectural element is a hall of columns designed to recall the poles and awning of a huge rectangular version of a tent shrine, a significant gesture towards the Egyptian myth of temple origins (see Chapter 2). The wall scenes feature the underworld god Seker, the royal Sed-festival, the ithyphallic form of Amun, the solar cult, and the cult of the royal ancestors. As with Egyptian temples generally there is little that is explicit about the purpose of the building, and this has led to considerably different interpretations. One of them, which takes account of the Osirid statues of the king flanking the entrance, holds that the main

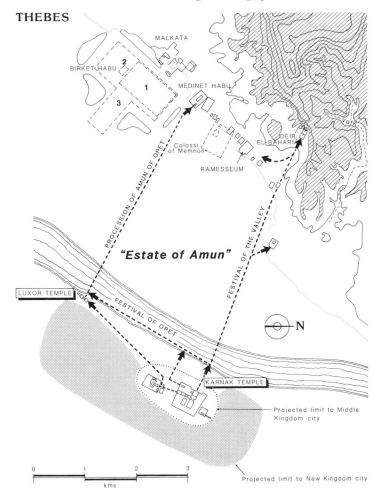

Figure 71 Map of Thebes, the 'Estate of Amun', in the New Kingdom, showing main temples and processional routes. The rectangles marked along the western desert edge are royal mortuary temples. 'VofK' = Valley of the Kings. For Malkata and the Birket Habu see Figure 74, p. 214, and Plate 8, p. 215. The numbered parts of the latter are: 1) hypothetical first basin; 2) palace for the first *Sed*-festival; 3) probable second basin, defined by earth mounds.

purpose was the celebration of the renewal of the divine king through identification with the resurrecting god Seker and the solar gods Horus and Ra, and through the rituals of the *Sed*-festival. The ongoing, ever-renewed powers of the king were thus made an integral part of the architectural symbolism and of the annual cycle of ritual of Egypt's main temple of Amun. Certainly the wall-reliefs show that the well-being of the reigning king and of his ancestors, as represented by statues, was catered for in the charged religious atmosphere of this enclosed building. The various royal statues, evidently located in different parts of the building, were themselves the object of a procession which carried them out to the nearby temple of the goddess Mut.[34]

Somewhere in the grounds of Karnak temple lay a royal palace.[35] Its position changed during the New Kingdom as the temple was enlarged. It must have been built of mud brick for nothing has been found either of foundations or of loose stone blocks. But we are sure of its existence from references in inscriptions. In the case of Queen Hatshepsut they are sufficiently explicit to suggest an actual location: in front of the 18th Dynasty temple façade, on the north side. References to a palace at Karnak continue through the New Kingdom, even though by the mid-18th Dynasty kings were no longer residing at Thebes. The texts themselves make it clear, however, that this was no ordinary domestic palace, but a ceremonial building used, for example, during a royal coronation. The king visited Thebes as the divine son of Amun. Wherever he was accommodated took on the character of a sacred building. We have more direct clues as to what one of these palaces looked like. The Karnak building programme of the reforming King Akhenaten included a palace, and fragmentary pictures of this have survived on carved blocks. They suggest a building without domestic quarters: primarily one or more columned rooms for banquets, storerooms, and a balcony for public appearances (the 'Window of Appearance' discussed on pp. 212–13). We are probably dealing with a cross between the standard small palace attached to the Theban mortuary temples (see pp. 211–13), and a larger version actually of Akhenaten's time at Amarna (the King's House, see Chapter 7). These buildings were not very large.

The Hatshepsut texts reveal the political value of the Amun cult at Karnak. On various festivals the portable barque containing Amun's image was carried out of the main temple, borne on poles resting on the shoulders of priests. This could be made the opportunity for Amun to perform a 'miracle'. Some movement from the heavy wooden barque would be communicated to the shoulders of the bearers, and magnified so that a distinct deviation from the prescribed course occurred, and sometimes a dipping forwards of the shrine. The texts also claim that speeches were communicated from the god, but by what means is unclear. In this way Hatshepsut was publicly picked out by Amun and the miracle interpreted as being a divine choice of the next monarch.[36] Subsequently Tuthmosis III claimed that by a similar miracle at Karnak he also had been chosen by Amun.[37] How should we react to claims of this kind? Should we be cynical and say it was all made up afterwards for propaganda reasons? Should we be more broad-minded and consider that chosen people in a state of excitement might actually hear voices, or voice openly the urgings of their conscience? Or was there a device by which the god's voice was made to speak? The question is made more acute by a case where a king (Tuthmosis III again) claims that in the important cord-stretching ceremony during the foundation rituals preparatory to building a new temple at Karnak (his 'Festival Hall'), 'the majesty of this revered god [i.e. Amun] desired to do the extending of the line himself'.[38] How much deeply felt religious experience as against cynical use of stereotyped religious phraseology we think was present will depend very much upon the individual reader's own state of mind. It is not something that scholarly research can properly answer. What we can say is that statements of this kind make an ideological point, stressing the particular importance of the event in question. The reader is informed that the choice of the next king or the laying out of a temple (or the various other acts sanctioned by Amun's oracle) has the greatest authority that mind and vocabulary can convey. They demonstrate the legitimizing role of Amun and the use of the Karnak temple precinct as the proper arena for it.

Perhaps the most dramatic illustration of how Karnak lay at the heart of the ideology of the New Kingdom state is to be seen in the reign of King Akhenaten, who carried through a fundamental, though short-lived, reform of the theology of the state and the imagery of kingship in the late 18th Dynasty. This involved the total rejection of Amun, and the creation of temples to the visible sun (the Aten) built along novel lines and with novel decoration. Akhenaten began his programme at Karnak itself, with the construction of several of the new temples and a palace, and the celebration of a grand Sed-festival.[39] By choosing to begin at Karnak he was proclaiming as powerfully as he could that the new style of kingship and state theology, which amounted to a new deal struck between king and god, emanated from the established seat of authority in such matters. At the same time, of course, he was admitting the continued importance of the old home of Amun, but within a short time he was to change that, too, by creating a new city for his sun cult at Amarna. But that will form the subject of a subsequent chapter.

The parading of the divine image was a basic part of temple life in ancient Egypt, Thebes in particular. We know this from the architecture at Karnak, as much as from the scenes and inscriptions on the temple walls. From the New Kingdom onwards almost as much attention and resources were directed towards laying out processional routes as to the temples themselves. Processional routes were, ideally, paved with stone, lined on both sides with sphinxes or similar statues, and punctuated at intervals by rest-stations: small formal shrines or temples set perpendicular to the route and designed to accommodate a portable boat shrine on a square stone pedestal. They, too, were called 'tent shrines of the god' (seḥ-netjer). The physical demands of reverently carrying a heavy wooden boat shrine may perhaps have dictated the intervals between rest-stations if not the actual practice itself. At Karnak one such route ran from the front of the temple westwards towards the river, ending in a stone quay above a basin at the head of a canal. In the 19th Dynasty this was shortened by the building on its line of the Great Hypostyle Hall and the Second Pylon, which became the new front to the temple. A second processional route was laid out in the 18th Dynasty to run southwards from the then temple front (see Figure 65, p. 187). It was given a particularly handsome and impressive appearance. By the time of Horemheb it consisted of four pylons separating as many courts, with obelisks, flag-poles, and colossal royal statues in front of the pylon towers, and a rest-station and royal jubilee hall built into the courtyard sides. Beyond the last pylon (no. 10 in the Karnak series) the route continued for a further 350 metres, lined with ram-headed sphinxes of the reign of Horemheb and flanked with two rest-stations, until it reached a completely separate temple, belonging to the goddess Mut who, in the New Kingdom, was held to be Amun's consort. A third avenue, lined subsequent to the New Kingdom with reused stone rams of Amenhetep III's reign, ran on an almost parallel course from the temple of Khonsu, who, as the son of Amun and Mut, completed the Theban holy family. The present building dates to the 20th Dynasty. This avenue is thought also to have ended in a quay above a basin connected to the Nile.[40] Close by lay the beginning of another processional route which ran southwards for a distance of 3 km, finally ending in front of the temple of Luxor. The sphinxes which now line this route date only to the 30th Dynasty, but a source from

Hatshepsut's reign shows that the route must have been marked in some way in the New Kingdom.

The festivals of Thebes were many, and the larger ones involved the temples in considerable extra expenditure in food 'offerings', which, by a ceremony called the 'Reversion of Offerings', were distributed as extra rations to the temple personnel and others involved in the festivals. As examples we can quote a damaged text of Tuthmosis III from his Festival Hall at Karnak which listed fifty-four feast days each year;[41] this compares with the sixty listed at Medinet Habu in the time of Rameses III;[42] and for the quantities of offerings the Calendar of Feasts and Offerings at Medinet Habu gives us as a minimum basis for some of the regular monthly feasts 84 loaves of bread and 15 jars of beer, but rising steeply for more favoured feasts to 3,694 loaves, 410 cakes, and 905 jars of beer in the case of the feast of the god Seker.

The processions of images of the holy family of Thebes and of other sanctified beings (including statues of kings of olden times) setting forth from the huge, brightly painted temples, and making their slow progress along formally arranged avenues with carefully stage-managed halts at intermediate stations, and the occasional excitement of a 'miracle': all this brought to the city as a whole spectacle and munificence which regularly reinforced the physical and economic dominance of the temples. And for the greatest of the festivals the king came to Thebes in person to be at the centre and to absorb some of the power that the occasion generated.

The most important was the festival of Opet.[43] It came round every year, in the second month of the season of Inundation. In the mid-18th Dynasty it lasted for eleven days. By the end of the reign of Rameses III in the 20th it had been lengthened to no less than twenty-seven days. At that time at Medinet Habu the festival was celebrated by the distribution of 11,341 loaves, 85 cakes, and 385 jars of beer. The core of the festival was an unusually long procession of images of the holy family of Thebes. The route lay between Karnak itself and the temple of Luxor, lying 3 km to the south (see Figure 71). In the time of Hatshepsut the outward journey was made by land, using the newly built southward extension of courts and pylons at Karnak and pausing at six rest-stations on the way, whilst the return journey was by river. By the late 18th Dynasty both the outward and the return journeys were being made by river. Each of the deities travelled in a separate barge, towed by smaller boats and by gangs of men on the bank, who could include high court officials. It was one of the occasions when the public could present pleas to the gods before their portable barques, and before colossal ka-statues of the king. Detailed scenes of the processions, depicting also the soldiers, dancers, and musicians who followed the progress of the barges from the bank, were carved on the walls of Luxor temple, the destination of the festival.

The present Luxor temple is largely the work of Amenhetep III and Rameses II. In facing towards Karnak rather than towards the adjacent river it proclaims its dependence upon Karnak. Indeed, the temple seems to have existed primarily to create a suitably monumental setting for the rites in which the annual Opet festival culminated (Figure 72).[44] These rites addressed themselves to the fundamental problem which sublime authority inevitably creates: how to reconcile the humanity of the current ruler with the divinity of his office.

We have already examined the process by which divinity was first infused into a mortal child destined to become king. It was explained in a rather literal way, as

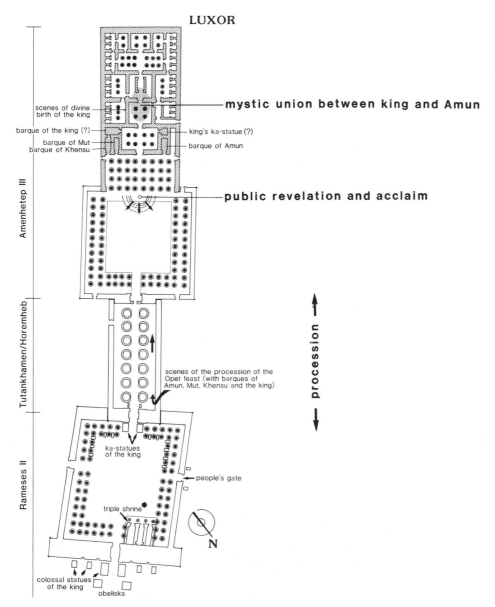

LUXOR

mystic union between king and Amun

scenes of divine birth of the king

barque of the king (?)

king's ka-statue (?)

barque of Mut
barque of Khensu

barque of Amun

public revelation and acclaim

Amenhetep III

Tutankhamen/Horemheb

Rameses II

procession

scenes of the procession of the Opet feast (with barques of Amun, Mut, Khensu and the king)

ka-statues of the king

people's gate

triple shrine

N

colossal statues of the king

obelisks

Figure 72 Luxor temple: centre of the mystic relationship between king and the god Amun, and focus of the Opet festival. The cross-hatched part at the rear is the earliest, and remained the sacred precinct in which the mysterious union between king and god took place each year. An asterisk marks the triple shrine in the outer court, originally a way-station from the time of Queen Hatshepsut, containing more *ka*-statues of kings, and a place for prayers and petitions by the people, hoping for an oracular response. The temple served as a place of coronation for at least one king, Horemheb.

brought about by a sexual union between his mother and the god Amun who had temporarily assumed the form of his father. One set of scenes illustrating this is part of the decoration of the inner part of Luxor temple. However, the nature of that divine essence was also separately identified: it was the royal *ka*. All persons had a *ka*, fashioned at their birth from the invisible continuum of life-force and destined to exist for ever. But, just as living kings belonged to the restricted uppermost band of the social hierarchy, so the *ka* of the king was part of the divine essence shared by gods and by the royal ancestors. Each new royal *ka*, created at the moment of the future king's conception (and depicted thus in the scenes of the king's divine birth), represented the next encapsulation of divine power in the sequence which stretched back through the long line of ancestral kings to the period when the gods had ruled in person. The indestructible royal *ka* existed in parallel to the life of the living king, its earthly manifestation, and gave the king his legitimacy. It was, of course, only an idea. But like all important religious ideas it was given a greater semblance of reality through the performance of ritual. Luxor temple was the focus of that ritual, its decoration giving great prominence to the king's *ka*. The mighty procession of the Opet festival took the king to the temple. Leaving the crowds outside he entered and proceeded in the company of priests to the enclosed chambers at the back. There, in a charged incense-laden atmosphere and the mystic presence of the god Amun (and his ithyphallic fertility manifestation Amun-Min), the king and his *ka* were merged, and the king's person transformed. When the king reappeared, he did so miraculously transformed into a divine being, 'Foremost of all the living *Ka*s'. His reappearance in public freshly transfigured was the real climax, the moment of cheering which implied that the miracle had worked and had been accepted as having worked. Luxor temple was, in the words of its original builder (Amenhetep III), 'his place of justification, in which he is rejuvenated; the palace from which he sets out in joy at the moment of his Appearance, his transformations visible to all'. Luxor temple provided for the king the essential setting for the interplay between the hidden and revealed aspects of a divinity that other temples provided for images of the gods.

The annual festival centred on the the presence of the king in person. By the mid-18th Dynasty kings were no longer residing at Thebes. They lived for the most part in the north of Egypt, particularly in the palaces at Memphis. The royal participation every year in the Opet festival thus came to involve a state progress upstream that spread the public acclamation further, and grew into an institution in itself. The job of feeding the court during the many overnight stops there and back fell to the mayors of provincial towns, and by the late 18th Dynasty this had become a burden which required a royal edict to correct.

The merging of the king with the god Amun and all his pageants had the important consequence of drawing a line between politics and myth. The royal succession could go badly wrong, some could even plot to kill the king and replace him with another (as happened with Rameses III). But behind visible reality lay an immensely weighty edifice of myth, festival, and grand architectural setting that could absorb the petty vagaries of history and smooth out the irregularities. It guaranteed the continuity of proper rule that was so important an element in the Egyptians' thinking. In particular it could convert usurpers (or new blood, depending on one's point of reference) into models of legitimacy and tradition. Horemheb is a prime example. The 18th Dynasty ended with the royal line petering out in the aftermath of the Amarna Period. The throne passed to a military strong-man, General Horemheb, who had risen to prominence in the reign of Tutankhamun. By lineage he was not royal. He was part of the court at Memphis, and during this time saw to the completion of a handsome tomb for himself and his family in the court cemetery at Sakkara. His elevation to the kingship is recorded in formal texts. These go so far as to recognize the early part of his life when he was 'supreme chief of the land' and an adviser to the king. When, through the machinations of court politics, and the leverage which his leadership of the army bestowed, he became king himself, his coronation was carried out at Karnak and Luxor as part of the festival of Opet of that year. As the texts describe it the whole coronation ceremony was integrated with the Opet festival so that the great Karnak-Luxor procession became a celebratory parade for the newly validated king.[45]

The Theban city of the dead

Karnak, Luxor, and the city of Thebes proper lay on the east bank of the Nile. Across the river on the west bank the New Kingdom witnessed the large-scale development of a city of the dead. From the beginning of the 18th Dynasty kings abandoned the building of pyramids in the Memphite area. They sited their tombs at Thebes and their successors continued to do so until the very end of the 20th Dynasty. But now the nature of the royal tomb was very different. The new-style burial place was a catacomb dug into the desert hills in the Valley of the Kings, and quite separate from the all-important offering-cult which was now housed in a temple lying separately beside the alluvial plain. It is easy to explain this change in practical terms: the tombs in the Valley of the Kings were more difficult to rob, initially because their location was, as far as possible, kept secret, and for the most part because of close policing of the area. The new style of burial and commemoration did, however, also involve a fundamental revision of the symbolism of the royal tomb, and it may well be that it was this rather than practical ends which dictated the result. The principal difference concerned the relationship between king and supreme deity. In the new tombs the king's body and statue cult were no longer subsumed into a gigantic image of the sun-cult, the pyramid. The only gesture now made to the cult of the visible sun was an open court containing a platform and stairs built into the back of the new mortuary temples. Instead, the new temples proclaimed the centrality and supremacy of Amun.

Although we are accustomed to speak of these as being royal mortuary temples, they were in reality dedicated to a specific form of the god Amun with whom the king became fused both in death, through the presence of his images within their own shrines, and in life during his visits to the temple.[46] At Deir el-Bahari there was Amun 'Holy of Holies', at the Ramesseum (mortuary temple of Rameses II) Amun 'within United-with-Thebes' (the ancient name for the Ramesseum), and at Medinet Habu Amun 'of United-with-Eternity', the ancient name for Medinet Habu. Each of the mortuary temples was really an Amun temple in which the form of a particular king had taken up residence. This is very apparent from the architecture of the better-preserved ones. Those of the 19th and 20th Dynasties (of Seti I, Rameses II, and Rameses III) reserved the rear central chambers, the holiest part of the temple, for the cult of Amun, not only in a permanent image but, more importantly, in a portable boat shrine kept within a pillared hall with central pedestal. For the 18th Dynasty only the temple of Hatshepsut preserves sufficient of its masonry, and here, behind the centre of the upper terrace, a rock-hewn sanctuary housed the image of Amun. The mortuary temples catered for other aspects of ideology, too. As just noted, the old cult of the visible sun was given an open court on the north side equipped with a stone platform reached by steps, a construction which the Egyptians rather oddly called a 'Sunshade', and from the top of which solar hymns were declaimed; and a room or suite of rooms to the south of the Amun sanctuary accommodated the cult of historical continuity, in the form of the king's father and sometimes his ancestors as well.[47] Yet another portable boat shrine stood here.

The network of Amun's connections to the west bank of Thebes was expressed through more processions. Once a year, roughly five months before the Opet festival, the 'Festival of the Valley' took place.[48] In this the images of Amun, Mut, and Khonsu, the holy family of Thebes, were brought from Karnak and ferried immediately over the river. Once across they continued their journey either by road or canal to Deir el-Bahari, site of the ancient mortuary temple and tomb of King Menthuhetep II of the 11th Dynasty and of the recent mortuary temple of Queen Hatshepsut. Deir el-Bahari lies almost exactly opposite to Karnak so that the whole journey could have been accomplished along a single line. However, as the New Kingdom progressed the route was extended so that the portable barques with their statues could rest overnight in the mortuary temple of the reigning king. On the next day the procession returned to Karnak. Although it was a much shorter festival than that of Opet it was highly regarded and was the occasion for families with relatives or ancestors buried in the Theban hills to make their own journey to the family tomb, to have a meal there, and to stay overnight.

A lesser but more frequent connection between east and west banks was maintained at a small temple built (or rebuilt) at the southern end of the Theban necropolis in the time of Tuthmosis III (*c.* 1475 BC), beside the space which later would be occupied by Rameses III's mortuary temple of Medinet Habu.[49] The shape of the temple was standard for its day, but its innocuous form disguised the fact that it was regarded as embodying yet another of the primeval mounds on which creation had first taken place. It was 'The Genuine Mound of the West', a name which probably also conveyed the notion that original creation and the rebirth of the dead in the western desert cemetery were linked. Inscriptions from the 21st Dynasty reveal that every ten days (the normal length of a working 'week' in ancient Egypt) the image of Amun of Opet (Luxor) was brought across to visit this temple, and it is likely from inscriptions at Luxor itself that this custom extends back to at least the time of Rameses II.

When the routes of all these processions – the festivals of Opet and of the Valley and the regular trip to Medinet Habu – are marked on a map they form a definite pattern: a processional perimeter to Thebes (see Figure 71, p. 203). To see the Theban temples on east and west as parts which fit a master-scheme is not just modern fancy. Certain brief texts, particularly names specifying certain buildings or building parts, reveal a distinct parallelism in Egyptian thinking between the mortuary temples on the west and Karnak and Luxor on the east, a parallelism which the processions of boat shrines articulated.[50] The master-scheme, the unitary overview of the sacred places of Thebes, is summed up in the simple fact that all of them belonged to the 'Estate of

Plate 7   Part of the small palace attached to the south side of the mortuary temple of Rameses III at Medinet Habu. The walls are partly restored.

Amun'. This was what the processional perimeter really defined. Its realization on the ground, however, also reveals the limits of New Kingdom area planning, something that will become very clear indeed in Chapter 7, on the city of Amarna. There was no attempt to build on the legacy of the Middle Kingdom by extending the overall planning of a settlement to the premeditated arrangement of a huge religious complex of temples and tombs. Individual Theban temples impress us with their carefully symmetrical layouts. But their particular locations seem to have depended largely on local factors of sanctity or convenience, giving rise to an *ad hoc* landscape of religious architecture. This was where the processional avenues made their contribution, binding the disparate parts together and creating a semblance of unity.

Just as Karnak and Luxor provided an important ceremonial opportunity for the king, so also did the mortuary temples on the west bank. From the time of Horemheb onwards each contained a small palace situated near the front of the temple (Plate 7, see also Figure 68, p. 192).[51] It offered limited but evidently adequate accommodation for the king and his entourage during parts of his normally infrequent visits to Thebes. The best-known example, at Medinet Habu, has two entrances to the inner part of the palace and each is graced with a scene of the king making an entrance, in the one case

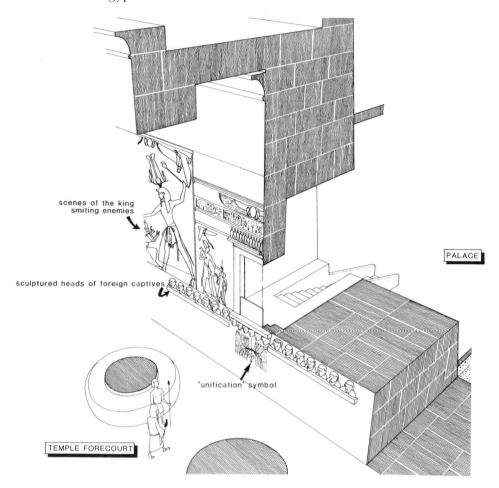

scenes of the king
smiting enemies

sculptured heads of foreign captives

PALACE

'unification' symbol

TEMPLE FORECOURT

Figure 73   Theatrical setting for the 'appearance' of the king: the symbol-laden ornamental palace balcony, the 'Window of Appearance' of Pharaoh. This slightly restored version is from the first palace at Rameses III's mortuary temple, Medinet Habu, west Thebes, after U. Hölscher, *The Mortuary Temple of Ramses III*, Part I, Chicago, 1941, Chapter II. See Plate 7, p. 211, for a photograph of the remains of the palace.

'to see his father Amun in his feast at the beginning of Opet', and in the other 'to cause his father Amun to appear in the Feast of the Valley'.[52] The mortuary temple palace was always on the south side, and at this point where it faced into the temple forecourt or towards the avenue leading into the temple it possessed a formal balcony, the 'Window of Appearance' (Figure 73).[53] This was the setting for a reward ceremony which, in view of the Theban festival programme, would have occurred no more than once or twice a year. A cushion was laid on the sill of the window itself, courtiers and high officials were led before it, and rewards and honours bestowed on them. This Theban reward ceremony was only a local version of a general gift-giving ceremony which later New Kingdom Pharaohs indulged in. The Edict of Horemheb describes in glowing terms how the army unit temporarily serving its ten-day period of guard-duty in the palace was given special extra rations at a reward ceremony performed at the Window of Appearance.[54] More will be said on this topic in Chapter 7, on the city of Amarna.

The rarity of the king's presence at Thebes must have ensured that the reward ceremony here was very much a special occasion reserved for particularly outstanding cases of merit. There was also a ritual overtone. Prior to Horemheb only one royal mortuary temple has survived to any significant extent: Hatshepsut's at Deir el-Bahari. This, too, has a Window of Appearance, but not as part of a small attached palace. This window is in the rear part of the temple proper (on the south side of the upper court) and thus an integral part of the area given over solely to religious ritual.[55] There are no scenes or texts with it, but its location implies that it provided a setting for the 'Appearance' of the Queen in the context of a ritual attended by priests. Inevitably the later Windows of Appearance in the small palaces inherited the ritual aura of the original occasion, and it is probably true to say that any formal appearance of a king was charged with ritualistic atmosphere, providing again a counterpart to the revelation of the portable image of a god in temple processions.

Amenhetep III's Sed-festivals

The Egyptians had a genius for adapting old styles to new requirements. New Kingdom Thebes was the product of a society which had changed significantly since the great age of pyramid building. But in the appeal to traditions the Egyptians found legitimacy for novelties.

As was discussed in the earlier chapters, some of the first intelligible monuments of kingship to have survived concerned the celebration of the earthly power and vigour of kings, the Sed-festival. In the New Kingdom it was still as prestigious an occasion as ever, but typically, although they would never openly admit to it in formal texts, the Egyptians invented new forms of pageantry and adapted the symbolism to the changed environment. The best-known case is the set of three Sed-festivals celebrated by King Amenhetep III (c. 1391 to 1353 BC) in the 29–30th, 34th, and 37th years of his reign.[56] The choice of these particular years was not wholly a personal matter. The Sed-festival had come to be, perhaps always had been, a celebration of thirty years of reign in the first instance. But thereafter, kings were free to hold repeats at frequent intervals. Amenhetep III's jubilees are of special interest because of the survival of the actual site where at least the first two were celebrated. It now bears the name Malkata, and lies on the west bank of Thebes, to the south of the line of mortuary temples and the Theban processional perimeter (Figures 71 and 74).[57] In being a kind of festival showground created for great pageants of kingship it offers a vivid and somewhat unconventional example from archaeology of the profligacy in the use of resources characteristic of despotic states at the height of their powers.

The classic Sed-festival was, as pointed out in Chapter 1, itself an amalgamation of two separate rituals, the Sed-festival proper and the ceremony of territorial claim. Early royal funerary architecture, best exemplified by the Step Pyramid at Sakkara, created a setting for both festivals in which one crucial part was a large arena where the king would run a sacred course. At Malkata this part was transformed into a water ceremony. A huge artificial basin was dug where the floodplain met the desert, designed in the shape of a modern letter T. This was the common shape for small tanks and pools

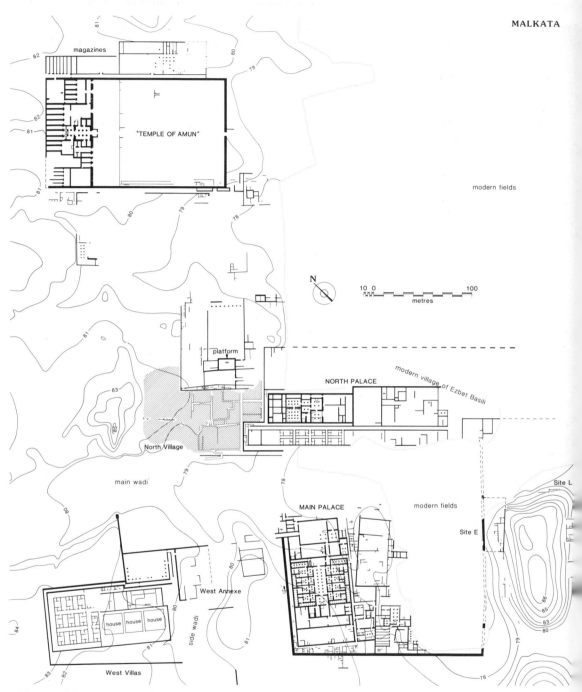

Figure 74 A setting for pageantry: Amenhetep III's constructions at Malkata, west Thebes, probable site of the celebrations of the king's first and second *Sed*-festivals. The map has been built up from a variety of sources, including aerial photographs, and notes and measurements made during a survey of the site for the University Museum of Pennsylvania. It includes the results of excavations carried out in 1973.

Plate 8   Aerial view of part of ancient Egypt's largest earthwork: landscaped mounds of spoil from the digging of Amenhetep III's ceremonial lake at the Birket Habu site, Malkata.

containing pure ritual water. By the end of the king's reign the Malkata basin had been enlarged to the extent that the main part measured 2 km long by 1 km wide. The earth dug out from this stupendous hole in the ground was partly spread out to make an artificial terrace on which the king's mortuary temple and part of the adjacent palace stood, and was partly heaped up into rows of artificial hills. Remnants of this early example of landscaping still survive (Plate 8). A contemporary Theban tomb, belonging to a high court official called Kheruef, has left a brief and very stylized description of the principal event from the king's first jubilee:

> The glorious appearance of the king at the great double doors in his palace, 'The House of Rejoicing'; ushering in the officials, the king's friends, the chamberlain, the men of the gateway, the king's acquaintances, the crew of the barge, the castellans, and the king's dignitaries. Rewards were given out

in the form of 'Gold of Praise', and ducks and fish of gold, and they received ribbons of green linen, each person being made to stand according to his rank. They were fed with food as part of the king's breakfast: bread, beer, oxen and fowl. They were directed to the lake of His Majesty to row in the king's barge. They grasped the towropes of the Evening Barge and the prow rope of the Morning Barge, and they towed the barges at the great place. They stopped at the steps of the throne.

It was His Majesty who did this in accordance with the writings of old. [Yet] past generations of people since the time of the ancestors had never celebrated such jubilee-rites.[58]

The Evening and Morning Barges carried divine statues, and were so called because they were intended as imitations of the heavenly barges in which the sun-god made his daily journey. Elaborate river processions had become part of the tradition of celebration at Thebes, and now provided the model for the *Sed*-festival. The last piece of the text catches the Egyptian approach well: it was novel, an invention of the day, yet in accord with people's feeling for tradition.[59]

The ability to invent with sound historical taste is illustrated by another of Kheruef's scenes of Amenhetep's *Sed*-festivals. In this the king is shown ceremonially raising into an upright position a carved pole called a *Djed*-pillar.[60] The pillar had the form of a hieroglyph which wrote a word which meant something like 'stability', and the act of raising it belonged to the range of symbols and ceremonies which encouraged orderliness in society. More specifically, by this time it was regarded as a symbol of resurrection and was thus associated with Osiris, god of the dead. Amenhetep III's master of ceremonies evidently felt it to be entirely fitting to add the *Djed*-pillar ceremony to the jubilee festival, although historically there was probably no connection. This interchangeability of ritual and associated ideas made it relatively easy to invent new combinations by stirring the pot of tradition. However, scenes of the festival in Amenhetep's own temples (as distinct from those in Kheruef's tomb) appear to be far more traditional and to shy away from the novelties.[61]

The texts mention a palace. Another scene in Kheruef's tomb shows king and queen emerging from it.[62] Their first appearance at the palace door on jubilee day, clad in the special jubilee costume, was another vital moment imbued with great significance. It was also truly traditional, since at the Step Pyramid this moment of first emergence from the palace seems to be commemorated. It was not the regular royal palace, however. Malkata was a site specially developed for this festival. So beside the ceremonial lake a special palace was built, of mud brick, its walls brightly painted with scenes and colourful designs. The food and drink for the celebrations were delivered to it in pottery amphorae whose tall mud stoppers bore the impressions of wooden stamps which recorded the great occasion. The festival day arrived, the amphorae were opened by having their tops expertly knocked off in one piece, the celebrations took place, and then the palace was closed for the last time. Within a short time work resumed on the lake, to enlarge it in time for the next jubilee. The palace stood in the way, so it was demolished and its rubble, mixed up with all the broken amphorae, was carried across to the desert and dumped there. This mixture of bricks, painted wall plaster, and broken empties was partially excavated in 1973.

For the next jubilee, four years later, a new ceremonial palace was built, again of mud brick. This one was left standing. The ruins, still with hundreds of fragments of left-over amphorae from the king's jubilee meal, were excavated in 1916. The plan of the building resembles a temple, complete with a small hypostyle (i.e. pillared) hall and group of sanctuaries, and this likeness was made explicit by stamped bricks used in the construction which refer to 'The Temple of Amun in the House of Rejoicing'. This last element in the name, it will be recalled, occurred in the Kheruef text quoted above. On such an august occasion the distinction between king and god, and the architecture which went with each, became quite arbitrary, just as at Luxor temple which was built primarily as a setting for an annual royal ritual. It also emphasizes how, even in the ancient *Sed*-festival rites which had no historical connection with either Thebes or its gods, Amun had been inserted to play the dominant role.

The royal family, the court, the servants who fed them, and the workers who kept them supplied with whatever was necessary – including glass vessels and glazed trinkets – were housed for the duration of the celebration in a large central complex of palaces, villas, and huts. The main palace contained the king's bedchamber and bathroom behind a formal arrangement of halls which included several suites for individual members of the royal family. Much of this building was painted with scenes from nature. Not far away a natural elevation of the desert formed the base of a brick dais facing a courtyard where perhaps the king could receive the more important visitors to his feast.

A pageant on water, distribution of gifts and a special meal, the erection of festival buildings and the assembling of dignitaries and foreign envoys and representatives: here are the ingredients for the archetypal state jamboree. Nor was it necessary to wait for a king blessed with longevity to reach his thirtieth year. The festivals of Opet and of the Valley were almost as grand.

The integration of king and temple cult of Amun enveloped the person of the king in an elaborate cocoon of mystery and pageant. It successfully blurred the difficulty that people might have in reconciling the divine and earthly aspects of a ruler who was also the head of a series of powerful institutions. For a brief time, however, it looked as though this compromise was only an intermediate stage in the evolution of a charismatic monarchy which sought the same level of adulation, but now directly focused on the king without the obscuring veil of religious mystery. This brief time was the reign of King Akhenaten, late in the 18th Dynasty. It will be described in Chapter 7. For the moment it can be pointed out that although Akhenaten's twin visions of a monarchy worshipped for itself, and of a theology that was so simple as to release the king from the shrouds of mystery, failed to convince his contemporaries and died with him, it offered a glimpse of a future that is still with us. Akhenaten's kingship provides an unintended caricature of all modern leaders who indulge in the trappings of charismatic display. The Egyptians themselves did not like what they saw. It evidently offended their sense of good taste. After his death they returned to intellectual compromise and wrapped again the nakedness of monarchy in the shrouds of high theology.

Secular powers in the land

Akhenaten's reign of seventeen years without the support of the traditional priesthood and all the colourful shows that it could provide, and the failure of this new style after his death which can by no means be described as the triumph of the priesthood, brings into focus two further institutions within New Kingdom society: the palace and the army.

In terms of bricks and mortar the term 'palace' is useful for any distinctive building in which a king or important royal relative stayed.[63] The Egyptian kings travelled inside their country quite extensively. If the journey was not on a regular route temporary accommodation could be found in a tented encampment, as was used by Akhenaten on his first prospecting visit to el-Amarna.[64] But for scheduled journeys where something was built to provide accommodation, be it only for an overnight stop, it would of necessity have a certain degree of formality (with e.g. a throne room) which attracts the modern word 'palace' when the remains are excavated. There were probably at any one time in ancient Egypt a very large number of 'palaces', ranging from overnight lodges or rest-houses which could be quite small to great sprawling complexes at major cities which a Pharaoh might have thought of as 'home'. When one adds to this the fact that from their unique position kings can build palaces stamped with an individuality lying outside the norms of the architecture of the day, reflecting considerations that may amount to whimsy, it is hardly surprising to find that the excavated New Kingdom palaces do not fit into the kind of standard pattern that one can recognize in temples and tombs.

Most journeys within Egypt used the river extensively. The small overnight palaces on royal routes were therefore sometimes called 'the mooring-places of Pharaoh'. The term 'rest house' perhaps renders the sense best into English.[65] River travel did not necessarily cramp the king's style: one model letter commanding preparations for the king's arrival at the riverine rest-houses shows that a force of chariotry was expected to be with him.[66] Provisioning the rest-houses exposed an administrative problem: how to cater for the occasional and not necessarily regular excesses of a brief royal passage. A partial solution lay in allocating to them farmland so that a permanent income maintained a small staff and could be stored in granaries ready for the direct feeding of the king's party and presumably for use in barter to purchase the extras which the farm did not produce itself. A group of 'mooring-places of Pharaoh' in Middle Egypt is known from the Wilbour Papyrus, a massive document on land-rents.[67] One lay near the harem-palace of Medinet el-Ghurab, another was at the city of Hardai on the Nile. This one owned 401 arouras of land. It is hard to imagine, however, that such a simple device solved the problem. Some kings were more extravagant than others, or might travel with a harem of excessive demands (remembering that the harem was a semi-independent institution with its own officials). The model letter of command to a local official in charge of some royal rest-houses is notable for the amazing range of its list of demanded commodities. Being a model letter we can suspect an element of vocabulary practice, but New Kingdom Pharaohs were not modest in their tastes. This is the sort of point at which the only solution for the hard-pressed official in charge was to go out and to commandeer extra supplies from other institutions and risk the appalling penalties laid down in royal decrees intended to protect individual institutions (such as the Nauri Decree, described in Chapter 6).

A good compromise was simply to make the mayor of the local town responsible. An excessive use of this device was corrected in the Horemheb Edict (see Chapter 6). Ancient Egyptian mayors are an interesting group. In earlier periods they had been all-powerful locally, commonly holding the office of chief priest in the town's temple as well. To some extent they lay outside the regular bureaucratic systems, and did not possess a hierarchy of their own officials. Their power must have lain in the respect and influence they commanded by virtue of local landownership and family ties and a network of patronage and obligation. Although they had no bureaucracy of their own, they were normally responsible for seeing that local taxes were collected and delivered to the vizier, the king's chief representative. They presumably acted as a buffer between the external demands of the state and the well-being of the local community of which they were the symbolic head. For making up a shortfall in supplies for a sudden royal arrival, who better to lean on than the local mayor? Another example of mayoral responsibility for keeping the palace in food will be cited shortly.

What did these royal rest-houses look like? A fair guide is probably to be found in the small palaces attached to the west bank mortuary temples at Thebes, adding in a magazine and some kitchens and small houses for servants and caretakers (see Plate 7, p. 211, and Figures 68, p. 192, and 73, p. 212). The model letter just cited refers several times to the existence of a special window at the 'mooring-place', which we should probably take as a 'Window of Appearance'. The fact that this was a standard feature of the west bank mortuary temple palaces strengthens the case for using them as a model for this type of provincial royal rest-house. One example of a rest-house, used apparently as a hunting-lodge, has actually been discovered and excavated, but never properly published. It dates to the time of Tutankhamun and lay close to the Great Sphinx at Giza. Why here? By the New Kingdom the Great Sphinx – originally a statue of Khafra, the king who built the second pyramid at Giza – had been reidentified as a statue of the sun-god Horemachet (another example of theological invention). Kings and private individuals rendered acts of piety to it. Amenhetep II built a special little brick temple not far from it. The site had an added attraction, too. The large stele in Amenhetep II's temple records how, when still a prince, he had exercised his chariot over the nearby desert. His son, the later Tuthmosis IV, went hunting for game, including lions, over the same ground. Just to the south of the Sphinx and incorporating the ruins of the ancient Valley Temple of Khafra, 18th Dynasty kings maintained a small palace. Tragically, it was destroyed by early archaeologists too interested in Old Kingdom monuments with very little record being made.[68] A plan of part of it suggests that it consisted of a group of buildings which resembled the larger houses at el-Amarna (Figure 75). One of them contained an inscribed stone door-frame bearing the cartouches of Tutankhamun later usurped by Rameses II. Several wine-jar stoppers were recovered. One description of a 1907 excavation may refer to a brick enclosure wall with square external towers at regular intervals.

A small rest-house with a similar purpose – chariot exercise – stands on the desert edge south of Malkata, at a site known as Kom el-'Abd. Built by Amenhetep III, its main feature was a flat-topped brick platform reached by a ramp (Figure 76). It has been hypothesized that tents were erected on top.[69]

The archaeology of New Kingdom palaces is best illustrated at el-Amarna, to which site Chapter 7 is partly devoted. Outside Amarna the excavated evidence is less rich

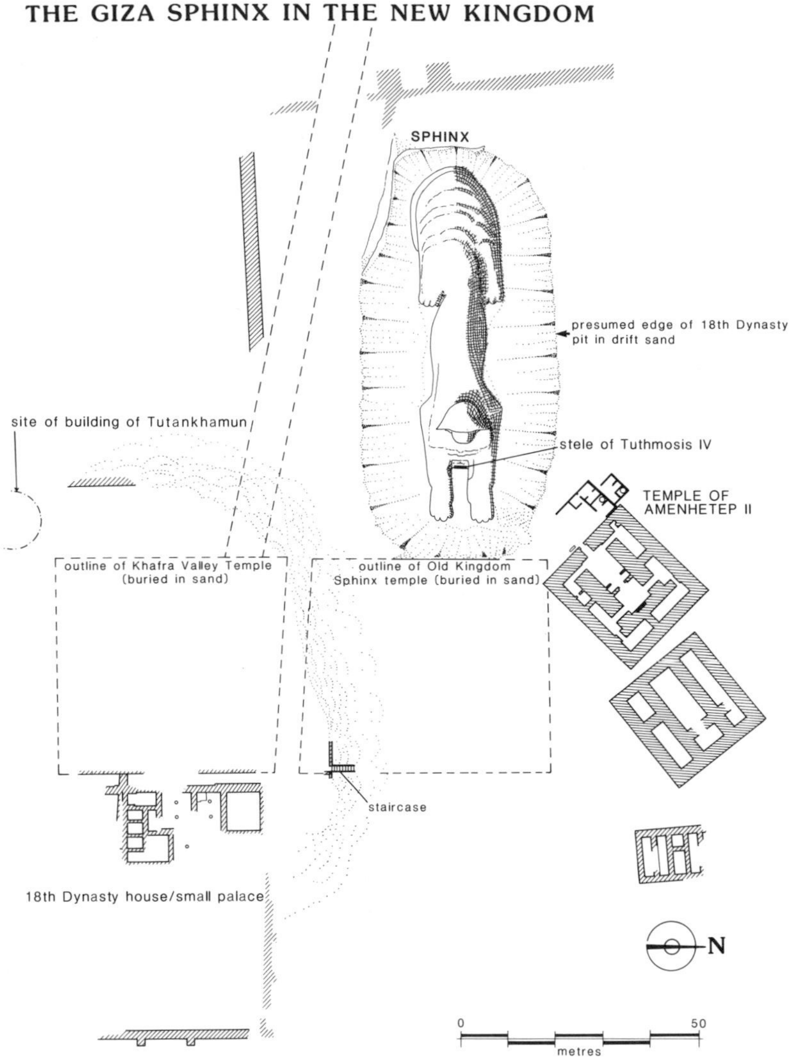

Figure 75 A royal rest-house at a sacred site. By the 18th Dynasty, the body of the Great Sphinx at Giza (then 1,000 years old and evidently neglected) had been buried by sand, which had also mounded up over the two contemporary stone temples in front. The Sphinx was now designated as an image of the sun-god Horemakhet (Horus on the Horizon). Amenhetep II built a small brick shrine facing the Sphinx's face, and following a dream whilst resting in its shadow, Tuthmosis IV cleared the sand from around the statue's base and commemorated this with a granite stele erected between the statue's front legs. The royal interest was not, however, wholly spiritual. Texts show that the desert area behind, around the pyramids, was being used by kings to exercise their chariots and practise archery (in the same way that the area today is a centre for horse-riding). A royal rest-house was also constructed here as well, around the flat-topped mound of sand in which the Valley Temple of Khafra (the original creator of the Sphinx) lay buried. The whole complex, itself buried by sand and even later buildings, survived in reasonably good condition until modern times, when it was mostly destroyed with little record being taken by archaeologists obsessed with finding sculpture and Old Kingdom stonework. After U. Hölscher, *Das Grabdenkmal des Königs Chephren*, Leipzig, 1912, Blatt XV; Selim Hassan, *The Great Sphinx and its Secrets*, Cairo, 1953; H. Ricke, *Der Harmachistempel des Chefren in Giseh* (Beiträge zur Ägyptischen Bauforschung und Altertumskunde 10) Wiesbaden, 1970; and conversations with M. Lehner. See also J. van Dijk and M. Eaton-Krauss, 'Tutankhamun at Memphis', *Mitteilungen des Deutschen Archäologischen Instituts, Abteilung Kairo* 42 (1986), 39–41.

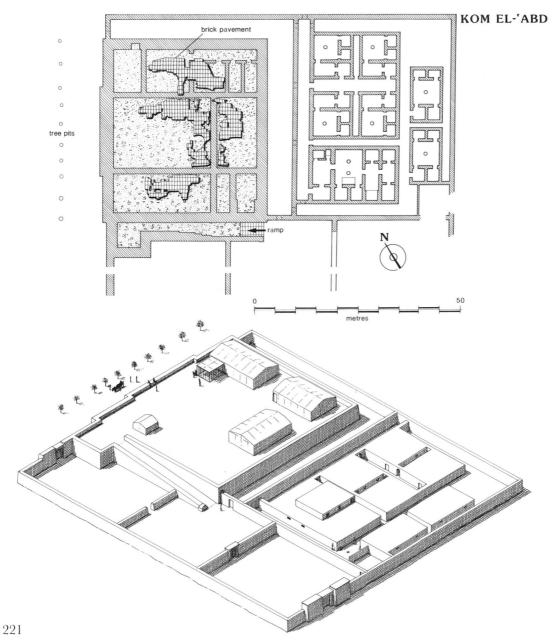

KOM EL-ʿABD

brick pavement

tree pits

ramp

N

0   50
                    metres

221

Figure 76 A royal rest-house at Kom el-ʿAbd, near Malkata, built by Amenhetep III. The use of brick platform for supporting tents is hypothetical. After B.J. Kemp, 'A building of Amenophis III at Kôm El-ʿAbd', *Journal of Egyptian Archaeology* 63 (1977), 74, Fig. 2, 79, Fig. 3.

than one might have hoped. We know from texts and from general historical circumstances that large residential palaces existed at Memphis and, from the reign of Rameses II onwards, at Per-Rameses (near the modern town of Khatana) in the eastern Nile Delta. So far the Per-Rameses palaces are represented by lengths of massive brick wall and the disembodied remains of a glazed throne dais; Memphis has fared a little better: a fine reception hall with all the proportions and dignity of a temple building belonging to King Merenptah was excavated early in this century.[70] The clearest picture we have of the extent of a real residential palace outside Amarna comes from Malkata, put up to accommodate Amenhetep III's huge entourage when it moved up to Thebes for his jubilee festivals (Figure 74, p. 214).

One motive in the siting of some palaces seems to have been to create a retreat, away from the pressures of the full court and its administrators. One clear case of this is the palace at Medinet el-Ghurab, on the desert edge close to the entrance to the Fayum.[71] Built by Tuthmosis III it remained in use through the Amarna Period. It is a particularly interesting palace because it housed the senior royal ladies, with their own officials, servants, and staff of weavers. It was a harem-palace where the occupants could live a secluded private life, and also bring up some of the royal children. At least one important Ramesside prince was buried there. The hot atmosphere of personal scheming and political intrigue which such a place could engender need not be left only to the imagination. The greatest Pharaoh of the 20th Dynasty, Rameses III, vanquisher of foreign hosts, including the 'Sea Peoples', fell victim to a plot hatched in one of them. We know this from a surviving summary of verdicts from the trial of the conspirators.[72] Thirty-one men were implicated, together with six of their wives. All except four were executed or allowed to take their own life. The plot centred, however, on the women of the harem, and one named Teye, whose son the conspirators evidently hoped to make king. Although the son was amongst those found guilty the harem women themselves seem to have been left alone. The composition of the group is most revealing: eleven were officials of the harem itself, twelve were officials or courtiers with other titles, only five were military men, and there was one solitary priest. One of the soldiers, a captain of bowmen of Nubia, was involved because his sister who was in the harem had written to him urging him to start an uprising.

Another retreat palace, or rather set of two palaces with accompanying villages, was built by the early 18th Dynasty kings in the desert at Ballas, just 22 km north of Thebes.[73]

Provisioning the royal household involved not only getting supplies to a travelling pocket of gross consumption but also supporting permanent communities at the larger palaces which served as home bases. One of these was at Memphis. We have an important set of documents from the administration of the Memphis palace bread supply in the time of Seti I (c. 1300 BC).[74] States one heading: 'Receiving wheat from the granary of Pharaoh in Memphis, in order to make it into loaves in the bakery which is under the authority of the mayor of Memphis, Nefer-hetep, to be sent over to the storehouse of Pharaoh.' There follow lists of daily amounts of between 100 and 180 sacks (about 7,300 and 13,000 litres). A complementary list picks up the trail: 'Receiving the bread of the bakery which is under the authority of the mayor of Memphis, Nefer-hetep, at the storehouse of Pharaoh.' The quantities, received every few days, were usually between 2,000 and 4,000 small loaves. Note the way that the mayor of Memphis had been made responsible for the difficult part – the running of the actual bakehouse, a labour-intensive place (as the excavated evidence at el-Amarna will show) where the system of keeping tabs on the flow of commodities was very vulnerable as grain was turned into flour and then made into loaves. This was separately documented in these papyri. We learn that 3.5 sacks of flour make 168 standard loaves or 602 small loaves, with separate notations for weight and for losses of weight during the baking process. A sack of flour seems to be the product of about two sacks of grain, but no one is allowed to take an average ration for granted. Measurement took place at every step and the discrepancies were noted. Milling was traditionally a woman's job, and there is one brief entry illustrating this: on one day three women, representing a group of twenty-six, collected 10.5 sacks of grain and turned it into 7.25 sacks of flour. The rate of issue of wheat would have amounted to some 50,000 sacks each year, which would have required a granary about one-quarter of the size of that at the Ramesseum, although we also have to allow for a separate and substantial amount of cereal used for brewing beer. But since the wheat was for immediate baking we must also accept the existence of a substantial dependent population, running into many hundreds, if not the low thousands.

The palace was, of course, much more than just architecture and provisions. Decisions of state and matters of dynastic succession must have been much more in the minds of those who lived there, and what they concluded and did provides the historian with the raw material for his profession. The harem conspiracy of Rameses III's time is a case in point.

The area which most consistently illustrates the political realism with which business at court was conducted is foreign affairs. The New Kingdom saw a great change in Egypt's international position. Conquest and empire moved to the forefront of real policies as well as of ideology. The result was an empire which took in much of the northern Sudan, and to the north-east Palestine and parts of Syria. The reality of significant conquest boosted the portrayal of the king as mighty conqueror, something done with much vigour and total lack of embarrassment on temple walls and in many other contexts (Figure 77). Success in battle, however, also led to deadly political gamesmanship with powerful enemies even further afield, whom Pharaoh could never hope to conquer. A study of New Kingdom foreign relations becomes the most important window open to us for observing the existence, at the highest level, of instinctive political acumen coping pragmatically with difficult real situations far removed from the cosmic tramplings of kings as depicted simultaneously in Egyptian art.

The prime source is a cache of clay tablets from a government office in the centre of Akhenaten's capital, el-Amarna, written in cuneiform script employing a dialect form of Akkadian.[75] Amongst the texts are a few intended to help Egyptians learn Akkadian, and vice versa. The bulk of the tablets are letters from western Asiatic courts, and copies of letters sent from the Egyptian court in return. In political terms the letters fall into two main groups which immediately delimit the real sphere of Egyptian power abroad. One is correspondence between Egypt and other states of great-power status where the mutual mode of address is 'brother'. These are the states of Babylonia, Assyria, Mitanni, Hatti, and Alashiya (Cyprus). The content is mainly personal, but might include a political element, as with the King of Alashiya's advice not to align with the kings of Hatti and Babylon (EA 35). With the letters went exchanges of

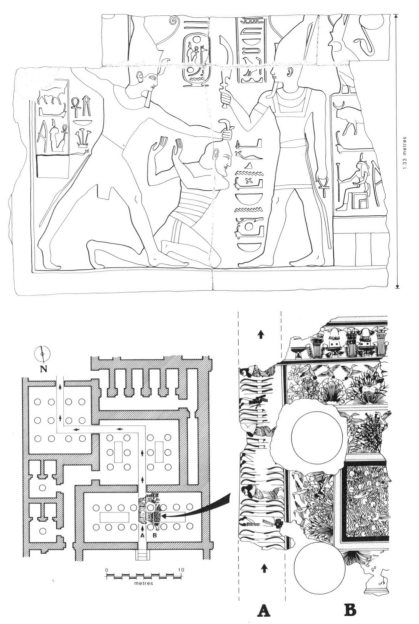

Figure 77 Imperial images. *Above*. God's blessing for Pharaoh's conquests. Rameses II smites a Semitic victim, whilst god, in the form of Atum Lord of Tju (=Tjeku, a local place), offers him a sickle-sword to legitimize the act. From a temple at Tell el-Retaba, eastern Delta, after W.M.F. Petrie, *Hyksos and Israelite Cities*, London, 1906, Plates XXIX, XXX. *Below*. Pharaoh Akhenaten tramples his enemies, within the security of his palace. *Right*. A section of painted pavement from the Great Palace at Amarna, depicting two themes – a rectangular pool surrounded by vegetation (B), and a central path of bound foreign captives alternating with groups of three bows, symbolic of the king's enemies in general (A), after W.M.F. Petrie, *Tell el Amarna*, London, 1894, Plate II. *Left*. Outline plan of part of the Great Palace showing the context of the painted pavement, and how the painted pathway continued. As the king strode from hall to hall he crushed his enemies underfoot. After J.D.S. Pendlebury, *The City of Akhenaten* III, London, 1951, Plate XIIIA, and comments on p. 40.

presents, a practice taken very seriously and about which kings were most sensitive in balancing what they gave against what they received. Arranged diplomatic marriages were one such delicate area.[76]

The second group of letters concerns the city-states of Palestine and Syria, their princes and their resident Egyptian officials. They address Pharaoh as 'my lord'. Those closer to Egypt had little prospect of an improved alternative, but the Syrian princes were in a position to make choices of major importance for themselves. Their aims have been summarized as: preservation of their own local autonomy, extension of their own rule over neighbours, maintenance towards the Egyptians of a show of loyalty to secure men and money, and either opposition or submission to the Hittite king according to circumstances.[77] Their letters tend to have the form of a long introductory protestation of absolute loyalty couched in obsequious language:

> This is the message of a slave to his master after he had heard what the kind messenger of the king [said] to his servant upon arriving here, and [felt] the sweet fragrance that came out of the mouth of Your Majesty towards his servant.

Thus Abimilki of Tyre (EA 147). In such cases the direct political message tends to be reserved for a brief final sentence or two, although some writers, notably Rib-addi of Byblos, could sustain loquacious pleas for support for much of their letters. A constant element is denunciation of a neighbouring prince on grounds of disloyalty to the king of Egypt. Since the accusations at times extended to the murder of one prince by another (e.g. EA 89, also 73, 75, 81, 140), these were not necessarily to be dismissed as inventions.

The obvious conclusion to be drawn from this material is that, although no trace has survived of anything like an objective comment on an international situation, behind the façade of total military supremacy Egypt's foreign relations were politically based, required careful interpretation and judgement, and involved discussion of situations in terms of human motives. For this one may assume that the Egyptians were well equipped. In the first place they tended to write letters to their superiors in a not dissimilar exaggerated style. Secondly, the giving of legal judgements in Egypt (something which was not confined to a class of professional judges but was probably a basic attribute of holding a significant office), although it might well involve reference back to documentary archives, was essentially a matter of resolving conflicting testimonies and assessing human behaviour. People who could pronounce judgement in a convoluted case of disputed land ownership going back over several generations had the right frame of mind for reading between the lines of diplomatic letters.[78]

The letters, however, had another and more insidious dimension. They created a mental world of their own, into which all the correspondents were drawn. For the king of Egypt, more or less at the end of the letter-writing line in geographical terms, it was a world of maybe fifty members, each one a ruler or occasionally another member of a ruler's family. The members rarely if ever met. They wrote to each other with long intervals in the correspondence, but there were enough of them to sustain at the Egyptian court (and doubtless in many courts elsewhere) a permanent office and secretariat to deal with them. As they read letters and dictated replies they must have formed in their minds shadowy images of one another which were frequently very wrong

Figure 78 Fear of the outside world. The outside world as viewed from Egypt was a place of hostile and threatening chaos. The Middle East, in particular, bristled with fortified towns and cities ruled by (to the Egyptians) devious and untrustworthy princes. Here one of them, the city of Dapur in northern Syria and an ally of the Hittites, is attacked by Rameses II's army. The Egyptian soldiers (who include four named princes), with round-topped shields, mount an assault from behind the protection of temporary shelters (*below*) and are beginning to scale the walls with a ladder. Some of the defenders retaliate with bows and arrows or by hurling stones, whilst hapless civilians caught outside either sue for peace (*bottom left*), or seek the safety of their city by being hauled up the outside face of the walls. From a scene in the Ramesseum, Rameses II's mortuary temple, after W. Wreszinski, *Atlas zur Altaegyptischen Kulturgeschichte* II, Leipzig 1935, 107–9 (redrawn by S. Garfi).

Figure 79 A further danger was posed by unsettled populations, some of them properly nomadic, others dispossessed and displaced, who were drawn as predators towards the urbanized societies of the Middle East. By the 20th Dynasty, swelled by an exodus from Anatolia which increased as it took in families in Syria, the existence of Palestinian and ultimately of Egyptian society was threatened. In this scene, of a battle by Rameses III's army *c.* 1186 BC, part of this migration is halted. Egyptian soldiers (A, F, H) wield spears and oblong shields with rounded tops, and are assisted by Mediterranean mercenaries, Sherden (C), who wear a distinctive helmet decorated with disk and horns. The Anatolian warriors (B, E, G, J) have spears, long triangular swords, and round shields, and wear what looks like a feathered head-dress. They fight on foot and in chariots (G), and protect their ox-carts (B). Three ox-carts appear (B, D, I) with wicker bodies and solid wheels, drawn by humped zebu-oxen. The carts carry women and children. From the temple of Medinet Habu, after H.H. Nelson and U. Hölscher, *Medinet Habu Reports* (Oriental Institute Communications 10), Chicago, 1931, pp. 19–20, Fig. 13 = University of Chicago, Oriental Institute, Epigraphic and Architectural Survey, *Medinet Habu* I Chicago, 1930, Plate 32. See also N.K. Sandars, *The Sea Peoples*, London, 1978, pp. 120–24.

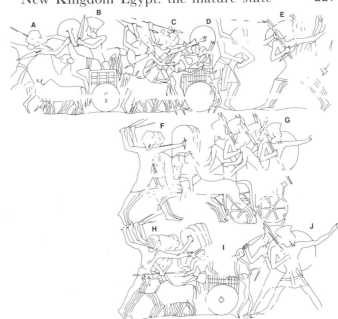

in detail, but which captured the essence of the situation: that they were all players on a political stage and had a broadly similar motivation. Although they usually wrote to gain a specific end, their letters also represented moves in a game where the stakes were measured in prestige and dignity. In this artificially constructed world of long-distance communication a king might blush or rage at thoughts of what had been said about him in a distant court that he would never see and could not punish, thoughts conjured up by the words of a letter of clay and the tales of the envoy that brought it. The Egyptian battle scenes on temple walls reduced international conflict to a level of absolute simplicity. Backed by the gods Pharaoh smote helpless and impotent foes with impunity. The letters, however, drew the same Pharaoh into a world of international vanity in which the price of acceptance as a star player was exposure to competition. Here he was no longer a god.

The empire brought to Egypt a new militarism. In earlier periods civil wars had been fought and territories conquered, particularly in Nubia. A striking level of specialist military architecture for the defence of towns had been developed (Chapter 4). But all the evidence suggests that the fighting was done by militias raised for a specific campaign, sometimes stiffened by Nubian desert warriors (Medjay people). Battlefield weaponry remained strangely crude – clubs and flint spears even in the Middle Kingdom. All this changed dramatically in the New Kingdom. Faced with the need to battle much more seriously against the well-equipped armies of western Asia the Egyptians borrowed technology and tactics, and seem for the first time to have established a standing army of long-serving soldiers and officers.[79]

Armies have a clear and straightforward purpose and much of what can be said about them takes the form of a catalogue of weapons, a listing of ranks and units, and a chronicle of particular fights. The army of the New Kingdom was no exception in this. From our point of view a much more interesting concern is the following: all institutions have a place in the state, are part of the system by which power is wielded at home; where did the Egyptian army fit into the government of the New Kingdom?

Because of the nature of the Egyptian administration – basically an extended cluster of centres of activity potentially in rivalry with one another – it is by no means clear that members of one 'profession' felt themselves to be part of a group with a common interest and thus, potentially at least, possessed of political power. Even the priesthood was probably no exception; the army, however, may well have been. We can call the New Kingdom army professional not merely on the grounds of general business-like appearance. It took in young recruits and put them into training camps, and campaigns and garrison duty were fairly regular. Army units were stationed within Egypt. The Horemheb Edict, for example, speaks of two corps of the army, one in the south and one in the north. Its soldiers had the chance to be in the palace to guard the king personally. The Edict also reaffirms the custom of employing as the king's bodyguard a group of soldiers from the provinces which was changed every ten days (the Egyptian 'week'), the changeover marked by the distribution of special extra rations at the Window of Appearance.[80] For veterans there is evidence from the 18th Dynasty as well as from the late 20th that they were settled with grants of land.[81] By the very nature of its life the New Kingdom army was a body of men, an institution, with its own sense of identity arising from its separateness from normal life. This separateness was heightened as the New Kingdom progressed by the increasing practice of recruiting foreign mercenaries: from Libya and from the countries of the eastern Mediterranean. They, too, enjoyed grants of land in Egypt.

In considering the role of the army – institutionalized armed force – we have to ask ourselves a very basic question: who really were the kings of Egypt? Where did they come from? The Egyptians themselves put up a great and very effective screen around this question. The elaborate array of pageant, ritual, myth, insignia, and sycophantic language that surrounded kings from coronation to death and beyond represented in total an overwhelming intellectual and behavioural assault on society to the effect that the reigning king's position was unquestionable and unassailable. Granted that within the confines of the court the question of which royal male would succeed next offered opportunities for scheming, for long periods the royal succession remained within a single family, a dynasty. Even when dynasties changed the newcomer might seek legitimacy by marrying a lady from the ousted royal house. But dynasties did change. The origins of the newcomers, except when foreign, are almost invariably hard for us to trace simply from a general lack of evidence. Sometimes they seem to have been already prominent at court, sometimes they arose from the provinces. What we have to accept is that they saw the office of king for what it really was: a goal for an ambitious man to grab at a time when the great screen of divine kingship was temporarily lowered, making such a step seem practicable. Usurpers and founders of new lines were not summoned from a state of innocence by priests or by mysterious voices or supernatural signs. They responded to crude ambition. Before the New Kingdom there appears not to have been a professional standing army. But if militarism was less of a factor in previous periods, so also was people's experience of it. This simply means that intimidation could be achieved by less. The 11th Dynasty, and the historical prominence of Thebes, arose from victory in a civil war. The background to the change from the 11th to the 12th is not very clear, but the successful usurper, Amenemhat I, himself fell victim to assassination. And if we go back to the very beginning of Egyptian history the sources show that kingship arose from a period of internal warfare, which reappeared at the end of the 2nd Dynasty. The screen of divine kingship maintained kings and dynasties in power for long periods of political stability, but ultimately kingship was the outcome of force.

The New Kingdom developed from the defeat of foreign armies. To the new militarism in society the portrayal of kingship responded with a greatly reinforced image of military leadership. The greater power of arms was matched by the king being presented as a military hero; some of them responded to this with a taste for the battlefield. Whereas in the past armed force could be mustered in the service of ambition, now the armed force was there all the time, dispersed through the provinces both at home and abroad. It became the source of ambition itself. This came to maturity at the end of the 18th Dynasty. In the Amarna Period, so we have to imagine, the religious changes of Akhenaten alienated the priests of the old cults, especially those of Amun, whose very existence Akhenaten tried to destroy. But in the aftermath the group whose representative became king – in the person of the general, Horemheb – was the army. In succession to him the throne passed to a military family from the eastern delta who founded the Ramesside line of kings.[82]

Yet militarism was evidently not characteristic of educated Egyptian society as a whole. The army and the empire in the end depended on the civil administration, from whose ranks also came politically powerful individuals. At school, through the texts which served as models for copying, young scribes were taught a disdain for all professions other than their own. This extended to military careers, and scorn was poured on the soldier and chariot officer and on service abroad. These texts evince no positive side other than selfishness – being a scribe 'saves you from toil, it protects you from all manner of work'[83] – but simply in preferring power through orderly administration to glory through action and adventure people who had accepted this ethos must have been a source of counter-arguments to those of the military. The creation of colonies in Nubia modelled on Egyptian temple-towns of the New Kingdom extended Egyptian-style administration over one complete sector of the empire, leaving western Asia to provide the main scope for military shows, though even here, as the Amarna letters imply, identifying the enemy was itself a task for home-based officials.

We can see the shadowy outline of two opposed interest groups in the New Kingdom: army and civil scribes, the latter with well-placed representatives amongst the courtiers. The harem conspiracy in the time of Rameses III involved many, and the leaders had sought the support of the army (though not of a priesthood). This conspiracy was 'political' in the narrow sense that those involved plotted and acted in accord with a pragmatic evaluation of risks and rewards.

Where does this leave the priesthood? In the case of the most important office, that of

High Priest of Amun at Karnak, we can follow its fortunes through most of the New Kingdom.[84] For the 18th Dynasty and the 19th into the reign of Rameses II each high priest was a royal appointment drawn from the ranks of officialdom (two, Ptahmes and Paser, had been viziers) or from people with a background of temple service, though not necessarily at Karnak or even Thebes. The priesthood in the later 19th and the 20th Dynasties was, however, largely dominated by two families (with a marriage connection) who managed to monopolize the office of high priest and many lesser ranks in the Amun cult at Karnak, forming veritable dynasties of priests. Their power base, however, was civilian: the dignity of high office, the family connections, the patronage at their disposal. In the last resort they themselves were only tolerated. They fail the ultimate test: families of priests did not provide future kings. The break between the two families coincided with some civil unrest connected with the dynastic dispute that led to the coming of the 20th Dynasty. For a time in the early 20th the office of high priest was held by one Bakenkhonsu, son of a man who had been in charge of the military garrison which by now the estate of Amun at Thebes maintained. But the full extent of the dependence of civilian power on the military came only at the end. The penultimate high priest of the second family, Amenhetep, was actually ejected from his office for eight or nine months during a veritable civil war in Upper Egypt involving the viceroy of Kush at the head of a Nubian army. This man established himself at Thebes and, for a short time, put himself in charge of the grain deliveries to the estate of Amun (an act which seems to have stabilized previously erratic grain prices).[85] When the dynasty ended the office of high priest was taken over by a military commander, Herihor. The ensuing three centuries were a time of private armies. The Thebaid became a semi-autonomous province governed by the high priest of Amun who was both commander of an army and frequently a prince of the reigning house in the north of Egypt, the same fusion of religion and secular power as was embodied in kingship.

It was a triumph not so much of either army or priesthood but of political realism. Herein lies an important lesson. Religious awe was not a basis of power in itself: its images of power were an illusion unless they articulated the political determination of people who, either by birthright or ambition, felt the urge to rule. They would probably not have seen it or put it so crudely themselves. For one thing, there was no ready vocabulary of politics and cynicism. But if they accepted the pious language and concepts they also bent the images in their direction and projected themselves into their centre. A powerful civilian priesthood was tolerated by the real men of power only so long as it did not get in their way.

And so we return to the opening sentiments of this chapter. I live in Britain, and am well aware that in my society pageantry and ceremony are not a symbolic articulation of political power. Much of this resides with the prime minister, a figure around whom the pomp is subdued. Things have clearly changed a great deal since antiquity. But wait. The audience at whom the pomp of Pharaohs was directed commenced with the court, spread to lesser officials, and probably included by the New Kingdom at least token groups of the people at large. But the notion of collective power was hardly born. The audience was for the most part politically neutral. People complained of unjustified tax demands, and demonstrated when rations failed to arrive, but they did not form political parties or revolutionary mobs. The pageantry was not buying off a real threat. Those who most represented a threat to the king were individuals closest to him, on the 'inside' of the pomp, who probably helped to organize it and were thus least impressed by it.

We are right to look for essential communications on ideas of rule within court pageantry, couched in the understood terms of the day, for the terms themselves may have had little existence independent of the celebration itself, and the preparations for it. Could we claim, for example, that the *Sed*-festival existed independently of its celebration (or anticipated celebration)? The means of communication was itself ideology. Pageantry and ceremonial were a reciprocal therapy, an 'in-touch' form of expression which all concerned found satisfying to indulge in, including the theoreticians – presumably priests – who devised the meaning, and for whom, without the performance, there would have been no meaning. Not only was the audience embraced by it, so also were the key performers.

Modern society, in democratizing pageantry and ceremonial and offering it as well to heroines and heroes of entertainment, usefully reveals that pomp is a collective social event sustainable in a manner that is independent of political power. In the ancient world the merging of roles tends to obscure this, but it must still have been true. Who ruled, who rose in favour, and who fell, what wars were fought and taxes raised, what new edicts were issued: the exercise of real power, behind the screens, was irrelevant to the pomp and the ceremonial.

6
The birth of economic man

It is possible to compile a 'Who's Who' of ancient Egypt for certain periods. The New Kingdom is one of them. If we look at the result, one very clear fact will emerge: no one who was prominent and successful claimed to be so on a basis independent of the state. Everyone was an 'official'. You could rise from a humble background to be the most powerful man in the land next to the king, but only because the king recognized your merits, one of them being loyalty. We will find no self-made men of trade or of manufacture, no merchants or moneylenders, or makers of other people's tombs. At least, that is what the inscriptions, the ideal autobiographies carved in tombs, tell us. As a consequence, on the basis of the formal written and pictorial evidence, we can conclude that the effective part of Egyptian society consisted only of institutions.

As always, however, we must be on our guard against confusing myth with structure. It is equally true to say that ancient Egypt possessed no politicians, in the sense that that word is used now, i.e. to refer to people who make it their business to articulate and to struggle for the interests of one particular group. But the Egyptians were not politically innocent. Within the framework of the loyal hierarchy of officialdom ambitious individuals pushed themselves forward and plotted to undermine those who stood in their way. The politics of self-interest most definitely existed, contained within the single system of administration. It was a later world, more given to abstract thought and less internally cohesive, that provided the political schemer with the 'cause' and the special-interest group, and thus the opportunity to reveal politics as an independent subject and calling.

Economics offers a roughly similar picture. No one thought 'economics' or pursued it as an independent goal, yet should we conclude that the Egyptians were economically naïve? The matter is clouded by the existence of a body of broad theory which encompasses both ancient and 'primitive' societies, and which tends to claim just this economic innocence. For ancient Egypt the influence of this special area of economic theory has been slow to arrive, but it has already left its mark. Essentially it represents a delayed response to the work of the Hungarian-American economic historian Karl Polanyi (1886–1964).[1] Polanyi's own works had little to say about ancient Egypt, but his name has come to signal a particular kind of approach to economic history and anthropology generally. The following discussion is thus not really of Polanyi's own views, but of those of others who in recent years have formulated opinions on the ancient Egyptian economy under the influence of his ideas.[2] Characteristic of this approach is a careful and self-conscious distancing of the historian from the modern economic world. We must not take for granted, for example, the basic experience of valuing our transactions in terms of profit and loss. This is because the economic systems of the ancient past were significantly different from those of the present. We can construct models of how they worked only from the ancient sources themselves, from a judicious use of ethnographic literature, and from certain points of reference which seem to be generally valid for economies in early complex societies. We must be alert, according to this view, to the dangers of implanting into the past the motivations and the means of the economies that we ourselves are familiar with. This is a valuable, indeed essential, discipline, yet if left here it runs the risk of unnecessarily isolating the past and impoverishing the discussion. In particular it depicts ancient systems as static entities devoid of mechanisms of adjustment to changing circumstances.

Furthermore, if the contrast between present and past is so crucial, it is important to have an informed basis of just what does constitute 'the present'. Herein lies another source of weakness. In discussions of this kind the economic systems of the present are made synonymous with 'market economies', the product of mercantilist thinking and practice of recent centuries which had their beginnings in the west. This is a false basis from which to begin. At the level of individual states the modern world contains no examples, nor has it ever, of an economic system based fully on market forces. Even for those politicians who most desire it, it remains an unattainable goal. All macroeconomic systems represent a balance, a compromise, an uneasy truce between two forces: the urge of the state to provide itself with a secure base for its own existence and plans, and the fragmented pressure of private demand.

At one end of the spectrum we have those states which, for reasons of ideology (or sometimes the exigencies of war), institute a wholly administered economy. The Soviet bloc countries are the most obvious examples. They use modern means to achieve something now familiar from studying ancient systems: 'redistribution' (a word which, in archaeology, has come to mean widespread centralized collection of produce which is subsequently disbursed on a similarly large scale). Economic transactions are intended to achieve egalitarian social goals and are thus 'embedded' (a key Polanyi term) within a political ideology which aims to engineer a particular set of social and economic relationships (i.e. socialism). For such a system to work as its creators intend it must be sufficiently sensitive in its prediction of personal demands and circumstances, and flexible in its response with the supply of goods and services to make all people content. All modern systems fail to meet the immensity of the task, and where failure occurs a market solution arises, although the modern world misleadingly renames a normal market response within a controlled economy a 'black market'. The 'black market' simply fills the interstices within a megalithic system.

Then there are those states dedicated to market freedom. This philosophy is in its application, however, invariably restricted. It flourishes most obviously in the manufacturing and retailing of consumer products. Modern states of this kind retain huge administered sectors – civil service, armed forces, defence procurement, farm price support, unemployment benefit, social insurance schemes, and control of the banking system – within which the free market operates. Modern market-sector states are large employers and (through welfare schemes) supporters of people, and large purchasers of many things, including money, yet are themselves not commercial organizations ruled by the maximization of profit and minimization of loss. At anything other than the local scale, the self-regulating, price-fixing market responsive wholly to supply and demand is an illusion. Modern market mechanisms are also embedded within, and draw for part of their performance on, the administered state sector, not least the state's almost invariable control of the banking system, levels of taxation, and supply of money, which is itself embedded within broader notional considerations such as 'national interest', 'party political considerations', 'social and moral responsibility', and so on.

What has this to do with the study of the ancient past? All modern macroeconomic systems, despite huge differences in philosophy and practice, represent different mixes of the same two basic ingredients: state ambition on the one hand, and private demand for more than an egalitarian share-out of the state's resources on the other. Whether we focus on states devoted to free enterprise which may wish to withdraw from final economic control, or those with an entirely contrary philosophy, we find in reality that they merely shift the boundaries between the two zones. We are thus entitled to ask of past systems: do they, too, represent a mix of their own within a universal and inescapable macroeconomic structure created when the first states emerged, allowing for the possibility that, like the modern 'black market', some aspects may appear in a different guise?

No doubt attaches itself to one side of the ancient mix, that directed by institutional administration, of the redistributive kind. This is not the case, however, with the other side, the satisfaction of individual demand, where the emphasis of the Polanyi view is to minimize its economic power. If, as we are encouraged to do with ancient states such as Egypt, we regard the administered economy as overwhelmingly dominant, we have to accept that one of two conditions was present: either the system itself was able constantly to assess every individual's real needs and satisfy them, or the needs of very large sections of the population remained not so much static as passive, offering a mirror-image of fluctuations within the state system: that is, when the state had less to give out, people resigned themselves to receiving less. For the first condition, had it ever existed it would have to be regarded as one of the lost arts of antiquity, since it would represent a level of economic management that eludes the grasp of all modern governments. For the second, however, we have to consider both the nature of ancient demand and the extent to which ancient systems were static.

The state sector: its power and its failings

The administered, redistributive side to the Egyptian economy is too well known to require much explanation. Several papyri or groups of papyri document specific instances in considerable detail for the various periods,[3] and to these major sources we can add a host of minor ones. Chapter 3 covered some of the relevant ground. We can utilize archaeological evidence, including huge granaries, witnesses to the scale of the state's maintenance of buffer-stocks of grain, which evened out fluctuations in supply brought about by varying harvest yields over the years.[4] To illustrate their magnitude, in the last chapter attention was directed towards one particular example, at the Ramesseum (see Figure 68, p. 192). Their passive economic weight should not be underestimated. Economic performance is a cyclic affair, and in the modern world state control of key sectors acts to bridge the gap between the inevitable peaks and troughs. We understand far too little of pure economic interactions in the ancient world to be able to model the changing economic climate which we must recognize was a major and ever-present factor, but in the case of Egypt we can be sure of one cyclic element: that of the volume of Nile waters. The annual inundation, the key to agriculture, not only varied from year to year, but was also subject to broader climatic cycles which, over a period of time, would have had inexorable consequences on the agrarian economy. The intervention of the state (palace and temples) would have had a powerful cushioning effect.

It was not a monolithic system: as we have seen, alongside the palace and its various centres of administrative authority there was a complex network of quasi-autonomous pious foundations or religious institutions where the focus of attention was the cult of statues of gods and kings, the latter including those belonging to the royal tombs and their associated temples.[5] All of these institutions were, to varying degrees, collectors of revenue, storing part and distributing part as rations or wages. The number of people who benefited seems sometimes to have been deliberately multiplied through the phyle-system, which shared out temple duties (and benefits) on a part-time basis.[6] As we have noted, it was the Middle Kingdom which seems to have progressed furthest down this particular road.

An important general point arises here. In recent years archaeologists have shown an interest in regarding aspects of ancient societies as 'systems'. Their component parts and lines of interaction can then be identified and laid out diagrammatically like a modern management flow-chart. It is a valuable perspective, but it carries a semantic pitfall. We may identify systems in the workings of ancient societies, but they need not have been at all systematic, for the latter word implies a prominent degree of reason and order. The workings of the Egyptian administration at its various periods are reasonably apparent, but they seem not to be the product of an abstract concept of administration elegantly applied across a broad spectrum of activities. Far from it. The system ran in channels of authority. Within any one channel the procedures could be remarkably effective (though not efficient) in achieving a given target, such as quarry, transport, and erect a colossus of a particular size. This is where bureaucratic talents flourished. But we will look in vain for evidence of conscious integration of the individual parts into a general scheme of management.

One document from the New Kingdom brings out very clearly the way that ancient government consisted of an accumulation of individual institutional arrangements of very restricted scope. This is the Edict of Horemheb (c. 1320 BC).[7] When the Edict was issued the Amarna Period had just ended, and the military leader Horemheb had become king. It might be anticipated that this would be a time of reorganization throughout the country, and of the reassertion of royal power of a traditional form. But the first part of the Edict is a collection of individual royal decrees directed against specific cases of wrongful or excessive collection of revenues by various groups of persons responsible to the king. They give the distinct impression of being responses to individual petitions of complaint rather than of being the result of a considered exercise in overhauling the administration generally. In so doing they imply that there was no codified system of revenue collection as we might understand it. In its place there was a range of individual practices sanctified by tradition. One group of officials did this, another did that. In one case the tradition was of recent memory. A separately mentioned authority in the Edict is the royal harem which had its own revenue-raising powers. Every year the king and some of his household travelled upstream to Thebes for the festival of Opet. The job of feeding them *en route* had been passed on, in the time of Tuthmosis III, to the mayors of local towns. The officials of the queen and of the royal harem had turned this into a predatory affair which the Edict now tried to correct. It is tempting to imagine an irascible queen making up for the boredom of a long journey away from the comforts of her own palace by preying on hapless provincial mayors and thereby creating a little administrative tradition. But to do this is to reveal an uncomfortable truth about academic scholarship: it takes on life only when it breathes in the vapours of historical fiction.

Because ancient Egypt was for long periods successful as a complex society we have to accept none the less that some kind of overall economic balancing act prevailed. Part of the process lay in what was, in effect, a massive delegation of short-term management through the pious foundations. We have already, in Chapter 5, commented on the symbiotic relationship between temples and palace. Their status as religious centres embedded within the overall ideology of the state, and their internal bureaucracies gave them the authority and means to function effectively but not divisively. In the longer term, however, they were subject to a process of piecemeal adjustment in which older and less prestigious foundations lost their benefactions to new foundations. The notion that cults were founded for eternity was a myth which did not hinder state interference. In revenue and expenditure terms the sum of their activities plus a general level of royal expenditure on court life, on large and thus long-term building programmes, and on the military, represented a general 'budget' or balance-sheet for the country. It was probably never seen in quite so abstract a way. But complaints from below of insufficient resources would have signalled to senior officials a degree of imbalance, which they could then have sought to correct.

The basic level of royal expenditure was maintained partly through the income of lands and other productive resources directly owned, partly through revenue-raising powers bestowed on particular officials of particular institutions, and partly through a country-wide tax levy. From time to time this was recalculated, presumably in response to perceived shortfalls in revenue.[8] The one detailed record we have of a general tax levied on provincial towns and districts for the benefit of the king (through his vizier) is the taxation scene in the tomb of Rekhmira at Thebes (Figure 80).[9] This source implies, however, that the amounts raised in this way were very modest. Yet particular circumstances regularly created extra if short-lived demands. The procedure then was simply to pass them down the administrative channels. Ideally such a demand would be accompanied by an order to release some of the state's buffer stocks from the magazines of a convenient institution to cover the demand. In practice, however, this did not always work. An *ad hoc* solution was expected, and this could be found either by a peremptory local demand on whomsoever was vulnerable, or by raiding the resources of another area of administration.

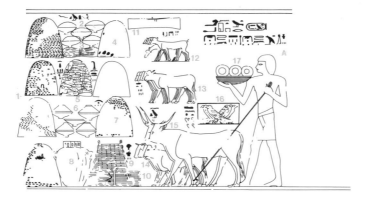

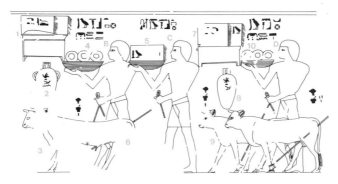

Figure 80 Paying in kind: local taxation in a cashless economy, illustrated by a portion of the revenue scene from the tomb of the vizier Rekhmira at Thebes, mid-18th Dynasty. Not all commodities can be identified. *Top.* (A) Taxes delivered by the 'mayor of (the town) of Huwet-weret-Amenemhat' (south of Abydos). 1: four heaps of barley; 2: cakes; 3: rope; 4: dôm nuts; 5: cakes; 6: spices (?); 7: carob beans; 8: honey (?); 9: sacks; 10: reed mats; 11: grass mats; 12: 6 goats; 13: 5 calves; 14: 4 head of cattle; 15: 2 head of long-horned cattle; 16: 500 pigeons; 17: 2 gold, 1 silver ring-ingots. *Bottom.* (B) 'The recorder of the town of Wah-set' (south of Abydos), and (C) 'The scribe of the recorder of the town of Wah-set'. 1: 2 lengths of linen cloth in a chest; 2: honey; 3: 1 head of cattle; 4: 3 gold ring-ingots. 5: 1 linen garment; 6: 1 head of cattle; (D) 'The recorder of Abydos'; 7: 1 length of cloth and 1 garment in a chest; 8: honey; 9: 1 head of cattle; 10: 2 gold, 1 silver ring-ingots. After N. de G. Davies, *The Tomb of Rekh-mi-rè at Thebes*, New York, 1943, Plate XXXIV; P.E. Newberry, *The Life of Rekhmara*, London, 1900, Plate VI.

The ill-feeling generated by the tangle of individual systems of revenue collection, by which institutions and groups of officials quite literally lived off the land, is illustrated by a second document from the New Kingdom, the Nauri Decree of Seti I. It belongs to the reign of one of the 'great' kings and is thus lifted above the charge that it reveals a good system going wrong under a bad king. One of the great pious works of Seti I was the building of a sumptuously decorated and equipped temple for Amun and Osiris at the holy city of Abydos. As was customary he donated sufficient land and other sources of income to make the temple a permanently wealthy institution. Some of the land lay far away in the conquered territories of the Sudan. The purpose of the decree was quite simply to protect the new donations from other official institutions whose agents might arrive at some distant farm or cattle station and demand payment of a tax. For such officials the punishments were fierce: heavy fines, beatings, and mutilations. Every year, too, a flotilla of ships set off from the Nubian lands on the long journey downstream not only to replenish the huge storerooms attached to the temple with the year's Nubian harvest, but also to bring exotic trade goods purchased through barter by 'traders' employed by the temple. On its long journey downstream the flotilla passed Egyptian fortresses whose real job was to protect Egyptian life and property. One must have lain near Nauri, a lonely, isolated place:

> As for any commander of the (local) fortress, and scribe of the fortress, any inspector belonging to the fortress who shall board a boat belonging to the Temple and shall take gold, [ivory, ebony?], leopard and other animal skins, giraffes' tails, giraffes' hides, etc., any goods of Kush which are brought as revenue to the Temple, punishment shall be meted out to him in the form of one hundred blows, and he shall be fined on behalf of the Temple in terms of the value of the goods at the rate of eighty to one.[10]

The remoteness and isolation of Nauri do not, in themselves, make the decree an exception. The full text makes it clear that the Nauri version was only one copy of a decree which applied to the open farmlands of Nubia where Egyptian colonial towns had been built and a full Egyptian-style administration functioned. Nor is the decree itself unique for its period. Others are known from other reigns, including one of Rameses III from Elephantine and others from the Ramesside period from Armant and Hermopolis.[11] Indeed, the tradition of decrees to protect individual institutions from the exactions of others goes back to the Old Kingdom.[12]

Government in ancient Egypt was by royal decree, the system of administration was the sum of these decrees, and the resulting overlaps and confusions of responsibility were tackled by fresh decrees in response to specific complaints. This cycle of decision–petition of complaint–redress was a basic part of bureaucratic life, to the extent that collections, of model letters used in the training of scribes often contained a model letter or petition of complaint.[13] The universal picture of the rapacious tax-collector and the suffering peasant is joined in ancient Egypt by the picture of the predatory official victimizing his colleague.

The state sector of the Egyptian economy existed to satisfy institutional demands, and must have had very limited flexibility. If it also satisfied most private demand, that demand must have been of low intensity. We need to look next, therefore, at the real pattern of private demand.

The power of private demand

When we turn to the record of archaeology, especially that from cemeteries, it is very clear that during the latter part of the Predynastic Period Egyptian society entered that crucial stage of social and psychological significance: conspicuous consumption. The creation of large and striking private tombs and the accumulation of burial goods affected the whole of Egypt geographically, and created an aspiration that penetrated deeply into society. If we adopt the Polanyi approach we can find that the redistributive economy and conspicuous consumption are not incompatible. Social obligation brings the two together: the king rewards his great men, many of them having provincial connections. They in turn pass on bounty to poorer relatives and dependants. Everyone is satisfied (or unable to articulate his dissatisfaction in economic terms), and in death takes his place in a cemetery which likewise reflects the social and economic order: local leaders in centrally placed handsome tombs surrounded by myriads of smaller tombs of lesser folk (Beni Hasan and Naga ed-Deir providing fine examples from the Old and Middle Kingdoms respectively).[14] We can make Egypt into a model of the redistributive economy.

At a political level (i.e. in the wish to exercise power), however, the Old Kingdom shows that the ideal of consensus is an illusion. Provincial governors (nomarchs) appear, and when, at the end of the 6th Dynasty, occasion allowed, the more ambitious amongst them strove by any means to carve out larger territories for themselves, in some cases bringing about civil war.[15] The politics of self-interest were well and truly alive. The sense of social obligation was not lost, the classic example being Ankhtify of Hierakonpolis who, having taken over the neighbouring nome of Edfu, found himself distributing famine relief over a huge territory. Ankhtify, having seized lands, was, for a short time, in effect ruling a miniature state.[16]

Famine relief is a special case of obligation. Would Ankhtify have also headed an administration capable of satisfying normal demands? We lack the archaeological evidence from contemporary cemeteries in his own area which would enable us to see for ourselves how people in his territory fared. Further north, however, in Middle Egypt we have a particularly well-documented cemetery record for this and the preceding periods. This derives from the work of the archaeologist G. Brunton in the Qau/Badari/Matmar/Mostagedda area.[17] In the First Intermediate Period this belonged to the frontier zone between the warring dynasties of Herakleopolis and Thebes, although the role of the local nome administrator is nowhere made clear in the surviving sources. The period is particularly well represented by burials, so much so that it has been suggested that the combination of famine and civil war could have sharply increased the mortality rate.[18] Yet the grave goods show no sign of general impoverishment. Brunton addressed himself particularly to this point:

> In the cemeteries at Qau and Badari the tombs with the most objects are precisely those of the vii-viiith dyn. period. Here we find the greatest profusion of beads and amulets; no diminution in the number of alabaster vases, and all the alabaster head-rests; the greatest number of mirrors of any period; and the least number of simple shallow graves. The workmanship of the glaze amulets may show great delicacy; the carnelian legs are the best of their kind; and the animal-backed seal-amulets are cut with skill and care.[19]

Brunton then showed that more gold beads and amulets occurred in this period as well. It is unreasonable to argue that this was mostly material robbed from earlier graves because much of it is in styles peculiar to the period. Nor were these graves clustered around large, centrally placed tombs of leaders and providers. They occur in a series of small cemeteries spread out along the edge of the desert as if representing the burials of a wide scatter of villages. It strains credulity to suppose that these people were passive recipients of a state redistributive system, which was, by its nature, of limited flexibility.

Fortunately, the First Intermediate Period has also supplied us with some grass-roots personal papers, in the form of the Hekanakht archive. Hekanakht lived just to the south of Thebes, within the state created by the Theban rulers of the 11th Dynasty which by now incorporated the whole of Egypt. Hekanakht was a small farmer who, on trips away from home, wrote testy letters back to his family. These display a strong urge to maximize family income by means of shrewd deals with neighbours and others, with no reference at all to an outside system or authority.

> He was able to pay rent for his lands in advance, could, in addition, lend substantial amounts of grain and had at his disposal copper, oil, and cloth woven from the flax raised on his farm, all of which could be used to make purchases. He cultivated more than was needed for the immediate requirements of his household, and had substantial capital reserves.[20]

He also possessed a herd of thirty-five animals. Towards members of his household he displayed an obligation of a strict kind, issuing everyone including his mother with a monthly ration, and so repeating on a tiny scale the precise system of ration distribution so familiar from administrative texts. But to the outside world the relationship was one of calculated gain. He urges one of his household, for example, to retain one bull in a herd about to be sent out because a chance of a particularly good sale had arisen: 'his price has increased by half'.[22]

It has to be pointed out that Hekanakht was living in difficult times. He makes explicit references to famine. But this is irrelevant to the central issue: Hekanakht displays the mentality of one who survives by shrewd personal dealing rather than of one whose fortunes depend upon his position within a system of social obligation and administered support.

Hekanakht coped in a time of change which, in its magnitude, was unusual in the course of Pharaonic history. But although ancient economies never experienced the prolonged volatility of modern times it is a mistake to think of them as static. A single generation separated Hekanakht from the centralized Memphite administration of the early 12th Dynasty. Overall, between say 2100 and 1500 BC, the boundaries of state power ebbed and flowed in two cycles of great magnitude. And at the best of times, when famines and civil war were no more, the state system still had to adjust to change, particularly demands made by ambitious kings. New temples, new fleets of ships, the re-equipping of the army for fresh campaigns: these could create sudden demands both for the redirection of existing resources and for additional revenue. Any economic system that we propose for ancient Egypt has to be able to account for the apparently successful adjustments which local communities made to changes of different magnitudes within a relatively crude state system of economic direction.

What reasons other than avarice would Hekanakht have had to accumulate wealth? One commentator, Klaus Baer, has already tentatively supplied at least part of the answer: a fine burial.[23] Whether one set things aside during one's life, or left it to one's heirs to select from what was available, the effect was the same: theoretically a bottomless hole into which a proportion of the country's goods were cast, creating a constant demand for replacement – theoretically, because tomb robbery constantly brought some of it back in a clandestine recycling. In the case of the most favoured officials the royal resources might well assist at least in providing the labour for cutting and decorating the tomb itself. This is claimed in inscriptions.[24] But for the majority, the cost of burial was a private matter. Private responsibility for a good burial was enshrined within the law: '"Let the possessions be given to him who buries", says the law of Pharaoh.' So declares one New Kingdom party in a case of disputed inheritance. This document, with others, shows that the normal pattern of inheritance of property was subject to the proviso that the whole inheritance would go to whomsoever undertook to have the actual burial carried out.[25] A potential heir would disinherit him- or herself by ignoring this. The practice, and the kind of costs involved for non-officials, are illustrated by the case of the man Huy (from Deir el-Medina), buried by his wife Iy. She apparently inherits from him since she orders a coffin and pays for it with a house originally belonging to her husband. In relative terms this was a heavy expense involving the sale of a house, although the hope of inheritance must have made the weight of obligation easier to bear.

A good burial, however, was only part of the economic pressure in private demand. A prospering official might seek to build a new house for himself. This is promised in New Kingdom school texts,[26] but we also have a real letter on the subject written by a provincial mayor (possibly of Armant) of the 18th Dynasty called Menthuhetep to a friendly and, as deputy to a 'chief of works', usefully placed official at Thebes, a 'scribe' called Ahmose. The subject: instructions on the early stages of building a new house for Menthuhetep, a house which, to judge from its dimensions, was to be an impressive one. Here we probably have a case of a provincial dignitary setting up a second house in a royal city, in this instance Thebes, and clearly paying for it himself. For at the end of the letter he adds: 'have the price of the land for the house given to its owner, and make sure he is happy with it. See to it that when I come he doesn't have words with me' (Papyrus B.M.10102).[27]

Then there were the goods which daughters and sons needed to acquire to create the joint properties which formed the basis of a marriage contract; there were pious outlays at shrines, possible gifts or bribes for advancement, and the general competitive display of wealth engendered by the existence of an ostentatious and lavish court. Apart from the property and goods which the excavation of settlements and cemeteries reveals, other sources tell us that officials maintained fleets of Nile boats (Figure 81),[28] and, in the New Kingdom, horses and chariots as well. People were surrounded by reasons to accumulate wealth, which might arise quite suddenly. The effects of a relatively free play of competitive acquisition unconnected with burial customs can be seen at the New Kingdom city of Amarna, where wealth and status were advertised by a finely graded array of house sizes and architectural status symbols (see Chapter 7).[29] In their own way they imply the existence of an economic system finely tuned to individual ambition and circumstances.

The answer of the Polanyi approach to the existence of demand for things that were not merely peripheral to life is economic passivity laced with optimism: working honestly, and waiting patiently for loyalty, hard work, and the social obligation of others to bring better times. Something like this was held up anciently as an actual ideal: 'A cup of water quenches thirst, a mouthful of herbs fortifies the heart' is the ascetic advice of the sage Kagemni.[30] The elements we have pointed to so far, however, do not exemplify this philosophy. We can identify areas of strong private demand that

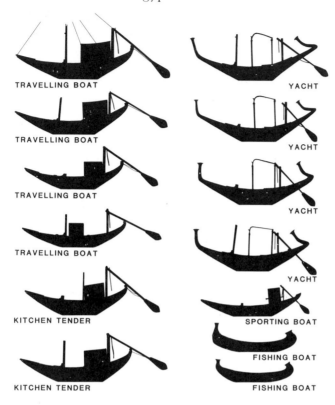

Figure 81 Affluence: the Chancellor Meket-ra's river fleet. Silhouettes of the wooden boat models from his tomb at Thebes, 11th Dynasty, after H.E. Winlock, *Models of Daily Life in Ancient Egypt*, New York, 1955, Figs 70–82.

continued to be satisfied irrespective of the effectiveness of the state system. The First Intermediate Period is of great significance here, implying that resignation towards one's place in the social and therefore economic order was not characteristic of all. Many made the best of whatever chances for enrichment came their way.

The late New Kingdom provides some spectacular documentation (in the form of an archive of papyri dealing with investigations and trials) on the promise of instant enrichment through theft.[31] Nothing was sacred: temple grain supplies were quietly siphoned off, tombs were robbed, temple equipment and fittings were plundered. Although tomb robbery attracted people of mainly lowly status, less arduous forms of theft and dishonesty drew in officials as well, including temple priests. Indeed, the scale of the thefts often required official participation. Apart from depicting the seamier side to the crumbling fabric of late New Kingdom society and also the processes of law when they were eventually invoked, the papyri illustrate in a highly coloured way motives and means in the contemporary economy. They dramatize the existence of a crude urge for self-enrichment, which in more orderly circumstances would have been sublimated by participation in the market-place, selling goods, renting or leasing land, making loans bearing interest, all of them practices explicitly documented. They also reveal the fate of the stolen goods as they re-enter the economy of the living, and in so doing add usefully to our restricted knowledge of the economic behaviour of the time.

The thieves generally, even when of lowly status, were town or village dwellers and householders, many apparently living in the medium-sized town of Maiunehes which lay in and around the mortuary temple of Rameses III (Medinet Habu; see Chapter 7). Much of what they stole they simply kept as part of the household property. Apart from the gold and silver the lists of recovered goods include a fair quantity of linen pieces and garments, vases of oil, coffin trimmings, and pieces of wood. Copper and bronze in any form were much favoured. A set of copper carrying-rings prised off a wooden chest was the haul from a temple theft (Papyrus B.M.10402). One whole list of recovered goods consists almost entirely of these metals. Sometimes the item is specified – 'a wash-bowl of bronze equal to 20 *deben*' – but mostly a figure of how many *deben* were involved is given, and the amounts could be quite small: 'The lady Aref of the Necropolis, wife of the workman Hori: 1; the lady Takiri of the Necropolis: 1' (Papyrus B.M.10053, Recto 2.18–19). One *deben* was only half the price of a pair of sandals.

In the end, however, material wealth was the means of purchase. The wife of one of the thieves confesses: 'I took my husband's share and put it aside in my storeroom, then I took one *deben* of silver from it and used it to buy grain' (Papyrus B.M.10052, 6.6–7). Another wife, smarter (or perhaps more honest), when asked how she bought servants if not by stolen silver, replied: 'I bought them in exchange for garden produce' (Papyrus B.M.10052, 10.14–15). Though her words may sound naïve she clearly hoped to be believed and was, in effect, basing her case on being able to grow cash crops on a significant scale, a most important point in itself. An equally positive defence was given by another wife when asked to explain the origin of a quantity of silver: 'I got it in exchange for barley in the year of the hyenas, when there was a famine' (Papyrus B.M.10052, 11.5–8). Here the claim is based on scarcity driving up the price of a basic commodity, a classic supply–demand relationship. A more elaborate case is provided by the confession of another priest and temple gardener Ker on the subject of stripping gold foil from off the temple doors:

> 'We went yet again to the door-jambs . . . and we brought away 5 *kite* of gold. We bought corn with it in Thebes and divided it up. . . . Now after some days Peminu our superior quarrelled with us saying: "You have given me nothing." So we went again to the door-jambs and brought 5 *kite* of gold from them, and exchanged it for an ox and gave it to Peminu.' (Papyrus B.M.10053, Verso 3.10–13).

This case is particularly interesting: Peminu preferred good farm livestock to a suspicious quantity of gold foil.

Many more examples can be quoted to illustrate the variety of purchases. 'Charge concerning the shrine of cedar, both the image and the timber, which the scribe of the royal records Setekhmes stole. He sold it in Thebes and received its price' (Papyrus B.M.10053, Verso 5.5). The overseer of the field of the temple of Amun, Akhenmenu, gives '1 *deben* of silver and 5 *kite* of gold in exchange for land' (Papyrus B.M.10052, 2.19). The scribe Amenhetep called Seret, of the temple of Amun, gives '2 *deben* (of silver) in exchange for land, for 40 *deben* of copper, and for 10 *khar* of barley' (Papyrus B.M.10052, 2.22). The servant Shedbeg disposes of quite a list of commodities 'in payment for the slave Degay' (Papyrus B.M.10052, 2.23–25). Another confesses: 'I gave 5 *kite* of silver to the incense-roaster Penementenakht of the temple of Amun in exchange for 10 *hin* of honey' (Papyrus B.M.10052, 2a.1; cf. also lines 4–14). The confession of the herdsman Bukhaaf begins: 'The lady Nesmut came to where I was and said to me:

"Some men have found something that can be sold for bread. Let's go so that you can eat it with them'" (Papyrus B.M.10052, 1.8–10). We can recognize Theban slang here: 'bread' must mean 'fine goods' or something similar.

Sometimes the loot was needed to buy services, in the form of protection: 'Now when we were arrested, the district scribe Khaemipet came to me . . . and I gave him the 4 *kite* of gold which had fallen to my lot' (Papyrus B.M.10054, Recto, 1.11–12). And in another case: 'But the scribe of the royal records, Setekhmes, had overheard and threatened us saying: "I am going to report it to the chief priest of Amun." So we brought 3 *kite* of gold and gave it to the scribe of the royal records, Setekhmes' (Papyrus B.M.10053, Verso, 3.13–14). Some disposals were probably to settle obligations or to gain favours:

> Charge concerning the 4 boards of cedar belonging to the 'Floor of Silver' of King Usermaatra-Setepenra [Rameses II], the great god, which the scribe Sedi gave to the lady Teherer, wife of the god's father Hori: he gave them to the carpenter Ahauty of the funerary chapel of Hui, and he made them into an inner coffin for her.
>
> (Papyrus B.M. 10053, Verso 4.15–17).

Perhaps the most provocative entry from the economic point of view is a list of gold and silver 'recovered from the thieving workmen of the Necropolis, which they were found to have given to the traders of every establishment' (Papyrus B.M.10068, Recto 4.1–18). Fourteen traders are listed, attached both to temples and to private households. It was the job of a 'trader' to maintain the supply–demand balance of an employer by trading surplus or unwanted commodities for whatever was required. These thieves, who would not have been in a position to have 'traders' in their own employ, were therefore latching on to a professional system for converting their loot into other commodities, doubtless for a fat commission. As urban dwellers in Maiunehes they had channels of communication with a wider world.

The rotten state of society at the end of the New Kingdom was cured, if only temporarily, by the imposition of military rule. The legal papyri of the time are not a guide to the state of affairs earlier in the period. They are relevant because they provide verbatim testimony to attitudes to material wealth and to the easy and natural recourse which people had to a free market in goods, slaves, livestock, food, and even land. It would be foolish to claim that the opportunities for exchange, the markets themselves, were created by the dishonesty of the day. In more orderly times people still received windfalls – from inheritance, gifts from the state – and had a similar range of choices in what they did with them, hoarding them at home or exchanging them for other things. The late New Kingdom robberies released a surge of wealth into society from, as it were, the bottom. The 18th Dynasty had done the same, from spoils of battle, but from the top and according to an administered system.

One discovery, at Amarna, does actually reveal that concentrations of liquid wealth were in circulation in this earlier time. In a small open space beside a public well in the North Suburb a pottery jar had been buried, containing twenty-three bars of gold and a quantity of silver fragments and roughly made rings, as well as a silver figurine of a Hittite god (Figure 82).[32] The gold bars had been made simply by pouring melted-down gold into grooves scooped by the finger in sand. The total weight of the gold was 3,375.36 grams, equivalent in ancient terms to 37 *deben*. The total weight of the silver

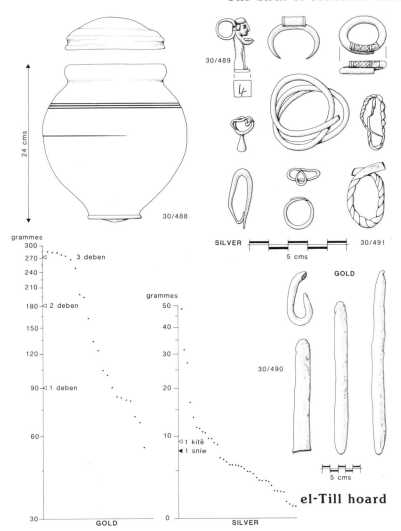

Figure 82 Part of a hoard of gold and silver buried in a pottery jar in a surburb of el-Amarna. The silver is made up partly of finished items (including the Hittite figurine, no. 30/489), and partly of coils and irregular pieces, some cut from vessels; the gold in crude bars. As the weight tables show, there is little to suggest that pieces of standard weight (proto-coins) were desired. Rather, with the coils, scraps and bars, pieces were cut off to meet a specific demand, their weight (and thus value) determined by weighing (as in Figures 85, p. 250, and 86, p. 254). After H. Frankfort and J.D.S. Pendlebury, *The City of Akhenaten* II, London, 1933, pp. 59–61, Plate XLIII, and original record cards.

came to at least 1,085.85 grams, or 12 *deben*. This represents a fair amount of wealth, though not a staggering sum. The most successful of the late New Kingdom tomb robberies, in the tomb of the 17th Dynasty King Sebekemsaf, netted the thieves 160 *deben* of gold. But some idea of its purchasing power can be obtained from the ratios of gold to silver (5:3 later becoming 2:1), and of silver to copper (1:100). Thus the silver could have been used to purchase, say, ten or twelve head of cattle. The archaeologist who made the Amarna find assumed that it was part of a thief's loot, and in view of the odd place in which it was found this still seems credible, although there are other possibilities. Stock from a jeweller's workshop has also been suggested.[33] Whatever its origin, however, it illustrates easily convertible wealth poised on the point of re-entering the economy at a private level.

The satisfaction of private demand for finished goods required an availability of raw materials. Official inscriptions are often taken to imply that a royal monopoly existed on those raw materials which lay outside the Nile floodplain. Inscriptions at mines and quarries do, indeed, reveal a scale of operation that only a state could undertake.[34] But these need not have been the norm. Take alabaster, for example. One prime source was the desert to the east of the Assiut-Minia area in Middle Egypt, the area which includes the Hatnub quarries.[35] Hatnub was one target for large expeditions dispatched by kings. It can, however, easily be visited by donkey in a single day.[36] If a group of people took with them a few days' supply of water and food, some baskets and simple tools, they could bring back a sizeable load of small lumps of alabaster suitable for vase making, perhaps using pieces left behind by the major expeditions. Simple operations of this kind could leave few archaeological traces behind them. A further indication that written sources are not a full guide to the procurement of raw materials is that certain substances are excluded altogether. We have no records of expeditions to quarry the soft rock that was the basis for the marl clays widely used in pottery manufacture,[37] and the same is true for natron and for gypsum. These operations had no need for military-style expeditions. They could be accomplished by small groups of hardy labourers camping and working in a primitive manner (such as at the Fayum gypsum quarries, Figure 83).[38] By invoking a simple mode of supply we can easily explain the continued availability of raw materials during times of internal weakness. There was, for example, no shortage of small pieces of alabaster for the vase-makers of Middle Egypt in the First Intermediate Period.

In the Graeco-Roman Period natron was, like some other commodities, the subject of state monopoly. Monopoly is a word which is sometimes used for the Pharaonic Period as well.[39] Its earlier existence is, however, a matter of inference rather than of documentation, and does not accord with the general picture of people's attitudes in Pharaonic Egypt. The political stability and cultural coherence of ancient Egypt over long periods of time are part of its abiding image. They must reflect a broad acceptance of the ideas and ideals which originated within the court. But beneath this bland law-abiding exterior lurked a predatory instinct directed towards property rather than persons. Institutionalized vigilance pursued elaborate schemes of checking, and threatened fearsome punishments. When it slipped, dishonesty quickly flourished. The tombs of kings and commoners faced robbery, and temples the misappropriation of furnishings and property. In this atmosphere no monopoly could have relied upon a tacit acceptance of its validity. It, too, would have required enforcement by decrees and punishments. Within the corpus of administrative documents we will look in vain for such references.

Even with foreign trade we should be cautious in using the term 'monopoly'.[40] It is not, for example, the natural interpretation to place on the famous scene in the tomb of the nomarch Khnumhetep III at Beni Hasan which shows the arrival of a small Palestinian group from Moab bringing a quantity of eye-paint (*msdmt*) with them

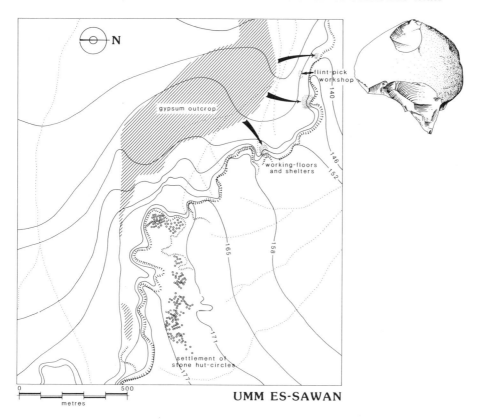

Figure 83 Low-level exploitation of a mineral resource: the gypsum quarries of Umm es-Sawan (north Fayum) of the early Old Kingdom. The seasonal encampment of about 200 circular stone shelters occupies the top of a ridge along the edge of an escarpment overlooking a broad surface outcrop of gypsum on the desert plain below. The gypsum was dug out, using crude flint picks, in part as lumps for the making of vessels, and in part as powder to be used as mortar. The workshops for the vessels were in more sheltered places against the escarpment face. The flint picks were made on the spot, from flint nodules brought in from outside. Other types of flint tools were used in the vase making. The informal nature of the settlement should be contrasted with the planned Middle Kingdom workmen's village at Kasr es-Sagha, (see Figure 59, p. 167). After G. Caton-Thompson and E.W. Gardner, *The Desert Fayum*, London, 1934, Plate LVIII.

(Figure 84).[41] Although one of Khnumhetep's titles, 'administrator of the eastern desert', suggests some formally recognized responsibility for the adjacent desert area, the general intention of the scene is clear enough. The Palestinian group represents just one part of the broad range of products of Khnumhetep's 'estate', which included game hunted in the desert as well as agricultural produce from the Nile floodplain. Indeed, the Palestinians are introduced by a 'chief of the huntsmen'. Here again we have a means of low-level satisfaction of local demand for products out of the direct reach of industrious valley dwellers: small trading groups from further afield making their way along the desert wadi-systems to provincial points of contact within the Nile Valley. One tomb scene does not make a pattern, but it does point to a possibility which can only be denied by having recourse to the dogmatic statement: 'foreign trade was a royal

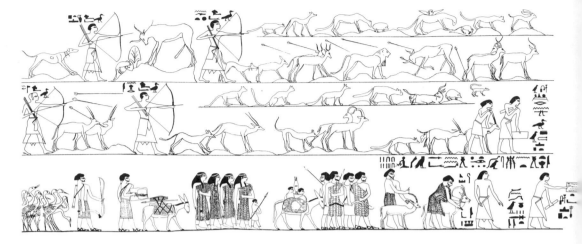

Figure 84 Produce of the eastern desert received by the nobleman appointed to control it, the nomarch of the Oryx Nome and 'Overseer of the Eastern Deserts' in the 12th Dynasty, Khnumhetep. The produce is mainly in the form of hunted game, but also (bottom register) includes a Palestinian trading party bringing eye-pigment, who are introduced by an Egyptian official, 'Chief huntsman, Kheti', a title which illuminates the status of the Palestinian group in Egyptian eyes. From tomb no. 3 at Beni Hasan, after P.E. Newberry, *Beni Hasan* I, London, 1893, Plates XXX, XXXI.

monopoly', a statement which can be given no direct support. The availability of raw materials and imported finished goods in ancient Egypt is potentially a further exemplar of where the balance lay from period to period between state and the private domain.

Economics without money

The methods of small-scale economic transaction are well known for the New Kingdom, particularly from the wealth of data from the workmen's village of Deir el-Medina (Plate 9).[42] Acquiring and disposing of goods was done by barter, but not just by an impulsive gesture of the kind: I'll swap you a pig for two pairs of sandals. Everything had a value, expressed in various units which coincided with quantities of certain commodities: weights of silver and copper/bronze, and units of capacity of grain and sesame-oil (Figure 85). Metals were themselves used in exchanges but not as coinage. The nearest step on the road to money is to be found in the stone weights which, when used in the pans of scale balances, checked the weights and thus the values of metals, precious and otherwise. One group of the thieves of Thebes scrupulously kept in a house a stone weight which they had used in dividing up the spoil from one tomb (Papyrus B.M.10052, 3.8–13; cf. also 5.20). Prices varied from occasion to occasion, and the ratios of commodity values changed (e.g. that of silver to copper declined late in the New Kingdom at Thebes from 1:100 to 1:60, perhaps because of the flood of silver from the spate of robberies). In a typical transaction a policeman buys an ox from a workman, and pays for it with a jar of fat worth 30 *deben*, 2 tunics worth 10 *deben*, scraps of copper/bronze weighing (and thus worth) 5 *deben*, and 10 *hin* of vegetable oil worth 5 *deben*.[43] The total is 50 *deben* (of copper), and the little receipt calls the total 'silver',

Plate 9 The setting of village life: part of the village of necropolis workmen and artists at Deir el-Medina, western Thebes, late New Kingdom. The photograph is taken looking north-west down the central line of one house, no. III.NE. More houses continue beyond a transverse road, and in the background are terraces which originally supported tomb chapels. The walls are partly restored.

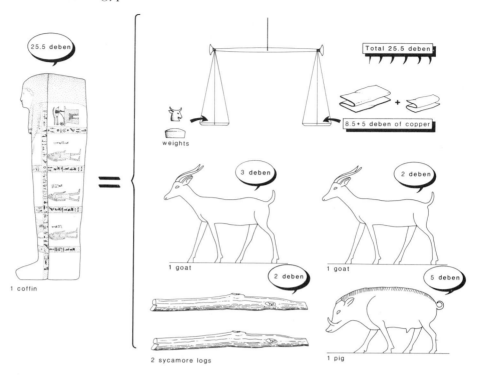

Figure 85 Buying and selling by barter-exchange, illustrated by an example from Deir el-Medina, 20th Dynasty. On one side of the exchange is a coffin, notionally valued at 25½ *deben* of copper. The buyer has to make up a set of commodities of equal value, and does so partly with other items with notional values in copper *deben* (two goats, a pig, and two logs of wood, perhaps raw material for coffin making), and partly with actual copper items or scraps where the *deben* value was obtained by direct weighing on scales, using small stone or bronze weights sometimes carved in animal shapes (as in Figure 86, p. 254). The example is from Ostracon Deir el-Medina 73, verso, from J.J. Janssen, *Commodity Prices from the Ramessid Period*, Leiden, 1975, p. 10.

which word was used colloquially to mean something very close to the modern word 'money'. This system of values also covered the price of labour and of raw materials. Stringing a wooden bed cost 1 *khar* of grain, actually making it cost about 5 *khar*, decorating it cost 1.5 *khar*, whilst the wood might cost 3 *deben*. With 1 *khar* of grain approximately equal to 1 *deben*, the total is about 18 *deben*. To buy a ready-made bed would cost between 12 and 25 *deben*, which is a rational reflection of the labour plus material costs.[44]

Did the state play any role in the fixing of prices? We can be sure that it did not explicitly regulate them. There is no direct evidence for kings or other officials ever doing this, and the study of the prices themselves, although it throws up broad regularities, also reveals too many variations. Prices fixed themselves. However, from the very fact that, at least during periods of strong centralized administration, the institutions were heavily involved in paying wages and collecting, storing, and releasing commodities held as buffer-stocks, we can deduce that general levels were implicitly maintained. This is, however, a general framework within which all modern economic systems work no matter how active their 'free' market sector.

The fixing of prices for raw materials and other commodities, from grain to servant girls, takes us to the heart of the difficulties which we experience in coming to terms with ancient economies. Some people are tempted to draw a contrast between how this might have been done anciently and what is regarded as the modern solution to fixing prices: by means of a free market in which the relationship between supply and demand does it automatically. This modern process seems to attract an unnecessary degree of mystique. The rise of consumerism – the constant purchase by private individuals of new products often with a very short life – has so vastly increased the number of trans-actions in society that they come to reflect arithmetic regularities, something further enhanced by the speed with which information is transmitted. These regularities are often, misleadingly, called economic 'laws'. In the street-market selling of home-made jams, bankrupt stock, and second-hand books, however, the abstract constructions of modern economics begin to dissolve. Although a rare second-hand book sold at auction can illustrate, through competitive bidding, a fixing of price by demand greatly exceeding supply, unimportant books are priced at what the seller thinks intuitively is a general value, but which in individual cases the buyer may regard as an amazing bargain, although other buyers might not agree.

The very personal concept of 'value' – do I think that something is worth a particular price? – provides an overall limitation on all marketing, the supply and demand relationship acting within it with an intensity that varies with circumstances. It is a relationship which basically reflects a general human preference for buying cheaply, coupled with thresholds of resistance against prices which seem to be high against an intuitive appreciation of the 'value' of a thing. How values are formed is ultimately a psychological question outside the scope of economics altogether, which exists as a modern rigorous discipline only because, given sufficient examples of any phenomenon, statistical regularities are bound to occur.

When we consider ancient societies, since the level of trading and speed of communication must have been far less than in modern times, the occurrence of the statistical regularities which appear to be 'laws' in economics is bound to evaporate. A more irregular and unpredictable pattern of prices is what one should expect if prices were freely fixed. Such a pattern is not evidence against marketing and exchange of goods by people motivated towards coming out of a deal with a sense of having done well, given that, if they knew each other already, friendship or obligation may have tempered the vigour with which they pursued their deal.

The price data from ancient Egypt are more or less neutral as a source of evidence on how they themselves were fixed, in that they can be used to support widely differing interpretations. Janssen's magisterial study of village economics at Deir el-Medina uses them as evidence for a general lack of economic awareness on the part of the people involved, and for prices having little self-regulatory power. But they can just as easily be fitted into a scheme in which economic forces play a more active role. Thus the prices for a pair of sandals:[45] over nearly 150 years they remained within a range of 1 to 2 *deben*, occasionally 3. Janssen sees this stability as evidence that 'tradition' played a large part in price fixing. True: but this does not exclude an underlying rationale. We can also say that, lacking modern machinery for mass production, the price of a pair of sandals reflected a floor price of subsistence for the sandal-maker. Prices were held at this level by the resistance of the buyer, who, if faced with a high price, could normally hobble far enough away on his worn-out sandals to buy from another sandal-maker at the usual price. 'Tradition' represented a supply and demand equilibrium.

A particularly interesting set of prices is that for grain (wheat and barley), a commodity generally prone to volatile price movements and thus the object of huge intervention schemes in modern 'free-market' economies. Intervention in the form of massive storage capacity creating buffer-stocks was standard in ancient Egypt, too, both at the institutional level and within the economies of private estates whether in times of peace and plenty (e.g. the Amarna estates) or in times of famine and unrest (e.g. Ankhtify). This was a passive intervention which did not extend to official attempts to regulate prices. The New Kingdom price data show many prices of between 1 and 2 *deben* per *khar*, which presumably reflected a fair return for all those involved in farming, although the margin of difference was no small one where large consignments of grain were involved. But the buyer's resistance threshold could be much lower, driven there by the prospect of hunger. In the economy of western Thebes in the late 20th Dynasty prices show great volatility, ranging from some near-normal to far higher levels, reaching, during the reigns of Rameses VII–IX, 8 and even 12 *deben*. This was not a case of general 'inflation' of the kind so familiar from the modern world, since other prices fail to display a similar trajectory, and there is no evidence for alterations in the units of measurement themselves. One clue is the famine reference quoted on p. 243: the woman who claimed to have sold barley for silver 'in the year of the hyena, when there was a famine'. Unfortunately the source fails to say what quantities were involved, but the way that she phrases her reply implies that a barley/silver exchange made during that famine was a distinctive transaction, and a high price is the natural interpretation. Actual prices from around this time (the first part of the reign of Rameses XI) show a common doubling of the traditional maximum price, i.e. 1 *khar* equal to 4 *deben*. We can also look to the repeated complaints of food shortages by the Deir el-Medina community from the reign of Rameses III onwards to explain the volatility of the grain prices in later Ramesside times, though a cause-and-effect connection has to remain circumstantial.[46]

Some commentators show concern that the Egyptians, as well as other ancient peoples, did not refer to 'profit' explicitly, or even possess a suitable word in their vocabulary. We should not read too much into this, however. For the abstract notion of profit from sales is a rationalization of the result of making a successful transaction, of getting a good price. The latter belongs to the realm of intuitive survival strategies that are part of being human. Hekanakht seems to have been at home here, and the absence from his mind of the idea of 'profit' did not hinder him from distinguishing a good from a bad price, and should not hinder us from crediting him and the people of ancient societies generally with an adequate business sense. The Egyptians lived economics rather than thought it. They aimed not for profit as an abstract measure of success in trading or making things, but for a surfeit of good things that made you feel satisfied and the envy of others. The results were, however, not much different from those of their modern counterparts who are more economically aware.

The Deir el-Medina records of transaction are devoid of locale, as are, in general, the confessions of the Theban thieves. Some transactions must have arisen because buyer and seller, in the same village, knew each other. This would apply when manufacturing was involved. If you wanted to obtain a new footstool you presumably knew where a carpenter lived, and the transaction took place at a house, either his or yours depending on your relative status. But would informal and personal contacts suffice entirely to match demand with supply? Were there recognized market-places in which sellers spread their wares? One of the accused women in the robbery papyri sets a telling scene: 'Now I happened to be sitting hungry [begging?] under the sycamores, and the men happened to be trading copper as we were sitting hungry' (Papyrus B.M.10403, 3.5–7). Where the sycamores were in terms of the topography of western Thebes we do not know. But some markets at Thebes were on the river bank.[47] This we know from tomb paintings. There are no texts to explain these pictures. Our understanding of them depends on correctly interpreting the mime that the artist has used to convey the meaning.

One of them comes from the tomb of a Deir el-Medina sculptor named Ipy, who looked forward to the next world and the life of the scribal ideal (Figure 86).[48] The centre of the scene is a river boat bringing the annual grain harvest to the private granary, as well as bundles of papyrus and what are probably bundles of fodder. As the unloading takes place some of the sacks of grain, as well as the green-stuff, are sold. The buyers are simultaneously sellers: women who sit with a single basket of produce in front of them. In return for grain they sell fish, loaves, and vegetables. Behind a bread seller a shelter has been erected shading two jars of drink. The logic of the picture is that this also is a saleable commodity.[49] The scene complements well the testimony of some of the robbery papyri: the role taken by many women in buying and selling for the household, including cash crops.

The second scene, although similar in design, depicts transactions at a significantly different level. It comes from the tomb of Kenamun, an 18th Dynasty mayor of Thebes who was also in charge of the granaries of Karnak temple (Figure 86).[50] The subject is the arrival at Thebes of a fleet of sea-going ships from Syria and the Aegean. They unload their cargo and, in a further portion of the scene, present their goods to Kenamun himself. Herein lies the first ambiguity. Is Kenamun, who as mayor would have been a leading and wealthy citizen, receiving the goods for himself, acting out the line in the school text where the scribe's ship 'has returned from Syria laden with all manner of good things'? Or is he receiving goods destined for, say, the temple treasuries? As with Ipy's painting, *en route* to their destination some of the goods are sold, presumably on the river bank. The buyers are, inevitably, sellers also, but no longer housewives with a single basket of foodstuff. Two of the three traders are men, and all three sit beneath shelters, offering a range of goods: sandals, lengths of cloth, some with fringes, bread and other food, and what may be metal fish-hooks. One transaction is shown: a Syrian proffers a stoppered jar of wine. The male traders hold little scale balances in their hands. These are occasionally found in excavations (two came from one small house in the North Suburb at Amarna),[51] and are sometimes depicted in use in more detail. One (perhaps their main) purpose was to weigh metal against stone weights of known values on the *deben* scale. The implication of their appearance in this scene is that metals were part of the transaction, with the foreigners perhaps carrying their own sets of weights as a safeguard against being cheated. The Egyptian traders look much more professional than the housewives in the tomb of Ipy. But who were they really? This is a crucial area of ambiguity. Were they 'traders' as the Egyptians used the word, that is, commercial agents for officials? Or were they trading

Figure 86 Scenes of barter-exchange in New Kingdom tombs. *Above*. Traders in booths make deals with Syrians unloading their wares at the river bank, from the tomb of Kenamun at Thebes, after N. de G. Davies and R.O. Faulkner, 'A Syrian trading venture to Egypt', *Journal of Egyptian Archaeology* 33 (1947), Plate VIII. *Below*. Workers unloading a grain barge use sacks of grain to buy fish and vegetables from village women, from the tomb of Ipy, after N. de G. Davies, *Two Ramesside Tombs at Thebes*, New York, 1927, Plate XXX.

for themselves? If we knew the answer we would have an important piece of knowledge on the Egyptian economy of the period. For in the latter case they would have been, in effect, shopkeepers, living from buying and selling and thus from the profit between transactions. But even without this knowledge we must admit that these scenes do not illustrate *ad hoc* exchanges between neighbours in a village. They display the kind of purposeful behaviour on the part of the sellers which belongs to proper markets in which buyers are not necessarily from the same community at all, and thus not necessarily much influenced by social obligation: the very kind of mechanism that is required for an economic model which allows greater scope to private enterprise.

These New Kingdom scenes have a long history behind them, with important predecessors in several Old Kingdom tombs, which have received much discussion in recent years.[52] Like their later counterparts, however, they are to be explained as much from how we perceive the general economic framework as from any specific details within the scenes themselves, which remain, on their own, ambiguous. There is one social change to notice: in the Old Kingdom scenes the sellers are normally men. There is also one unusually explicit accompanying text: in a sale of cloth the statement is made: 'xx cubits of cloth in exchange for 6 *shat*'. Although the exact nature of the *shat* at this time is not known, it must be a unit of absolute value similar to the New Kingdom units of copper, grain, oil, and so on.[53]

Deir el-Medina was an atypical community in two respects: though a small village, it was in contact with senior officials and wealthy clients and thus with affluent living, which rubbed off on the villagers' own expectations; and its basic needs were supplied as rations by the state. This latter circumstance, however, only adds interest to the evidence for private enterprise on the part of the villagers: exchanging goods with each other and with outsiders, manufacturing beds, selling their specific skills as artists in the making of statues and coffins, hiring or lending donkeys for exorbitant interest or rental, and generally directing part of their lives towards accumulating wealth, part of which ended up in their well-appointed burials.[54] The villagers show in their lives that the state, even when in the position of supplier of needs, could do so only in a rough-and-ready way, through regular grain rations and a few other perks, leaving the details of individual demand to local and private transactions, i.e. to a market. A good example of where the boundary lay between public and private provision is the water-supply for the village, which had no nearby natural source of its own (although an attempt, possibly unsuccessful, was finally made to dig a well not far from the village, see Chapter 7). A group of water-carriers was thus provided for the village. It was feasible for a man to carry water in a pottery amphora either on his shoulder or slung on a pole (tomb scenes depict both), but easier to use a donkey. So the water-carriers, who were poor men, regularly hired donkeys from the Deir el-Medina workmen themselves.[55]

Deir el-Medina had an equivalent at the late 18th Dynasty city of el-Amarna, at the Workmen's Village lying out in the desert to the east of the city. Excavation there has produced negligible written material, but by contrast the site has proved to be unusually rich in basic archaeological data of the kinds that are missing from so many Egyptian settlements, including Deir el-Medina itself. One of the issues raised by the excavation is the boundary between state provision and private enterprise. The state built the square walled enclosure within which the villagers were to live, and laid out the basic house plans. Thereafter, however, it is evident that the villagers were left to their own resources to complete their houses and to build chapels and other

Plate 10 A poor man's industry: a pig-pen at the Workmen's Village, el-Amarna. It is one from Building 300, looking north. The scale is 1 metre long. By courtesy the Egypt Exploration Society.

constructions for themselves. This they did by substituting for the normal mud bricks made from Nile alluvial mud, bricks made from desert clays quarried just outside the village walls. The most extraordinary discovery of the villagers' own industry has been of a pig farm.[56] The animals had been born and raised in sets of specially constructed pens (Plate 10). They had been fed on grain, and most of the litters had been slaughtered in their first or second year. The butchering, salting and packing of meat in pottery jars had been done in special areas coated hygienically with white gypsum. The whole complex represents a well-organized operation that so far has no parallel in the main city, nor, for that matter, at Deir el-Medina. The relative care and degree of organization devoted to the farm imply that it was more than a sideline run by some of the villagers for the food requirements of their own community; rather, that it also served to supplement income by sales into the main city.

The occupants of workmen's villages were limited in means, status, and ambition, and no amount of evidence from such communities can fully describe the Egyptian economy. The crucial area of contact between state system and private need was the lives of the officials, the group most exposed to competitive pressures. Although in receipt of rations and other rewards from the state, they also owned or rented lands which brought in an income well in excess of subsistence. What did officials do to satisfy the demands that a limited state system could not, by its very nature, achieve? These were men and women too busy or proud to haggle over the price of a donkey with a ragged neighbour, but nevertheless possessed of wealth stored in plenty in and around their houses.

The answer is provided by a class of persons already encountered, tied up in dealings with the robbers of western Thebes. They are the men with the title *shuty*, a word best translated as 'trader'.[57] They appear always in the employ of someone else, either a temple or an official, and must have been commercial agents, to whom was delegated the job of buying what was needed in exchange for accumulated wealth. The employer overlap between temple and private household is itself revealing as to the essentially common nature of the economic basis of both. Both accumulated farm produce and manufactured goods (mainly but not exclusively linen cloth in the case of households) from regular income but were not wholly self-sufficient and needed to purchase from suppliers of one kind or another. In the robbery papyrus referred to earlier (P. B.M.10068, Recto 4.1–18) gold and silver had been recovered from fourteen 'traders of every establishment'. No less than seven of them (two of them brothers) belonged to the household of a high-ranking soldier, a chief of Hittite troops called Amen-nefer; two belonged to the daughter of another officer, a lady called Isis who was also a temple singer; two more belonged each to military officers; and the remaining three belonged to temples, and were responsible to a named priest. Elsewhere in these papyri a group of eight traders appears from the town of Merwer, at the entrance to the Fayum. This was where one of the principal harem-palaces for royal ladies was situated, and it could have provided a suitably safe outlet for stolen treasure.

The status of traders varied. They could be rich enough to own their own slave, or poor enough to be at the same time a slave to their employer. Their contacts enabled them to do business for themselves on the side: not only receiving stolen goods but also, in a satirical school text, lending grain to the poor peasant who is unable to discharge his debt even by offering his wife to them.[58] The picture that is painted by a variety of texts is that the 'trader' – the commercial agent, the arranger of deals – was a ubiquitous figure of New Kingdom Egypt. To find the right markets they plied the Nile in boats: 'The traders fare downstream and upstream, as busy as bees [lit. copper] carrying goods from town to town, and supplying wants' (Papyrus Lansing, 4.8–4.9). Their journeys took them abroad. 'Your ship has returned from Syria laden with all manner of good things' (Papyrus Anastasi IV) says a scribal school text day-dreaming over the good life open to a successful official.[59] This long-distance aspect to trading emphasizes the point made in connection with the tomb scenes of marketing: there can have been little if any sense of social obligation between trader and customer.

Internal mobility provides, in fact, a weighty argument against the view that personal economic transactions were so often cosy reciprocal exchanges between relations and neighbours as to form the only serious alternative to redistribution. Two aspects are particularly telling. One was the provincial origin (and continuing links) of some officials who based themselves in a royal city (something explored in the next chapter). When the mayor Menthuhetep moved into his new house at Thebes (see p. 241), built on land purchased from a stranger, those with whom he came to do business would not have belonged to his own social nexus, and there would have been no grounds for the idea of 'reciprocation' to skew prices demanded and prices paid. The other was the well-documented long-distance internal trading initiated by large institutions and conducted through their 'traders', as just outlined. The implication of a range of sources is that internal riverine movement of goods was a major factor in the life and economy of Egypt, probably at times overshadowing the local movement of produce at village level. The fact of 'internal cosmopolitanism' invalidates too great a reliance on case studies of modern peasant communities to provide the social and economic models for ancient Egypt. To do so is to accept too parochial a horizon and to ignore the power of the River Nile, not only to sustain life, but also to provide a channel of communication.

A sizeable majority of the population, who lived circumscribed lives in villages or urban neighbourhoods, may have remained largely cut off from this dynamic side to Egyptian life. But Egypt generally was a rich country, offering a way of life well above subsistence level to a significant official class, who must often have been far less embedded within a local social matrix than were peasants or artisans. It is on this class that we must focus if our picture of the ancient Egyptian economy is to be complete. It is unfortunate that in doing so we have to relegate to the periphery the major source of written economic documents from the New Kingdom, those from the Deir el-Medina community.

This comment becomes very pointed when we consider how the overwhelming majority of documents recording transactions depict barter in which the buyer trades a motley collection of goods for his purchase. This is probably, however, a distorted picture simply because so many of them derive from a single source, the village of Deir el-Medina, with a social status below that of a broad range of city-based officials. We have already seen from the robbery papyri that people of modest status at Thebes did not hesitate, when they had the chance, to use gold and silver for buying things. This must have been more common amongst people of greater wealth and standing. Not only does common sense tell us this when, for example, a building plot in Thebes was being bought, but occasional written sources say so too. One group of papyrus fragments from the 18th Dynasty (Papyrus Bulaq XI=P. Cairo 58070) records a series of transactions in which a supplier of meat (possibly but not necessarily a temple) sells individual joints of meat (and occasionally jars of wine) to 'traders' in exchange for amounts of gold and silver.[60] A common amount is 1 *seniu* of gold, a twelfth part of a *deben*, thus about 7.6 grams. The same trader bought a fair quantity of meat on a daily or near daily basis. His employer is not stated but must have had a large and well-fed household to support, unless the trader was actually employed by another institution. At this level of expenditure the gold in the buried hoard from Amarna would have lasted for well over a year. The question can be asked: if large households and institutions maintained their own herds of cattle, why buy meat in joints? The answer is simple: a daily supply of fresh meat required the daily slaughter of an animal. Very few had herds of that magnitude. A good plump ox of the kind that the Egyptians regarded as ideal would have enough meat on it to feed one or two hundred people. We know that it was a common practice to preserve meat joints, but, even so, a slaughtering probably attracted a range of buyers, some of them poor and hoping for the scraps and less pleasant parts that the rich disdained.

One part of the cycle remains to be completed. From where did the officials obtain their supplies of gold and silver? The palace was one source. In the New Kingdom the flow was institutionalized through a reward ceremony at the Window of Appearance, feeding into the private sector and ultimately maintaining the supply of precious metal.[61] But for the extent of circulation that is implied for New Kingdom society we also have to accept that officials – through their traders – sometimes sold for gold and silver, too: surplus grain, occasional livestock and joints of meat, and – dare we also think it – some of the 'good things' brought from Syria. In other words, we should accept that a substantial amount of gold and silver was always in circulation. This would explain, for example, the gold found in the First Intermediate Period tombs of the Qau area commented on on p. 239. It would also explain how gold and silver featured prominently amongst the commodities used by provincial towns and districts for paying local taxes to the vizier's office, as depicted in the tomb of Rekhmira (see Figure 80, p. 237).[62]

The status of the trader was a lowly one. No one who had made a success of his life used the word as a title. For this reason we cannot translate it as 'merchant'. It is here that the ancient and modern worlds divide on economics. Trading was akin in status to making sandals. Rich people enjoyed the benefits of trading but did not pursue it as an occupation, whilst the idea that the activity could bring wealth and position on its own terms was literally unthinkable to all concerned. There were no merchant princes just as there were no princes of sandal-makers. Officials – 'scribes' – maintained the monopoly of power, prestige, and wealth. It was not a conspiracy. The attitudes were held, so one imagines, unthinkingly.

The economic system of ancient Egypt is tolerably clear, if we allow logic to create the framework into which textual and archaeological evidence can be set. The beginning of understanding is an acceptance that ancient Egypt was, by the standards of the ancient world, a rich country. In stable times it had wealth in plenty stored and in circulation, offering to all the prospect or the dream of a life far above subsistence level. This created the phenomenon of private demand: powerful and widely spread from the late Predynastic Period onwards. When the state was strong and well organized many people gained much from its redistributive mechanisms, which must, in these same times, have acted as a general control over the whole economy simply on account of their magnitude. But for those demands which could not be met by state hand-outs (and this would amount to virtually everything in times of weak government) marketing provided the answer: both local face-to-face dealings sometimes skewed by social obligation and wider-ranging exchanges involving employed intermediaries – 'traders'. Social values obscured the reality of the process, leaving a blind-spot over the concept of profit. But any ancient Egyptian who could feel the difference between a good price and a bad price was a representative of 'economic man'.

This provides us with a far more challenging role for economic history within ancient Egypt. The descriptive approach to the Egyptian economy defines two spheres – peasant exchanges and state redistribution – and leaves neither with a dynamic which fits it for a role in history. But, as we have seen, this approach fails to account both for the manifest integration of materially ambitious officials within the system, and the equally evident capacity for adjustment which the system as a whole possessed. These we can accommodate by accepting the existence of a relatively dynamic private sector. We can therefore say that one of the principal themes of political history – the ebb and flow of centralized power *vis-à-vis* provincial assertion – must have had its economic counterpart in the expansion and contraction of the private sector, partially manifested in local and regional marketing. Here we have a truly dynamic theme couched in economic terms, and thus the basis for real economic history.

The attempt to identify ancient economies as a special type of economic system containing special modes of transaction and interrelationships may be a useful means of grouping sources and focusing attention, but it also leads to arguments about nothing. Within the single framework of macroeconomics, which embraces all states which have ever existed, the goal of research is to identify the ways in which the two forces – institutional and private – satisfied their interests, both in terms of the means employed and the disguises in which they were clad. It is likewise misleading to view ancient economies as a stage in an evolutionary process: for there is sufficient variety of economic systems in the modern world to make the choice of evolutionary line an arbitrary one. Rather, they should be seen as further variations of a single theme, different solutions to a common problem: how do large communities, inevitably made up of competing interests, remain in existence for long?

7

Egypt in microcosm: the city of El-Amarna

In developed societies religion is never stationary for long. The stimulus of creative thought is essential to the human mind. This is true for those religions – principally Judaism, Christianity, and Islam, the religions 'of the book' – which are based upon a sacred text. Although appearing to be closed systems of thought all three have a long history and a huge literature of speculation about the significance of their revelations, which has often drawn upon the inheritance of the late 'pagan' Hellenism of Neoplatonic philosophy. Egyptian religion was no exception. Indeed, in being an open system of thought, essentially a theological language for pursuing speculation on the hidden aspects of the world, it was particularly open to change. By the Late Dynastic Period Egyptian religion had grown to be significantly different from that of earlier periods, responding to deep-seated psychological changes in the population at large. If Egypt had remained a more isolated country and had not been swamped by influences from the Hellenistic world the old religion would doubtless have continued to change and might well have survived to the present as a viable system of thought.

The instrument of change lay in the scholarly work of priests who read and copied old texts, sometimes adding explanatory glosses, and who from time to time felt stimulated to compose fresh material which was, however, always couched in the theological language which drew upon a large store of traditional images. For the New Kingdom we have fine examples of the scholarly work of the day preserved in the painted decoration inside the tombs of the Valley of the Kings.[1] This perfectly illustrates the interweaving of old and new material, which aimed partly at ensuring the well-being of the dead king in a cosmic afterlife, and partly at illustrating the forces and processes at work in the cosmos.

The names of those responsible are not known. This was the proper work of the priests and the fruits of their labours probably went over most people's heads. Educated Egyptians were, on the whole, far more impressed with people who offered sensible advice on conduct and morals, or who were particularly noted for practical achievements. The way to fame and to becoming a household name generations later was either to be a great constructor,[2] or to write an 'instruction', which had little to say on theology but provided a message that people generally could understand, or at least find arresting. Most of the admired teachings spoke straightforwardly. One, by a Middle Kingdom sage called Ipuwer, offered an apocalyptic view of the world in chaos but with such drama and vivid detail that it haunted people's imagination and remained an irresistible read centuries after it was composed.[3] In the New Kingdom the Egyptians still lived in so secure and confident a world that theology was left to priests following a path of free-thinking which always produced acceptable answers because of their enormous innate respect for their own traditions. Respectful evolution was the process by which change occurred. Something might be new, but it was just what the ancestors would have approved of. And, as noted in the Introduction, this opens up a yawning trap for us, in that by the act of explaining Egyptian theology we are almost certainly adding to it.

The founder: Akhenaten, 'the heretic king'

In the history of Egyptian religion there is, in fact, only one name, and that belongs to a king of the late 18th Dynasty: Akhenaten, son of Amenhetep III. Using the great power and wealth at his disposal he made a bold departure from the traditional career of kings in Egypt: he attempted religious reform.[4] How and why Akhenaten came to step outside the mentality of his time remains a mystery that we are unlikely ever to resolve. But he sought to create from the religious traditions of Egypt a new and simpler cult. The nature of Egyptian theology has been commented upon more than once in previous chapters. It was built around a fascination with names and words. One result was a composition which appears on the walls of some of the royal tombs at Thebes. Known as the Litany of Ra it invokes the sun-god Ra under his seventy-five names, which are those of other gods.[5] Thus he is the 'body' (substance?) of Atum, Shu, Tefnut, Geb, and Nut, the deities who are the main elements of nature. In this developed form of theological word-game, involving the handling of the names of gods as entities of logic, a balance and harmony of thought were sought in which the potential incompatibility of the historical multiplicity of divinities on the one hand, and the perceived unity of divine power on the other, was avoided. The idea of many gods was held within a mental shell of ultimate singleness whose essence was the power of the sun.

The inherited complexity of Egyptian theology provided priests with a challenge to be resolved by intellectual means which did not violate respect for the past. Akhenaten seems to have found violation necessary in order to bring about a resolution of a quite different order of simplicity. Much of the inherited system he simply ignored. But the main accretion to the sun cult – the god Amun or Amun-Ra of Thebes, whose form was human – he rejected. The name and image of Amun were methodically defaced in an organized campaign of administered iconoclasm. In the place of everything from the past he put the visible disk of the sun, to which the Egyptians commonly gave the name: the Aten. Its image was a disk from which many rays descended, each one ending in a little hand. Like a king, the Aten was also given two names written in cartouches. Its temples were to be great open courts filled with altars. Traditional temples wrapped the image of god in darkness and secrecy inside windowless halls. The Aten could be seen directly in the sky, without mystery, and needed temples only as settings for the pageantry of the king's worship. This he performed on the 'Sunshades', the platform-altars already familiar from the Theban mortuary temples.

Akhenaten saw the Aten as the universal creator of all life, and celebrated this in several hymns which have survived amongst the carvings in the rock tombs of some of his courtiers at Amarna.[6] Their sentiments were not themselves new in Egypt. A well-known hymn on a papyrus in the Cairo Musuem dated to before Akhenaten's reign addresses the Theban god Amun in similar terms of universal power and solar imagery.[7] Where Akhenaten's hymn differs is in the absence of references to other gods which, in the older hymns, were seen as complementary aspects of Amun. Akhenaten's originality lay in his perception of the simplicity of solar religion, and thus the irrelevance of much of the traditional theological language-game. The sun's disk, devoid of human features, became the only divine image in Akhenaten's new temples and in the decoration within his own tomb at Amarna. The elaborate depictions of a universe populated by divine beings were wholly banished. The visualization of the king's birth from a union between his mother and the sun-god incarnate in human form became impossible. Religious language-game and its pictorial counterparts were more or less dead.

Since the early days of Egyptology, people have been fascinated by the question: is this monotheism? It is a fascination which in the past has been fuelled by the parochial western view that belief in one god is superior to belief in several. The question is, however, almost impossible to answer sensibly in these terms. Religion is too elaborate a phenomenon to be handled by simple labels. Developed forms of Christianity and Islam have far more subtle and complex approaches to manifestations of divinity and paranormal authority than are implied by the term 'monotheism'. Indeed, as an outsider I find it illogical that Christianity should be classed as a monotheistic religion. If I wander around a major European church, seeing it with the eye of an archaeologist, the number and variety of sacred images in stone, wood, brass and stained glass will lead me to reconstruct a very elaborate and many-centred system of belief which includes a Trinity or Triad of divine entities. The Christian believer escapes from the inconsistency by means of an impressive mental adjustment founded on the notion of 'mystery', a way of thought from which I, as an unbeliever, am excluded. The intelligent ancient Egyptian did the same, converting religious sensation into the linguistic terms of his culture. In this way the term 'polytheism' as applied to the Egyptians falls wide of the mark by suggesting that Egyptian religion was fragmentary and incoherent. In practice the question resolves itself into a comparison between Akhenaten and Old Testament Judaism.

Akhenaten lived well before the establishment of the kingdom of Israel, yet the imagery in the Hymn to the Aten has distinct echoes in one of the biblical Psalms. Furthermore, in both sets of thinking we see the same desperately serious intention: to reach out for concise statements of finite definition on the nature of god. Both mirror a sense of dissatisfaction. But the lack of contemporary background evidence from the region prevents us from knowing if this represented a more widespread intellectual ferment manifesting itself in divergent forms and spread through the ancient Middle East. The results were in any case very different. They could scarcely have been otherwise given the great contrast in cultural milieu. The Aten was a force presiding benignly but remotely over a stable and familiar world; it was not an irascible god prepared to intervene in the affairs of man and dictate behaviour. Moral teaching was already long established in Egypt, and tended to be separate from theology, where the prime interest was in how the universe functioned. Akhenaten's religion was in this tradition: his concern was not in man's destiny or condition – that was not really a subject which occupied the Egyptians much in normal times – it was in the source of life itself. In the Aten he found a simple, unintellectual answer: the source was nothing but what he could see for himself, the disk of the sun. Mystery – the promise that there was always more to be discovered – vanished from theological writings and from temples. Akhenaten spoke of being the sole knower of the Aten's mysteries, but even in the privacy of his own burial at Amarna we can detect no sign of anything not already widely publicized.

Mosaic Judaism, with its distinctive code of living, was a positive force for the host society, giving the Israelites a sense of identity in a hostile world. It became a means of rejecting the cultures of others. By contrast, the Aten robbed Egyptians of a tradition of explaining the phenomena of the universe through an extraordinarily rich imagery which, to those who studied it, managed to contain the concept that a unity, a oneness, could be found in the multiplicity of divine forms and names. Akhenaten was telling the Egyptians something that they knew already, but in a way that made further serious speculation pointless. It is easy to understand why the Egyptians rejected the king's religion after his death. He had tried to kill intellectual life.

In our own modern perceptions of the world, traditional ancient Egyptian theology and language-game have no place. They form a colourful and interesting example of pre-scientific thought. Akhenaten can appear to us as a remarkable and somewhat tragic figure because he seems to have perceived the irrelevance of much of the thought of his day, yet was unable to put into its place anything that satisfied man's universal desire for complexity in thought. Nor were there people around him who were stimulated by the intellectual vacuum he created to advance beyond the confines of religion in the search for explanations of phenomena.

We know of no later stories or traditions concerning Akhenaten, and after his death his ideas were forcefully rejected and his monuments smashed or demolished. He became a non-person. That we know about him at all arises from the sheer quantity of the sculpture of his reign which later generations reused in foundations for other buildings, and from his creation of a complete city on a desert site which lay abandoned until modern rediscovery. Because Akhenaten had been a prolific builder his existence could not be obliterated. But this points to one question which we can never hope to answer: did Akhenaten represent a small and usually undemonstrative, but nevertheless enduring, tradition of intellectual dissent? Did his uniqueness lie simply in being king and thus able to bring an alternative vision into the public domain?

The lack of background sources cripples the historian. It has proved impossible to write a history of Akhenaten's reign which does not embrace an element of historical fiction. It is as if one has to decide which actor would best play the part: an effete, limp-wristed dreamer, or a fearsome, despotic madman. If the religious idealism points to the former, his approach to his own position and the simple fact that he achieved what he did takes one to the opposite pole. For Akhenaten's escape from the past had its limits. Kingship in Egypt was embedded within theology, and it was not Akhenaten's intention to diminish the power of Pharaoh. Quite the reverse. Between the simple vision of a life-giving sun on the one hand, and humanity and nature on the other, stood the king and his family as sole intermediaries. Here, too, there was innovation, and it is in the portrayal of the king and his family that a simple interpretation of the king's mind breaks down. The royal family, in which his principal queen, Nefertiti, was pictured as if with a dominant role (though whether this was really her character we cannot tell), was given a new style of presentation. Mysticism was mixed with informality amounting to lethargy in a manner often verging on the grotesque, and alien to the Egyptians' own conceptions of good form.

To claim 'mysticism' is, in itself, to align oneself to a particular interpretation of why the features of the king and his family are portrayed in the way that renders the art of his reign unique. The remains of his temples at Karnak show that this was something developed very early in his reign. The peculiarities amount to a list of distortions: long forward-leaning neck, pendulous jaw, narrowed eyes, and swollen belly and hips. The king always wears a crown, but when the characteristics are transferred to other members of his family they also include a rear elongation of the skull. This strange physique is most impressively seen in colossal statues where the viewer stands below, easily overwhelmed by the sheer weirdness of the overall effect; it is less successfully translated into two-dimensional wall carvings.

Many people have seen in the distortions to his body a faithful attempt to portray the effects of a serious disease from which the king suffered. It is a more plausible alternative, however, that it represents a bold attempt to portray kingship as a force with characteristics that place it outside the normal plane of human experience. There was little tradition in Egypt of using sculpture to convey an intellectual sensation more complex than that the life-force that animated in varying degrees gods, kings, and ordinary humans was materialized in the form of the ideal, youthful human body. What normally distinguished the statue of a god from that of a king or of a high official was the name written somewhere on the statue, and items of dress and insignia. They were to be experienced, however, in the same straightforward and rather innocent way. Akhenaten's self-images were experimental and surreal, made against a particularly unsuitable cultural background. And it is a central point in assessing his intentions that this attempt to portray the mystery of superior force through surreal art rather than through word-game was confined to himself and his family. The shape of the Aten held no mystery. The divine force that passes understanding was revealed to mankind through the Aten's earthly agent: the king. Hence the paired cartouches: large ones for the Aten, small ones for the king – god and the son of god, ruling together.

The colossal statues of the king stood making their statement through their form. In two-dimensional art – wall reliefs and stelae – the royal family group was portrayed in scenes of relaxed informality, but these scenes were themselves the object of devotion by courtiers and officials. This warm family life of the king seems not to have been intended as an example or as an encouragement for greater contact between the royal family and the rest of society. It was used, one might think perversely, to set them apart as a loving group so perfect as to warrant veneration. In the prayers of courtiers Akhenaten and Nefertiti were invoked as gods alongside the Aten.[8] The new cult offered no channel for personal piety amongst the people. For them it was not a democratic cult, only a revised and eccentric focus for loyalty. We can match his place in the history of thought as an early rationalizer with an equally precocious niche in the history of rule: that of the glorious dictator. More will be said shortly on Akhenaten's rewriting of the mental script for kingship.

The composition of the royal family group is itself noteworthy. Apart from Akhenaten it is entirely female. For in addition to Nefertiti up to six daughters are shown as well. The eldest of these was Meritaten, who was intended as the heiress, and was given, during Akhenaten's reign, increasing prominence, presumably as she came of age. The next in age was Meketaten, who died young and was buried in the Royal Tomb at Amarna, in a separate suite of her own; then came Ankhsenpa-aten who, with the changed name Ankhsenamun, eventually married Tutankhamun, and for a short time became Egypt's principal queen; the last three are only names to us: Nefernefruaten the Younger (Nefernefruaten being Nefertiti's first cartouche name), Nefernefrura, and Setepenra. It is possible that this exclusively female group is a faithful depiction of the full extent of Akhenaten's own family. Good evidence exists, however, for making Tutankhamun a son of Akhenaten, though not necessarily by Nefertiti, since Akhenaten is known to have had more than one wife.[9] If this is so, emphasis on femininity may itself be a facet of Akhenaten's ideology.

One further traditional religious concept was retained by Akhenaten, and even emphasized. This was *maat*, which can be translated 'truth' or 'justice', and really embraced the whole correct order of the universe.[10] In a characteristic transformation of an abstract into something tangible the Egyptians had made Maat into a goddess, daughter of the sun-god Ra. Although the goddess herself received little attention from Akhenaten, the old-established epithet 'who lives on *maat*', which once was a prerogative of the gods, was used by Akhenaten regularly to describe himself. 'Who lives on truth' is one of the set phrases of Akhenaten's inscriptions, the words meaning that 'truth' was a substance which he consumed. Although the Egyptian's normal use of the word did not carry the stark and binding power which the word has in modern usage, it would be perverse, given the nature of Akhenaten's interests, not to recognize that, however the word may have been used previously, the 'Truth' was now the new and superior revelation of the nature of god. 'Truth' was on its way to having the force which it has come to have in modern creeds.

In Chapter 5 it was pointed out that Akhenaten's first major initiative in establishing the new cult was carried out at Karnak, at the centre of the cult of Amun. This took the form of building a series of temples of likely open-plan type more suited to the worship of the visible sun and decorated with statues and wall scenes in the startling new style, the whole operation brought to a climax by a royal *Sed*-festival years before its proper time. Tens of thousands of small loose stone building blocks have been recovered from these early temples, as well as pieces of colossal statues of the king. These are in the most extreme artistic style of his reign, and show that it was developed at the very beginning.[11]

The foundation: Akhetaten, 'Horizon of the sun-disk'

In the fifth year of his reign Akhenaten chose to build an entirely new royal city and centre for his cult: a city built around temples to the Aten and palaces for his family in the novel style which could stand unchallenged by the works of the past. Its name was

Akhetaten, 'The Horizon of the Aten'. The site for this lay roughly half-way between Memphis and Thebes: a complete slice of the Nile Valley, from a broad tract of farmland on the west to a flat and apparently unoccupied stretch of desert on the east where most of the building would be done. His visionary intentions are recorded on a series of tablets (the Boundary Stelae) carved at intervals in the cliffs on both sides of the Nile (Figure 87).[12] They state that the Aten had led him to the site and selected it, and that it had previously belonged to no other god or goddess. Within the limits of the tablets the temples and palaces would be built, and the existing fields and villages on the opposite bank of the river found themselves part of the grand scheme. One year later he paid another state visit to the site, and a second set of tablets was carved into the hills. They contain an oath of the King:

> My oath of truth, which it is my desire to pronounce, and of which I will not say: 'It is false', for ever and ever: Akhetaten extends from the southern tablet as far as the northern tablet, measured between tablet and tablet in the eastern mountain, likewise from the south-west tablet to the north-west tablet in the western mountain of Akhetaten. The area within these four tablets is Akhetaten itself; it belongs to Aten my father: mountains, deserts, meadows, islands, high ground and low ground, water, villages, men, animals and all things which the Aten my father shall bring into existence eternally and forever. I will not neglect this oath which I have made to the Aten my father eternally and forever.

On two of the tablets a second similar oath was repeated after another two years, perhaps at the time that the King came into residence. One passage in the tablets has sometimes created the impression that Akhenaten swore never himself to leave the confines of the city. This, however, is a misunderstanding. The relevant passages, in stating that he will not go beyond the boundaries, mean that he will not extend the limits of Akhetaten beyond them. Another of the passages contains the very clear provision for his death when outside the city: 'If I die in any town of the north, south, west, or east, in the multitude of years, I will be brought, and my burial be made in Akhetaten.'

The ultimate sign of Akhenaten's sincerity and his break with the past was this promise to site tombs for himself and for his family in the eastern hills, a new Valley of the Kings. His courtiers were expected to do the same.

The city was built in great haste, and occupied by a substantial population. Its life was, however, to be brief. The king died in his seventeenth regnal year. What happened immediately afterwards remains obscure, but the eventual successor was Tutankhamun and his wife, the third royal daughter, Ankhsenpa-aten.[13] During his nine-year reign the ideas of his father were rejected, and a complete return to religious orthodoxy took place. This is made very explicit by his decree re-establishing the cult of Amun at Karnak.[14] Interestingly, it was issued from Memphis, a sign of how much Memphis had come to replace Thebes as the main royal city during the New Kingdom. Akhenaten's preparation of a tomb at Amarna shows that he had the faith that the city and his ideas would be lasting. His faith was misplaced. He was rejected by later generations as not having been a legitimate king, and came to be referred to as 'that enemy from Akhetaten' and suchlike.[15] The rapid abandonment of his ideas meant that the city, too, had little future. A sizeable population lingered on for a while, probably well into the

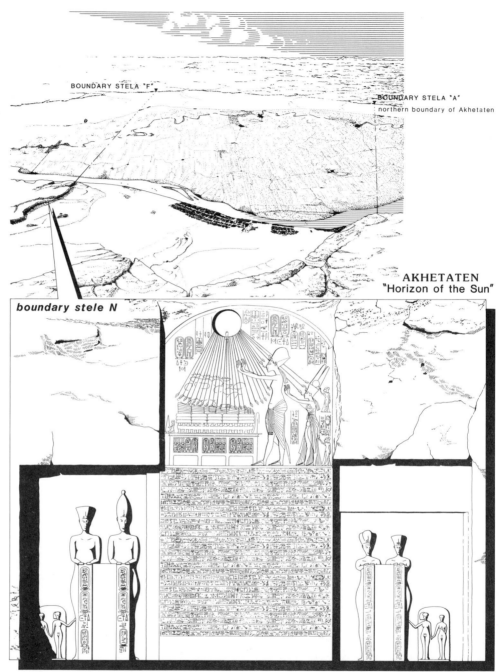

Figure 87 Akhenaten's new city, Akhetaten, 'Horizon of the Sun'. *Above*. Reconstruction of the 18th Dynasty landscape showing the extent of cultivated land on the west side of the river which lay between the boundary stelae. *Below*. Reconstruction of the original appearance of one of the boundary stelae, 'N'. The stele, 3.9 metres high, is flanked by statues. Each set depicts Akhenaten and Nefertiti holding in front of them a narrow vertical tablet inscribed with the names of the Aten and of themselves. They are accompanied by their two eldest daughters, Meritaten and Meketaten. Much of the stele and parts of the statues still survive.

reign of Tutankhamun, but thereafter, apart from an area beside the waterfront, it became a ghost city.

The nature of Amarna has gradually been revealed by excavation and survey which began last century, continued with breaks until 1936, and was resumed in 1977.[16] The city itself, apart from the information it gives us about Akhenaten's concepts, is a major site for the study of ancient urbanism generally. Few archaeological sites of this size exist in the pre-classical world where the ground plan is as clear or as well documented as this. Although the circumstances of its founding are unique, it forms an apt basis for considering certain aspects of ancient Egyptian society, and for illustrating the impact which kingship could have on it.

Amarna is the modern name for the city part of Akhetaten lying on the east bank (Figure 89). The ancient city limits, however, encompassed an area roughly 16 by 13 km, measured between the Boundary Stelae (Figures 87, 88). Clearly a good deal of farmland was present, but we can only guess at how much. It is worth making the attempt, however, because it then becomes possible to consider what the carrying capacity of the land was (i.e. how many people its agricultural produce would support) in terms of the likely population of the city.

We can be reasonably sure of one thing, that the present course of the river as it sweeps past Amarna is not very far from its 18th Dynasty course, since several of the tomb scenes are explicit in giving the central part of the city a waterfront. The floodplain is crossed from north to south not only by the Nile but by a parallel water-course to the west called the Bahr Yusef which used to diverge from the Nile in the region of Dairut.[17] If we limit the cultivable land of the New Kingdom to that which lay east of the Bahr Yusef – and particularly towards the south this could well produce a very conservative estimate – we have a total of around 162 sq. km, or 59,200 of the ancient land measure called an aroura. People have made estimates as to how large a population an aroura could support: a rural population of perhaps 0.5 per aroura, plus a non-farming population of a rather smaller size, perhaps 0.25.[18] We can estimate that the fields of Akhetaten could have supported a population as large as 45,000. As we shall see, estimates of the actual city population vary between 20,000 and 50,000.

We also have to consider what we mean by farming and non-farming elements in the population. The character of the Amarna houses strongly implies that many of the 'officials' who lived in the city were also receiving a farm income, either from their own more distant lands or from rented land across the river, on the fields of Akhetaten. The village population on the west, made up largely of labourers, may thus have been quite small. It is impossible without more reliable evidence to pursue this line of reasoning any further, but what the exercise does do is to suggest a very rough balance between the carrying capacity of the land and the population within the limits of Akhetaten. It was, however, also a general ideal to build up surplus grain stocks (grain mountains, in today's terms). In pursuit of this, local produce could well have been augmented by the produce of private estates outside the limits, and perhaps also by income for the Aten from other places. The Aten temples at Karnak were supplied by 'offerings' from very diverse sources, including provincial mayors.[19] But this was in the king's early days. The proclamations in the Boundary Stelae might mean that henceforth the Aten at Akhetaten was to be supplied only by the land that was his, the land demarcated by the Stelae. The allocation of a large contiguous block of land to one institution runs so

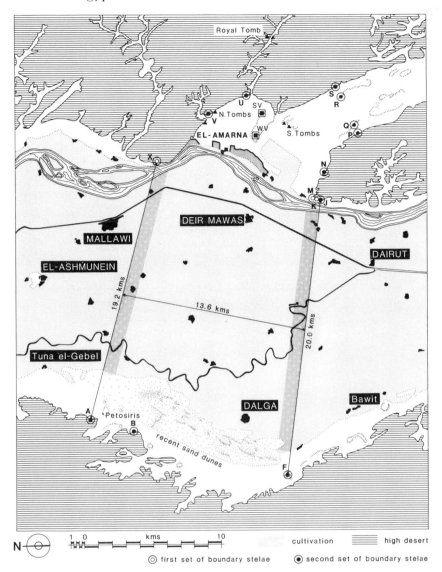

Figure 88   Map of the Nile Valley at el-Amarna showing the extent of Akhetaten, as defined by the Boundary Stelae. Behind el-Amarna are the two sets of rock tombs (the North Tombs and South Tombs), the Royal Tomb, and two outlying sites, the Workmen's Village (WV) and Stone Village (SV).

much counter to the normal pattern of institutional landholding that it might, in itself, mark an application of the novel simplicity that Akhenaten seems to have found attractive.

Excavation by archaeologists lays bare the outlines of ruined buildings, but the results may be a long way from how the city appeared to those who lived there. We are fortunate at Amarna in having pictures of the city as certain artists saw it, recorded in

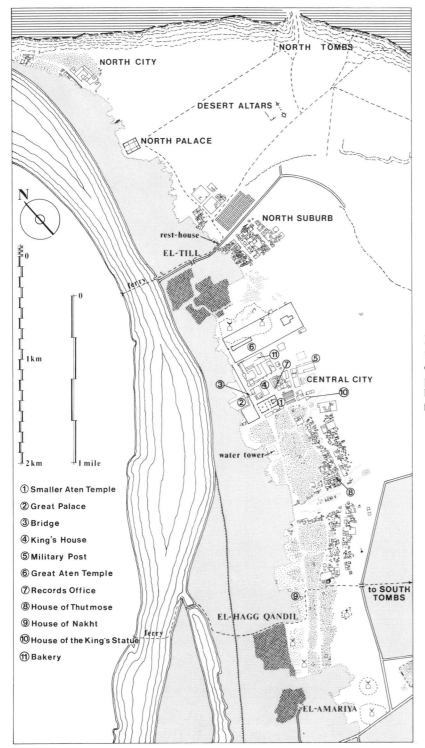

Figure 89 Map of the ancient city of Amarna showing principal excavated buildings and modern features.

NORTH TOMBS

NORTH CITY

DESERT ALTARS

NORTH PALACE

N

NORTH SUBURB

rest-house

EL-TILL

ferry

CENTRAL CITY

water tower

to SOUTH TOMBS

EL-HAGG QANDIL

ferry

EL-AMARIYA

0
1km
2km

0
1 mile

① Smaller Aten Temple
② Great Palace
③ Bridge
④ King's House
⑤ Military Post
⑥ Great Aten Temple
⑦ Records Office
⑧ House of Thutmose
⑨ House of Nakht
⑩ House of the King's Statue
⑪ Bakery

several of the rock tombs at the site.[20] Their perspective was very different from ours: their purpose was to record the visual sensations of being in certain important places, rather than to delineate them with topographical accuracy. Consequently they must be used with care. But they do show many important architectural features which would otherwise be unknown, and they show that the ancient Egyptians' love of trees and gardens was well represented in the city. It would have possessed a greenness which the present aridity of the site entirely lacks.

The rock tombs are in two groups, the North and the South, hewn in the cliffs and hills which border the site in a great arc to the east. They belonged to courtiers and officials. It is common at Thebes to find tombs left unfinished, but at Amarna it is the rule. But since it was standard ancient practice to bring in the decorators as soon as enough wall space was ready for them, a good deal of carved wall decoration was finished even when the masons might not have finished hewing out the inner chambers. The scenes are variations on a limited number of themes, most of which centre on the life of the royal family. The tomb owner appears only as a subordinate figure, except at the entrance to the tomb, where he was often allowed to occupy the side walls with figures of himself offering a long prayer, and at the rear of the tomb where, in a few cases, a statue of the owner has been started, and surrounded by little depictions of his family.

There is one further pictorial source of information. The new temples and the Great Palace were partly built of stone, their walls decorated with scenes which sometimes showed the same kinds of pictures of city life around the royal family as occur in the private tombs. In the time of Rameses II, between 50 and 100 years afterwards, Amarna was a largely empty city with its public buildings abandoned but still in good condition. They were too tempting a source for cheap building stone. With great thoroughness they were demolished and the stones taken away by the boatload for use in the king's huge programme of temple construction. Many made a short journey, to the city of Hermopolis (modern el-Ashmunein) across the river. Excavations have brought to light some 1,500 loose blocks, but this is likely to be only a fraction of the original quantity. They cannot be put together to form complete scenes, but singly or in small groups they are a useful source of information.[21]

On his Boundary Stelae Akhenaten promised tombs for himself and his family at Akhetaten. The new Valley of the Kings was in a peculiarly remote location to the east. From the city a trek of 3 miles (5 km) takes one to the entrance to the wadi which leads to the Royal Valley, but another 4 miles (6 km) lie ahead before the site of the royal necropolis is reached. Of the various tombs planned, only one was brought anywhere near to completion, and this was Akhenaten's own. It has the dimensions and character of the tombs in the Valley of the Kings at Thebes. Most of the decoration has been lost, but the few fragments surviving show familiar pictures of the royal family and the Aten. The really unusual feature of the design is that it was intended as the nucleus for a family tomb. When the second daughter, Meketaten, died she was buried in a separate series of chambers leading off from the main entrance corridor. Poignant scenes of the distraught royal family occur on the walls. Subsequently a second and much grander side-suite was begun, which shows all the signs of having been intended as a second royal tomb. A tempting suggestion is that this was for Nefertiti.[22]

Security for cemeteries was an age-long Egyptian concern. Tomb robbery was an ancient occupation, and a few generations after the Amarna Period the authorities at Thebes were busy investigating robberies in the Theban necropolis. At Amarna it would seem that the desert behind the city and around the cliffs was patrolled in an organized manner. This left behind on the desert a network of paths that are still visible.[23] They were made by sweeping desert stones to either side of the path to leave two bordering ridges. In daytime they might seem superfluous in the normally clear air. Their usefulness would have become apparent at night, when the faint light of the moon, or even of the stars, renders slight irregularities of the desert surprisingly visible. The paths cross from north to south, circle around two desert villages, converge on some kind of central point in the southern portion of the desert, and cross other roads running in straight lines directly to important rock tombs. One track followed the brink of the cliffs, being broken into separate sections by the deep valleys.

The creation of Akhetaten must have involved a labour force of workers and artists, but the presence of a large and regimented group of this kind is not obvious from the archaeological record. Perhaps many were simply the city inhabitants whose houses were to be found almost everywhere. An exception to this lies out in the desert behind the main city. A low plateau runs forward from the foot of the cliffs towards the main city, and in a little side valley lay a square walled village containing sixty-eight houses of identical size, plus a larger one, presumably for the official in charge. The village lies not too far from the southern group of rock tombs, and this may be an important clue for the reason for the village: it housed a community of men maintained by the government for cutting and decorating tombs. A similar village existed at Thebes, at the site of Deir el-Medina, although here the workmen's prime responsibility was the current royal tomb. We cannot be sure if this was true also for the people at the Workmen's Village at Amarna, for the Royal Tomb is a long way distant.

The Workmen's Village was the first site of the resumed modern excavations of the Egypt Exploration Society of Great Britain.[24] Much of the excavation was concentrated on the ground immediately outside the village walls, where substantial quantities of rubbish had anciently been dumped, and this, together with changes to buildings, discloses a degree of activity which is surprising when compared to the brevity of occupation. It runs well into the uncertain years following the death of Akhenaten. At this time, when Tutankhamun came to the throne, a new phase of building activity took place just outside the village. The inhabitants began to build chapels on the hillside intended as places for family gatherings. Some inscriptions have been found, and these mention mainly traditional gods, including Amun-Ra, whom Akhenaten regarded as an arch-enemy. At this place people evidently stayed on for a longer period after Akhenaten's death than is often supposed, perhaps looking after the tombs, either until their precious contents were removed, or perhaps just in case a further turn in history brought the court back again. Subsequent excavations in the Main City, at a place which supplied the village with its water and probably also with some of its pottery, have confirmed that the reign of Tutankhamun gave to some parts of Amarna a new lease of life, albeit short-lived.

Figure 90 The royal chariot drive. *Upper register.* Akhenaten and Nefertiti in a chariot leave one of the Aten temples (represented as a pylon entrance with flag-poles). They head towards a fortified building set between what look like fences, probably the North Riverside Palace (Figure 91), flanked by a running bodyguard headed by the 'Chief of Police of Akhetaten, Mahu'. *Lower register.* The royal couple drive along a road marked by what looks like the same fence, again accompanied by Mahu and his bodyguard. From the tomb of Mahu, after N. de G. Davies, *The Rock Tombs of El Amarna* IV, London, 1906, Plates XX–XXII.

The arena of royal display

The point was made in Chapter 5 that the sources for Akhenaten's kingship create, quite unintentionally, a caricature of the public role of the charismatic leader as it has survived from the Bronze Age to this day. The elements can be summarized thus:

1. the state procession
2. armed escorts
3. postures of special deference for those allowed to approach
4. the 'Appearance', alone or with family, at a palace balcony
5. the open-air review of troops and representatives of empire
6. public or semi-public acts of worship
7. pictures of the leader, alone or with family, in people's own homes (Figure 94).

Amarna provides us with a unique combination of sources which allows us to reconstruct the public showing of Egyptian kingship. We have the action pictures in the scenes in the rock tombs, and we have from excavation much of the actual physical setting. Samples of the elements 1) to 6) as they occur in tomb scenes will be found in Figures 90, 92, and 93. It remains to describe the layout.

Although the city was laid out on a relatively flat and unencumbered stretch of desert, the degree of forward planning was not great, and was largely confined to the official buildings which created this special setting. These are the elements we need to isolate (Figure 91). The backbone was a long, straight avenue, the so-called Royal Road, which connected the Central City to the North City. The choice of where its end-points were to be was influenced by the site's topography. Although we speak of the 'Amarna plain' it is not, in terms of the scale of human visitors, particularly flat. From north to south it has several broad undulations which make themselves felt to those travelling from one end to the other. The Royal Road linked two of them. The Central City stood on one, its peak the King's House on an eastwards-running ridge on which the police post was also built; at the other end the North City nestled tightly and securely on the foot of the slopes beneath the cliffs where they approach the river.

The North City (Figure 91) contained a substantial building, the North Riverside Palace, with massive fortified wall. This was probably the principal royal residence, private and separate from the rest of the city, and also well protected.[25] Part of this wall, pierced by a huge gateway, is still a prominent feature. Between the wall and the palace proper were magazines and other buildings which could well have been a barracks for the king's bodyguard. Across the road lay a group of houses, some of them the largest in the whole city and presumably for some of the courtiers closest to the king. The North City was closed at the north by a large administrative building terraced up into the lower slopes of the cliff, and containing a huge warehouse block for commodities, part of it perhaps a granary. This implies that the North City and the king's private residence were self-sufficient in food, with a supply independent from the sources which sustained the rest of the city. The whole site, because of the overshadowing cliff, has an atmosphere very different from the rest of the city, and was evidently as attractive a place to Akhenaten as it remains to visitors today.

The Royal Road began here, and then struck southwards across low open ground

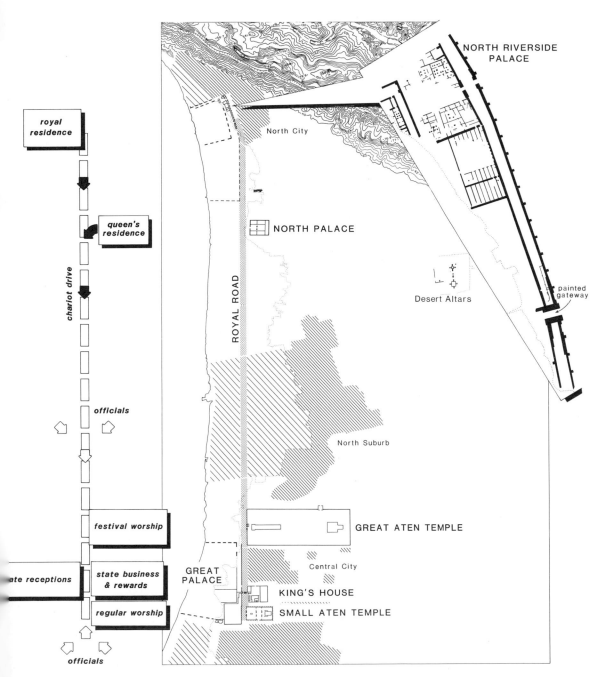

Figure 91 Diagram of the principal structural element at Amarna, the royal processional route.

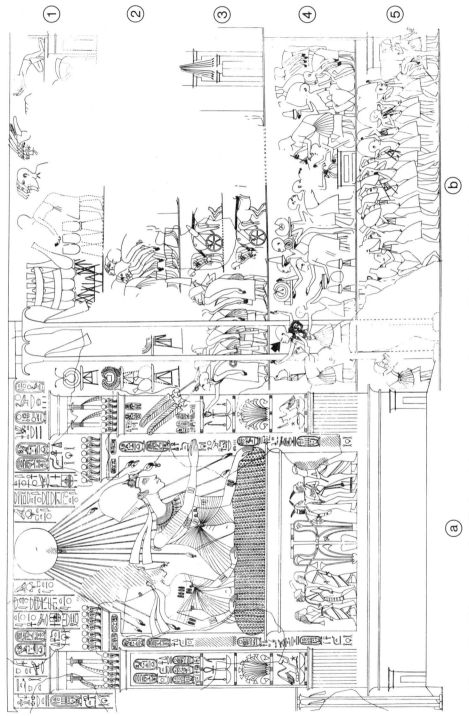

Figure 92 Akhenaten at the Window of Appearance, rewarding one of his loyal officials. Note the 'unification' symbol with bound captives which appears below the window in section (a), cf. Figure 73, p. 212. In register 4 of section (b), at the left end, the official Parennefer receives gold necklaces bestowed by the king, whilst to the right servants and scribes record and pack into a chest other gifts. Of particular interest in this scene is register 5, which shows amphorae and baskets of commodities being carried out, confirming that the Window ceremony involved the distribution of goods of a more basic, ration-like kind as well as the giving of special rewards. The upper registers (1–3) depict other officials and courtiers (awaiting their turn?), and some of their waiting chariots. For Windows of Appearance at Thebes, see Figures 68, p. 192, 73, p. 212. From the tomb of Parennefer, after N. de G. Davies, *The Rock Tombs of El-Amarna VI*, London, 1908, Plate IV.

towards the Central City. This was the route for the royal drive, a favourite amongst the tomb scenes. One of them actually shows the North Riverside Palace, drawn as a stylized fortress complete with battlements, as the point of the royal departure, and some kind of fencing along the sides of the great road (Figure 90). In Chapter 5 we saw how important to the city of Thebes were the processional festivals of its gods, how they provided a round-the-year public spectacle and a symbolic claim to the external world by traversing long distances. For the most important of them the king arrived to add and in a way submerge his person. The worship of the Aten stopped all this. There were no sacred boat shrines to carry any more. The Aten's disk made its own way across the sky, permanently in procession. Akhenaten had created another vacuum and tried to fill it with processions of himself as the focus for public adulation, replacing with military dash the stately, colourful, and noisy bearing of the divine images of old. Here again we catch a whiff of the world to come. King, queen, daughters, retainers in their chariots, the bodyguards running along in stooping posture (Figure 90): we can recognize the basis of the scene re-enacted today in capital cities and on state occasions the world over. The presidential limousine, the royal landau, motorcycle outriders, presidential advisers, and security guards, all are parts of a public performance acted out over the subsequent millennia as rulers and leaders have responded to the urge for public acclaim.

On its way south, the Royal Road passed an isolated building facing the river, the North Palace.[26] When excavated in the 1920s it was found to be a self-contained royal residence, with formal reception halls, a domestic suite with bedroom and bathroom, an open-air solar temple, and gardens and courts where the walls were painted with bright scenes from nature, and animals and birds were kept. The many fragments of inscriptions recovered show that the person for whom the North Palace was finally intended was the eldest princess and heiress, Meritaten. It may have become, when she came of age during her father's reign, her main residence. In its basic purpose – providing a quite separate palace for a major queen and her household – it conforms to the type of harem-palace documented both from texts and from the site of Medinet el-Ghurab (see Chapter 5), and in its formality it can be compared with, for example, the surviving fragment of the Palace of Merenptah at Memphis.

Beyond the North Palace, the Royal Road eventually ran through the first of the densely built-up areas of private houses, the North Suburb, and began the slight climb to the low plateau on which the Central City stood. The Central City was arranged around the terminus of the main stretch of the Royal Road (Figures 89, p. 271, 91, p. 277).[27] Along the entire western side and probably covering all the ground to the waterfront lay the Great Palace.[28] This included an intimate area of pleasant courts and halls, brightly painted (see Figure 77, p. 224, for a fragment of painted pavement). But the core of the building was an enormous courtyard surrounded by colossal statues of Akhenaten, and a complex of halls and smaller courts and monuments. These parts were constructed of stone, and since, after the city was abandoned, the stonework was systematically removed, it is now difficult to be sure how these parts appeared. Whatever the details were, however, the whole served to provide the king with a sumptuous, semi-religious setting which advertised his new religion and art and in which formal receptions and ceremonies could be held, including those, perhaps, for the most important envoys from foreign courts who would return to their masters with tales of

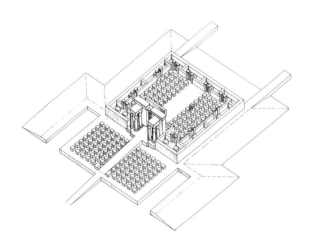

wonder at the extravagance and innovation of the new ruler. At the southern end of the Great Palace was an extraordinary addition, a hall built for Akhenaten's immediate successor, Smenkhkara, containing 544 brick columns, and with walls encrusted with glazed tiles. A bridge of brick across the Royal Road linked the Great Palace with a small residence, the King's House. This is a representative of the smaller palaces – the mooring-places of Pharaoh – discussed in Chapter 5. It served as the king's working premises, and as such contained the Window of Appearance, where the king and his family appeared in order to reward loyal officials and to announce their promotions to higher offices. More will be said about this window in the next section.

One state building in the centre has already been described: the Great Palace. Two more lay on the other side of the road, closing either end of the Central City. Both were temples, but, of the key elements built of stone, only their foundations survive. The more northerly was the Great Temple to the Aten.[29] This occupied a huge enclosure 229 metres wide and running back from the Royal Road for 730 metres. Much of the interior seems to have been open space, but we must suspect that this is simply because Akhenaten never completed his grand designs. At both temples there is evidence that the first constructions were in brick, just to create quickly the necessary settings for worship. A programme of replacement and enhancement in stone then followed. The Great Aten Temple enclosure gives the distinct impression of being a huge ceremonial site still waiting for most of its complement of sacred buildings to be added. In the end only two were built, lying along the main east-west axis.

The temple enclosure was entered between two brick towers (or pylons) at the front, which led immediately to the first of the two stone buildings, called 'The House of Rejoicing'. Unlike normal Egyptian temples which began with an open court followed by roofed chambers, this building reversed the sequence by beginning with a columned hall which gave access to a series of open courts filled with stone offering-tables. At the rear of the building was an area separately designated: 'Gem-Aten', or 'The Aten is found'. This differed little from the rest of the temple except that some of the altars around the sides of the courts were protected by walls. The provision of many altars is a feature of Akhenaten's cult. Contemporary tomb scenes which depict the temples show the altars piled with food- and drink-offerings. This was the traditional way of serving the gods, but Akhenaten seems to have used it to demonstrate an excessive piety. It reached its height beside the 'House of Rejoicing', where several hundred offering-tables were laid out over a veritable field on the south side. In the rear part of the Great Temple lay the second stone building, where again the main feature was open courts filled with rows of offering-tables. We must remember in looking at plans and reconstruction drawings of these buildings that all that survives are the foundations, together with ancient depictions in the rock tombs at Amarna. They allow considerable scope for differing interpretations. For example, whereas the excavators visualized them

Figure 93   Semi-public worship of the Aten in one of the temples in the Central City. *Above*. The king stands on a platform within the temple making offerings. Within the temple are numerous small offering-tables. He is observed by some of his daughters, and by groups of obsequious onlookers. Note the animal slaughterhouse in the top left corner, with its tethering-stones. From the tomb of Panehsy, after N. de G. Davies, *The Rock Tombs of El-Amarna* II, London, 1905, Plate XVIII. *Below*. One reconstruction of the Sanctuary of the Great Aten Temple, after B.J. Kemp, *Amarna Reports* IV, London, 1987, p. 112, Fig. 8.7. Other reconstructions from available evidence are possible.

Figure 94   An official portrait of the royal family relaxing at home. The portrait was itself, however, an object of private veneration for it came probably from a chapel in the grounds of a private house. Limestone, height 32 cm. Akhenaten sits on the left, holding the eldest daughter and heiress Meritaten; Nefertiti sits opposite, with the second daughter Meketaten (soon to die) on her lap, and cradling the third daughter Ankhsenpa-aten (later the wife of Tutankhamun) in her arms. Berlin Museum 14145.

built more or less at ground level and surrounded by high walls it is possible to argue that they were, for the most part, constructed on platforms of gypsum concrete with their front parts open so that the king's initial acts of worship would be more widely visible, as is suggested in the tomb pictures (Figure 93).[30]

Another finished sacred structure within the enclosure was a free-standing monument, a *benben*-stone. Again we are indebted to ancient tomb scenes for giving us its shape (Figure 30(5), p. 87). It stood on a pedestal, and was a single piece of stone given a rounded top. As noted in Chapter 2, from early times this was the shape of a sacred sun symbol, the original possibly standing at Heliopolis, just outside modern Cairo. The origin of the shape and reason for its connection with the sun are not really known, but its retention by Akhenaten is one of many signs that in the form and presentation of his cult he relied heavily upon traditional ideas.

The Central City possessed a second, smaller temple to the Aten, called 'The Mansion of the Aten.' It lay immediately beside the King's House. It is essentially a compressed version of the Great Temple. Its enclosure was much smaller, and surrounded by a wall with towers at intervals on the outside face. This is something known from other temples of the New Kingdom, where the evidence shows that the towers were finished off at the top with battlements, to give the outside world the impression that the temple stood within a fortress (see Chapter 5). The entrance was between two pylon towers which are still a prominent feature of the landscape. Their outside faces were provided with grooves in which tall flag-poles were erected, streamers fluttering from their tops. A large 'Sunshade' platform stood in the centre of the first courtyard, beyond the entrance pylons. Behind two more sets of pylons came the stone sanctuary, which was almost a copy of that in the Great Temple. Recent re-examination of parts of this temple has illustrated very clearly how it was subject to a process of improvement during the Amarna Period. The 'Sunshade' came first, perhaps as the very first place at Amarna where the king could properly worship the Aten. Later it was demolished to its foundations, presumably to be replaced by the stone sanctuary further back. Only at this time were the pylons built, and they had to await the reign of Smenkhkara before stonemasons could be found to start the process of stone embellishment of the main entrance.[31]

This smaller temple, from its position in the heart of the city, was evidently the place where many of the king's acts of semi-public worship took place, and was thus essentially a chapel royal. Whether by coincidence or not, if one stands at the front of the temple pylons and looks directly along the temple axis to the distant cliffs, it will be found that the temple axis points roughly towards the entrance to the wadi which led to the Royal Tomb. One can argue from this that the temple was the equivalent to a mortuary temple, where statues of Akhenaten would receive a more concentrated degree of cultic attention than they might have done in other royal buildings. The presence in the second court of a small building which probably consisted of a robing-room and Window of Appearance adds some weight to this, for this feature was an essential element of the royal mortuary temples at Thebes.[32] So, too, does the use of the term 'Mansion', which was commonly, though not exclusively, used for funerary temples and shrines in the New Kingdom.

The cult of the royal image was an ancient part of the ideology of the Egyptian state, but in normal circumstances our evidence is limited to temples. The unique spread of excavated evidence from Amarna for once allows us to see how much further it could extend. The most important evidence comes from a building (R43.2) which lay where the official zone of the city met the southern residential area (Figure 95).[33] It was built of mud brick and possesses certain elements of traditional temple design: an open forecourt (with trees) and a larger and smaller columned hall, all elements arranged symmetrically round a central axis. In the centre of the inner hall had stood a wooden shrine carved and painted with scenes of the Aten and the royal family. An inscription mentions 'the great statue which the King caused to be made', which presumably stood inside the shrine. Parts of wooden statues and a small wooden sphinx were also found here, as well as numerous beads and pendants. One odd aspect of the building is the

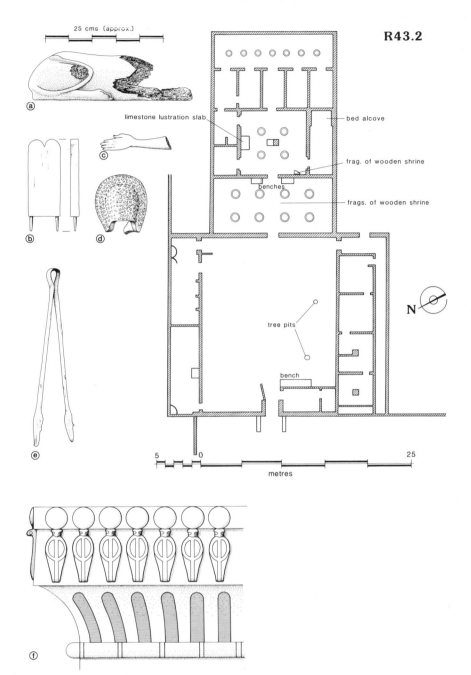

Figure 95 Chapel of the King's Statue at el-Amarna, showing the plan and some of the principal finds. After J.D.S. Pendlebury, *The City of Akhenaten* III, London, 1951, p. 141, Fig. 20, Plates XXII, LXXIX, and original record cards. (a) wooden sphinx; (b) wooden plumes from statue; (c) wooden hand from statue; (d) faience helmet from statue of Akhenaten; (e) bronze tongs; (f) reconstruction of cornice from wooden shrine.

apparent bedroom adjoining the statue chamber. We can only speculate as to the nature of the cult, although from the location of the building and its unpretentiousness it could have been a focus of private patronage.

Although this statue is lost, excavation in the residential parts of the city has brought to light other pieces of royal statuary which must have stood in small shrines which graced the gardens of a small number of the wealthier, or, in a few cases, stood actually inside the house itself. In place of a statue a stele carved with a picture of the royal family could suffice (see Figure 94, p. 282), and their picture was painted on shrine walls as well. These shrines are a striking feature of some (but by no means all) better-class houses. This suggests that it was in good taste, but not obligatory, to display and to pay respect to what was, in essence, a portrait of the king or the royal family. Such reinforcement of rulers' presence is still an esteemed practice in states which favour the cult of the great leader.

It is an obvious point to make that at Amarna we may be seeing a far more extreme manifestation of the cult of ruler than was normal in the New Kingdom, given Akhenaten's own preferences in this direction. But it was, all the same, only a matter of degree. A papyrus of the time of Amenhetep II refers to 'the statue of the lord (life, prosperity, health!) which is in the shrine in the house of the chief treasurer' at Memphis,[34] whilst the chief priest at Amarna, Panehsy, had brought with him to the city a stele of Amenhetep III and Queen Tiy to set up in a domestic shrine.[35]

The city proper ended by the modern village of el-Hagg Qandil, but this was still only about half-way along the line connecting the end boundary tablets in the cliffs. This left space for isolated buildings. The best-known was called Maru-Aten.[36] It consisted of two large, walled enclosures where the central features were shallow lakes. Carefully planted gardens surrounded them, and set within the gardens were pavilions and a group of shrines, including a group of 'Sunshade' platforms standing on an island surrounded by a shallow moat. A large number of wine jars was found stored in one building. The whole complex seems to exemplify the spirit of sun worship, providing an idyllic garden landscape of greenery and water presided over by the sun. It also exemplifies the wish for retreat, mentioned in the treatment of palaces in Chapter 5, and is symptomatic of the age in that a crucial part of it, the 'Sunshade' itself (and possibly the whole building), belonged to a leading royal lady. By the end of the Amarna Period the formal owner was the king's eldest daughter, Meritaten.

The most recent excavations at Amarna have led to the discovery of a second isolated temple complex to the south of the city, at the site now known as Kom el-Nana. Unlike Maru-Aten its central feature was a large stone temple, but this had been partly surrounded by a formal garden of small trees. Its principal distinguishing feature so far revealed, however, is a range of service buildings inside the extensive walled enclosure. These included a large bakery and probably workshops where other commodities were manufactured, which perhaps made it a self-supporting institution. It says much for our ignorance of the Amarna Period that the existence of this major building, still without its original name and ownership being known, should have remained unknown until so recently.

Prior to Akhenaten the Egyptian year was punctuated by religious festivals, some great (like the Theban festivals of Opet and the Valley) and many small. Regular periodic festivals were so fundamental an expectation that we are bound to frame the question: what did Akhenaten put in their place? We know from texts from his Karnak temples that generous provision was made for daily offerings, and a tantalizing fragment of a similar inscription is known from Amarna.[37] But these texts have so far failed to document periodic festivals. Here again we encounter a surprising vacuum. The worship of the sun provides a ready-made set of calendrical feasts, the solstices and equinoxes, the celebration of which can be built into temple architecture. Yet Akhenaten's conception of the sun seems to have been so simplistic (or pure, depending on one's point of view) that no attributes of the sun's annual behaviour were incorporated into theology. Even more surprising is the alignment of the temples and altars at Amarna. They are clearly dictated by the topography of the city, and not by celestial factors. This was true of New Kingdom temples generally (though not of the far earlier pyramids and their associated temples). The failure to set up a programme of celebration and feasting with popular appeal built around the Aten, as distinct from around the king, could well have been a most important reason for Akhenaten's failure.[38]

Only two great celebrations are documented at Amarna, and both focused on the king. One of these was a second Sed-festival,[39] the other a huge reception of foreign envoys and their diplomatic gifts and tribute held at Amarna in the king's twelfth year of reign.[40] For the former we have no expansive sources at all, and it remains entirely guesswork as to where we wish to locate the main ceremonial. For the latter, two private tombs record in great detail the contingents of foreigners as they are led before the royal family in order to render formal homage and offer exotic gifts. Egyptian soldiers are present as well, but whether in numbers greater than formed the normal royal bodyguard we cannot tell. The setting is depicted as an open space containing a number of small buildings: principally a platform reached by stairs and shaded by a roof supported on columns. This is where the royal couple sat to wave recognition to the advancing and retreating representatives. Not far away stood a standard group of three 'Sunshade' platforms, the largest one walled around and containing an offering-table. On either side of them are shown what look like two enclosures containing supplies of food and drink. It is very difficult to identify this place on the ground, for we cannot necessarily assume that the architectural setting is shown in full. If it is we can point to an isolated set of buildings in the desert between the North Palace and the North Tombs. It is known as the 'Desert Altars' (Figures 89, 91, pp. 271, 277).[41] In its final phase an area of desert approximately 250 by 300 metres was cleared of stones. A set of three buildings (I–III) was constructed inside, along a single axis. No. III is the brick foundation for a pavilion consisting of a platform reached by ramps. The intricate internal plan represents a pattern of foundations for lines of columns erected on top of the platform, showing that the building was roofed, and may well have contained an inner nucleus of walled or columned rooms as well. Building II is the group of three 'Sunshades'. The central one had been rebuilt at some stage, so that a single central offering-table was replaced by a pair. Building I was another platform reached by ramps but this time the platform was left open to the sky. In the centre a square, brick-lined depression may mark the original position of a standing stone (a benben-stone?) anciently removed.

Buildings II and III within their setting of something resembling a parade-ground look very much like the scene in the tomb of Huya. It is true that there is nothing to match the enclosures for food supplies and Building I does not appear. But it is possible that the site saw more use, in which, as the excavators thought, Building III was demolished. Thus Building I could have been built for some purpose after the reception of year 12, a purpose which saw the remodelling of the central 'Sunshade'. The whole site would then have been like Malkata on a small scale, an arena for celebratory architecture of short duration.

For the assembled emissaries from abroad the long wait in the sun was an ordeal. From one such occasion the representatives of the king of Assyria, Ashuruballit I, later complained of this to their master, who subsequently and with sarcasm passed their complaint back to Akhenaten:

> Why are my envoys kept standing out in the open sun? They will die out in the open sun. If it does the king good to stand in the open sun, then let him stand out in the open sun himself, and let him die himself. Then will there be profit for the king![42]

But, as the tomb scenes clearly show, by means of sunshades and canopies Akhenaten took good care to protect himself from long exposure to the rays of his god.

We are still left, however, with an important gap between daily ritual largess and occasional great ceremonies. If there were periodic festivals through the year we can scarcely doubt that they focused on events in the life of the king and his family.

The archaeology of institutions at Amarna

Akhenaten's interests were directed towards intellectual and ideological goals. Although political consequences came in their wake, and one set of institutions – the temples – must have been badly disrupted, there is no sign that he attempted to change the nature of the state itself, or of Egyptian society. We have many sources for the workings of the state in the New Kingdom. At Amarna we possess a physical profile, a kind of giant theatre, of what this might mean on the ground.

Behind the evidence for palaces and chariot drives lies an important general point on the tenor of royal government: the physical as well as symbolic separation of the king and his family from the outside world. They lived away north in the great fortified palace in the North City, emerging – how frequently and regularly we cannot tell – to descend in splendour on the King's House in the Central City. This was their base for worship in the temples, meeting and rewarding their senior officials and holding reviews. The King's House provided for the routine face-to-face contact with working ministers. Many of these lived almost as far away in the opposite direction. The vizier Nakht, for example, resided nearly 2 km away in the south, and some other houses of the very largest size lay even further beyond. It is interesting in this connection to observe that even those officials closest to the king – those with the decorated rock tombs – still depicted their main contact with him as taking place in the King's House.

The King's House lay at the heart of a complex of buildings which catered for the worldly business which the king was obliged to conduct (see Figure 89, p. 271). Administrative linkage tied these buildings to the King's House so that they formed parts of a greater 'palace', although no architectural recognition was given to this essential unity of purpose. There was no wall to surround them and bind them together.

An unpretentious spread of little offices intended to house the archives and officials of those departments which worked directly beneath the king lay immediately behind the King's House. Except in two cases, little in detail is known of which departments occupied which offices. One exception is the 'Bureau for the Correspondence of Pharaoh'. Late in the 19th century AD, the local villagers discovered inside it the hoard of little clay tablets now known as the Amarna Letters, the archive of diplomatic correspondence briefly discussed in Chapter 5. The other building in this group the purpose of which we know from labels stamped into the bricks was called 'The House of Life'. By this term the ancient Egyptians referred to an institution where scrolls on religious and other serious topics (medicine, astronomy, etc.) were studied and copied. Its copies of old texts would have made it into a library, and it is noteworthy that Akhenaten did not dispense with this traditional centre of learning.

This technical apparatus of government was housed very modestly. Much more space was given over to servicing the patrimonial side of kingship: the distribution of goods and rations. The King's House consisted of three principal parts: a small palace, a courtyard with a formal avenue of trees, and a large set of storerooms or magazines. There were several entrances, but the principal ones were on the west either from the Royal Road or from the Great Palace via a bridge, and on the north between a pair of pylon towers. The small palace may have been of more than one storey, in which case we have lost all information about the upper parts which are likely to have been more private. The ground floor seems to have consisted of several small robing rooms (distinguished by their brick screens), storerooms, and a large columned hall. In a side hall a platform had been built against the north wall. On the outside of the wall at the very same point the surface had been decorated with a painted panel, depicting bound foreign captives. This is a key piece of evidence, for it serves to locate the Window of Appearance which so often appears in the private rock tombs at Amarna, with just such a decorated panel beneath it.[43] The window must have been an opening in the wall immediately above, furnished with a balcony, the royal family standing partly within the opening and partly on the platform immediately behind. The reward ceremony took place in the great courtyard, the recipient entering between the pylons and making his way towards the window down the avenue of trees. The depictions of the ceremony concentrate on special occasions: gifts of gold and other precious things, or the formal announcement of a promotion to higher office (see Figure 92, p. 278). However, we know from the Horemheb Edict cited several times in previous chapters that the reward ceremony at the window could also be used for regular distribution of rations. This served as a repeated ceremonial reinforcement and reminder of the dependence of high officials on the king. The proximity of the large storehouse block is thus explained. It was used to store the commodities issued as rations to the king's officials. Part of it, perhaps much of it, must have been a granary. We can tell this from the brick compartments for the storing of grain, exactly reproduced in one of the Amarna tombs.

The floor space of this granary is about 2,000 sq. metres, thus about one quarter of that at the Ramesseum considered in Chapter 5, but capable of storing grain for the support of several thousand people, though still only a fraction of the city's likely total population. The order of magnitude belongs with that suggested by the Memphite palace bakery records of Seti I also mentioned in Chapter 5. An interesting little problem enters here. In the best-documented community of the period, the village of

Deir el-Medina, the workmen were paid in grain, and used grain as one medium of barter-exchange. But records of large-scale ration distribution, some from palaces and major temples under the heading of 'offerings', list bread and beer as the form in which cereals were distributed. On what grounds the decision was made to prefer loaves over sacks is not known. Perhaps the former were reserved for a supplementary or short-term ration rather than a permanent and total sustenance paid throughout the year. But the preference of temples for bread and beer points to an interesting gap in the evidence. Even where temple layouts are well preserved (as at the Ramesseum), no bakery is present, despite the very distinctive traces that ancient bakeries leave: numerous ovens, deposits of ash, and large amounts of broken pottery bread-moulds. The nature of such deposits probably explains their absence. Bakeries were smoky places, producing soot, ash, and sherds, and better kept outside sacred precincts. Somewhere in the vicinity of the Ramesseum, therefore, but outside the walled enclosure, a large bakery and brewery must have lain that have so far escaped detection.

At Amarna, however, where the ground outside temple enclosures is as accessible as the ground inside, two large institutional bakeries have been excavated. They occupied long ranges of narrow parallel chambers, running close beside the southern enclosure walls of the two Aten temples (Figure 96).[44] Each chamber was a single baking unit, containing one or more circular ovens of standard domestic design at the back. Various brick bins lined the walls. The total number of baking chambers in the bakery beside the great Aten temple amounted to more than a hundred. Details of what went on inside are illustrated on one of the Hermopolis blocks (Figure 96), depicting part of a bakery. From one side of a courtyard two chambers open. The curvature across the top of each one probably depicts a vaulted roof. In each chamber a man tends an oven. Behind the one on the left, flat round loaves are stacked on a table; behind the other, the table bears instead long cylindrical bread moulds. This reflects the two basic Egyptian baking methods: flat loaves baked on round mud trays, and tall narrow loaves baked inside cylindrical pottery moulds. Fragments from tens of thousands of such moulds are not only heaped on the desert behind the central Amarna bakery, they seem largely to bury the baking chambers as well.

The pottery moulds are a distinctive type, easily recognizable amidst a collection of ancient sherds. A study of the pottery recovered from the huge excavations at Amarna reveals, however, that their distribution was very uneven. They were rare in the residential areas, and common around the central bakeries. What was so special about mould-baked loaves? By the New Kingdom they seem to have denoted a sense of occasion, in particular of religious occasion. It may not be coincidence that in both cases these bakery blocks adjoin not only the king's particular domain but also the Aten temples. These were nominally the owners of the tract of land which supplied the nucleus of the city's food. Yet unlike normal New Kingdom temples, no granary was built within their precincts. The only large granary that can be definitely identified in the Central City is that belonging to the King's House. This suggests a very direct royal control of temple wealth, something consistent with the general tenor of Akhenaten's reign. The Aten temples were his very personal creations, and evidently, to judge from the Central City layout, an extension of the domain of the palace.

The form of these bakeries is very revealing of the Egyptian approach to organization. Here was a major challenge: how to bake bread in industrial quantities? A modern

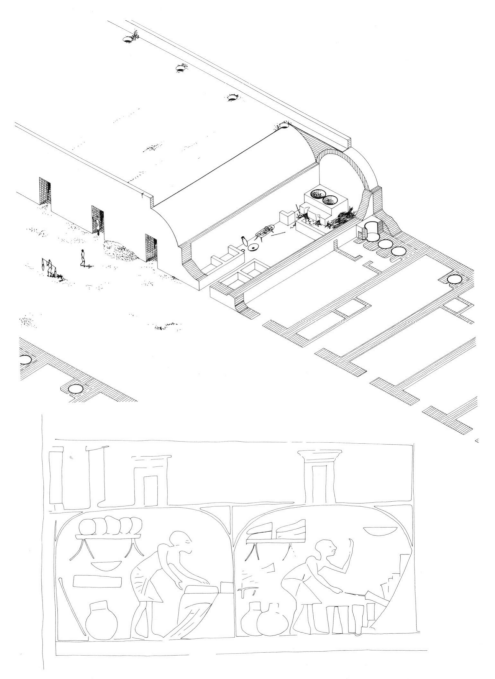

Figure 96   The temple bakeries in the Central City, a rare example of large-scale factory production though characteristically arranged in the form of repeated cellular units. The scene below, from an Amarna block found reused at Hermopolis, is after J.D. Cooney, *Amarna Reliefs from Hermopolis in American Collections*, Brooklyn and Mainz, 1965, p. 73.

approach might be to rethink the whole organization of the process and to redesign the ovens, giving them larger capacity, so that the ratio of loaves to manpower would be improved. This is the mentality of 'productivity' and 'efficiency'. The Egyptian solution was very different. It was simply a repetition, over and over again, of the basic domestic kitchen until the necessary capacity was obtained. This presumably involved a simple multiplication of the necessary number of people as well, subdivided into as many teams as there were chambers, each chamber under its overseer, and all working under the responsibility of an official. This seems also to be the system behind the bakery records from Memphis from the reign of Seti I, less than fifty years afterwards, discussed in Chapter 5.[45] There the responsibility for baking rested with the mayor of Memphis. It is worth noting that Amarna had its own mayor, too, although the location of his house is not known, only that of his tomb (no. 13).[46] This cellular approach to a large-scale operation offers a paradigm for the whole ancient system. It was a system based on a ready supply of cheap labour. This is why we can say that in organization the ancient Egyptians could be very effective, but we cannot say that they were at all efficient.

The city's water supply illustrates the same phenomenon. The demand for water was substantial, for it had to serve not only the inhabitants and their livestock, but also the trees and other vegetation that grew in the gardens of the larger houses. Although the city lay alongside the Nile, many houses were more than 1 km distant, and so it was given an independent water supply through the provision of numerous wells, although some of them lay only 350 metres from the likely line of the ancient river bank. Our general lack of excavated town and city sites from Egypt makes comparison difficult, but such evidence as there is does not parallel Amarna in the number of its wells. The whole large town of Kahun, for example, must have been supplied with water carried in from a source outside the town walls. Malkata, Deir el-Ballas, and Medinet el-Ghurab seem to tell the same story. Deir el-Medina similarly had to rely on water brought in by donkey, although attempts were made in the 20th Dynasty to remedy this by sinking a rectangular shaft provided with a continuous staircase in the vicinity of the village, which reached the astonishing depth of 52 metres.[47] The unique density of wells at Amarna could represent another of Akhenaten's novel schemes, in this case to provide his new city with a supply of water independent of the Nile.

The design of the wells – the large ones at administrative centres, the small ones in private estates or for public use amongst the houses of the poor – had one notable feature in common: they relied on the human carriage of water for part of their depth. They seem to have been regarded as deeply sunk water-holes: the vertical distance for water to be lifted by means of a rope and vessel or, in the case of the large administrative wells, use of the *shaduf*, was kept as low as possible by sinking the mouth of the shaft itself into the ground, so that it had to be reached by a spiral staircase in a large circular pit. Some restored examples can be seen in Figure 98, p. 295.

The excavation of one large administrative well in 1987 also revealed a serious technical problem which faced the well diggers, at least in this instance.[48] Dig down into the desert at Amarna and the thin layer of surface sand and gravel is found to cover hard marl bedrock. Continue cutting down through this, and eventually one breaks into a thick stratum of soft pale grey sand. This is the aquifer which contains the fresh water. At this particular point it began about 7 metres beneath the surface. The sand is so soft, however, that on exposure it rapidly collapses. A modern solution would be to aim for a narrow well shaft lined with a good solid material, such as stone or fired brick, and to raise the water with ropes and perhaps a labour-saving lifting device. The ancient solution was, as just noted, quite careless of labour. The water was to be raised by porters who carried it up in pottery vessels on their shoulders. Thus for most of its depth the well was a large open pit, 9 metres square, provided with sloping ramps. Just above the soft sand aquifer the pit narrowed to a shaft, and the only means used to inhibit its collapse was to plaster around the sides an irregular layer of sand and clay. It was not particularly effective, and must have been seen as such. The difference between the width of the shaft and of the upper part allowed some leeway for the gradual collapse of the former, and thus its gradual widening until it began to undermine the rock walls of the latter. At this point the well would have become progressively more unsafe and would eventually have had to be abandoned. By the end of the Amarna Period this one sample well was approaching this point.

The King's House was the centre of conspicuous consumption for many officials. Most of what they received here they took home with them, but still a residue of richer-than-usual rubbish accumulated. The principal place for disposal was a tract of waste ground on the edge of the Central City, beside the main police post.[49] When examined by Flinders Petrie in 1892 it was found to be rich in broken glazed finger-rings bearing the cartouches of kings and fragments of little bottles made of coloured glass, and also to contain large numbers of broken pottery jars imported from the Aegean or east Mediterranean, the prototype design coming from Mycenae. As imports they may well have contained oil.

The scenes of the king's public life which dominate the decoration of the rock tombs give a conspicuous place to soldiery. Wherever the king goes we see contingents of Egyptian and foreign units from the army. This is in keeping with the strong military element in New Kingdom society, and fits some of the statements in the Horemheb Edict, where a constantly changing royal bodyguard is referred to. Yet in the city layout military architecture is notably absent. The North Riverside Palace looked from the outside like a great fortress, and in its outer parts we can perhaps detect the outlines of a barracks for the king's own bodyguard. But there is nothing like this in the Central City or in the housing areas. What we do find on the far eastern edge of the Central City is a set of buildings evidently for a force of men and chariots, the horses kept in a set of stables with cobbled floors, mangers, and tethering-stones. Outwardly, however, the buildings remained plain and unfortified. We know from the rock tomb of the chief of Medjay-police, Mahu, that order was kept in the city by a force of police equipped with chariots who were separate from the normal army.[50] There has to be a strong presumption that these buildings were the Medjay-headquarters. A smaller police post, again without the architectural trappings of fortification, lay in the desert a short way behind the South Suburb.[51]

We can deduce from the spread of evidence at Amarna that although the army formed part of the barrier between the king and the outside world, and although the king generally travelled as part of a military contingent and saw the world framed as much by soldiers' spears as by the rays of the Aten, militarism and contact with the army were not part of the normal experience of city life in the New Kingdom. One might have a military officer as a neighbour, but in his house he would have led a civilian-style life (cf. the neighbourhood plan, Figure 97).

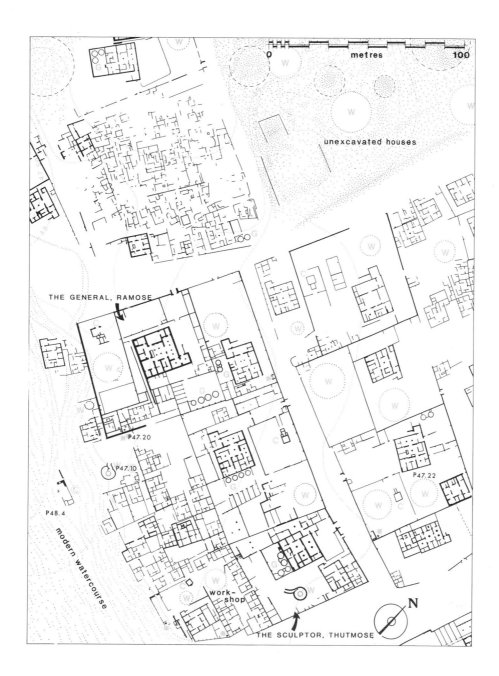

Figure 97 Plan of a characteristic part of a residential area at Amarna, in the Main City. The famous painted bust of Queen Nefertiti was found in the house of a sculptor, whose name may have been Thutmose. The letters on the plan are: W: (well); C: (chapel; the two in a circle were public chapels); G: (granary). The asterisk indicates the probable presence of a pottery kiln. Figure 98 is based on part of this map.

Our picture of the Central City depends largely on excavations carried out in the 1930s, but although conducted on a large scale they by no means exhausted the ground covered by 'official' buildings. These continued for a considerable distance along the sides of the southward prolongation of the Royal Road. Although never excavated in modern times their outlines are visible on old maps, aerial photographs, and to the discerning eye today. They appear to be primarily storehouses and perhaps granaries.[52] Whereas those around the King's House can be fitted within the important redistributive function of kingship in Egyptian society, the context and therefore the meaning of this range of buildings are largely unknown, and to this extent our picture of the city is incomplete.

Suburban life

Most of the resident population of Amarna lived in two large housing areas north and south of the Central City: the North Suburb and Main City. The Middle Kingdom had seen the growth of a tradition in Egypt of simple grid planning, applied to the streets and houses of settlements up to the scale of full-size towns. But in the New Kingdom the idea of total planning lost its attraction. We have already seen this, in effect, at Thebes, in the contrast between the rigid symmetrical planning of individual temples, and their casual interrelationships which were disguised by linking processional routes. In Amarna, outside the corridor of royal buildings, planning petered out altogether. Instead of a grand unitary design we find a few broad but far from straight streets running more or less parallel to the Nile to join the suburbs to the centre, while narrower streets cross at right-angles. The overwhelming impression is of a series of joined villages. The individual house plots interlock in complex patterns, creating distinctive neighbourhoods (Figures 97, 98). Sometimes groups of larger or smaller houses occur, but the two types are often intimately mixed. Within them rich and poor lived side by side. There was little concept of prime location, other than frontage to one of the main north-south thoroughfares. Exceptionally in the North City a group of unusually large houses lay adjacent to the main palace (the North Riverside Palace), and from this we can guess that they housed people with a particularly close relationship to the king. But otherwise proximity to the Central City or to the Royal Road seems to have held little if any attraction. It has already been pointed out that one of the king's most senior officials, the vizier Nakht, lived almost as far away from the king as he could. The house of the High Priest Panehsy (one of the favoured few with a large tomb in the northern group as well as an official residence beside the Great Aten Temple) lay in the Main City well back from the Royal Road; another priest, Pawah, lived in a large house in the middle of the Main City. Business in the Central City and with the king meant commuting, by chariot. This is also faithfully recorded in the tomb scenes.

The plans of individual Amarna houses are remarkably uniform, irrespective of size.[53] Although it is rare to find two identical houses, the same elements are constantly repeated in slightly different combinations (Figure 97). The main feature is a square, central living-room. At one end stood a low brick dais, where the owner and his wife would sit to receive guests. Against another wall was sometimes a plastered stone

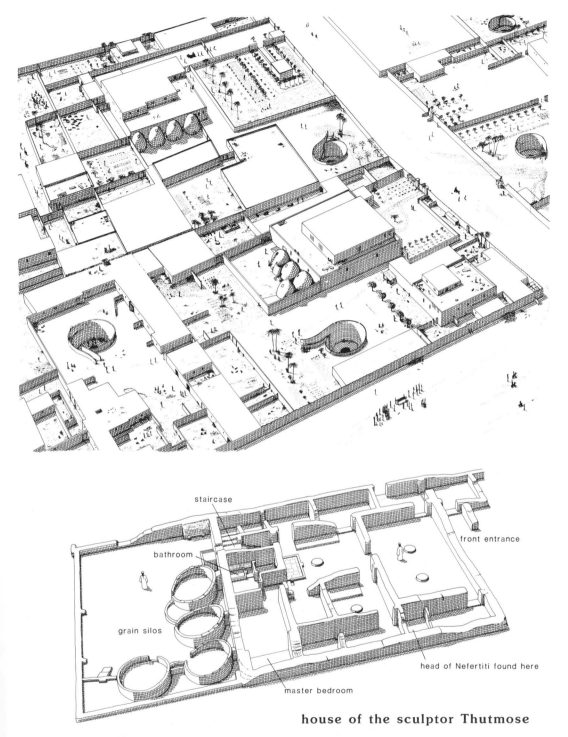

staircase

bathroom

grain silos

master bedroom

front entrance

head of Nefertiti found here

house of the sculptor Thutmose

Figure 98 Perspective reconstruction of part of the area of Figure 97. The house of Thutmose is shown in the condition in which it was found when excavated in 1914.

washing-place. One or more wooden columns would have raised the ceiling sufficiently to allow windows to be inserted high up in the walls. In large houses such windows took the form of stone grilles. Around the central room were grouped others: an outer reception room, storage rooms, and the more personal domestic quarters. One principal bedroom served the owner, in which a wooden single bed stood at the back in a raised alcove. Beside it, ideally, was a bathroom and lavatory. Liquid waste disposal, however, was of the simplest kind. There is no trace at all of a public drainage system within the city.

As far as we can tell, the houses bore little decoration. Outside and inside walls might be plastered and whitewashed with gypsum, but beyond this the richer houses contained only very limited areas of conventional paintings, mostly geometric designs. And as for the lifestyle and activities of the people who lived in these houses, archaeology is helped out by other sources, including a few ancient pictures (Figures 99, 100).

One problem faces archaeologists everywhere. If we find only the ruins of a building, how can we tell if it had more than one storey? It is generally accepted that in Amarna the houses were of one storey only. The windows beneath the raised ceilings of the central room guarantee this for the central part. Many houses, however, also possessed an internal staircase. It is commonly assumed that this led just to the roof, a useful area for storage and summer sleeping, except in the case of large houses where an upper room may have lain over the front part of the house. This offered a greater degree of privacy suitable for the important behavioural sphere of womanhood. Recent excavations at the Workmen's Village, however, have shown that this upper room may have been far more widespread.[54] It is a point which future excavations should clarify.

The ideal house stood within its own grounds, surrounded by a wall which could reach at least 3 metres in height, its main entrance marked by a pair of low projecting walls which guided chariots in at right-angles and so prevented the projecting ends of the axles from catching the door posts. The loose arrangement of elements in the compounds stands in marked contrast to their carefully prearranged place in the formal Middle Kingdom layouts discussed in Chapter 4 and exemplified at Kahun. Many details of usage are still not clear but the general outline is tolerably so. The list of basic elements is:

1. granaries: up to a certain individual capacity they were tall, circular constructions of brick, in diameter about 2.5 metres on average, and with domed tops (Plate 11). The principal grains were wheat and barley, and they were poured in at the top and withdrawn through a trap-door at the bottom. However, over a certain size they were replaced by long vaulted rooms of the kind that form the basis of 'magazines'. Then, since other commodities were stored in them as well, it becomes much more hazardous to estimate stored grain capacity;
2. animal byres: generally identified as sheds with roof supported on several square brick pillars;
3. a well;
4. a garden with trees, presumably for both vegetables and flowers;
5. kitchens: they often lay at the southern end, downwind of the prevailing north wind, which reduced nuisance from smoke (except to neighbours). They were simple

Figure 99 The activities of a large house, as seen by an Egyptian artist at Thebes. At first sight the picture portrays a multi-storey house, but it is also possible that the main parts on the left follow one another laterally at the same level. The principal scenes show: (1) spinning linen thread and weaving linen at an upright loom, whilst at the right-hand edge a figure leans over a quern grinding flour; (2) the main reception room, where the house-owner sits on a chair on a low dais and is waited on; the rectangles running along the top of the wall are likely to be windows; (3) an inner room where the house-owner is evidently conducting business with two scribes who squat on the floor; (4) a row of grain bins; (5) a butcher at work cutting meat on a table and hanging joints on a line to cure. After N. de G. Davies, 'The town house in ancient Egypt', *Metropolitan Museum Studies* 1, 1929, pp. 234–5, Figs. 1A, 1B.

    affairs: small groups of circular clay ovens used primarily for baking bread. When cooked meals were prepared an open fireplace was used, again outside the house, with cooking probably done in bronze or copper basins;

6.   sheds and enclosures of uncertain purpose, though in some cases they could have been used for craft activities. Sculptors, whose debris archaeologists can easily identify, are one group whose workshops were in and beside their house compounds;

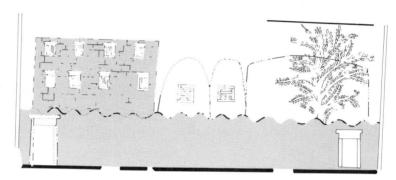

Figure 100   Two ancient views of houses. *Below.* A house in its grounds, surrounded by an enclosure wall with a wavy finish to the top. Two grain silos and the roof of another building are visible above. From the tomb of Anena at Thebes, after N. de G. Davies, *Scenes from Some Theban Tombs (Private Tombs at Thebes, IV)*, Oxford, 1963, Plate XXIII. *Above.* Outline of an Amarna house from a limestone block reused at Hermopolis. After J.D. Cooney, *Amarna Reliefs from Hermopolis in American Collections*, Brooklyn and Mainz, 1965, p. 74.

7.   a shrine, which in the houses of the richest stood in its own formal grounds with ornamental lake and separate pylon entrance to the street;

8.   separate accommodation, including a porter's lodge at the gate, but most importantly a completely separate house. It remains a mystery who occupied this house: a steward, a married son, servants?

Houses of rich and poor are distinguished more by size than by design, although larger houses did possess features, such as an entrance porch, which denoted status in themselves. If we take the size of a person's house as even a rough-and-ready measure of his status in society, the spread of house sizes provides a general profile of the kind of society we are dealing with.[55] An easy way to view the whole mass of data is in tabular form (Figure 101). Although there are some jumps and gaps the overall pattern of the data fits a single curve in which, beyond a point of very basic housing, ever-larger houses grow steadily rarer. There are no obvious breaks or plateaux. If we remember that this was a time of great national prosperity, the gulf between rich and

Plate 11 Private wealth: the bases of circular brick granaries in a private estate at el-Amarna, house U24.1, looking north-east. The diameter of each silo is about 3.5 metres. By courtesy the Egypt Exploration Society.

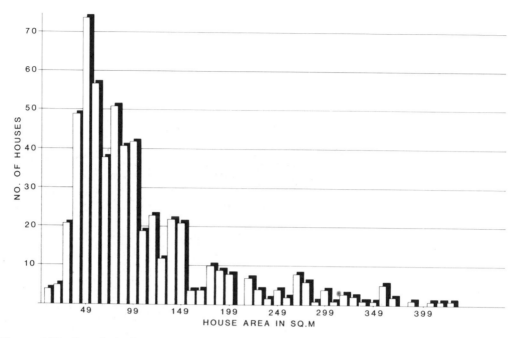

Figure 101   Bar-chart showing the frequencies of houses of varying sizes within the Main City at Amarna. House sizes are given in steps of 10 sq. metres. The regularity of the curve of distribution is striking. After Piers Crocker, unpublished dissertation, University of Cambridge, and cf. 'Status symbols in the architecture of El-'Amarna', *Journal of Egyptian Archaeology* 71 (1985), 52–65.

poor in this respect was not as great as we might expect. The rich and powerful lived in large houses, not in palaces. The great gulf was between the king and everyone else.

Maps of the city which mark walls and spaces as black lines and white background create a clinical effect which can be misleading. So do reconstruction drawings which turn Amarna into a pleasant garden suburb. To gain a true impression of what it was like to be there we need to begin by making a record of the total debris of human occupation. Figure 102 is a small section of a modern plan which aims to do just this. It shows a section of the city before excavation, although some parts have been disturbed by the probings of treasure hunters in the last century. The surface undulates, forming a very complex pattern of mounds and depressions, here portrayed by contours. On first walking over the ground the effect is very confusing. Greater familiarity, however, leads to some understanding, particularly from subtle variations in the composition of the surface. These enable one to distinguish between mounds of rubble and sand which cover unexcavated houses, and those which are the remains of ancient rubbish heaps. The latter are shaded in Figure 102. We must allow for them having spread out in the three millennia that have passed since they were formed, and also for some loss of volume as sand and dust have been blown away. We are then left with a picture in which, away from the broad north-south thoroughfares, prominent heaps of domestic refuse had formed in more or less every available open space outside the walled compounds of the better-off. They loomed close to public wells, and must have reduced access to the smaller houses down to narrow paths winding amongst them. They may spoil the image we have of Akhenaten's city but we should not mind them. The original occupants accepted them (they could, after all, have carried their rubbish further away) and for the archaeologist they are now of great importance. In earlier days of archaeology at Amarna people excavated houses in the hopes of finding the things that the original occupants had left behind. The results were often disappointing, for two reasons. The city was not abandoned in a great rush: people seem to have had plenty of time to pack up their belongings; and, in any case, Egyptians were given to sweeping their houses out regularly. But what they swept up they didn't carry far. Figure 102 includes part of the large house and compound of one of the senior officials at Amarna (Q46.1). The front gate lay on the east, opening on to the main road; the back gate looked out on to a small area of waste ground. Just to one side is a large rubbish heap, originally banked against the compound wall. It is strongly tempting to identify this as the main rubbish heap from the big house. The big house was excavated in 1914, the rubbish heap is still undug. If we want to complete our record of what the occupants left behind we must dig here as well.

Akhenaten stripped away the cloak of institutionalized religion, and in so doing exposed for a short while the raw bedrock of general belief. In these unique circumstances we can examine how people responded, both during Akhenaten's reign, and later, when, for a while in the reign of Tutankhamun, large parts of the city continued to be lived in and the threats to the old order had been lifted. As we have seen, the cult of the king fared well, even in back gardens. Those who could afford a walled garden frequently included within it a little shrine to the royal family. But how it was used by the inhabitants and what it represented emotionally to them we do not know. It may have been more than lip service or an empty gesture of expediency, for in the ensuing Ramesside Period the cult of royal statues patronized by officials reached its peak.[56] Furthermore, statues of Akhenaten in the private garden shrines appear not to have been in the grotesque style favoured by the royal buildings. Akhenaten was manipulating a real and strong source of power. Pharaoh had always been a god, and the cult of the new royal image may have found a real emotional target. So, too, with the Aten. For lack of evidence and from the eventual failure of Akhenaten's ideas to survive his death it is easy to conclude that the cult of the Aten had little popular following. Yet in the midst of this negative picture stand two unique papyrus letters written by a minor official from Amarna to his relatives on entirely private matters. In them the Aten is freely used as a bestower of blessings, just as Amun and other deities were in the letters of other periods.[57] If history had run a different course, and subsequent kings had maintained the cult of the Aten, it is possible to imagine from evidence such as this that the Aten would have developed a truly popular aspect.

As we saw in Chapter 5, the big traditional temples had little peripheral shrines on the outside of the walls where people who were not priests could make contact with a great deity and leave a votive offering. This satisfied the urgings of piety, and at the same time, if the donation were a statue or something similar, it became a statement of one's ability to command such a thing and thus enhanced one's prestige in the community. It is impossible to identify equivalents at the Aten temples, but certainly the opportunity for private temple donations remained. This is well illustrated by a group of bronze vessels discovered in the Sanctuary of the Great Aten Temple. One of them had been dedicated by a military officer, a 'standard-bearer' named Ramose.[58]

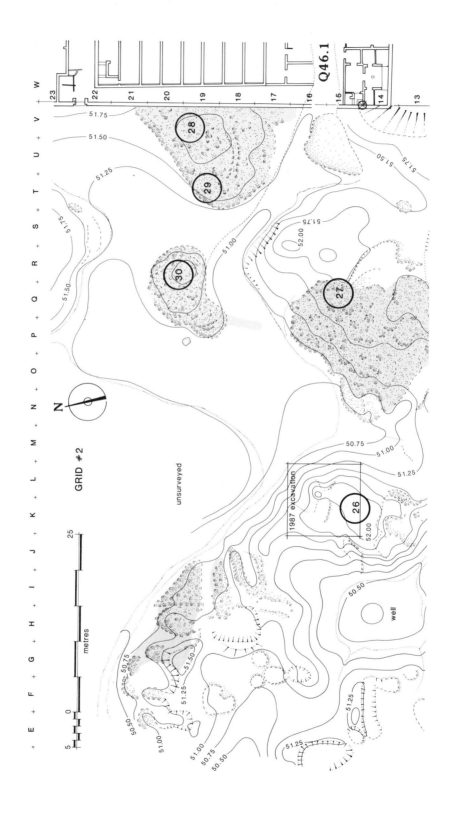

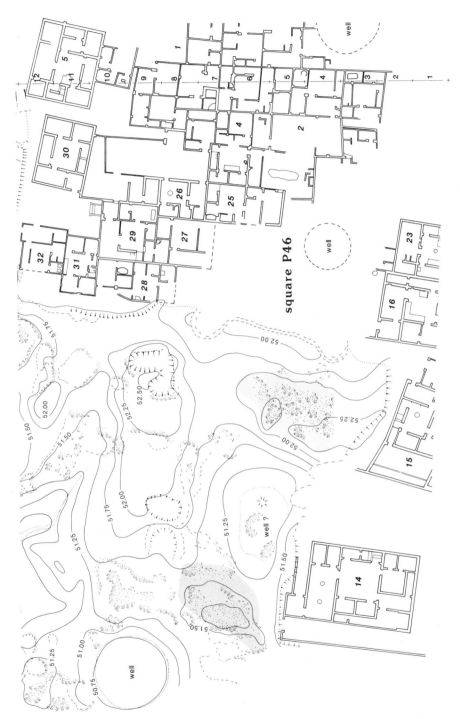

Figure 102 The residential part of Amarna as archaeological site. The plans of houses excavated in the 2nd and 3rd decades of this century are shown in outline. The remainder of the area must continue in the same way, with some of the mounds marking the positions of unexcavated houses. Other areas, however, can be distinguished as ancient rubbish mounds, and these are shaded. Heavily drawn numbered circles are sherd samples. Unpublished plan.

The general tenor of Akhenaten's religion was that the king would serve as the focus for prayer, and in the temple to the king's statue (R43.2) on the edge of the Central City, we have a likely venue for this level of cult (see Figure 95, p. 284). There were, however, other centres of spiritual interest in Egyptian lives largely independent of institutionalized religion.

At the Workmen's Village, a community tied particularly closely to the state, the families built their own chapels just outside the village walls.[59] In time they would have become places of burial and memorial for deceased members of the family and we would have called them tomb chapels. But their first function was to serve as centres where family meals could be eaten on certain occasions in a calm and sanctified atmosphere. This was close to an abiding ideal for Egyptians generally. As we shall see in the next section, a great many of the citizens of Amarna probably retained very close links with other towns and cities. This was where most family tombs were and we are entitled to imagine that in the course of a year a pilgrimage home for a special meal at the ancestral tomb was an event anticipated with much relish. But this is not the end of the story. Many of the Workmen's Village chapels were built after Akhenaten's death. The villagers felt free to choose to commemorate the gods they favoured. Whom did they choose? The evidence is small, but does consist of a few references to Amun and Amun-Ra in short prayers painted on the walls, and limestone stelae to the goddess Isis and Shed 'the Saviour', who offered protection against accidents, such as scorpion sting. But the Aten is present, too, demoted from his unique status but certainly not ignored.

One way generally of defining the area of non-priestly, i.e. non-professional, belief in ancient Egypt is to look at private votive material, which is the result of personal choice involving some effort or expenditure. Amarna does provide some, although not in the quantities and concentrations that accumulated in the old cities around the temples. One little group of stelae comes from the porch around one of the southern rock tombs, which belonged to a scribe called Any.[60] The donors were evidently friends of his and his brother, and the subject of their dedication was the deceased Any himself. They reflect an ancient custom of honouring on the fuzzy borderline between respect and worship the spirit of a man who had achieved great eminence in the community (the antecedents of modern sheikhs), and who could in a few rare cases, e.g. Amenhetep son of Hapu, go on to become minor gods.

The remaining votive material from Amarna mostly consists of a thin scatter of flakes and small slabs of limestone bearing designs in ink or in rough carving.[61] The subject matter includes figures of divinities: the baboon-god Thoth (patron of writing), Ptah (particularly associated with Memphis), a sacred ram, and Thöeris (goddess of childbirth); and representations of the process of gaining attention: a figure of a man making offerings before an altar, and a set of crudely painted ears by which the god's hearing was aided. If we look for concentrations of this kind of material hoping to identify actual shrines in the city the results are largely negative. A stele showing a man before an altar came from a collection of rooms beside one of the public wells in the North Suburb (T36.67), but the plan of the walls tells us little: they have neither the character of a house nor of a shrine. Evidence from the Main City is a little better. Again beside a public well a little building was excavated (P47.10) which looks from its plan like a shrine, although no votive material accompanied it (see Figure 97, p. 293).[62] Not far away, apparently in the same open space although the context had been largely destroyed by denudation, the same excavation uncovered a small building which is the strongest candidate of all for a shrine in a public place (P48.4, see Figure 97, p. 293). Apart from its shrine-like plan, a well-made limestone stele was discovered depicting a man adoring before a table of offerings, and above him a group of three deities, the holy family of Elephantine: Khnum, Satis, and Anukis.[63]

Most of the votive material, however, and it is not numerous, comes from houses, small and large, and raises the question as to whether it was intended for some special little place in the house itself. A few of the larger houses had small platform altars inside, but the one collection of votive material found in position (house N49.21) came from the tiny room beneath the stairs.[64] It consisted of a stele showing a woman and girl before Thöeris, parts of two female figurines and two model pottery beds. The last items represent a much more numerous category of evidence for an area of domestic cult that centred on the ambience of womanhood and the danger and mystery of childbirth.[65] It embraced the goddess Thöeris and the dwarf and demonic god Bes, a popular subject for tiny glazed pendants strung on necklaces. At the Workmen's Village Bes and Thöeris appear on wall paintings, and there is some evidence that an upstairs room with special wall paintings supplied the focus for domestic femininity.[66] Domestic cults included a cobra deity, probably the goddess Renenutet, to whom little statuettes and figurines moulded into the bottom of pottery bowls were made.[67]

A pattern emerges at Amarna which has probably a general validity for New Kingdom religious practice. We can discern four basic directions of attention: towards images of the king (and in normal circumstances statues of major gods in extra-mural shrines at large temples) as a source of great but remote authority which can sometimes be beneficially tapped; towards the family chapel which contained the family tomb and which gave status and sanctity to the concept of family-with-ancestors; towards cults centred in the household and especially that of domestic femininity; towards a varied collection of deities and occasional revered humans who drew out feelings of respect and could offer that general sense of hopeful well-being that is contained in the English word 'blessing'.

Profiling Amarna's population: direct and indirect evidence

How large a population lived in the city, and perhaps of more real interest, what kind of people were they? The first question has to be disposed of briefly because of inherent technical difficulties. Enough of the city has been excavated, and enough of the remainder can be traced in outline on the desert, to form the basis for an estimate of how many houses were originally present altogether. From this we can proceed to a further estimate of how many people they housed. This is the real point of difficulty. There is surprisingly little direct evidence for average household size in ancient Egypt,[68] and the best we can do is to use figures both from recent village communities in the Middle East, and turn-of-the-century census returns from Egypt, which themselves show wide variations from place to place. Furthermore we have to consider the possibility that ancient Egyptian households embraced not only a nuclear family but also an assortment of dependants. The best that we can attempt, therefore, is a general order of magnitude for Amarna. Two such exercises in estimation have been carried out, producing figures of between 20,000 and 30,000 in one case (and using an average household figure that is perhaps too modest), and upwards from 50,000 in the other.[69]

In considering the composition of this sizeable population we are focusing our attention on the basic profile of ancient Egyptian society in general, and at the same time exposing the serious limitations of our evidence. In a tiny proportion of cases a house will have a direct element of personal identity. Usually this is because we know the name of the owner. It was the custom for leading citizens to frame their front doors in stone or wood on which their names and official titles were carved. Unfortunately, when the city was abandoned it would seem either that most people took such expensive fittings with them, or that termites have thoroughly consumed the wood, so that only rarely do we know who lived where. The most important person in this category was the vizier, or chief minister, named Nakht, already noticed, with a particularly large house with extra columned halls but which was still tiny compared to the royal palaces. We have also noted the houses of two priests, Panehsy and Pawah. Military officers had houses scattered through the city: Ra-nefer, a chief charioteer, owned a quite modest house on a corner in a neighbourhood of small houses or workshops; a commander of troops, Ramose, had a somewhat larger house a few streets away (see Figure 97, p. 293). The owners of two more houses must have been involved in Akhenaten's construction works. One, an overseer of builders, Maa-nakhtutef, had an unpretentious house in the Main City. Away in the north, in the North Suburb, an overseer of works, Hatiay, was close to completing a new house for himself on the outskirts of the city when the call came to abandon everything and leave. The handsome painted door lintel was left lying in front of its intended destination, the front door. The most famous occupant from the point of view of modern public interest, however, was one Thutmose, a sculptor (see Figure 97, p. 293).[70] His studio, close to his house, lay in a part of the Main City where other sculptors lived and had their workshops. The workshops were simple courtyards with little huts built against the walls. When the city was abandoned, unfinished sculptures and pieces used as models were left lying about or were packed away in the sculptor's house. One such piece was the famous painted head of Queen Nefertiti.

Such examples of individuality are, however, exceptional. The city remains for us generally an anonymous place, but this simply means that we must work harder with such evidence as we can muster. And this means casting our net over written and other evidence from a broader background than the Amarna Period alone, always remembering that Egyptian society changed over time and from one province to another.

We can begin by setting up an expectation – or a model – of what kind of population we would find in a New Kingdom town. One of the Ramesside robbery papyri used in the last chapter to illustrate the movement of sudden wealth contains a list of the households to be found in western Thebes (excluding Deir el-Medina).[71] In all, 179 are listed, and of these 155 belonged to a single settlement called Maiunehes. There can be no reasonable doubt that Maiunehes was the name of a town which had grown up in and over the ruins of the buildings which surrounded the inner enclosure of Rameses III's mortuary temple, Medinet Habu. A fragment of this settlement survived into the early years of this century and was excavated. Each household is defined by the name and occupation of the male head. The absence of women (in, for example, the category of widow) could well be a coincidental aspect of this one community since women had a property-owning role which was overtly recognized. Each 'house' would have had its own population, consisting of the nuclear family and probably its servants, too, since servants and slaves are not listed separately. We must therefore multiply the number of households by a suitable factor (around 6), to arrive at an estimate of the population of this town, which would then have been of around 1,000 persons. We can group the occupations of the householders into eight categories. They comprise: 7 senior civil officials, 32 priests, 12 scribes, 12 'military' (policemen and stablemasters), 13 junior officials, 31 urban craftsmen, 47 with rural occupations, and 1 with no occupation specified. This provides the first observation: all except one of the householders had a title or defined occupation. As just noted, there are no 'houses' of servants or slaves, which leads one to suspect that such people (probably not numerous in medium to small households) were accommodated within or beside the owner's building or buildings. There is one case of servitude, a small farmer who belongs to a scribe, but the scribe himself (who is named) did not live in the town.

We can look at this information in two ways: grouping occupations together to create an outline sociological profile, and considering whether the list has a topographic aspect. For the first, we have to remember that any divisions or groupings that we make will inevitably be arbitrary, a reflection of the relative social fluidity of ancient Egypt. The list itself illustrates this perfectly: two priests were also coppersmiths, and two of their colleagues had other civil jobs, one as an inspector and one as a chief guard. If, nevertheless, we make a rough division into two broad groups: 'officials' (including priests) who were paid to do a non-productive job, and those engaged in manufacture and agriculture, the result is a surprising fifty-fifty split (76:78).[72] This is to some extent accounted for by the presence of no less that thirty-two priests of various ranks. We can use the presence of the Medinet Habu temples to argue that this was a peculiar community, but other data (including the Wilbour lists of landholders, see p. 311) imply that in the later New Kingdom priest was a common occupation generally. This is not, of course, a sign of unusual spirituality, for being a priest was a job rather than a vocation.

Nearly a third of the householders of Maiunehes were engaged in agriculture and related tasks, but the proportions of the various subdivisions at first sight show that herding was more important than cereal crop-growing (represented by only six small farmers or 'cultivators' or possibly 'agricultural agents'[73]). This, however, could be misleading. There is abundant evidence (including the Wilbour Papyrus) to show that people of all occupational categories owned or rented farmland, both cereal fields and vegetable plots. This does not answer the question of who actually worked the land, the choice being between paid labourers and children, and less fortunate relatives who were members of the landholder's family. Maiunehes itself does not seem to have contained a significant labouring population divided into its own households. We might argue that such people lived dispersed in the adjacent lands and therefore did not find a place in the list, were it not for the fact that no less than twelve householders were fishermen. Even if they were fishing in back-swamps near the desert (drained and vanished in modern times)[74] rather than in the Nile, they are people whom one might have expected equally to have been living outside the town. Since children and poor relatives were cheaper than paid labourers, the families of Maiunehes could have resembled that of

Hekanakht who had lived in the area nine centuries before (Chapter 6). On his lands the agricultural work was done by the five men who were part of his household, and who were also probably his sons. Belonging to a household, either as a relative or as a receiver of patronage, seems to have been an important Egyptian wish, and if this were significantly the case at Maiunehes then the number of people that we put into the 155 households would rise well beyond the 1,000 mentioned earlier, and some of the households, as officially recognized, could have been represented on the ground by several houses in a contiguous group, as can frequently be picked out in the Amarna suburbs.[75] This also points to a major question in the social history of the ancient world which we are unable to answer: when did cities begin to acquire a significant urban proletariat, a population of men, women, and children who were simply workers, and who looked for their employment to a source outside their own household? The rise of this group would have been at the expense of the 'households' which seem to have been of great importance to the Egyptians, but we cannot be sure even if there was any change at all on this front during Pharaonic times.

The scribe who compiled the household list of Maiunehes did so without an obvious system of ordering. We can see this, for example, by looking where the Medjay-police occur. The seven members of this distinctive group are distributed singly throughout the list. This makes it at least plausible that the list was compiled on a street and neighbourhood basis.[76] If we look at the list in this light it makes very good sense. The scribe started from the group of perhaps five large houses of the leading men of the town: an army scribe, the mayor himself, and three others. We cannot know how he then proceeded along the tortuously winding streets, quite likely unintentionally separating households which were in fact neighbours of each other. Nevertheless several other groups survive (two groups of five priests, one of four sandal-makers, one of five and one of four herdsmen and goatherds), as well as pairs (e.g. of brewers, two of washermen, fishermen, coppersmiths, and scribes of the divine records). The list suggests a tendency towards occupational clustering, perhaps involving families who were also related by blood, yet no rigid segregation since most occupations are also found adjacent on either side to others, often of very different status.

This very generalized impression of Maiunehes fits the Amarna suburbs very well. There is a tendency towards clustering of larger as against smaller houses, but no more than that, certainly no rigid separations. It is also possible to distinguish amongst the smaller houses contiguous groups, as if belonging to a family network. If such a group of small houses containing several related poor families were treated administratively as a single household it would explain the lack of a labouring and menial class in the Maiunehes list.

Occupational clusterings at Amarna are harder to locate. A conspicuous occuption in terms of its debris was that of sculptor. Several workshops have been found, and these seem by and large to have been confined to one zone withing the Main City, though with insufficient density to merit the term 'sculptors' quarter'. Another workshop of apparently similar form (and not far away) but with a very different output was partially excavated in 1987.[77] In plan it consisted of a rectangular enclosure surrounded by a buttressed wall lying adjacent to the large well described earlier. A series of rooms had been built against the inner face, surrounding an open central space. Amidst the ash and rubbish in which the building had been progressively buried as it was used was evidence for manufacturing of various kinds, including glazing and pottery making. The excavated area also actually included the factory where the pottery had been made. The evidence that had been left behind was of four kinds: one or possibly two puddling pits where the potters' clay was first prepared; an actual potter's wheel found thrown into a pit; several hundred mud sherds from unfired vessels, many of them cast away by the potter after faulty manufacture; and pottery kilns. The surviving kilns number two: one abandoned after much use and filled with later rubbish; the other one replacing it and never actually used. The mud sherds are particularly interesting for they show the range of vessel types being manufactured, which was surprisingly wide, and included cobra bowls and also female figurines. Furthermore, whilst most of the sherds had been made from Nile silt, some seem to have been made from desert marl clays. Red and yellow colouring was also found on some.

This discovery not only clarifies the manufacturing processes of New Kingdom pottery, it has wider implications for the city as a whole. In knowing what one set of kilns and its associated debris look like, it has become profitable to search for further examples in the plans and descriptions of previous excavations. Several likely kilns have been identified amidst the houses, and some of them actually re-excavated. This has confirmed that simple pottery kilns lay within the grounds of some of the larger private houses, P47.20 and P47.22 (see Figure 97, p. 293). Surprising to our point of view is that the latter one lay quite close to where a private chapel stood. We can also add to this evidence the observation that pieces of vitrified kiln occur widely over the main suburban area, creating a strong presumption that pottery-making was quite common and widespread at Amarna, and not only within special factories that we can suspect were run by the state, but also within the grounds of private houses. The same was also probably true for the making of little glazed rings and other ornaments widely worn at this time, whilst it has long been established both by actual finds and by ancient tomb pictures (see Figure 99, p. 297) and models that the spinning and weaving of cloth was another standard domestic industry.

Amarna was not a city of quiet garden suburbs. Quite apart from the rubbish that filled every open space in the main suburb, the houses were busy centres of private manufacture as well as of the storage and handling of farm produce. They were generators of part of the city's economic substance.

The farm-centre aspect is well documented, for the larger Amarna houses look like little farms, and in so doing both reflect the commodity-based nature of the Egyptian economy, and at the same time make an important contribution to the debate about private economics in New Kingdom Egypt. We can estimate that the capacity of an average silo not filled to its entire capacity was about 9,500 litres, equivalent in ancient terms to about 125 *khar* of emmer-wheat.[78] At the Theban necropolis Workmen's Village of Deir el-Medina a skilled artisan's annual wage for his family included a maximum of 48 *khar* of emmer, whilst the foreman received 66. For guards and porters the annual rate was 24 and 12. The payments in barley seem to have been about a third. Thus two or three of these silos, a not uncommon number in the Amarna house compounds, would appear to suffice a family with a purchasing power somewhat larger than a Deir el-Medina foreman's. However, the Deir el-Medina householders did not have large silos to store their grain in. They were paid monthly and evidently consumed most of it, either as food or as a medium of exchange. They did not, in other words, accumulate grain balances. To be able to do that was a significant mark of status. The groups of silos at Amarna thus indicate two possibilities (as alternatives or present together): either storage of an annual harvest, or a monthly receipt of ration payments far in excess of basic needs.

To form a better judgement of what lies behind the silos we must turn again to outside data, and consider certain aspects of the agrarian economy and landscape of the New Kingdom, beginning with the extent and nature of private landholding in the New Kingdom. Hereditary possession of land was possible. A text known as the Inscription of Mes introduces us to a parcel of land granted by King Ahmose at the beginning of the 18th Dynasty to an 'officer of ships' as a reward for military service.[79] About three centuries later, in the reign of Rameses II, we find the same land still in the hands of the same family, descendants of the original hero, now squabbling over its division into lots, and appealing to a duplicate set of government land records, kept by the treasury and by the department of the granary, wherein was recorded the history of ownership. A papyrus of the time of Rameses IX (Papyrus Valençay I) is even more explicit in drawing a distinction between *khato*-lands of the Pharaoh and privately-owned land whose taxes were paid independently to the treasury.[80] We must add to this the evidence (particularly from the Wilbour Papyrus, discussed on p. 311) for the widespread leasing of temple lands, with hints that this might have been a hereditary practice. Put the evidence together, and we have the outline for the private sector of a highly complex pattern of landholding in which a 'farm' was not a single discrete parcel of agricultural land, but a whole series of scattered plots held in more than one way: either owned outright or rented from a temple or from some other landowner.

And the 'farmers'? They were none other than people with official titles who, for a position of respect and comfortable living, needed the income of a small estate. The school exercise texts make this very clear. In addition to the model letters they contain pieces which dwell on the benefits accruing to the successful literate man. They cast his lot not as a constant round of important duties in official surroundings but as a life of bucolic ease in one's villa, surrounded by the produce of a well-stocked and well-managed farm.

> You go down to your ship of fir-wood manned from bow to stern. You reach your beautiful villa, the one you have built for yourself. Your mouth is full of wine and beer, of bread, meat and cakes. Oxen are slaughtered and wine is opened, and melodious singing is before you. Your chief anointer anoints (you) with ointment of gum. Your manager of cultivated lands bears garlands. Your chief fowler brings ducks, your fisherman brings fish. Your ship has returned from Syria laden with all manner of good things. Your byre is full of calves, your weavers flourish. You are established whilst (your) enemy is fallen, and the one who spoke against you is no more.[81]

The emphasis on the self-made aspect of the official is notable. No hint here of the good life being handed down from the king in return for loyal service. This is also, of course, the ideal portrayed in many tomb pictures of the New Kingdom and earlier periods. Officials of whatever kind looked forward to an eternal life which featured prominently the pleasures of watching with serenity happy peasants working the fields of the estate.[82]

Our need to sharpen the focus of generalized pictures of this kind is again served by

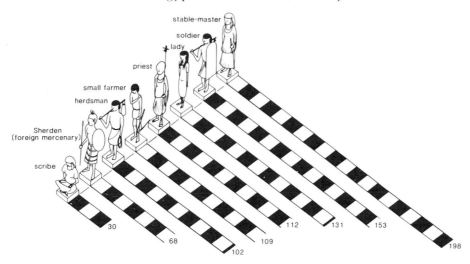

Figure 103 A social profile: categories of persons renting land in Middle Egypt in the 20th Dynasty (after Wilbour Papyrus). Each square represents ten persons.

occasional written statistical data. Thus the Wilbour Papyrus (see p. 191) offers a little profile of the categories of person who rented fields from temples in an area of Middle Egypt late in the New Kingdom (Figure 103). This has some surprising features, the high proportion of women being one. The numbers of soldiers (including Sherden mercenaries) is probably a local peculiarity, though it well reflects the practice of settling army veterans on the land.[83]

The appearance of the rural landscape in ancient Egypt has to be left very much to the imagination. Archaeology gives us direct evidence for towns, and the continuity of landscape and farming practices from ancient to recent times provides a good basis for picturing the rural scene in a very general way. But as to how much settlement there was outside the towns, and of what kind, we have only a hazy outline. As noted early in this chapter, the Amarna Boundary Stelae refer to 'villages' across the river, but we lack any evidence as to how many and who lived in them. Perhaps the closest we can come to a New Kingdom source for rural landscape and settlement is the Wilbour Papyrus.

This huge document is a register of measurement and revenue assessment for certain categories of agricultural land in a stretch of some 150 km in Middle Egypt in year 4 of Rameses V (1142 BC), thus towards the very end of the New Kingdom.[84] It is not a list of places, but in referring to plots of land it makes frequent reference to places large and small. It is almost certainly not a complete account of the area, and how the places lay in relation to one another is something that is extremely difficult to decide. But there is still no other source which approaches it for detail. About 416 settlement names are given, and these can be assigned to each of four zones. With the most important places, judged by the amount of land they owned or controlled, we can go some way towards locating them on a map. For the rest, all we can do is to assign them as blocks to a particular zone. The nature of the place names is very much like that of modern Egypt. Some are 'proper' names, but a large number are compounds in which the first element is descriptive. In modern Egypt the commonest are *Kôm* (mound), *Bet* (house), *Ezbet* (originally a settlement for a landowner's peasants), *Naga* (properly an originally Arab Bedouin settlement), *Zawiyet* (a hamlet), and *Deir* (a Coptic Christian monastery). Amenhetep III's palace at Malkata, for example, stands today beside a modern village called Ezbet Basili, named after a prominent landowner of former times with the Coptic-Greek name of Vasili, who actually lived in Luxor, across the river. Wilbour gives us *Iat* (mound), *At* (house), *Wehit* (hamlet), *Bekhen* (an official's villa), and *Sega* (tower). Altogether there are 141 of these places, subdivided as follows: 51 mounds, 37 houses, 29 hamlets, 17 villas, and 7 towers. They are not, however, spread evenly through the four zones. 'Houses' tend to be more numerous in zones where there were fewer larger towns, whilst 'villas' and 'towers' cluster in zones marked by larger towns. For our enquiry the most interesting of the groups is the villas (*bekhen*). This is the very term used in the scribal exercises for the official's residence so abundantly stocked with farm produce. The same texts say of the ideal villa that it is 'upon the ground of your city' in one case, and 'in your city' in another. Wilbour territory saw a concentration of these in zones of larger towns, specifically near the provincial capital of Herakleopolis.

Wilbour territory has another contribution to make to our understanding of who lived in a 'capital' city. The place names just discussed have as their second element a personal name, 'The villa of so-and-so'. They are thus the ancient equivalents of Ezbet Basili. These names are common Egyptian names without titles so that, lacking the local knowledge which the people of the day had, we can learn nothing more from them, except in one case. One of the villas was 'of the vizier'. We can insert here one further small source for one of the zones: the cemetery for Herakleopolis itself, which lay on the nearest piece of desert in an area now known as Sidmant el-Gebel. Several New Kingdom tombs excavated early this century bore evidence of who their owners were.[85] Some were people prominent in local society, which in practice meant the priesthood of the local temple. We have an Amenhetep, who was a priest of the local god Heryshef, and an Amenemhat, who was a divine father in the same cult. There is also a record of a mayor called Menena. The remainder, however, are officials of court or army: Nebenkemt (chief of bowmen and fanbearer on the royal boat Khaem-maat), Sety (general, overseer of attendants of the Lord of the Two Lands, ambassador in all lands), Pahemneter (deputy commander of chariotry, chief of bowmen), and Rahetep and Parahetep (viziers), and possibly an earlier vizier called Tuthmosis. These are just the ranks of officials whom we find at Amarna and could probably have been found at Thebes, Memphis, and Per-Rameses.

Amarna itself provides a classic instance, in the person no less of the man who was to become king after Tutankhamun, Ay. A strong case can be made out for regarding Ay as a member of a prominent family whose home was the city Akhmim, in Upper Egypt. His parents would have been a couple, Yuya and Tuyu, whose tomb in the Valley of the Kings was discovered early in this century. They had earned this honour because their daughter had married Amenhetep III and had become his principal wife, the queen Tiy. Typically for this as for other periods, the family had leading positions in the local Akhmim priesthood and in the army. Ay himself took over the army titles. When he finally became king he was able to make an impressive gesture towards Akhmim, having a small rock-cut temple hewn in the cliffs behind the city.[86] This is symptomatic of another aspect of New Kingdom Egypt. As pointed out in Chapter 5 this was the first time for many provincial towns or cities to possess a prestigious stone-built temple.

Embellishing it or adding to its lands provided important people with a fine opportunity for munificence to their home town, recorded in a dignified way for posterity.

In the New Kingdom the key mode of entry for a young person to high position was to be brought up at court. For a man this brought the honorary title 'child of the Nursery', and for a woman, 'king's ornament'. As far as we can tell entry was by personal contact and recommendation. But it is clear that whilst there were doubtless families whose main base and permanent home was a royal city, many officials must have come from families based in the provinces. One member at court opened up a channel for others. The degree of attachment to home must have varied, but the Herakleopolis cemetery shows that even viziers could feel it so strongly as to arrange to be taken home to be buried. Now it becomes clear why in Wilbour territory so many officials from all ranks all the way up to the vizier leased land. Even if their rank linked them closely to the court or to campaigning army units many of them had strong home ties extending to a villa with its agricultural lands. The Herakleopolis viziers were among those who maintained a villa in the nearby countryside.

We can now better understand the social and economic basis to Amarna. For some of the officials the houses that we see must represent all that they had in terms of property, and when this included silos and stockyards they were to store the produce of the lands which they managed, which were probably not too far away. Akhetaten included the large tract of agricultural land on the west bank. It would have been typical of the Egyptian way of doing things for this land, although presumably expropriated by Akhenaten for the Aten, to have been leased out to officials with a house in the city. For others, and how large a proportion we cannot tell, the city villa was not everything. They retained the provincial links of their origin and this inevitably included property rights and hopes of further inheritance. In view of the sudden changes of fortune that could occur when a new king came to power it was probably very prudent to maintain these links and to look forward to an eventual retirement and burial in the place of one's birth. Indeed, there may well have been a sense of exile in setting up home in a royal city.

Links with a provincial and semi-rural base were easy to maintain. Egyptians were inveterate letter-writers, and regular Nile travellers. Two letters written by an 'oil-boiler' called Ramose from Amarna have actually survived, intended for his brother, a treasury scribe at Thebes, and for his sister.[87] We can tell from their contents that they were part of a regular correspondence. A boat was amongst the range of desirable personal possessions. Visits – vacations – were also formalized in two ways. One was the sporting expedition, for fishing and fowling, which was a full family outing, as tomb pictures frequently show. The other was the pilgrimage to the family tomb: to inspect it, arrange for further work, and to sit down to a special meal in the spiritual company of ancestors. We have already seen that at Thebes the 'Beautiful Festival of the Valley' was used as a general occasion for a pilgrimage and night vigil at tombs. We can hardly doubt that provincial towns and their cemeteries had their equivalents (there is a well-attested Middle Kingdom case at Asyut).[88]

When we examine Amarna houses we find not only a great variety in individual capacities to store grain, but also that this variety does not particularly match the size of the attached house.[89] The two signs of status and wealth – house size and silo/magazine size – are to some extent independent. We can explain this by saying that villa economies reflected both the income of the owner and the extent of provincial ties. The full property list of the vizier Nakht, for example, may have included not only the house in the Main City at Amarna but properties at his home town, wherever that was. One of the school texts makes just such a distinction between the urban context of the ideal villa and agricultural holdings at one's village:

> I will build for you a new villa upon the ground of your city, surrounded with trees. Its stalls are inside, and its granaries are full of barley and emmer-wheat. . . . I will tend for you five *arouras* of cucumber-beds to the south of your village, and the cucumbers, carobs and [translation uncertain] will be as abundant as the sand. Let ships come to load them up.[90]

Continuing provincial connection also explains a much more flagrant anomaly at Amarna. Akhenaten's Boundary Stelae declare that amongst the works to be done at Akhetaten is the making of tombs for officials, to be located in the eastern desert. From this declaration two groups of rock tombs emerged, the North Tombs and the South Tombs. Their numbers, however, fall far below the number of officials who, so we can estimate, lived in the city. For this estimate we can take the smallest house known to have been occupied by an official, which is actually N49.18 (the chariotry officer Ranefer). We can then assume that all houses of this size and above are likely to have belonged to such people. They actually number sixty-five. The excavated housing zones represent something like 50 per cent of the total likely residential area, so that we must think in terms of around 130 as at least an order of magnitude for officials of more than modest rank. This may well be too exclusive, however. As already noted, there are no jumps in house sizes as one moves up the social scale. But certain features do appear with houses of increasing size. One of these is an entrance porch. If we take this as a sign of ownership by people of some status, i.e. of officials of more than the most minor rank, the excavated total rises considerably. One study has shown that of the 120 largest houses only 15 lack this feature.[91] If we take the figure 120 as a base for houses of 'officials', and still this is only 15 per cent of the total number of houses excavated (and a small proportion compared to the households of Maiunehes), and allow for the excavated sample being only about half of the original, the number of those who might have been expected to provide a decorated tomb for themselves and their family rises to 240.

Nearly all the tombs at Amarna remained unfinished when the city was abandoned. Starts had, however, been made on forty-three. They varied a good deal in size and elaboration, reflecting the varying status and resources of their owners. Despite their unfinished condition we can still make one subdivision: between those intended to have an internal columned hall (or more than one), and those which were not. We have sixteen of the former, twenty of the latter, and seven where we just cannot tell at all. The pattern of ownership of the two groups reflects what we might expect. People who, by their position, we would expect to be important have tombs in the former category, with the columned hall. They include the vizier Nakht(pa-aten), the mayor of Akhetaten Neferkheperu-her-sekheper, the chief priest Merira, the personal stewards of Nefertiti (Merira II) and of the queen mother Tiy (Huya), the chamberlain Tutu who may well have been in charge of correspondence with foreign powers and client rulers in western Asia, and the chariotry officer Ay, subsequently to become king.

The total of forty-three rock tombs is obviously a lot smaller than the total number of officials who had houses at Amarna. Furthermore, the number of those who were established early enough to see much progress made on their tombs was a good deal less, around twenty-five at the most, although the same must have been true to some extent in the city: it continued to grow until the end as more people moved in to start a career there. But the imbalance remains. An explanation which fits the known pattern of New Kingdom society is not hard to find.

When a king came to the throne he brought with him a circle of people who had shared his upbringing. This must have signalled a change in several key posts of power, the ousted holders perhaps retiring to their place of origin if they came from the provinces. This change of faces must have extended some way downwards into the ranks of officialdom before petering out. At Amarna the rock tombs were a sign of closeness to the king or to his favoured officials, and a statement of commitment to the new order. That there were relatively so few we can perhaps take as a sign that even in the extreme circumstances surrounding this particular accession the change of faces was very restricted in numbers, although not necessarily in influence. We are talking about an exclusive royal coterie of between twenty to thirty men at any one time. Most of those who moved to Amarna and who did not belong to this exclusive circle left behind roots either in a royal city or in the provinces, roots which included a family zone within a cemetery, and, for a wealthy minority, a rural estate to enjoy in retirement. Indeed, the move to Amarna probably encouraged burial plans to be made around the old family tomb. The tombs that were made at Amarna carried in their decoration the stamp of the new king's preferences. The tomb owner, instead of basking in the attentions of his family, whiling away the hours on his estate, and making sure that he was familiar with some of the gods of the underworld, now looked on in humility and adoration whilst the royal family worshipped the Aten and paraded themselves around the capital. In the privacy of your tomb Akhenaten's new scheme threatened to be with you for ever.

A royal city was populated in part by families whose permanent home it was, in part by people from the provinces there for a career, hoping that their foothold would provide future access for sons and other relatives. In Akhenaten's time the main royal cities were Memphis and Thebes. Where did most of the Amarna population come from? In the first four years of his reign Akhenaten must have spent much time at Thebes, both to supervise the construction of the new temples and for the celebration of his *Sed*-festival, held uncharacteristically early in his reign. His reliefs show a palace in the city of Thebes proper. His father, Amenhetep III, had likewise spent much time at Thebes in the later years of his life. To this end he built the Malkata palace which was large enough to accommodate the court for the periods of weeks, perhaps even months, that they spent there. But Malkata was nowhere near the scale of a royal city, and apart from a token presence of caretakers was probably not used much after Amenhetep III's death. The Theban evidence does not really support the idea that the 18th Dynasty kings lived there for long enough to warrant the permanent establishment of houses for the full range of officials and their dependants who ran the king's business. The nearest thing to a 'home base' for the kings was Memphis, and much of the officialdom which served the king's interests lived there permanently. Akhenaten's interests must have been partly identical to his predecessors' and, in the staffing of the Aten temples, partly new. Where the latter personnel were drawn from we do not know, although there can scarcely have been a suitable group available who lay outside the stratum of society which normally filled official posts. But for many, their most likely previous place of residence was Memphis, even if their family roots were in the provinces, including at Thebes itself. (The two unique private letters written from Amarna which were mentioned earlier were destined for relatives living at Thebes, where the letters were found, one to a brother, a 'scribe of the treasury'. They were, incidentally, found in a tomb. Would the writer also have hoped to be buried amongst his Theban relatives?). And when the experiment was over and Tutankhamun left Amarna and issued a decree of restoration for the temples, it was issued from the royal residence in Memphis even though the temple of Amun at Thebes was the main beneficiary.[92]

In Chapter 6 it was pointed out that the ancient Egyptian economy is regarded by many scholars as a two-tier edifice: an administered collection and redistribution of commodities as rations at the top, overlying the closed domestic economies of villages lying outside the state's various institutions, leaving no room for the existence of a free market for goods, not even a restricted one. For New Kingdom society in general, and for Amarna in particular, we have to ask ourselves: could such a system account for all that we see?

We have already had occasion, in Chapter 4, to draw attention to one of the physical consequences of an ancient structured view of society, one consisting of a small number of top bureaucrats and a large number of others, the latter economically dependent upon the former: the town of Kahun (and probably many others of the Middle Kingdom). This offers a physical counterpart to the two-tier economic system outlined above. This kind of model community was also, in Chapter 4, contrasted with Amarna. As we have now seen in more detail at Amarna the more or less continuous gradient of house size and other status indicators (see Figure 101, p. 300), as well as the interlocking horizontal pattern of houses of different sizes, suggests a pattern of economic relationships of some complexity. The residential parts of the city look for all the world like an aggregate of villages and neighbourhoods, each with its many layers of dependence, economic and otherwise. Yet if the city plan implies the existence of a great variety of individual household demands and circumstances, it follows that the two-tier economic model would have to offer an equally flexible and finely tuned means of supply, primarily from the overwhelming state sector. This defies common sense, as well as such evidence as we have for the New Kingdom. For, if anything, the New Kingdom seems to have been somewhat less orientated towards extended bureaucracy than the Middle Kingdom.

We can be in no doubt that the private means existed to satisfy a demand side to the economy. It is all too evident in the substantial though varying provisions for the storage of grain and other commodities at private residences. The surpluses could have come from the owner's harvest (on owned or rented lands), and/or from ration handouts from the state. We must also accept that a proportion of officials at Amarna had links with more distant estates and houses in their home provinces. The more successful officials were, therefore, institutions in miniature. Their households also, to varying degrees, engaged in manufacture. In foodstuffs and goods, private estates had surpluses to dispose of, through gifts and also through sales, the latter sometimes delegated to the 'traders'. This mixed economic system was effective, for it spread resources in a fairly even gradient throughout this large city.

Amarna was not a typical Egyptian city. No royal city ever could be. Memphis, Thebes, Per-Rameses in the delta must each have had its individuality from the initiatives of ambitious kings. Yet the remains at Amarna still manage to illuminate New Kingdom society at all levels, from top to bottom. Two aspects need particularly to be stressed. One is the great coherence of Egyptian society, through the intimate ties which linked urban populations to the country and so made even a great capital city an aggregate of villages. The wealthy had prestige and patronage, but they were not remote from ordinary life. Nor can we identify, or even suspect, the existence of an urban proletariat living and working outside this tightly knit neighbourhood pattern. The city in ancient Egypt was not an alien place, although internal mobility brought many encounters and juxtapositions between strangers. It was firmly embedded within Egyptian society as a whole. The second aspect is the separation, almost the removal, of the king and royal family from real life. They lived physically isolated in a corridor of buildings which in their size and style frequently bore little relation to the domestic surroundings of even their high officials. They lived psychologically isolated in a charged atmosphere of sycophancy, religious ritual, and militaristic pageant. Contact there had to be with officials, but this was institutionalized at the King's House, which stood at the centre of a web of economic and political tics, well represented on the ground by a range of different buildings.

Outside the royal areas, in the teeming city neighbourhoods, the king and his entourage recede into the background, and icons are the main reminders of his presence. In the larger houses we see the officials living, or struggling to achieve, the good life of private income and state donation promised by the school texts, dividing their time and loyalty between their city house and their family home in the provinces, writing letters and making visits to keep in contact. In the small houses crowd a range of people of lower status, some servants, some holders of minor office, many making things for sale: sandals, linen, beds, baskets, beads; perhaps near the river bank fishermen and boatmen ferrying into Amarna sellers of vegetables, fodder, pigeons, honey. More boats bring in the grain, livestock, wine, and other produce from the estates of establishments: the larger private households and the palace and temples. And all the time exchange: the haggling of lesser folk buying their heart's desire with a basket or sack of trinkets, the deals of traders at institutional magazines buying with gold and silver, or in the grounds of their employer's home selling grain or meat.

Busy people, idle people, doubtless some desperate and many harassed people: much of the city their world, independent even of an eccentric monomaniac king. This was to be the long-term reward for rulers seeking a life of sublime separation, surrendering their realm to economic man.

Epilogue: Onwards from the Bronze Age

The Egypt that we leave with the Amarna Period belongs to the last phase of the Bronze Age in the eastern Mediterranean. We should not quibble over the relative frequency of bronze versus iron at this time: the term Bronze Age has come to refer conveniently to the period of the first well-established states. In them we can see distinct reflections of ourselves and of our own societies. As such they form an important benchmark in assessing human progress. How has humanity, how have we, fared since then?

Civilization contains a paradox. It is the outcome of behaviour which, when personally encountered, can be nasty, but when distant we forgive because we approve of the end-product. This ambivalence in values is apparent when we consider the 'great rulers' and 'great periods' of the past.

In the last few years the field of Egyptology has seen the appearance of no less than three books on the life and times of the New Kingdom Pharaoh, Rameses II, 'the Great'. All are serious works, and one is a magnificent study of the society of the times written by an unquestioned master of the original sources.[1] All, though to varying degrees, accept that this was a glorious era, and that we should admire its triumphs, and at times cheer when the Egyptians win. The authors subscribe to a particular philosophy of history: that 'great' kings are a good thing, and that greatness is a sum of respect abroad won through military valour, and wealth and stability at home, celebrated by public works that render into permanent form the sense of achievement at large in the country. By such judgements we put ourselves on the winning side and reinforce this philosophy. Rameses II is great because when we read about him we look at the world through his eyes and like what we see: victory and success. Our own philosophy in this case is one that descends in a straight line from the ancients themselves. This is the way they viewed things, too.

The image of the wise put powerful ruler, stern with justice but benevolent to those who respect him, is an ideal that men have applauded down to the present day, even though their enemies will have looked to their own leaders in the same terms. Indeed, the parochial nature of this ideal undermines it as a philosophy of general benevolent progress. Anyone setting out to write such a history of one of the countries or peoples that Rameses II preyed on will see his 'triumphs' in a very different light.

There is, in fact, just such a study, on Nubia.[2] The author, W. Y. Adams, adopts the conscious philosophy of writing from a Nubian point of view. Nubian society prior to Egyptian conquests is a 'pastoral ideal', the Egyptians become the destroyers and Rameses II the 'megalomaniac pharaoh'. The problem for this view of Nubian history comes later. In the end the Nubians learned their lesson and became imperialists themselves, conquering Egypt and ruling for a time as the 25th Dynasty. Subsequently the successors of these Sudanese Pharaohs, whom historians call the kings of Meroe, must have extended their sway over many a simple pastoral people of the vast Sudanese plains. In the future an archaeologist whose speciality is these people may come to write a history of them in which the Meroitic kings are the vainglorious predators. It is a truism of history that, given the chance, the underdog imitates his master.

Yet the reader, whilst nodding in agreement, may also feel, in response to a commonsense view, that only under 'great' kings has civilization been nurtured. Their role in presiding over a society where artists and thinkers flourished outweighs in the long view of history the casualties amongst those who had to foot the bill. The fact that I am writing and the reader reading, instead of both of us gathering wild cereal grains, is possible only because in past times kingdoms and empires carved out oases of leisure for the gifted and the learned. Without the will to coerce his neighbours man would live in a perpetual Stone Age.

This cannot be denied. Paradoxically, however, it is the development of those attitudes, institutions, and traditions which inhibit absolute power and prescribe a universal morality for the conduct of affairs, and in so doing undermine the cosy ancient paternalistic view of the ideal ruler, that offers the principal claim to the existence of progress in the history of civilization. But whereas the great ruler and his admirers take care of themselves, the forces of rational opposition require nurturing.

Civilization got off to a good start, and Egypt is a good exemplar of its first products. Quite apart from mesmerizing achievements in the arts, and an oddly attractive open mode of intellectual speculation (which we see as religion), the Pharaonic state in its heyday had developed (as we can see with hindsight) a governing system of some rationality which, by massive institutional intervention in the agricultural economy, maintained stability of grain supply and of grain price and thus of the general economic structure and of the country's general economic well-being. It also had, and widely used, the power to direct labour on public works projects, offering in return a basic wage in the form of a grain ration at subsistence level and above. It acquiesced in the multiplication of part-time 'officials', so spreading the benefits of rank and extra income. It gave opportunities to those who were gifted. It allowed a limited private economic sector to flourish. As an answer to the problems of creating and holding together a 'state' we can call it, for convenience, the Egyptian Solution. Its apparatus was in many ways crude and it was built around a powerful ideology peculiar to its place and time, and one which now looks suspect: it was all for the glory of kings and gods. It was also not a unique evolution. It had counterparts elsewhere in the world, in Mesopotamia, the Indus Valley, China, and the pre-Columbian Americas. But despite the crude and the exotic elements we can recognize in the general shape the precursor to a common type of modern provider state. It was a solution to the question of how the state and its people should relate to each other that still, in different guises, has widespread acceptance.

Yet there is no direct and continuing rational line of evolution. By the New Kingdom in Egypt the evolutionary process in this direction had stopped. New Kingdom Egypt was a more loosely structured state, and subsequently Egypt moved on to become just one part of a Mediterranean world characterized by the chaotic and heady mixture of state power and individual assertiveness of which the modern west is the product. The Egyptian Solution seems to be a tendency which develops to an extreme degree in the course of the evolution of a society, and then moderates and sinks back into a more complex world of compromise between state and people. Logic is on the side of the provider state. It can achieve much in material terms if the people identify themselves with, or at least passively accept, the goals. But individual assertiveness allows logic on this scale only temporary victories.

Progress has made the modern world in many respects unrecognizable compared to antiquity or even the more recent past. Yet much of the progress in knowledge and in technology has revealed itself to be amoral. As many lives are diminished as are improved. The instant recognition that we have of 'great' rulers of the past is itself a sure sign of how little some very basic things have changed. It mirrors a current world scene that is alive with pointers to the undiminished power of this atavistic image, and the continuing virility of symbols and ideology, dogmas, rituals, and appeals to weird traditions, the whole spectrum of those devices by which people have been manipulated in the mass since the Bronze Age.

If we dare to accept that the progress of civilization is to be measured in the rise of those factors which inhibit or humanize the exercise of the power which started the process in the first place, what does make us different from our ancient ancestors? We should be suspicious of religion. For the west and for parts of the east the main religions of today are themselves rooted in the ancient Middle East, reflecting its limitations, and their personal ethics are nothing special. In their intolerance and willingness to join the forces of state formation they introduced a new aggravation of human unpleasantness, creating a celestial version of the 'great ruler'.

Where we really differ from the past is in possessing choice in the nature of our myths, and in understanding, even if imperfectly, the role that myth plays in our minds. At the two poles of our lives – our intuitive personal strategies to survive, and our direction by the ideologies and instruments of our states and communities – we remain as we have been since complex society first emerged. We still live in the shadow of the Bronze Age. The societies of the remote past, such as that of ancient Egypt, reveal this starkly. We can see in them the bare bones of human existence ever since. It is in the growth of rational myth and the parent bodies of stored knowledge that we are differently placed. And the most important knowledge is the objective view of mind, and the nature and role of myth itself. It is within our ability to make ourselves objects of scientific study, and to view ourselves and our own societies as products of an earlier world, isolating and seeing for what they really are the elements that survive from irrational and original myth, the divisive, parochial, and atavistic ideologies that we are still invited to support. The 'great ruler', with his panoply of visual aids, was a necessary instrument to start the process of civilization. Now he has been unmasked. We can set him within his proper context. As we begin to understand the process and choose rational humanitarian myths as our goals he should be needed less. The true study of man is a subversive subject.

Notes

List of abbreviations

AEL: M. Lichtheim, *Ancient Egyptian Literature: a Book of Readings* (3 vols), Berkeley,Los Angeles, London, 1973–80

AJA: *American Journal of Archaeology*

AJSL: *American Journal of Semitic Languages*

ANET: J.B. Pritchard (ed.) *Ancient Near Eastern Texts, Relating to the Old Testament*, Princeton, NJ, 1950

ASAE: *Annales du Service des Antiquités de l'Egypte*

BAR: J.H. Breasted, *Ancient Records of Egypt: Historical Documents*, (5 vols), Chicago, 1906–7

BibOr: *Bibliotheca Orientalis*

BIFAO: *Bulletin de l'Institut Français d'Archéologie Orientale*

CdE: *Chronique d'Egypte*

GM: *Göttinger Miszellen*

JAOS: *Journal of the American Oriental Society*

JARCE: *Journal of the American Research Center in Egypt*

JEA: *Journal of Egyptian Archaeology*

JESHO: *Journal of the Economic and Social History of the Orient*

JNES: *Journal of Near Eastern Studies*

JSSEA: *Journal of the Society for the Study of Egyptian Antiquities* (Toronto)

KRI: K.A. Kitchen, *Ramesside Inscriptions: Historical and Biographical* (7 vols), Oxford, 1968–in progress

LD: C.R. Lepsius (ed.) *Denkmaeler aus Aegypten und Aethiopien* (6 vols in 12) Berlin, 1849–58

Lexikon: W. Helck and E. Otto (later W. Helck and W. Westendorf) (eds) *Lexikon der Ägyptologie* (6 vols), Wiesbaden, 1975–86

MDAIK: *Mitteilungen des Deutschen Archäologischen Instituts, Abteilung Kairo*

MDIAAK: *Mitteilungen des Deutschen Instituts für Ägyptische Altertumskunde in Kairo*

MDOG: *Mitteilungen der Deutschen Orient-Gesellschaft zu Berlin*

NARCE: *Newsletter, American Research Center in Egypt*

NSSEA: *Newsletter of the Society for the Study of Egyptian Antiquities* (Toronto)
OMRO: *Oudheidkundige Mededelingen uit het Rijksmuseum van Oudheden te Leiden*
PM: B. Porter and R.L.B. Moss, *Topographical Bibliography of Ancient Egyptian hieroglyphic Texts, Reliefs, and Paintings* (6 vols), Oxford 1927– second edition still in progress
PSBA: *Proceedings of the Society of Biblical Archaeology*
RdE: *Revue d'Egyptologie*
SAK: *Studien zur Altägyptischen Kultur*
Urk IV: K. Sethe, *Urkunden der 18. Dynastie*, Leipzig, 1905–9
ZÄS: *Zeitschrift für Ägyptische Sprache*

1 The intellectual foundations of the early state

1 In general, see D.B. Redford, *Pharaonic King-lists, Annals and Day-books: a Contribution to the Study of the Egyptian Sense of History*, Mississauga, 1986.
2 Now in the Louvre, E13481 bis. See PM 2(2), pp. 111–12; also D. Wildung, 'Aufbau und Zweckbestimmung der Königsliste von Karnak', GM 9 (1974), 41–8; D. Wildung, 'Zur Frühgeschichte des Amun–Tempels von Karnak', MDAIK 25 (1969a), 212–19.
3 Now in the Cairo Museum, CG34516. See PM 3(2), 2.2, p. 666; D. Wildung, *Die Rolle ägyptischer Könige im Bewusstsein ihrer Nachwelt* I, Berlin 1969b, Taf. I; Sir A.H. Gardiner, *Egypt of the Pharaohs*, Oxford, 1961, p. 49, Fig. 8; J. Málek, 'The special features of the 'Saqqara King-List', JSSEA 12 (1982), 21–8.
4 G. Posener, *Littérature et politique dans l'Egypte de la XIIᵉ dynastie*, Paris, 1956, pp. 1–3; D. Arnold, *Der Tempel des Königs Mentuhotep von Deir el-Bahari* I, Mainz, 1974, pp. 92–5; Gardiner, op. cit., p. 127.
5 Sir A.H. Gardiner, *The Royal Canon of Turin*, Oxford, 1959. J. Málek, 'The original version of the Royal Canon of Turin', JEA 68 (1982), pp. 93–106, provides a provocative analysis of the text and the way in which texts of this kind could have given rise to Manetho's dynasties.
6 B. Gunn, 'Notes on two Egyptian kings', JEA 12 (1926), 250–1; Posener, op. cit., pp. 31–3; Wildung, op. cit., 1969b, pp. 104–52.
7 BAR IV, p. 228, §471; KRI VI, p. 19 ll.12–13.
8 E.g. AEL I, pp. 215–22.
9 Herodotus II, 124–7; W.G. Waddell, *Manetho*, Cambridge, Mass., 1948, pp. 47, 49.
10 G. Posener, 'Le conte de Néferkarè et du général Siséné (Recherches littéraires, VI)', RdE 11 (1957), 119–37; *Lexikon* V, p. 957.
11 AEL I, pp. 149–63.
12 ANET, p. 12.
13 Waddell, op. cit., pp. 61, 63.
14 AEL I, pp. 139–45.
15 D.B. Redford, 'The Hyksos invasion in history and tradition', *Orientalia* 39 (1970), 1–51.
16 BAR I, pp. 332–7; R. Anthes, *Festschrift zum 150 jährigen Bestehen des Berliner Ägyptischen Museums*, Berlin, 1974, pp. 15–49.
17 H.G. Evers, *Staat aus dem Stein*, Munich, 1929; C. Aldred, 'Some royal portraits of the Middle Kingdom in ancient Egypt', *Metropolitan Museum Journal* 3 (1970), 27–50.
18 AEL I, pp. 51–7, III, pp. 4–5; F. Junge, 'Zur Fehldatierung des sog. Denkmals memphitischer Theologie, oder Der Beitrag der ägyptischen Theologie zur Geistesgeschichte der Spätzeit', MDAIK 29 (1973), 195–204.
19 J.-E. Gautier and G. Jéquier, *Mémoire sur les fouilles de Licht*, Cairo, 1902, pp. 30–8. Good

photographs of two of the throne sides are in K. Lange and M. Hirmer, *Egypt: Architecture, Sculpture, Painting in Three Thousand Years*, 3rd edn, London, 1961, pp. 86, 87; also E. Otto, *Egyptian Art and the Cults of Osiris and Amon*, London, 1968, Plate 5.

20 On Seth, see H. te Velde, *Seth, God of Confusion*, Leiden, 1967.

21 Sir A.H. Gardiner, *Ancient Egyptian Onomastica*, London, 1947.

22 Chapter 15, Papyrus of Ani, as quoted by A. Piankoff, *The Litany of Re*, New York, 1964, p. 46. R.O. Faulkner, *The Ancient Egyptian Book of the Dead*, London, 1985, p. 40, translates differently. Another good example built around the name of Osiris is 'Osiris-Apis-Atum-Horus in one, the Great God', cited in H. Frankfort, *Kingship and the Gods*, Chicago, 1948, pp. 146, 196; also in S. Morenz, *Egyptian Religion*, London, 1973, p. 143. Pages 139–46 of the latter deal with the general phenomenon of individuality/plurality in Egyptian divine names, as does E. Hornung, *Conceptions of God in Ancient Egypt: the One and the Many*, London, 1983, Chapter 3.

23 Morenz, op. cit., p. 145.

24 T.G. Allen, *The Book of the Dead or Going Forth by Day*, Chicago, 1974, pp. 118–20. A similar invoking of the manifold forms of Ra (seventy-five in all) is contained within the Litany of Ra, see Piankoff, op. cit., pp. 3–9, which discusses the phenomenon of name plurality in other religions, including Islam.

25 AEL I, pp. 52–3; Frankfort, op. cit., Chapter 2.

26 Useful discussions here are J. Gwyn Griffiths, *The Conflict of Horus and Seth*, Liverpool, 1960, pp. 130–46; B.G. Trigger, *Beyond History: the Methods of Prehistory*, New York, 1968, Chapter 6, 'Predynastic Egypt'; also the references cited in Note 44.

27 For the somewhat enigmatic Mesopotamian connection, see H. Frankfort, *The Birth of Civilization in the Near East*, London, 1951, pp. 100–12; Frankfort, 'The origin of monumental architecture in Egypt', AJSL 58 (1941), 329–58; P. Amiet, 'Glyptique susienne archaïque', *Revue d'Assyriologie* 51 (1957), 121–9; H.J. Kantor, 'The early relations of Egypt with Asia', JNES 1 (1942), 174–213; Kantor, 'Further evidence for early Mesopotamian relations with Egypt', JNES 11 (1952), 239–50; Kantor, 'The relative chronology of Egypt and its foreign correlations before the Late Bronze Age', in R.W. Ehrich (ed.) *Chronologies in Old World Archaeology*, Chicago, 1965, pp. 1–46; W.A. Ward, 'Relations between Egypt and Mesopotamia from prehistoric times to the end of the Middle Kingdom', JESHO 7 (1964), 1–45, 121–35; A.L. Kelley, 'Cylinder seals in predynastic Egypt', NSSEA 4, no. 2 (1973), 5–8; Kelley, 'The evidence for Mesopotamian influence in predynastic Egypt', NSSEA 4, no. 3 (1974), 2–11; R.M. Boehmer, 'Orientalische Einflüsse auf verzierten Messergriffen aus dem prädynastischen Ägypten', *Archäologische Mitteilungen aus Iran* 7 (1974), 15–40; Boehmer, 'Das Rollsiegel in prädynastischen Ägypten', *Archäologischer Anzeiger* 4 (1974), 495–514; W. Needler, *Predynastic and Archaic Egypt in the Brooklyn Museum*, The Brooklyn Museum, Brooklyn, 1984, pp. 14, 26, 30–1.

28 The subject of motives and means in the ancient Egyptian economy of Pharaonic times will be treated in Chapter 6.

29 W.M.F. Petrie and J.E. Quibell, *Naqada and Ballas*, London, 1896; W. Kaiser, 'Bericht über eine archäologisch – geologische Felduntersuchung in Ober- und Mittelägypten', MDAIK 17 (1961), 14–18; B.J. Kemp, 'Photographs of the Decorated Tomb at Hierakonpolis', JEA 59 (1973), 36–43; W. Davis, 'Cemetery T at Nagada', MDAIK 39 (1983), 17–28; *Lexikon* IV, pp. 343–7.

30 A.H. Gardiner, 'Horus the Beḥdetite', JEA 30 (1944), 23–60, discusses in some detail the problems of Behdet and related matters.

31 But note a 1st Dynasty representation of Horus in a boat astride a pair of wings in the sky, the whole above the Horus figure surmounting a king's name. R. Engelbach 'An alleged

winged sun-disk of the First Dynasty', ZÄS 65 (1930), 115–16; Gardiner, op. cit., 1944, p. 47, Plate VI.4.

32 J.E. Quibell, *Hierakonpolis* I, London, 1900; J.E. Quibell and F.W. Green, *Hierakonpolis* II, London, 1902; B. Adams, *Ancient Hierakonpolis* (with Supplement), Warminster, 1974; W. Kaiser, 'Zur vorgeschichtlichen Bedeutung von Hierakonpolis', MDAIK 16 (1958), 183–92; W. Kaiser, op. cit., 1961, 5–12; W.A. Fairservis, K.R. Weeks, and M. Hoffman, 'Preliminary report on the first two seasons at Hierakonpolis', JARCE 9 (1971–2), 7–68; M. Hoffman, 'A rectangular Amratian house from Hierakonpolis and its significance for predynastic research', JNES 39 (1980), 119–37; M.A. Hoffman, *The Predynastic of Hierakonpolis*, Giza and Macomb, Ill., 1982; B.J. Kemp 'Excavations at Hierakonpolis Fort 1905: a preliminary note', JEA 49 (1963), 24–8. These contributions are primarily to the local archaeology of Hierakonpolis. The broader cultural context of Hierakonpolis is discussed by J. A. Wilson in 'Buto and Hierakonpolis in the geography of Egypt', JNES 14 (1955), 209–36.

33 Quibell and Green, op. cit., pp. 20–2, Plates LXXV–LXXIX; [F.W. Green], *The Prehistoric Wall-painting in Egypt* [London British School of Egyptian Archaeology, 1953]; H. Case and J.C. Payne, 'Tomb 100: the Decorated Tomb at Hierakonpolis', JEA 48 (1962), 5–18; J.C. Payne, 'Tomb 100: the Decorated Tomb at Hierakonpolis confirmed', JEA 59 (1973), 31–5; B.J. Kemp, op. cit., 1973, 36–43.

34 B.J. Kemp, 'The early development of towns in Egypt', *Antiquity* 51 (1977), 185–200; M. Bietak, 'Urban archaeology and the "town problem" in ancient Egypt', in K. Weeks (ed.) *Egyptology and the Social Sciences*, Cairo, American University, 1979, pp. 110–14.

35 Gardiner, op. cit., 1944, 32; C. M. Firth and J.E. Quibell, *The Step Pyramid* II, Cairo, 1935, Plate 41.

36 See Note 40 for the results of recent fieldwork which have located Predynastic and Early Dynastic strata.

37 S. Hendrickx, 'The Late Predynastic cemetery at Elkab (Upper Egypt)', in L. Krzyżaniak and M. Kobusiewicz (eds) *Origin and Early Development of Food-producing Cultures in Northeastern Africa*, Poznań, 1984, pp. 225–30.

38 The best summary of the older fieldwork at Merimda, Fayum, and the Maadi area is W.C. Hayes, *Most Ancient Egypt*, Chicago, 1965, Chapter 3, pp. 91–146. The more recent German excavations are the subject of a series of volumes, not yet completed, beginning with J. Eiwanger, *Merimde-Benisalâme* I, Mainz, 1984; also a series of preliminary reports by J. Eiwanger: 'Erster Vorbericht über die Wiederaufnahme der Grabungen in der neolithischen Siedlung Merimde-Benisalâme', MDAIK 34 (1978), 33–42; 'Zweiter Vorbericht über die Wiederaufnahme der Grabungen in der neolithischen Siedlung Merimde-Benisalâme', MDAIK 35 (1979), 23–57; 'Dritter Vorbericht über die Wiederaufnahme der Grabungen in der neolithischen Siedlung Merimde-Benisalâme', MDAIK 36 (1980), 61–76; 'Die neolithische Siedlung von Merimde-Benisalâme: Vierter Bericht', MDAIK 38 (1982), 67–82; also F.A. Badawi, 'Die Grabung der ägyptischen Altertümerverwaltung in Merimde-Benisalâme im Oktober/November 1976', MDAIK 34 (1978), 43–51.

39 I. Rizkana and J. Seeher, 'New light on the relation of Maadi to the Upper Egyptian cultural sequence', MDAIK 40 (1984), 237–52; Rizkana and Seeher, 'The chipped stones at Maadi: preliminary reassessment of a predynastic industry and its long-distance relations', MDAIK 41 (1985), 235–55; W. Kaiser, 'Zur Südausdehnung der vorgeschichtlichen Delta-kulturen und zur frühen Entwicklung Oberägyptens', MDAIK 41 (1985), 61–87; also L. Habachi and W. Kaiser, 'Ein Freidhof der Maadikultur bei es-Saff', MDAIK 41 (1985), 43–6; B. Mortensen, 'Four jars from the Maadi Culture found in Giza', MDAIK 41 (1985), 145–7.

40   For the recent Buto exploration, see T. von der Way, 'Untersuchungen des Deutschen Archäologischen Instituts Kairo in nördlichen Delta zwischen Disûq und Tida', MDAIK 40 (1984), 297–328; T. von der Way and K. Schmidt, 'Bericht über der Fortgang der Untersuchungen im Raum Tell el Fara'in/Buto', MDAIK 41 (1985), 269–91.

41   D. Wildung, 'Terminal prehistory of the Nile Delta: theses', in Krzyżaniak and Kobusiewicz, op. cit., pp. 265–9.

42   Wildung, op. cit., 1969b, pp. 4–21; Lexikon IV, pp. 46–8.

43   Waddell, op. cit., pp. 26–33.

44   Important discussions of this difficult period are J.H. Breasted, 'The predynastic union of Egypt', BIFAO 30 (1931), 709–24, where the upper register of the Cairo fragment of the Palermo Stone is properly published; W. Kaiser, 'Einige Bemerkungen zur ägyptischen Frühzeit.II.Zur Frage einer über Menes hinausreichenden ägyptischen Geschichtsüberlieferung', ZÄS 86 (1961), 39–61; Kaiser, 'Einige Bemerkungen zur ägyptischen Frühzeit.III.Die Reichseinigung', ZÄS 91 (1964), 86–125. P.F. O'Mara, The Palermo Stone and the Archaic Kings of Egypt, La Canada, Calif., 1979, has argued that the Cairo fragment is actually a modern forgery, although there is little sign that this view is being taken seriously. A particularly good summary of the current picture of Predynastic Egypt and the evolution to the Pharaonic state is Needler, op. cit., Chapter I; and the important synthesis by Kaiser, op. cit., 1985, 61–87.

45   J. Vandier, Manuel d'archéologie égyptienne I.1. La préhistoire, Paris, 1952, Chapters X, XI; J. Capart, Primitive Art in Egypt, London, 1905; H. Asselberghs, Chaos en beheersing, Leiden, 1961; H. J. Kantor, 'Ägypten', in M.J. Mellink and J. Filip (eds) Frühe Stufen der Kunst (Propyläen Kunstgeschichte, 13), Berlin, 1974; W.M.F. Petrie, Ceremonial State Palettes and Corpus of Proto-dynastic Pottery, London, 1953; H.G. Fischer, 'A fragment of late Predynastic Egyptian relief from the Eastern Delta', Artibus Asiae 21 (1958), 64–88; A.L. Kelley, 'A review of the evidence concerning early Egyptian ivory knife handles', The Ancient World (Chicago) 6 (1983), 95–102.

46   Lexikon II, pp. 146–8 ('Feindsymbolik'); Lexikon VI, pp. 1009–12 ('Vernichtungsritualen'), pp. 1051–4 ('Vogelfang'); M. Alliot, 'Les rites de la chasse au filet, aux temples de Karnak, d'Edfou et d'Esneh', RdE 5 (1946), 57–118; H.W. Fairman, 'The kingship rituals of Egypt', in S.H. Hooke (ed.) Myth, Ritual, and Kingship, Oxford, 1958, pp. 74–104, esp. 89–91; a scene of this kind also occurs in Hatshepsut's temple at Deir el-Bahari in a context which strongly implies a symbolic reference to triumph over hostile forces, E. Naville, The Temple of Deir el Bahari VI, London, 1908, p. 8, Plate CLXIII.

47   Kaiser, op. cit., 1964, 113–14, Abb. 7; Kaiser and G. Dreyer, 'Umm el-Qaab. Nachuntersuchungen im frühzeitlichen Königsfriedhof.2.Vorbericht', MDAIK 38 (1982), 262–9, Abb. 14.

48   The earliest evidence for the pairing of Horus and Seth is almost as ancient, from the reign of King Djer of the 1st Dynasty. In a queen's title 'She who sees Horus and Seth' the king is presented as an embodiment of the two gods (Gardiner, op. cit., 1944, p. 59, note).

49   Kaiser and G. Dreyer, op. cit., 1982, 242–5, discuss the importance of unusually large and well-appointed graves as evidence for the existence of political elites, and draw attention to Petrie's Abadiya cemetery. B. Williams, 'The lost Pharaohs of Nubia', Archaeology 33 (1980), 14–21; Williams, 'Forebears of Menes in Nubia: myth or reality?' JNES 46 (1987), 15–26; Williams, Excavations between Abu Simbel and the Sudan Frontier, Part 1: the A-group Royal Cemetery at Qustul: Cemetery L, Chicago, 1986, publishes an elite cemetery from Lower Nubia (Qustul), although with an overstated case for its importance, cf. W.Y. Adams, 'Doubts about the "Lost Pharaohs"', JNES 44 (1985), 185–92.

50   The basic excavation reports are W.M.F. Petrie, The Royal Tombs of the First Dynasty I, London, 1900, and W.M.F. Petrie, The Royal Tombs of the Earliest Dynasties II, London, 1901.

A fundamental re-examination of early royal tombs partly based on a re-excavation at Abydos is W. Kaiser and G. Dreyer, op. cit., 1982, 211–69; cf. also Kaiser, 'Zu den Königsgräbern der 1. Dynastie in Umm el-Qaab', MDAIK 37 (1981), 247–54; Kaiser, 'Zu den königlichen Talbezirken der 1. und 2. Dynastie in Abydos und zur Baugeschichte des Djoser-Grabmals', MDAIK 25 (1969), 1–21; B.J. Kemp, 'The Egyptian 1st Dynasty royal cemetery', *Antiquity* 41 (1967), 22–32.

51   The basic publication is in E.R. Ayrton, C.T. Currelly, and A.E.P. Weigall, *Abydos* III, London, 1904, Chapter I. The articles in Note 50 include discussions of its significance.

52   Documentation is conveniently summarized in W.B. Emery, *Archaic Egypt*, Harmondsworth, 1961, and discussed by B.J. Kemp, 'Architektur der Frühzeit', in C. Vandersleyen (ed.) *Das alte Ägypten* (Propyläen Kunstgeschichte, 15), Berlin, 1975, pp. 99–112. Good examples of later funerary architecture which preserve the style of decoration are J.E. Quibell, *The Tomb of Hesy*, Cairo, 1913, Plates VIII, IX; L. Borchardt, *Das Grabdenkmal des Königs Ne-user-re*, Leipzig, 1907, Bl 24; S. Hassan, *Excavations at Gîza, 1929–1930*, Oxford, 1932, Plates LXI–LXV.

53   The basic publications are C.M. Firth and J.E. Quibell, op. cit.; J.-Ph. Lauer, *La Pyramide à degrés*, Cairo, 1936. A valuable and detailed summary is J.-Ph. Lauer, *Histoire monumentale des pyramides d'Egypte* I, Cairo, 1962; some remarkable architectural drawings of the timber and matting architecture prototypes are in H. Ricke, *Bemerkungen zur ägyptischen Baukunst des Alten Reiches* I, Zurich, 1944.

54   Firth and Quibell, op. cit., Plates 15–17, p. 104. J.-Ph. Lauer, *Monuments et Mémoires* (Fondation Eugène Piot) 49 (1957), 1–15, discusses and illustrates points of detail.

55   A.J. Spencer, 'Two enigmatic hieroglyphs and their relation to the Sed-Festival', JEA 64 (1978), 52–5.

56   H. Frankfort, op. cit., 1948, Chapter 6; *Lexikon* V, pp. 782–90; Fairman, op. cit., pp. 83–5; C.J. Bleeker, *Egyptian Festivals: Enactments of Religious Renewal* (Studies in the History of Religions 13), Leiden, 1967, Chapter V; E. Hornung and E. Staehelin, *Studien zum Sedfest* (Agyptiaca Helvetica 1), Geneva, 1974. A.M. Blackman, *Studia Aegyptiaca* I (Analecta Orientalia 17, 1938), 4–9, has interesting comments on one 1st Dynasty depiction.

57   In Chapter 5 we shall examine one particular set, those of Amenhetep III of the 18th Dynasty.

58   The most explicit early reference occurs on the Palermo Stone in a 1st Dynasty entry (possibly for King Adjib). It shows the double-throne dais and accompanies it with the legend: 'Appearance of the King of Upper Egypt, Appearance of the King of Lower Egypt: *Sed*-festival'. See H. Schäfer, *Ein Bruchstück altägyptischer Annalen*, Berlin, 1902, p. 19. All early references to the *Sed*-festival are conveniently gathered in Hornung and Staehelin, op. cit., pp. 16–20.

2 The dynamics of culture

1   C. Robichon and A. Varille, 'Médamoud. Fouilles du Musée du Louvre, 1938', CdE 14, no. 27 (1939), 82–7; D. Arnold, 'Architektur des Mittleren Reiches', in C. Vandersleyen (ed.) *Das alte Ägypten* (Propyläen Kunstgeschichte, 15), Berlin, 1975, pp. 161–3, Abb. 36; D. Arnold, *Der Tempel des Königs Mentuhotep von Deir el-Bahari I; Architektur und Deutung*, Mainz, 1974, pp. 76–8.

2   C. Robichon and A. Varille, *Description sommaire du temple primitif de Médamoud*, Cairo, 1940; see also the comments by Arnold, op. cit., 1974, 76–8.

3   So far published in preliminary reports by W. Kaiser, G. Dreyer, G. Grimm, G. Haeny,

H. Jaritz, and C. Müller, 'Stadt und Tempel von Elephantine, Fünfter Grabungsbericht', MDAIK 31 (1975), 51–8; W. Kaiser, G. Dreyer, R. Gempeler, P. Grossmann, G. Haeny, H. Jaritz, and F. Junge, 'Stadt und Tempel von Elephantine, Sechster Grabungsbericht', MDAIK 32 (1976), 75–87; W. Kaiser, G. Dreyer, R. Gempeler, P. Grossmann, and H. Jaritz, 'Stadt und Tempel von Elephantine, Siebter Grabungsbericht', MDAIK 33 (1977), 68–83; and in one final report, G. Dreyer, *Elephantine VIII. Der Tempel der Satet; die Funde der Frühzeit und des Alten Reiches*, Mainz, 1986.

4 W. Kaiser, et al., op. cit., 1976, 78–80.

5 Dreyer, op. cit., 1986.

6 On this triad, see L. Habachi, 'Was Anukis considered as the wife of Khnum or as his daughter?' ASAE 50 (1950), 501–7. The blocks are in W. Kaiser *et al.*, op. cit., 1975, 45–50, 109–25; op. cit., 1976, 69–75.

7 Both figure in the scenes beneath the Step Pyramid at Sakkara, for example (cf. Figure 19, p. 58). See caption to Figure 20 for the references, particularly to the baboon cult and suggested explanations. Baboon and scorpion images were still included amongst the temple furniture of the pyramid of King Neferirkara of the 5th Dynasty at Abusir, see P. Posener-Kriéger, *Les Archives du temple funéraire de Néferirkarê-Kakaï (Les Papyrus d'Abousir): Traduction et commentaire*, Cairo, 1976, pp. 87–98.

8 J.E. Quibell and W.M.F. Petrie, *Hierakonpolis* I, London, 1900; J.E. Quibell and F.W. Green, *Hierakonpolis* II, London, 1902; B. Adams, *Ancient Hierakonpolis*, (with Supplement), Warminster, 1974; J. Weinstein, 'A foundation deposit tablet from Hierakonpolis', JARCE 9 (1971–2), 133–5; W.A. Fairservis, K.R. Weeks, and M. Hoffman, 'Preliminary report on the first two seasons at Hierakonpolis'. JARCE 9 (1971–2), 7–68; Dreyer, op. cit., 1986, pp. 37–46.

9 Principally the temple at Kasr es-Sagha, see Arnold, op. cit., 1975, p. 160; D. Arnold, *Der Tempel Qasr el-Sagha*, Mainz, 1979, pp. 22–3, where a Middle Kingdom date for the Hierakonpolis building is preferred.

10 The date of this image is not easily discernible from its style. One scholar has argued for a New Kingdom date, U. Rössler-Köhler, 'Zur Datierung des Falkenbildes von Hierakonpolis (*CGC* 14717)', MDAIK 34 (1978), 117–25. The archaeological context, however, demands a Middle Kingdom date or earlier.

11 Quibell and Petrie, op. cit., p. 6, Plate II; Quibell and Green, op. cit., Plate LXXII; R. Engelbach, 'A foundation scene of the Second Dynasty', JEA 20 (1934), 183–4; Adams, op. cit., Supplement, p. 17.

12 Quibell and Green, op. cit., p. 53, Plate LXXII; Adams, op. cit., Supplement, Frontis.

13 Quibell and Green, op. cit., pp. 10, 51, Plates LXVII, LXXII; Adams, op. cit., pp. 28–9.

14 W.M.F. Petrie, *Abydos* I, II London, 1902, 1903; B.J. Kemp, 'The Osiris temple at Abydos', MDAIK 23 (1968), 138–55; Kemp, 'The Osiris temple at Abydos. A postscript to *MDAIK* 23 (1968), 138–55', GM 8 (1973), 23–5; Kemp, 'The early development of towns in Egypt', *Antiquity* 51 (1977), 186–9; Dreyer, op. cit., 1986, pp. 47–58.

15 Sir R. Mond and O.H. Myers, *Temples of Armant*, London, 1940, p. 29, and section on Plate II.

16 Petrie, op. cit., II, pp. 7–8, Plate L.

17 A.J. Spencer, *Catalogue of Egyptian antiquities in the British Museum, V, Early Dynastic objects*, London, 1980, p. 67, Plate 55, no. 483.

18 Dreyer, op. cit., 1986, pp. 54–8. The single most important group is published by H.W. Müller, *Ägyptische Kunstwerke, Kleinfunde und Glas in der Sammlung E. und M. Kofler-Truniger, Luzern* (Münchner Ägyptologische Studien, 5), Berlin, 1964. A further note on date and provenance is provided by W. Needler, *Predynastic and Archaic Egypt in The Brooklyn Museum*, Brooklyn, 1984, p. 261.

19 W.M.F. Petrie, *Koptos*, London, 1896. For a general map of the location of the temple, see R. Weill, 'Koptos. Relation sommaire des travaux exécutés par MM. Ad. Reinach et R. Weill pour la Société française des fouilles archéologiques (campagne de 1910)', ASAE 11 (1911), 106, and folding plans, Plates I, II; B. Adams, 'Petrie's manuscript notes on the Koptos foundation deposits of Tuthmosis III', JEA 61 (1975), 102–13.

20 Petrie, ibid., p. 5.

21 On the lions, see B. Adams and R. Jaeschke, *The Koptos Lions* (The Milwaukee Public Museum, Contributions in Anthropology and History, 3), Milwaukee, January 1984.

22 Petrie or his sponsors seem to have been too embarrassed to publish illustrations of the torsos in the excavation report, and to this day no really detailed study has been published which does justice to these remarkable objects. Two are in the Ashmolean Museum at Oxford, and photographs appear in J. Capart, *Primitive Art in Egypt*, London, 1905, p. 223, Fig. 166; Sir E. Denison Ross (ed.) *The Art of Egypt through the Ages*, London, 1931, p. 86; E.J. Baumgartel, 'The three colossi from Koptos and their Mesopotamian counterparts', ASAE 48 (1948), 533–53, Plates I, II; H.J. Kantor, 'Ägypten', in M.J. Mellink and J. Filip (eds), *Frühe Stufen der Kunst* (Propyläen Kunstgeschichte, 13), Berlin, 1974, p. 255, Abb. 221. The Cairo statue, Journal d'Entrée 30770, appears never to have been illustrated. The head of one, its face missing, is also in the Ashmolean Museum, see Petrie, op. cit., 1896, Plate V.4; Baumgartel, op. cit., Plate III.

23 Adams and Jaeschke, op. cit., p. 21.

24 From the Turah quarries outside Cairo, according to Arkell, quoted by Baumgartel, op. cit., although one would like to have verification of this.

25 London, 1905, an English translation of a French-language edition published in Brussels in 1904.

26 K. Sethe, 'Hitherto unnoticed evidence regarding copper works of art of the oldest period of Egyptian history', JEA 1 (1914), 233–6; D. Wildung, *Die Rolle ägyptischer Könige im Bewusstsein ihrer Nachwelt* I, Berlin, 1969, p. 52, Note 3. Many references are on the Palermo Stone, H. Schäfer, *Ein Bruchstück altägyptischer Annalen*, Berlin, 1902, p. 15, Nr. 1; p. 16, Nr. 8; p. 17, Nrs 9, 10; p. 21, Nr. 14; p. 27, Nr. 4; p. 28, Nr. 10.

27 On the history of writing and literacy in ancient Egypt, see J. Baines, 'Literacy and ancient Egyptian society', *Man* 18 (1983), 572–99; J.D. Ray, 'The emergence of writing Egypt', *World Archaeology* 17 (1986), 307–16.

28 The most detailed and scholarly of introductions is H. Schäfer (translated and edited by J. Baines), *Principles of Egyptian Art*, Oxford, 1974. Others are M. Baud, *Les Dessins ébauchés de la nécropole thébaine (au temps du Nouvel Empire)*, Cairo, 1935; E. Iversen, *Canon and Proportions in Egyptian art*, 2nd edn, Warminster, 1975; G. Robins, *Egyptian Painting and Relief*, Shire Publications, Princes Risborough, 1986.

29 Kemp, 'The early development of towns in Egypt', 189–91.

30 *Lexikon* IV, 136–40.

31 For this last aspect see R. Germer, 'Die Bedeutung des Lattichs als Pflanze des Min', SAK 8 (1980), 85–7; M. Defossez, 'Les laitues de Min', SAK 12 (1985), 1–4.

32 G. Jéquier, *Le Monument funéraire de Pepi II* II, Cairo, 1938, Plates 12, 14; H. Goedicke, *Königliche Dokumente aus dem Alten Reich*, Wiesbaden, 1967, p. 43, Abb. 4.

33 Petrie, op. cit., 1902, p. 4, Plate III.48. Cf. also the probably 3rd Dynasty entry on the Palermo Stone, Schäfer, op. cit., p. 28, Nr. 10.

34 J. Baines, '*Bnbn*: mythological and linguistic notes', *Orientalia* 39 (1970), 389–404; *Lexikon* I, pp. 694–5.

35 J.D.S. Pendlebury, *The City of Akhenaten* III, London, 1951, Plate IX; N. de G. Davies, *The Rock Tombs of El Amarna* I, London, 1903, Plates XI, XXXIII; II, London, 1905, Plate XIX; III, London, 1905, Plate XXX.

36 *Lexikon* I, p. 680; LD II, Bl. 119.

37 Pyramid Texts, Utterance no. 600. R.O. Faulkner, *The Ancient Egyptian Pyramid Texts*, Oxford, 1969, p. 246; ANET, 3.

38 *Lexikon* I, p. 31.

39 The best general treatment of ancient Egyptian pottery is J. Bourriau, *Umm el-Ga'ab. Pottery from the Nile Valley before the Arab Conquest*, Cambridge, Cambridge University Press and Fitzwilliam Museum, 1981. It is profusely illustrated.

40 A.L. Kelley, 'Cylinder seals in predynastic Egypt', NSSEA 4, no. 2 (1973), 5–8; R.M. Boehmer, 'Das Rollsiegel im prädynastischen Ägypten', *Archäologischer Anzeiger* 4, (1974), 495–514. Also B. Williams, 'Aspects of sealing and glyptic in Egypt before the New Kingdom', in M. Gibson and R.D. Biggs (eds) *Seals and Sealing in the Ancient Near East*, Malibu, 1977, pp. 135–40.

41 H.G. Fischer, 'Old Kingdom cylinder seals for the lower classes', *Metropolitan Museum Journal* 6 (1972), 5–16. Large numbers are published by P. Kaplony, *Die Inschriften der ägyptischen Frühzeit* (3 vols), Wiesbaden, 1963, and for more, running through the Old Kingdom, P. Kaplony, *Die Rollsiegel des Alten Reichs* II, Brussels, 1981. A convenient selection is in W.M.F. Petrie, *Scarabs and Cylinders with Names*, London, 1917, Plates I–VII. Dreyer, op. cit., 1986, pp. 94–5, 151, Taf. 57, nos 449–51 are three faience tablets with similar designs from the Elephantine shrine deposits.

42 W.A. Ward, 'The origin of Egyptian design-amulets ('button seals')', JEA 56 (1970), 65–80.

43 N. Jenkins, *The Boat beneath the Pyramid; King Cheops' Royal Ship*, London, 1980; P. Lipke, *The Royal Ship of Cheops* (BAR International Series 225), Oxford, 1984; B. Landström, *Ships of the Pharaohs; 4000 Years of Egyptian Shipbuilding*, London, 1970, pp. 26–34.

44 G.A. Reisner, *A History of the Giza Necropolis II. The Tomb of Hetep-heres the Mother of Cheops*, Cambridge, Mass., 1955, pp. 23–7, Plate 5.

45 E.g. N. de G. Davies, *The Rock Tombs of Sheikh Saïd*, London, 1901, Plate XV.

46 Conveniently collected in A. Badawy, *Le Dessin architectural chez les anciens égyptiens*, Cairo, 1948, Chapters I and II; E. Baldwin Smith, *Egyptian Architecture as Cultural Expression*, New York and London, 1938, pp. 11–30.

47 Petrie, op. cit., 1903, II, Plate VII, nos 131, 132, Plate XI, no. 243; Müller, op. cit., A29a–c, A31; Dreyer, op. cit., 1986, pp. 64–5; W. Kaiser, 'Zu den ⌐o⋔ des älteren Bilddarstellungen und der Bedeutung von *rpw.t*', MDAIK 39 (1983), 275–8.

48 Some much later representations add this panelling to the sides of the carrying frame (cf. Kaiser, op. cit., 264–5, Abb. 1,2), but this could well be the kind of decoration from association of ideas which the Egyptians were so fond of.

49 A detailed discussion is provided by W. Kaiser, op. cit., 1983, 261–96; also Dreyer, op. cit., 1986, pp. 64–5. The human face with cow's ears which later became a symbol of the goddess Hathor was, in early times, a female divinity called Bat, see H.G. Fischer, 'The cult and nome of the goddess Bat', JARCE 1 (1962), 7–24; H.G. Fischer, 'Varia Aegyptiaca', JARCE, 2 (1963), 50–1; *Lexikon* I, pp. 630–2.

50 G. Legrain, 'Le logement et transport des barques sacrées et des statues des dieux dans quelques temples égyptiens', BIFAO 13 (1917), 1–76.

51 P. Spencer, *The Egyptian Temple: a Lexicographical Study*, London, 1984, pp. 125–30.

52 The remains of the early shrines at Abydos and Hierakonpolis are too incomplete for comparison. At Medamud the provision of two domains is evident in the earliest shrine, but the brick benches in the outer area do not look entirely suitable to be pedestals for the support of canopies for the revealed image.

53 See especially Fischer, op. cit., 1962, 12, and Note 39.

54 P. Spencer, op. cit., pp. 114–19.

55 A good and representative set of photographs of Edfu temple is in J.-L. de Cenival, *Living*

Architecture: Egyptian, London, 1964, pp. 147–59. An informative summary of the history and religious activity of the temple is H.W. Fairman, 'Worship and festivals in an Egyptian temple', *Bulletin of the John Rylands Library*, Manchester, 37 (1954), 165–203.

56   E.A.E. Reymond, *The Mythical Origin of the Egyptian Temple*, Manchester, 1969.

57   E. Naville, *The XIth Dynasty Temple of Deir el-Bahari* II, London, 1910, pp. 14–19, Plates XXIII, XXIV.

58   Arnold, op. cit., 1974, pp. 28–32, 76–8.

59   R. Stadelmann, *Die ägyptischen Pyramiden; Vom Ziegelbau zum Weltwunder*, Mainz, 1985, p. 229, Abb. 74.

60   Another good example is the reconstruction of a pair of obelisks and falcon statue perched on top of a shrine of tent shrine form at Gebel Silsila, see G. Legrain, 'Notes d'inspection', ASAE 4 (1903), 205–9, Figs 3, 4. As often happens, when such a reconstruction is reproduced in another book, the fact that it is only a reconstruction is overlooked, see G. Jéquier, *Manuel d'archéologie égyptienne I: les éléments de l'architecture*, Paris, 1924, p. 321, Fig. 218. Here the reconstruction becomes reality.

61   AEL I, pp. 115–18.

62   E.S. Bogoslovsky, 'Hundred Egyptian draughtsmen', ZÄS 107 (1980), 89–116; C.A. Keller, 'How many draughtsmen named Amenhotep? A study of some Deir el-Medina painters', JARCE 21 (1984), 119–29.

63   *Lexikon* III, pp. 145–8; D. Wildung, *Imhotep und Amenhotep – Gottwerdung im alten Ägypten*, Berlin, 1977; Wildung, *Egyptian Saints: Deification in Pharaonic Egypt*, New York, 1977.

64   AEL I, 6–7, 58–61; D. Wildung, op. cit., 1969, pp. 102–3; *Lexikon* III, pp. 290, 980–2.

3   The bureaucratic mind

1   Both passages are in Papyrus Chester Beatty IV, see A.H. Gardiner, *Hieratic Papyri in the British Museum. 3rd Series: Chester Beatty Gift*, London, 1935, p. 41. The first passage also occurs in Papyrus Anastasi II and Papyrus Sallier I, see R.A. Caminos, *Late Egyptian Miscellanies*, London, 1954, pp. 51, 317.

2   P. Posener-Kriéger and J.L. de Cenival, *Hieratic Papyri in the British Museum. 5th Series: the Abu Sir Papyri*, London, 1968; P. Posener-Kriéger, *Les Archives du temple funéraire de Néferirkarê-Kakaï (Les papyrus d'Abousir)*, 2 vols, Cairo, 1976.

3   A. Fakhry, *The Monuments of Sneferu at Dahshur II. The Valley Temple, Part I: the Temple Reliefs*, Cairo, 1961. A detailed study of all Old Kingdom sources of this kind is H. Jacquet-Gordon, *Les Noms des domaines funéraires sous l'Ancien Empire Egyptien*, Cairo, 1962.

4   Posener-Kriéger, op. cit., pp. 565–74; *Lexikon* IV, p. 1044; A.M. Roth, 'A preliminary report on a study of the system of phyles in the Old Kingdom', NARCE 124 (Winter 1983), 30–5.

5   Posener-Kriéger and de Cenival, op. cit., Plate XXXI; Posener-Kriéger, op. cit., pp. 429–39.

6   On Egyptian mathematics see T.E. Peet, *The Rhind Mathematical Papyrus*, London, 1923; R.J. Gillings, *Mathematics in the Time of the Pharaohs*, Cambridge, Mass., 1927; O. Gillain, *La Science égyptienne: l'arithmétique au Moyen Empire*, Brussels, 1927; G. Robins and C. Shute, *The Rhind Mathematical Papyrus*, London, The British Museum, 1987.

7   Rhind Mathematical Papyrus, Problem 42.

8   H.E. Winlock, *Models of Daily Life in Ancient Egypt*, New York, 1955, pp. 27–9, 88, Plates 22, 23, 64, 65.

9   B.J. Kemp, *Amarna Reports* III, London, 1986, pp. 2–5. A fine model quern emplacement was found in the tomb of King Tutankhamun, W.J. Darby, P. Ghalioungui and L. Grivetti, *Food: the Gift of Osiris*, London, 1977, p. 505, Fig. 12.2. This two-volume work contains much information on Egyptian baking and brewing.

10 F. Filce Leek, 'Teeth and bread in ancient Egypt', JEA 58 (1972), 126–32; Leek, 'Further studies concerning ancient Egyptian bread', 59 (1973), 199–204. Experimental milling was carried out at el-Amarna in 1987, see B.J. Kemp, *Amarna Reports* V, London, 1989, ch. 12.

11 H. Jacquet-Gordon, 'A tentative typology of Egyptian bread moulds', in D. Arnold (ed.) *Studien zur altägyptischen Keramik*, Mainz, 1981, pp. 11–24.

12 B.J. Kemp, *Amarna Reports* IV, London, 1987, Chapter 6. The connection between square ovens and bread moulds is also firmly established at the Middle Kingdom sites of Abu Ghalib and Mirgissa (H. Larsen, 'Vorbericht über die schwedischen Grabungen in Abu Ghâlib 1932–1934', MDIAAK 6 (1935), 51, Abb. 4, 58–60; R. Holthoer, *The Scandinavian Joint Expedition to Sudanese Nubia 5: New Kingdom Pharaonic Sites, The pottery*, Stockholm, 1977, Plate 72.2), and at the New Kingdom ovens beside the Treasury of Tuthmosis I at Karnak North (J. Jacquet, 'Fouilles de Karnak Nord. Quatrième campagne, 1971', BIFAO 71 (1972), 154, Plan 1, Plate XXXIV; J. Jacquet, *Karnak-Nord V: Le trésor de Thoutmosis Ier: étude architecturale*, Cairo, 1983, pp. 82–3).

13 N. de G. Davies, *The Tomb of Antefoḳer, Vizier of Sesostris I, and of his Wife, Senet*, London, 1920 pp. 15–16, Plates XI–XII.

14 Peet, op. cit., pp. 112–13; Gillings, op. cit., pp. 128–36. *Pefsu* is, in the latter book, called *pesu*, a possible alternative reading.

15 Rhind Mathematical Papyrus, Problem 75.

16 But not always, e.g. F.Ll. Griffith, *Hieratic Papyri from Kahun and Gurob*, London, 1898, p. 65, Plate XXVIa.

17 Experimentally verified at el-Amarna in 1987, see Kemp, op. cit., 1989, ch. 11.

18 D. Dunham, *Uronarti Shalfak Mirgissa (Second Cataract Forts, II)*, Boston, 1967, pp. 34–5, Plates XXVII, XXVIII; W.K. Simpson, 'Two lexical notes to the Reisner Papyri: *wḥrt* and *trsst*', JEA 59 (1973), 220–2.

19 An excellent treatment is D. Mueller, 'Some remarks on wage rates in the Middle Kingdom', JNES 34 (1975), 249–63.

20 Rhind Mathematical Papyrus, Problem 65.

21 G.A. Reisner, 'The tomb of Hepzefa, nomarch of Siût', JEA 5 (1918), 79–98; A.J. Spalinger, 'A redistributive pattern at Assiut', JAOS 105 (1985), 7–20.

22 Griffith, op. cit., pp. 45–6, Plates XVI, XVII.

23 Simpson, op. cit.; cf. B.J. Kemp, 'Large Middle Kingdom granary buildings (and the archaeology of administration)', ZÄS 113 (1986), 120–36.

24 On this subject and many related issues of land yields, see K. Baer, 'The low price of land in ancient Egypt', JARCE 1 (1962), 25–45.

25 Cited in Kemp, op. cit., 1986, p. 132.

26 W.K. Simpson, *Papyrus Reisner* I, Boston, 1963, pp. 83–5; W.K. Simpson, *Papyrus Reisner* III, Boston, 1969, pp. 13–15.

27 W.C. Hayes, *A Papyrus of the Late Middle Kingdom in the Brooklyn Museum*, Brooklyn, 1955. The quotation given is from p. 64.

28 G. Goyon, *Nouvelles inscriptions rupestres du Wadi Hammamat*, Paris, 1957, pp. 17–20, 81–5, no. 61; Mueller, op. cit., 256.

29 W.K. Simpson, *Papyrus Reisner* II, Boston, 1965.

30 What follows is essentially a summary of the work of the American archaeologist Mark Lehner. He provides a summary in 'A contextual approach to the Giza pyramids', *Archiv für Orientforschung* 32 (1985), 136–58, and partially in 'The development of the Giza necropolis: the Khufu project', MDAIK 41 (1985), 109–43, and I myself have learnt much from long discussions with him on the pyramid plateau itself.

31 N. Strudwick, *The Administration of Egypt in the Old Kingdom: the Highest Titles and their Holders*, London, 1985, pp. 237–50, covers the duties of the 'overseer of works', and his prime role in managing work-forces employed in a variety of tasks.

32   Herodotus II.124.
33   W.M.F. Petrie, *The Pyramids and Temples of Gizeh*, London, 1885, p. 34.
34   Abdel-Aziz Saleh, 'Excavations around Mycerinus pyramid complex', MDAIK 30 (1974), 131–54.
35   W.M.F. Petrie, *Gizeh and Rifeh*, London, 1907, p. 9.
36   K. Kromer, *Siedlungsfunde aus dem frühen Alten Reich in Giseh*, Vienna, 1978. A useful and clarifying review is by K.W. Butzer, JNES 41 (1982), 140–1.

4   Model communities

1   The best general account of Egyptian building methods is still Somers Clarke and R. Engelbach, *Ancient Egyptian Masonry*, London, 1930.

2   This is the approach of A. Badawy, *Ancient Egyptian Architectural Design: a Study of the Harmonic System*, Berkeley and Los Angeles, Calif., 1965.

3   To be appreciated by comparing the plan in J.E. Quibell and F.W. Green, *Hierakonpolis* II, London, 1902, Plate LXXIII, with the results of the 1967 and later American excavations, particularly W.A. Fairservis, K.R. Weeks, and M. Hoffman, 'Preliminary report on the first two seasons at Hierakonpolis', JARCE 8 (1971–2), 14–21, and accompanying plans and sections.

4   Still scarcely published. Some information is in B.J. Kemp, 'The early development of towns in Egypt', *Antiquity* 5 (1977), 185–200.

5   W. Helck, 'Bemerkungen zu den Pyramidenstädten im Alten Reich', MDAIK 15 (1957), 91–111; K. Baer, *Rank and Title in the Old Kingdom*, Chicago, 1960, pp. 247–73.

6   L. Borchardt, *Das Grabdenkmal des Königs Nefer-ir-ke-Re*, Leipzig, 1909.

7   K.A. Kitchen, *Pharaoh Triumphant: the Life and Times of Ramesses II, King of Egypt*, Warminster, 1982, pp. 103–9; Farouk Gomaà, *Chaemwese Sohn Ramses' II. und Hoherpriester von Memphis* Wiesbaden, 1973.

8   Papyrus Chester Beatty IV = P. British Museum 10684, AEL II, pp. 175–8.

9   Selim Hassan, *Excavations at Gîza IV (1932–1933)*, Cairo, 1943, pp. 1–62.

10   Primarily G.A. Reisner, *Mycerinus*, Cambridge, Mass., 1931, Chapter III; Hassan, op. cit., adds a further part of the plan. See also B. Trigger, B.J. Kemp, D.B. O'Connor, and A.B. Lloyd, *Ancient Egypt: a Social History*, Cambridge, 1983, pp. 92–4.

11   Ahmed Fakhry, *The Monuments of Sneferu at Dahshur I. The Bent Pyramid*, Cairo, 1959, pp. 114–17; II, Part II, *The Finds*, Cairo, 1961, contains a record of the pottery, largely Old Kingdom in date. See also Trigger *et al.*, op. cit., pp. 95–6.

12   W.M.F. Petrie, *Kahun, Gurob, and Hawara*, London, 1890, Chapter III; W.M.F. Petrie, *Illahun, Kahun and Gurob*, London, 1891, Chapters II and III; W.M.F. Petrie, G. Brunton, and M.A. Murray, *Lahun* II, London, 1923, Chapter XIII; A.R. David, *The Pyramid Builders of Ancient Egypt*, London, 1986.

13   The group discovered by Petrie is fully published in F.Ll. Griffith, *Hieratic Papyri from Kahun and Gurob*, London, 1898; the second group, from illicit excavations and now largely in Berlin, are variously dealt with in L. Borchardt, 'Der zweite Papyrusfund von Kahun und die zeitliche Festlegung des mittleren Reiches der ägyptischen Geschichte', ZÄS 37 (1899), 89–103; U. Kaplony-Heckel, *Ägyptische Handschriften*, Part I, ed. E. Lüddeckens, being part of the series W. Voigt (ed.) *Verzeichnis der orientalischen Handschriften in Deutschland* XIX, Wiesbaden, 1971; U. Luft, 'Illahunstudien I: zu der Chronologie und den Beamten in den 'Briefen aus Illahun', *Oikumene* (Budapest) 3 (1982), 101–56; 'Illahunstudien II; ein

Verteidigungsbrief aus Illahun. Anmerkungen zu P. Berol 10025', 4 (1983), 121–79; 'Illahunstudien III: zur sozialen Stellung des Totenpriesters in Mittleren Reich', 5 (1986), 117–53.

14 H.E. Winlock, *Models of Daily Life in Ancient Egypt*, Cambridge, Mass., 1955.

15 W.C. Hayes, *A Papyrus of the Late Middle Kingdom in the Brooklyn Museum*, Brooklyn, 1955, section IV.

16 Griffith, op. cit., pp. 19–24; also the discussion by D. Valbelle, 'Eléments sur la démographie et le paysage urbains, d'après les papyrus documentaires d'époque pharaonique', in *Sociétés urbaines en Egypte et au Soudan* (Cahier de Recherches de l'Institut de Papyrologie et d'Egyptologie de Lille 7) 1985, pp. 75–87.

17 D. Arnold and R. Stadelmann, 'Dahschur. Zweiter Grabungsbericht', MDAIK 33 (1977), 15–18, Abb. 2; Arnold, 'Dahschur. Dritter, Grabungsbericht', MDAIK 36 (1980), 15–17, Abb. 1; Dorothea Arnold, 'Keramikbearbeitung in Dahschur 1976–1981', MDAIK 38 (1982), 25–65.

18 J. Lauffray, Ramadan Saʿad, and S. Sauneron, 'Rapport sur les travaux de Karnak. Activités du Centre franco-égyptien en 1970–1972', *Karnak V (1970–2)*, Cairo, 1975, pp. 26–30, with plan on Fig. 13; J. Lauffray, 'Les travaux du Centre franco-égyptien d'étude des temples de Karnak, de 1972 à 1977', *Karnak VI (1973–7)*, Cairo, 1980, pp. 44–52; F. Debono, 'Rapport préliminaire sur les résultats de l'étude des objets de la fouille des installations du Moyen Empire et "Hyksôs" à l'Est du Lac Sacré de Karnak', *Karnak VII (1978–81)*, Paris, 1982, pp. 377–83; J. Lauffray, *Karnak d'Egypte*, Paris, 1979, pp. 197–209.

19 *Karnak VI (1973–77)*, pp. 153–65.

20 D.B. Redford, *Akhenaten, the Heretic King*, Princeton, 1984, pp. 95–8.

21 J. Jacquet, *Le Trésor de Thoutmosis Ier : étude architecturale*, Cairo, IFAO, 1983.

22 R. Fazzini and W. Peck, 'The 1982 season at Mut', NARCE 120 (Winter 1982), 44.

23 H. Larsen, 'Vorbericht über die schwedischen Grabungen in Abu Ghâlib 1932–1934', MDIAAK 6 (1935), 41–87.

24 M. Bietak, 'Tell el-Dabʿa', *Archiv für Orientforschung* 32 (1985), 130–5. For a general introduction to the site, see M. Bietak, 'Avaris and Piramesse: Archaeological Exploration in the Eastern Nile Delta' (Mortimer Wheeler Archaeological Lecture 1979), *Proceedings of the British Academy* 65 (1979), 225–90).

25 Good general histories of ancient Nubia and of Egyptian involvement are W.Y. Adams, *Nubia: Corridor to Africa*, London, 1977; B.G. Trigger, *Nubia under the Pharaohs*, London, 1976; also Trigger *et al.*, op. cit., pp. 116–37; Trigger 'The reasons for the construction of the Second Cataract forts', JSSEA 12 (1982), 1–6.

26 W.B. Emery, 'Egypt Exploration Society, preliminary report on the excavations at Buhen, 1962', *Kush* 11 (1963), 116–20, deals with the Old Kingdom town at Buhen. The sherds from Kubban are in W.B. Emery and L.P. Kirwan, *The Excavations and Survey between Wadi es-Sebua and Adindan, 1929–1931*, Cairo, 1935, p. 58, Plate 14.

27 A.W. Lawrence, 'Ancient Egyptian fortifications', JEA 51 (1965), 69–94; W.B. Emery, *Egypt in Nubia*, London, 1965, pp. 141–53; B.J. Kemp, 'Fortified towns in Nubia', in P.J. Ucko, R. Tringham, and G.W. Dimbleby (eds), *Man, Settlement and Urbanism*, London, 1972, pp. 651–6.

28 W.B. Emery, H.S. Smith, and A. Millard, *The Fortress of Buhen: the Archaeological Report*, London, 1979.

29 D. Arnold and J. Settgast, 'Erster Vorbericht über die vom Deutschen Archäologischen Institut Kairo im Asasif unternommenen Arbeiten (1. und 2. Kampagne)', MDAIK 20 (1965), Abb. 2, opposite p. 50; cf. A.R. Schulman, 'The battle scenes of the Middle Kingdom', JSSEA 12 (1982), 165–83.

30 J. Knudstad, 'Serra East and Dorginarti. A preliminary report on the 1963–64 excavations of

the University of Chicago Oriental Institute Sudan Expedition', *Kush* 14 (1966), 165–78.

31 G.A. Reisner and D. Dunham, 'The Egyptian forts from Halfa to Semna', *Kush* 8 (1960), 16, Plan 2; G.A. Reisner, N.F. Wheeler, and D. Dunham, *Uronarti Shalfak Mirgissa, (Second Cataract Forts II)*, Boston, 1967, Section II.

32 AEL I, pp. 118–20.

33 G.A. Reisner, D. Dunham, and J.M.A. Janssen, *Semna Kumma (Second Cataract Forts I)*, Boston, 1960, Section I.

34 ibid., Plates 17, 22.

35 ibid., Section II.

36 J. Vercoutter, 'Semna South fort and the records of the Nile levels at Kumma', *Kush* 14 (1966), 125–32.

37 A.J. Mills, 'The archaeological survey from Gemai to Dal – report on the 1965–1966 season', *Kush* 15 (1967), 206, Plate XXXVIIIb.

38 Marked on the map in J. de Morgan, U. Bouriant, G. Legrain, G. Jéquier, and A. Barsanti, *Catalogue des monuments et inscriptions de l'Egypte antique* Series I, Vol. 1, Vienna, 1894, p. 65; also more completely in J. Hawkes (ed.) *Atlas of Ancient Archaeology*, London, 1974, p. 163.

39 W.Y. Adams and H.Å. Nordström, 'The archaeological survey on the west bank of the Nile: third season, 1961–62', *Kush* 11 (1963), 23; Adams, op. cit., p. 183.

40 P.C. Smither, 'The Semnah Despatches', JEA 31 (1945), 3–10.

41 Adams, op. cit., p. 185.

42 J. Vercoutter, 'Le stèle de Mirgissa IM.209 et la localisation d'Iken (Kor ou Mirgissa?)', RdE 16 (1964), 179–91; Vercoutter, *Mirgissa* I, Paris, 1970, pp. 187–9.

43 B.J. Kemp, 'Large Middle Kingdom granary buildings (and the archaeology of administration)', ZÄS 113 (1986), pp. 120–36.

44 A. Badawy, 'Preliminary report on the excavations by the University of California at Askut (first season, October 1962–January 1963)', *Kush* 12 (1964), 47–53; Badawy, 'Askut: a Middle Kingdom fortress in Nubia', *Archaeology* 18 (1965), 124–31; Badawy, 'Archaeological problems relating to the Egyptian fortress at Askut', JARCE 5 (1966), 23–7.

45 J. Vercoutter, 'Kor est-il Iken? Rapport préliminaire sur les fouilles françaises de Kor (Bouhen sud), Sudan, en 1954', *Kush* 3 (1955), 4–19; H.S. Smith, 'Kor. Report on the excavations of the Egypt Exploration Society at Kor, 1965', *Kush* 14 (1966), 187–243; also Kemp, op. cit., 1986.

46 Reisner, Wheeler, and Dunham, op. cit., pp. 22–31, Plates XV–XIX, Map VI.

5 New Kingdom Egypt: the mature state

1 General discussions of the role of the temple in the society of the New Kingdom and later are J.J. Janssen, 'The role of the temple in the Egyptian economy during the New Kingdom', in E. Lipiński (ed.) *State and Temple Economy in the Ancient Near East* II, Leuven, 1979, pp. 505–15; B.J. Kemp, 'Temple and town in ancient Egypt', in P.J. Ucko, R. Tringham, and G.W. Dimbleby (eds) *Man, Settlement and Urbanism*, London, 1972, pp. 657–80; J.H. Johnson, 'The role of the Egyptian priesthood in Ptolemaic Egypt', in L.H. Lesko (ed.) *Egyptological Studies in Honor of Richard A. Parker*, Hanover and London, 1986, pp. 70–84.

2 K.A. Kitchen, 'Barke', *Lexikon* I, pp. 619–25.

3 K.A. Kitchen, 'Nakht-Thuty – Servitor of sacred barques and golden portals', JEA 60 (1974), 168–174; Kitchen, *Pharaoh Triumphant: the Life and Times of Ramesses II, King of Egypt*, Warminster, 1982, p. 172.

4 G. Legrain, 'Le logement et transport des barques sacrées et des statues des dieux dans quelques temples égyptiens', BIFAO 13 (1917), 1–76, is still a valuable documentary source

on the transport of sacred boat-shrines in the New Kingdom and later.

5   B.J. Kemp, 'Fortified towns in Nubia', in Ucko, Tringham, and Dimbleby, op. cit., pp. 651–6.

6   J. Jacquet and H. Wall-Gordon, 'Un bassin de libation du Nouvel Empire dedié à Ptah. Premiére partie. L'architecture/A New Kingdom libation basin dedicated to Ptah. Second part. The inscriptions.' MDAIK 16 (1958), 161–75; R. Anthes, *Mit Rahineh 1956*, Philadelphia, 1965, pp. 72–5, Plates 24–5.

7   See Note 31. Another example, at the gate of the temple of Soleb in Nubia, is documented in M.S. Giorgini, 'Sobeb, campagna 1959–60', *Kush* 9 (1961), 186, Figure 3.

8   The classic source for Nubian territories supplying an Egyptian temple is the Nauri Decree of Seti I, in favour of his temple at Abydos, see F.Ll. Griffith, 'The Abydos Decree of Seti I at Nauri', JEA 13 (1927), 193–208; W.F. Edgerton, 'The Nauri Decree of Seti I. A translation and analysis of the legal portion', JNES 6 (1947), 219–30; Sir A.H. Gardiner, 'Some reflections on the Nauri Decree', JEA 38 (1952), 24–33.

9   K. Baer, 'The low price of land in ancient Egypt', JARCE 1 (1962), 25–45, provides a good introductory discussion of sources and interpretations relevant to landholding in ancient Egypt. His comments on the Wilbour Papyrus have, however, been overtaken by subsequent articles, most recently J.J. Janssen, 'Agrarian administration in Egypt during the Twentieth Dynasty', BibOr 43 (1986), 351–66.

10 Sir A.H. Gardiner and R.O. Faulkner, *The Wilbour Papyrus* I–IV, Brooklyn, 1941–52; S.L.D. Katary, 'Cultivator, scribe, stablemaster, soldier: the Late-Egyptian Miscellanies in light of P. Wilbour', *The Ancient World* 6 (1983), 71–93; Janssen, op. cit., 1986.

11 Sir A.H. Gardiner, 'Ramesside texts relating to the taxation and transport of corn', JEA 27 (1941), 37–56.

12 Discussed in J.-M. Kruchten, *Le Décret d'Horemheb*, Brussels, 1981, pp. 92–3.

13 S. Schott, *Kanais. Der Tempel Sethos I. im Wadi Mia*, Göttingen, 1961, pp. 143–59; AEL II, pp. 52–7.

14 W. Helck, 'Eine Briefsammlung aus der Verwaltung des Amuntempels', JARCE 6 (1967), 135–51. The galena mines have been located, and a small and very crudely built shrine excavated: G. Castel, J.-F. Gout, and G. Soukiassian, 'Fouilles de Gebel Zeit (Mer Rouge). Première et deuxième campagnes (1982–83)', ASAE 70 (1984–5), 99–105; G. Castel and G. Soukiassian, 'Dépôt de stèles dans le sanctuaire du Nouvel Empire au Gebel Zeit', BIFAO 85 (1985), 285–93.

15 J.J. Janssen, *Commodity Prices from the Ramessid Period*, Leiden, 1975, pp. 455–9.

16 Gardiner, op. cit., 1941, 22–37.

17 W.F. Edgerton, 'The strikes in Ramses III's twenty-ninth year', JNES 10 (1951), 144; W. Helck, *Materialien zur Wirtschaftsgeschichte des Neuen Reiches*, Mainz, 1960–4, III, pp. 267–8; IV, p. 410; Sir A.H. Gardiner, *Ramesside Administrative Documents*, London, 1948, p. 64, lines 12 to p. 65, line 4.

18 T.E. Peet, *The Great Tomb-robberies of the Twentieth Egyptian Dynasty*, Oxford, 1930, p. 12, Note 1.

19 H.H. Nelson and U. Hölscher, *Work in Western Thebes 1931–33* (Oriental Institute Communications, 18), Chicago, 1934, pp. 46–51.

20 Pictures of temple magazines and granaries are N. de G. Davies, 'The graphic work of the expedition', *Bulletin of the Metropolitan Museum of Art*, November 1929, Section II supplement, 41–9.

21 U. Hölscher, *The Mortuary Temple of Ramses III* I, Chicago, 1941, pp. 71–82.

22 BAR III, p. 113, § 274.

23 J.J. Janssen, *Two Ancient Egyptian Ship's Logs*, Leiden, 1961, esp. pp. 101–2; see also Chapter 6.

24   AEL I, pp. 215–22.

25   E. Otto, 'Amun', *Lexikon* I, pp. 237–48; D. Arnold, *Der Tempel des Königs Mentuhotep von Deir el-Bahari I. Architektur und Deutung*, Mainz, 1974, pp. 78–80; F. Daumas, 'L'origine d'Amon de Karnak', BIFAO 65 (1967), 201–14.

26   H. Brunner, *Die Geburt des Gottkönigs*, Wiesbaden, 1964. The most easily accessible set of scenes is that of Hatshepsut at Deir el-Bahari, E. Naville, *The Temple of Deir el Bahari* II, London, 1896, Plates 47–55.

27   Naville, op. cit. III, 1898, Plate LXI.

28   On Coronation Days in the New Kingdom, see Sir A.H. Gardiner, 'Regnal years and civil calendar in Pharaonic Egypt', JEA 31 (1945), 25–8; *Lexikon* VI, pp. 532–3.

29   Papyrus Leiden I.350. A.H. Gardiner, 'Hymns to Amon from a Leiden papyrus', ZÄS 42 (1905), 12–42, esp. 20–2; C.F. Nims, *Thebes of the Pharaohs: Pattern for Every City*, London, 1965, p. 69.

30   For Thebes in general see Nims, op. cit. Descriptions of Karnak appear in guide books and books on Egyptian architecture, but more detailed treatments are: P. Barguet, *Le Temple d'Amon-Rê à Karnak: essai d'exégèse*, Cairo, IFAO, 1962; J. Lauffray, *Karnak d'Egypte: Domaine du Divin*, Paris, 1979.

31   Barguet, op. cit., pp. 219–42; C.F. Nims, 'The Eastern Temple at Karnak', in *Beiträge zur ägyptischen Bauforschung und Altertumskunde* 12 (Festschrift Ricke), Wiesbaden, 1971, pp. 107–11; L. Habachi, *Features of the Deification of Ramesses II*, Glückstadt, 1969, p. 20.

32   J. Yoyotte, 'A propos de l'obélisque unique', *Kêmi* 14 (1957), 81–91.

33   Barguet, op. cit., Chapter IV and pp. 283–99; J. Lauffray, 'Le secteur nord-est du temple jubilaire de Thoutmosis III à Karnak. État des lieux et commentaire architectural', *Kêmi* 19 (1969), 179–218; F. Daumas, 'L'interprétation des temples égyptiens anciens à la lumière des temples gréco-romains', *Karnak VI (1973–1977)*, (Cairo, 1980), 261–84; G. Haeny, *Basilikale Anlagen in der aegyptischen Baukunst des Neuen Reiches*, Wiesbaden, 1970, pp. 7–17, 81–93; Lauffray, op. cit., 1979, pp. 125–31; G. Björkman, *Kings at Karnak*, Uppsala, 1971, pp. 84–90; G.A. Gaballa and K.A. Kitchen, 'The festival of Sokar', *Orientalia* 38 (1969), 1–76, esp. 27–28.

34   Barguet, op. cit., pp. 179–82.

35   M. Gitton, 'Le palais de Karnak', BIFAO 74 (1974), 63–73; D.B. Redford, 'Studies on Akhenaten at Thebes. I. A report on the work of the Akhenaten Temple Project of the University Museum, University of Pennsylvania', JARCE 10 (1973), 87–90; R.W. Smith and D.B. Redford, *The Akhenaten Temple Project* I, Warminster, 1976, Chapter 9.

36   On oracles in ancient Egypt, see J. Černý, 'Egyptian oracles', in R.A. Parker, *A Saite Oracle Papyrus from Thebes in The Brooklyn Museum*, Providence, 1962, pp. 35–48; *Lexikon* IV, pp. 600–6. The Hatshepsut text: P. Lacau and H. Chevrier, *Une chapelle d'Hatshepsout à Karnak* I, Cairo, 1977, pp. 92–153; J. Yoyotte, 'La date supposée du couronnement d'Hatshepsout', *Kêmi* 18 (1968), 85–91; Gitton, op. cit.

37   Urk IV, pp. 157–62.

38   Urk IV, p. 837.3; see Björkman, op. cit., pp. 86–7.

39   D.B. Redford, *Akhenaten, the Heretic King*, Princeton, NJ, 1984, Chapter 7.

40   F. Laroche-Traunecker, 'Données nouvelles sur les abords du temple de Khonsou', *Karnak VII (1978–1981)*, (Cairo, 1982), 313–38, esp. 315.

41   Sir A.H. Gardiner, 'Tuthmosis III returns thanks to Amūn', JEA 38 (1952), 20–3; B. Cumming, *Egyptian Historical Records of the Later Eighteenth Dynasty* I, Warminster, 1982, p. 12.

42   Nelson and Hölscher, op. cit., pp. 24–5.

43   W. Wolf, *Das schöne Fest von Opet*, Lepzig, 1931; *Lexikon* IV, pp. 574–9.

44   L. Bell, 'Luxor temple and the cult of the royal *ka*', JNES 44 (1985), 251–94.

45   Sir A.H. Gardiner, 'The coronation of King Ḥaremḥab', JEA 39 (1953), 13–31; R. Hari,

Horemheb et la reine Moutnedjemet, Geneva, 1964, pp. 208–16.

46 H.H. Nelson, 'The identity of Amon-Re of United-with-Eternity', JNES 1 (1942) 127–55.

47 R. Stadelmann, 'Šwt-Rʿw als Kultstätte des Sonnengottes im Neuen Reich', MDAIK 25 (1969), 159–78; B. Lesko, 'Royal mortuary suites of the Egyptian New Kingdom', AJA 73 (1969), 453–8.

48 G. Foucart, 'Études thébaines. La Belle Fête de la Vallée', BIFAO 24 (1924), 1–209; S. Schott, *Das schöne Fest vom Wüstentale*, Wiesbaden, 1952; Kitchen, op. cit., 1982, p. 169.

49 W.J. Murnane, *United with Eternity: a Concise Guide to the Monuments of Medinet Habu*, Chicago and Cairo, 1980, pp. 76–7; *Lexikon* III, pp. 1256–8.

50 R. Stadelmann, 'Tempel und Tempelnamen in Theben-Ost und -West', MDAIK 34 (1978), 171–80.

51 R. Stadelmann, 'Tempelpalast und Erscheinungsfenster in der Thebanischen Totentempeln', MDAIK 29 (1973), 221–42.

52 Murnane, op. cit., p. 70.

53 Stadelmann, op. cit., 1973; B.J. Kemp, 'The Window of Appearance at El-Amarna, and the basic structure of this city', JEA 62 (1976), 81–99.

54 J.-M. Kruchten, op. cit., pp. 162–77, 199–200; J.-M. Kruchten 'Rétribution de l'armée d'après le décret d'Horemheb', in *L'égyptologie en 1979: axes prioritaires de recherches*, II (Colloques Internationaux du Centre National de la Recherche Scientifique, no. 595), Paris, 1982, pp. 144–8.

55 Stadelmann, op. cit., 1973.

56 The source material is conveniently listed in E. Hornung and E. Staehelin, *Studien zum Sedfest* (Aegyptiaca Helvetica 1), Basel and Geneva, 1974, pp. 33–6. See also W.J. Murnane, 'The Sed Festival: a problem in historical method', MDAIK 37 (1981), 369–76.

57 W. Stevenson Smith, *The Art and Architecture of Ancient Egypt*, 2nd edn, Harmondsworth, 1981, pp. 282–95; W.C. Hayes, 'Inscriptions from the Palace of Amenhotep III', JNES 10 (1951), 35–56, 82–111, 156–83, 231–42; B.J. Kemp and D.B. O'Connor, 'An ancient Nile harbour. University Museum excavations at the "Birket Habu"', *International Journal of Nautical Archaeology and Underwater Exploration* 3 (1974), 101–36.

58 The Epigraphic Survey, *The Tomb of Kheruef* (Oriental Institute Publications 102), Chicago, 1980, Plate 28, p. 43.

59 It is interesting to note that the earliest depiction of a Sed-festival element – the king seated on a high throne beneath a tent – occurs on one of the boats in the Hierakonpolis Decorated Tomb, see Figure 11, p. 40. However, we cannot be sure that a Sed-festival is meant. In depictions of the Early Dynastic Period and at the Step Pyramid boat imagery is absent.

60 The Epigraphic Survey, op. cit., Plates 56, 57, pp. 59–61.

61 The most important comparative source would have been the king's mortuary temple, of which little now survives. The Sed-festival fragments are published in G. Haeny, *Untersuchungen im Totentempel Amenophis' III*, Wiesbaden, 1981, Taf. 40–2. The Soleb temple scenes, LD III, Bl. 83, 84, also contain no reflection of the Kheruef scenes, although the ritual door-knocking is also a new element in the repertoire.

62 The Epigraphic Survey op. cit., Plates 42, 44, pp. 49–51.

63 A good general review of New Kingdom palaces is in Stevenson Smith, op. cit., Chapters 15 and 17.

64 As mentioned on the king's boundary stelae. For a discussion of royal tenting, see B.J. Kemp, 'A building of Amenophis III at Kôm El-ʿAbd', JEA 63 (1977), 77–8.

65 A.H. Gardiner (ed.) *The Wilbour Papyrus* II, Brooklyn and Oxford, 1948, p. 18; Kruchten, op. cit., 1981, 111–12.

66 R.A. Caminos, *Late Egyptian Miscellanies*, London, 1954, pp. 198–201.

67 Gardiner, op. cit., 1948, p. 18; Helck, op. cit., 1960–4, p. 235=1017.

68 U. Hölscher, *Das Grabdenkmal des Königs Chephren*, Leipzig, 1912, pp. 81–3, 86–7, Blatt XV, Abb. 75; Ahmed Bey Kamal, 'Rapport sur les fouilles du comte de Galarza', ASAE 10 (1910), 116–17. See also the aerial photograph in H. Ricke, *Der Harmachistempel des Chefren in Giseh* (Beiträge zur ägyptischen Bauforschung und Altertumskunde 10), Wiesbaden, 1970, Frontispiz. A staircase probably belonging to this palace is illustrated in Taf. 3, cf. p. xii.

69 Kemp, op. cit., 1977, 71–82.

70 A convenient plan is A. Badawy, *A History of Egyptian Architecture: The Empire (the New Kingdom)*, Berkeley and Los Angeles, Calif., 1968, p. 53, Fig. 29; see also D.G. Jeffreys, *The Survey of Memphis* I, London, 1985, pp. 15, 19–20, Fig. 63.

71 B.J. Kemp, 'The Harîm-Palace at Medinet el-Ghurab', ZÄS 105 (1978), 122–33.

72 A. de Buck, 'The Judicial Papyrus of Turin', JEA 23 (1937), 152–64.

73 Stevenson Smith, op. cit., pp. 278–81; P. Lacovara, 'Archaeological survey of Deir el-Ballas', NARCE 113 (Winter 1980), 3–11; Lacovara, 'Archaeological survey and excavation at Deir el-Ballas 1985', NARCE 129 (Spring 1985), 17–29; Lacovara, 'The Hearst Excavations at Deir el-Ballas: the Eighteenth Dynasty town', in W.K. Simpson and W.M. Davis (eds) *Studies in Ancient Egypt, the Aegean and the Sudan: Essays in Honor of Dows Dunham*, Boston, 1981, pp. 120–4.

74 W. Spiegelberg, *Rechnungen aus der Zeit Setis I*, Strassburg, 1896; Helck, op. cit., 1960–4, IV, pp. 633–41; A.J. Spalinger, 'Baking during the reign of Seti I', BIFAO 86 (1986), 307–52.

75 E.F. Campbell, *The Chronology of the Amarna Letters*, Baltimore, 1964. For samples of the style of the letters, see A.L. Oppenheim, *Letters from Mesopotamia*, Chicago, 1967, pp. 119–34. Each letter has its own modern identifying number and the prefix EA.

76 A.R. Schulman, 'Diplomatic marriage in the Egyptian New Kingdom', JNES 38 (1979), 177–93.

77 K.A. Kitchen, *Suppiluliuma and the Amarna Pharaohs*, Liverpool, 1962, p. 14.

78 The classic case is that of the Inscription of Mes, summarized in Kitchen, op. cit., 1982, pp. 128–9.

79 A.R. Schulman, *Military Rank, Title and Organization in the Egyptian New Kingdom*, Berlin, 1964; Y. Yadin, *The Art of Warfare in Biblical Lands*, London, 1963, provides a good illustrated summary of Egyptian military technology of the period.

80 Kruchten, op. cit., 1981, pp. 82–95, 162–77, also note 54 above.

81 'Militärkolonie', *Lexikon* IV, p. 135; D.B. O'Connor, 'The geography of settlement in ancient Egypt', in Ucko, Tringham, and Dimbleby, op. cit., p. 695. The land at the heart of the dispute in the Inscription of Mes provides another example.

82 The military background to the Amarna Period is discussed by A.R. Schulman, 'Some observations on the military background of the Amarna Period', JARCE 3 (1964), 51–69. On Horemheb's origins, see A.R. Schulman, 'The Berlin "Trauerrelief" (No. 12411) and some officials of Tut'ankhamūn and Ay', JARCE 4 (1965), 58–61. Subsequently Horemheb came to be regarded as the inaugurator of a new era: see A.K. Phillips, 'Horemheb, founder of the XIXth Dynasty? O. Cairo 25646 reconsidered', *Orientalia* 46 (1977), 116–21. For the origins of the 19th Dynasty, see Kitchen, op. cit., 1982, pp. 15–18; E. Cruz-Uribe, 'The father of Ramses I: OI 11456', JNES 37 (1978), 237–44. A. Kadry, 'The social status and education of military scribes in Egypt during the 18th Dynasty', *Oikumene* (Budapest) 5 (1986), 155–62, is also valuable.

83 In Papyrus Anastasi II and Papyrus Sallier I, see Caminos, 1954, pp. 51, 317.

84 *Lexikon* II, pp. 1241–9.

85 C. Aldred, 'More light on the Ramesside Tomb Robberies', in J. Ruffle, G.A. Gaballa, and K.A. Kitchen, *Glimpses of Ancient Egypt; Studies in Honour of H.W. Fairman*, Warminster, 1979, pp. 92–9.

6 The birth of economic man

1 For economic anthropologists and historians Polanyi's work remains a landmark in the formulation of concepts, even though specific case studies show that Polanyi has not supplied a set of ground rules for the full understanding of past economies. A detailed discussion of Polanyi's work, with biographical and bibliographical notes, is 'Symposium: economic anthropology and history: the work of Karl Polanyi', *Research in Economic Anthropology* 4 (1981), 1–93 (translated from *Annales: économies, sociétés, civilisations*, December 1974). A more recent discussion of Polanyi's general significance is R.H. Halperin, 'Polanyi, Marx, and the institutional paradigm in economic anthropology', *Research in Economic Anthropology* 6 (1984), 245–72. A case study critical of the Polanyi approach in an area crucial to Polanyi's arguments is B.M. Perinbam, 'Homo Africanus: antiquus or oeconomicus? Some interpretations of African economic history', *Comparative Studies in Society and History* 19 (1977), 156–78.

2 Three contributions which particularly prompted this chapter are R. Müller-Wollermann, 'Warenaustausch im Ägypten des Alten Reiches', JESHO 28 (1985), 121–68; J. Renger, 'Patterns of non-institutional trade and non-commercial exchange in ancient Mesopotamia at the beginning of the second millennium B.C.: Part I. Some remarks on Karl Polanyi's conception of marketless trading and the study of ancient economies', in A. Archi (ed.) *Circulation of Goods in Non-palatial Context in the Ancient Near East* (Incunabula Graeca, LXXXII), Rome, 1984, pp. 31–73. Egypt is dealt with on pp. 52–8; E. Bleiberg, 'The king's privy purse during the New Kingdom: an examination of *inw*', JARCE 21 (1984), 155–67, esp. 155–6. Behind these publications, however, stands the cogent and thoughtful work of J.J. Janssen, including: 'Prolegomena to the study of Egypt's economic history during the New Kingdom', SAK 3 (1975a), 127–85; 'Die Struktur der pharaonischen Wirtschaft', GM 48 (1981), 59–77; *Commodity Prices from the Ramessid Period*, Leiden, 1975b, Part III.

3 E.g. the Abusir Papyri for the Old Kingdom: P. Posener-Kriéger, *Les Archives du temple funéraire de Néferirkarê-Kakaï* (Bibliothèque d'Etude LXV), Cairo, 1976; P. Posener-Kriéger, 'Les papyrus d'Abousir et l'économie des temples funéraires de l'Ancien Empire', in E. Lipiński (ed.) *State and Temple Economy in the Ancient Near East* I, Leuven, 1979, pp. 133–51; and a newly discovered group, P. Posener-Kriéger, *Mélanges Gamal Eddin Mokhtar* (=Bibliothèque d'Etude 97/2), Cairo, 1985, pp. 195–210; Posener-Kriéger, 'Les nouveaux Papyrus d'Abousir', JSSEA 13 (1983), 51–7; for the Middle Kingdom and Lahun/Kahun Papyri: L. Borchardt, 'Der zweite Papyrusfund von Kahun und die zeitliche Festlegung des mittleren Reiches der ägyptischen Geschichte', ZÄS 37 (1899), 89–103; F.Ll. Griffith, *Hieratic Papyri from Kahun and Gurob*, London, 1898; and Papyrus Bulaq 18: A. Scharff, 'Ein Rechnungsbuch des königlichen Hofes aus der 13. Dynastie. (Papyrus Boulaq Nr. 18)', ZÄS 57 (1922), 51–68; A.J. Spalinger, 'Notes on the day summary accounts of P. Bulaq 18 and the intradepartmental transfers', SAK 12 (1985), 179–241; for the New Kingdom the Memphite palace accounts from the reign of Seti I: W. Spiegelberg, *Rechnungen aus der Zeit Setis I*, Strassburg, 1896; Spalinger, 'Baking during the reign of Seti I', BIFAO 86 (1986), 307–352. Also the texts published by A.H. Gardiner, 'Ramesside texts relating to the taxation and transport of corn', JEA 27 (1941), 19–73; M. Megally, *Le Papyrus hiératique comptable E.3226 du Louvre*, Cairo, 1971; *Recherches sur l'économie, l'administration et la comptabilité égyptiennes à la XVIIIᵉ dynastie d'après le papyrus E.3226 du Louvre*, Cairo, 1977; Janssen, op. cit., 1975a, 166–70.

4 A. Badawy, *A History of Egyptian Architecture: the Empire (the New Kingdom)*, Berkeley and Los Angeles, Calif., 1968, pp. 119–23, 128–47; B.J. Kemp, 'Large Middle Kingdom granary buildings (and the archaeology of administration)', ZÄS 113 (1986), 120–36.

5 Cf. B.G. Trigger, B.J. Kemp, D.B. O'Connor, and A.B. Lloyd, *Ancient Egypt: a Social History*, Cambridge, 1983, pp. 85ff.; B.J. Kemp, 'Temple and town in ancient Egypt', in P.J. Ucko,

R. Tringham, and G.W. Dimbleby (eds) *Man, Settlement and Urbanism*, London, 1972, pp. 657–80; Janssen, op. cit., 1975a, 180–2; J.J. Janssen, 'The role of the temple in the Egyptian economy during the New Kingdom', in Lipiński, op. cit., pp. 505–15; H. Goedicke, 'Cult-temple and "state" during the Old Kingdom in Egypt', in ibid. I, pp. 113–31; J.H. Johnson, 'The role of the Egyptian priesthood in Ptolemaic Egypt', in L.H. Lesko (ed.) *Egyptological Studies in Honor of R.H. Parker*, Hanover and London, 1986, pp. 70–84.

6   'Phyle', *Lexikon* IV, p. 1044; P. Posener-Kriéger, op. cit., 1979, II, pp. 565–74.

7   J.-M. Kruchten, *Le Décret d'Horemheb*, Brussels, 1981. It has also been pointed out that 'The duties of the vizier' text known from several New Kingdom tombs, whilst it has an internal logic of association which enables it to achieve its purpose of profiling the importance of the vizier, lacks the systematic presentation of the vizier's duties that we ourselves tend to expect of such a text. See G.P.F. Van den Boorn, 'On the date of "The Duties of the Vizier"', *Orientalia* N.S. 51 (1982), 369–81.

8   E.g. the autobiography of Weni, AEL I, p. 21; A.A.M.A. Amer, 'Tutankhamun's decree for the Chief Treasurer Maya', RdE 36 (1985), 18–20.

9   N. de G. Davies, *The Tomb of Rekh-mi-rè' at Thebes*, New York, 1943, pp. 32–6, 103–6, Plates XXIX–XXXV.

10   F. Ll. Griffith, 'The Abydos Decree of Seti I at Nauri', JEA 13 (1927), 193–206; Sir A.H. Gardiner, 'Some reflections on the Nauri Decree', JEA 38 (1952), 24–33; W.F. Edgerton, 'The Nauri Decree of Seti I. A translation and analysis of the legal portion', JNES 6 (1947), 219–30.

11   Elephantine: JEA 13 (1927), 207–8; Armant: R. Mond and O.H. Myers, *Temples of Armant*, London, 1940, p. 161; Hermopolis: H. Brunner, 'Das Fragment eines Schutzdekretes aus dem Neuen Reich', MDIAAK 8 (1939), 161–4.

12   H. Goedicke, *Königliche Dokumente aus dem Alten Reich*, Wiesbaden, 1967.

13   E.g. R.A. Caminos, *Late-Egyptian Miscellanies*, London, 1954, pp. 17–20, 273–5, 280–93, 325–8, 454–64.

14   Beni Hasan: J. Garstang, *The Burial Customs of Ancient Egypt*, London, 1907, esp. Plates III, IV; also B.J. Kemp, 'Egypt' in J. Hawkes (ed.) *Atlas of Ancient Archaeology*, London, 1974, p. 151; Naga ed-Deir: G.A. Reisner, *A Provincial Cemetery of the Pyramid Age: Naga-ed-Dêr, Part III*, Oxford, 1932; D.B. O'Connor, 'Political systems and archaeological data in Egypt: 2600–1780 BC' *World Archaeology* 6 (1974), 22–3.

15   Serious political intrigue amongst these locally powerful men is hinted at in the 6th Dynasty letter from Elephantine published by P.C. Smither 'An Old Kingdom letter concerning the crimes of Count Sabni', in JEA 28 (1942), 16–19. For the politics of the First Intermediate Period, see F. Gomaà, *Ägypten während der Ersten Zwischenzeit* (Beihefte TAVO B27), Wiesbaden, 1980.

16   For Ankhtify, see J. Vandier, *Mo'alla: la tombe d'Ankhtifi et la tombe de Sébekhotep*, Cairo, 1950; W. Schenkel, *Memphis, Herakleopolis, Theben*, Wiesbaden, 1965, pp. 45–57; Gomaà, op. cit., pp. 38–9; similar claims by other men of the time are conveniently translated in AEL I, pp. 87–90.

17   G. Brunton, *Qau and Badari* I, II, London, 1927, 1928; G. Brunton, *Mostagedda*, London, 1937; G. Brunton, *Matmar*, London, 1948; D.B. O'Connor, *World Archaeology* 6 (1974), 24–7.

18   D.B. O'Connor, 'A regional population in Egypt to circa 600 B.C.', in B. Spooner (ed.) *Population Growth: Anthropological Implications*, Cambridge, Mass., and London, 1972, pp. 78–100.

19   Brunton, op. cit., 1927, p. 76.

20   T.G.H. James, *The Ḥekanakhte Papers and Other Early Middle Kingdom Documents*, New York, 1962; K. Baer, 'An Eleventh Dynasty farmer's letters to his family', JAOS 83 (1963), 1–19; T.G.H. James, *Pharaoh's People: Scenes from Life in Imperial Egypt*, London, 1984, pp. 113–14,

242–7; U. Luft, 'Illahunstudien, III: zur sozialen Stellung des Totenpriesters im Mittleren Reich', *Oikumene* (Budapest) 5 (1986), 150–3.

21 Baer, op. cit., 12; cf. Luft, op. cit., 150.

22 Baer, op. cit., 19.

23 ibid., 16–17.

24 W. Helck, 'Wirtschaftliche Bemerkungen zum privaten Grabbesitz im Alten Reich', MDAIK 14 (1956), 63–75; 24. W. Helck, *Wirtschaftsgeschichte des Alten Ägypten im 3. und 2. Jahrtausend vor Chr.*, Leiden, 1975, Chapter 8. These sources also boast of private provision of elements for one's tomb.

25 J.J. Janssen and P.W. Pestman, 'Burial and inheritance in the community of the necropolis workmen at Thebes (Pap. Bulaq X and O. Petrie 16)', JESHO 11 (1968), 137–70.

26 Caminos, op. cit., *passim*.

27 S.R.K. Glanville, 'The letters of Aaḥmōse of Peniati', JEA 14 (1928), 294–312; James, op. cit., 1984, pp. 172–5. Papyrus BM10102

28 H.E. Winlock, *Models of Daily Life in Ancient Egypt*, New York, 1955, Section IV.

29 B.J. Kemp, 'The city of el-Amarna as a source for the study of urban society in ancient Egypt', *World Archaeology* 9 (1977), 123–39; P. Crocker, 'Status symbols in the architecture of El-Amarna', JEA 71 (1985), 52–65; C. Tietze, 'Amarna. Analyse der Wohnhäuser und soziale Struktur der Stadtbewohner', ZÄS 112 (1985), 48–84.

31 T.E. Peet, *The Great Tomb-robberies of the Twentieth Egyptian Dynasty*, Oxford, 1930.

32 H. Frankfort, and J.D.S. Pendlebury, *The City of Akhenaten* II, London, 1933, pp. 59–61. Plate XLIII. For the Hittite figurine, and a discussion of the circumstances of the find and its significance, see M. Bell, 'A Hittite pendant from Amarna', AJA 90 (1986), 145–51.

33 James, op. cit., 1984, p. 186, and Plate 11 (top).

34 Müller-Wollermann, op. cit., 163–4.

35 A. Lucas and J.R. Harris, *Ancient Egyptian Materials and Industries*, 4th edn, London, 1962, pp. 59–61; I.M.E. Shaw, 'A survey at Hatnub', in B.J. Kemp, *Amarna Reports* III, London, 1986, Chapter 10.

36 As is regularly done today by Egyptian Antiquities Organization guards responsible for Hatnub. The journey time is about three hours in each direction.

37 Dorothea Arnold, 'Ägyptische Mergeltone ("Wüstentone") und die Herkunft einer Mergeltonware des Mittleren Reiches aus der Gegend von Memphis', in D. Arnold (ed.) *Studien zur altägyptischen Keramik*, Mainz, 1981, pp. 167–91; P. Nicholson and H. Patterson, 'Pottery making in Upper Egypt: an ethnoarchaeological study', *World Archaeology* 17 (1985), 222–39.

38 G. Caton-Thompson and E.W. Gardner, *The Desert Fayum*, London, 1934, Chapters XXIII–XXVI.

39 *Lexikon* IV, pp. 197–8, 358; cf. Janssen, op. cit., 1975a, 163.

40 On foreign trade discussed from an archaeological background see R.S. Merrillees, *The Cypriote Bronze Age Pottery Found in Egypt*, Lund, 1968, pp. 173f., also 194; B.J. Kemp and R.S. Merrillees, *Minoan Pottery in Second Millennium Egypt*, Mainz, 1980, pp. 276 ff.

41 P.E. Newberry, *Beni Hasan* I, London, 1893, p. 69, Plates XXX, XXXI, XXVIII, XXXVIII; J.R. Harris, *Lexicographical Studies in Ancient Egyptian Minerals*, Berlin, 1961, pp. 174–6; W. Helck, *Die Beziehungen Ägyptens zu Vorderasien im 3. und 2. Jahrtausend v.Chr.*, 2nd edn, Wiesbaden, 1971, pp. 41–2. H. Goedicke, 'Abi-Sha(i)'s representation at Beni Hasan', JARCE 21 (1984), 203–10 argues against the view that the Asiatics were a trading mission at all, on two basic grounds: that galena was available to the Egyptians a lot closer (Red Sea hills deposits), and that it is an improbable route for Asiatics from Moab to have taken first to the eastern delta and then on to Beni Hasan. The first point, however, has little validity. If Asiatics were bringing galena this would have represented an easier source for the

Egyptians than gaining it by direct exploitation from the Red Sea margins, a dangerous area for Nile Valley dwellers. Furthermore the New Kingdom provides explicit references to galena from western Asia. Second, people living in south-east Palestine could have taken a route across central Sinai, perhaps via the Wadi el-Arish, to the head of the Gulf of Suez, so avoiding the likely Egyptian controls over access into the eastern delta. From here to Middle Egypt involves following the Red Sea coast southwards to the Wadi Araba, which provides a relatively easy journey to the Nile in the vicinity of Beni Suef. Beni Suef itself was outside Khnumhetep's own nome, but one can argue that the exercise recorded in his tomb portrayed his jurisdiction over the desert routes feeding into this key zone of Middle Egypt. Khnumhetep's role may have been to offer to these routes the same kind of control over immigration that others exercised over the eastern delta and the Second Cataract in Nubia.

42 Janssen, op. cit., 1975b; James, op. cit., 1984, Chapter 9. For the stone weights, see D. Valbelle, *Catalogue des poids à inscriptions hiératiques de Deir el-Médineh. Nos. 5001–5423*, Cairo, 1977; M. Cour-Marty, 'La collection de poids du Musée du Caire revisitée', RdE 36 (1985), 189–200.

43 ibid., 1975b, 9.

44 ibid., pp. 180–4.

45 Janssen, op. cit., 1975b, 292–8.

46 ibid., Chapter 2. For unrest blamed on hunger in the later Ramesside Period, see C.J. Eyre, 'A "strike" text from the Theban necropolis', in J. Ruffle, G.A. Gaballa, and K.A. Kitchen (eds) *Orbis Aegyptiorum Speculum: Glimpses of Ancient Egypt: Studies in Honour of H.W. Fairman*, Warminster, 1979, pp. 80–91. For Libyan raiders as another cause of Theban disruption, see K.A. Kitchen, 'Les suites des guerres libyennes de Ramsès III', RdE 36 (1985), 177–9.

47 Whether the well-known 'bank' (*mryt*) of western Thebes where trading and other activities took place was really by the river, or a different kind of place using the word 'bank' metaphorically, remains to be determined. See J. Černý, *A Community of Workmen at Thebes in the Ramesside Period*, Cairo, 1973, pp. 94–7, for the basic references.

48 N. de G. Davies, *Two Ramesside Tombs at Thebes*, New York, 1927, Plate XXX; James, op. cit., 1984, pp. 250–2, Fig. 25.

49 The jar on the left is fitted with a right-angled drinking tube, particularly used with beer, cf. James, op. cit., 1984, p. 252.

50 N. de G. Davies and R.O. Faulkner, 'A Syrian trading venture to Egypt', JEA 33 (1947), 40–6; James, op. cit., 1984, pp. 253–6. Fig. 26.

51 Frankfort and Pendlebury, op. cit., p. 19, Plate XXXIII.3 (House U.36.41).

52 A. Moussa and H. Altenmüller, *Das Grab des Nianchchnum und Chnumhotep*, Mainz, 1977, pp. 84–5, Taf. 24, Abb. 10; Müller-Wollermann, op. cit., 138ff.; James, op. cit., 1984, pp. 254–8, Fig. 27; cf. also S.I. Hodjash and O.D. Berlev, 'A market-scene in the mastaba of *Ḏꜣḏꜣ-m-ꜥnḫ (Tp-m-ꜥnḫ)*', Altorientalische Forschungen 7 (1980), 31–49.

53 For Old Kingdom cattle prices expressed in terms of vases of oil, see B. Vachala, 'A note on prices of oxen in Dynasty V', ZÄS 114 (1987), 91–5.

54 J.J. Janssen, 'Khaꜥemtore, a well-to-do workman', *OMRO* 58 (1977), 221–32; Janssen, op. cit., 1975b, pp. 533–8; E.S. Bogoslovsky, 'Hundred Egyptian draughtsmen', ZÄS 107 (1980), 89–116.

55 J.J. Janssen, 'The water supply of a desert village', *B Medelhavsmuseet* 14 (1979), 9–15; Janssen, op. cit., 1975b, pp. 448–9.

56 B.J. Kemp, *Amarna Reports* I–IV, London, 1984–7.

57 J.J. Janssen, *Two Ancient Egyptian Ship's Logs*, Leiden, 1961, pp. 101–4; James, op. cit., 1984, 247–8.

58 Papyrus Lansing 6.9–7.1 = Caminos, op. cit., p. 390; cf. Janssen, op. cit., 1961, p. 103.

59 Caminos, op. cit., p. 138; also the trader returning from Syria in ibid., p. 16 = Papyrus Bologna 1094, 5.5–5.6.

60 T.E. Peet, 'The unit of value *šʿty* in Papyrus Bulaq 11', *Mélanges Maspero* I, Cairo, 1934, pp. 185–99; Janssen, op. cit., 1975a, 162; James, op. cit., 1984, 260–1.

61 B.J. Kemp, 'The Window of Appearance at El-Amarna, and the basic structure of this city', JEA 62 (1976), 81–99; D.B. Redford, *A Study of the Biblical Story of Joseph (Genesis 37–50)*, Leiden, 1970, pp. 208–226; R.W. Smith and D.B. Redford, *The Akhenaten Temple Project* I, Warminster, 1976, pp. 123–34.

62 Davies, op. cit., 1943, pp. 32–6, 103–6, Plates XXIX–XXXV.

7 Egypt in microcosm: the city of el-Amarna

1   The most complete edition of one of the most elaborately decorated tombs is A. Piankoff and N. Rambova, *The Tomb of Ramesses VI*, New York, 1954. See also the article by A. Piankoff discussing these compositions in connection with the Amarna Period, 'Les grandes compositions religieuses du Nouvel Empire et la réforme d'Amarna', in BIFAO 62 (1964), 121–8.

2   Like Nakht-djehuty, builder extraordinary of sacred boats, see p. 185 and Note 3. He is one of a list of famous men in a tomb at Sakkara, K.A. Kitchen, 'Nakht-Thuty – servitor of sacred barques and golden portals', JEA 60 (1974), 172, Note 11.

3   For this and other didactic teachings see AEL I.

4   The literature on the Amarna Period is extensive. General surveys are C. Aldred, *Akhenaten, King of Egypt*, London, 1988; C. Aldred, *Akhenaten and Nefertiti*, New York, 1973; D.B. Redford, *Akhenaten, the Heretic King*, Princeton, NJ, 1984; D.B. Redford, *History and Chronology of the Eighteenth Dynasty of Egypt*, Toronto, 1967, Chapters 5 and 6; F.J. Giles, *Ikhnaton: Legend and History*, London, 1970; H.A. Schlögl, *Echnaton-Tutanchamun: Fakten und Texte*, Wiesbaden, 1983; R. Hari, *New Kingdom Amarna Period: the Great Hymn to Aten* (Iconography of Religions, Section XVI: Egypt, fasc. 6), Leiden, 1985; A.M. Blackman, 'A study of the liturgy celebrated in the Temple of the Aton at El-Amarna', in *Recueil d'études égyptologiques dédiées à la mémoire de Jean-François Champollion* (Bibliothèque de l'Ecole des Hautes Etudes, 234), Paris, 1922, pp. 505–27.

5   A. Piankoff, *The Litany of Re*, New York, 1964.

6   AEL II, pp. 89–100.

7   Conveniently translated in ANET, pp. 365–7.

8   J. Wilson, 'Akh-en-aton and Nefert-iti', JNES 32 (1973), 235–41.

9   On Tutankhamun's parentage, see J.D. Ray, 'The parentage of Tutankhamūn', *Antiquity* 49 (1975), 45–7; E.S. Meltzer, 'The parentage of Tutʿankhamun and Smenkhkarēʿ', JEA 64 (1978), 134–5; J. Vandier, 'Toutânkhamon, sa famille, son règne', *Journal des savants* (1967), 67–91.

10 R. Anthes, *Die Maat des Echnaton von Amarna* (Supplement to JAOS 14, April–June 1952).

11 See Aldred, op. cit., 1973; also C. Desroches-Noblecourt, *Monuments et mémoires* (Foundation Eugène Piot) 59 (1974), 1–44. See also the references cited in W. Stevenson Smith, *The Art and Architecture of Ancient Egypt*, 2nd edn, Harmondsworth, 1981, p. 461, Note 302.

12 N. de G. Davies, *The Rock Tombs of El-Amarna* V, London, 1908; AEL II, pp. 48–51. An important field collation of these texts has been carried out by W.J. Murnane, who has established the date of the earlier proclamation as being Akhenaten's fifth regnal year, not his fourth. See 'The El-Amarna Boundary Stelae Project: a preliminary report', NARCE 128 (Winter 1984), 40–52.

13 *Lexikon* VI, pp. 812–16.

14 J. Bennett, 'The Restoration Inscription of Tutʿankhamūn', JEA 25 (1939), 8–15; ANET, pp. 251–2.

15 In the Inscription of Mes, see G.A. Gaballa, *The Memphite Tomb-Chapel of Mose*, Warminster, 1977, p. 25; and in a 19th Dynasty letter, A.H. Gardiner, 'A later allusion to Akhenaten', JEA 24 (1938), 124.

16 *Lexikon* VI, pp. 309–19; C. Aldred, 'El-Amarna', in T.G.H. James (ed.) *Excavating in Egypt: The Egypt Exploration Society 1882–1982*, London, 1982, pp. 89–106. The principal excavation reports are W.M.F. Petrie, *Tell el Amarna*, London, 1894; L. Borchardt and H. Ricke, *Die Wohnhäuser in Tell el-Amarna*, Berlin, 1980; T.E. Peet and C.L. Woolley, *The City of Akhenaten* I, London, 1923; H. Frankfort and J.D.S. Pendlebury, *The City of Akhenaten* II, London, 1933;

J.D.S. Pendlebury, *The City of Akhenaten* III, London, 1951. Current work is summarized in the series B.J. Kemp *et al.*, *Amarna Reports* (London 1984–). See also H.W. Fairman, 'Town planning in Pharaonic Egypt', *Town Planning Review* 20 (1949), 32–51; A. Badawy, *A History of Egyptian Architecture: The Empire (the New Kingdom)*, Berkeley and Los Angeles, Calif., 1968, pp. 76–126; B.J. Kemp, 'The city of el-Amarna as a source for the study of urban society in ancient Egypt', *World Archaeology* 9 (1977), 123–39; Kemp, 'The character of the South Suburb at Tell el-'Amarna', MDOG 113 (1981a), 81–97.

17 *Lexikon* I, p. 601; K.W. Butzer, 'Archäologische Fundstellen Ober- und Mittelägyptens in ihrer geologischen Landschaft', MDAIK 17 (1961), 62–5, Abb. I. See also D. Kessler, *Historische Topographie der Region zwischen Mallawi und Samalut* (Beihefte TAVO B30), Tübingen, 1981.

18 The most informed estimates are bound to be very approximate. See the discussions in K. Baer, 'The low price of land in ancient Egypt', JARCE I (1962), 39–45; Fekri A. Hassan, 'Environment and subsistence in predynastic Egypt', in J.D. Clark and S.A. Brandt (eds) (*c.* 1984) *From Hunters to Farmers: the Causes and Consequences of Food Production in Africa*, Berkeley and Los Angeles, Calif., *c.* 1984, pp. 57–64, esp. p. 63.

19 Summarized in Redford, op. cit., 1984, 134–6. See also Ramadan Saad and L. Manniche, 'A unique offering list of Amenophis IV recently found at Karnak', JEA 57 (1971), 70–2; W. Helck, 'Zur Opferliste Amenophis' IV', JEA 59 (1973), 95–9.

20 A reasonably complete edition is N. de G. Davies, *The Rock Tombs of El-Amarna* I–VI, London, 1903–8.

21 G. Roeder, *Amarna-Reliefs aus Hermopolis*, Hildesheim, 1969; R. Hanke, ibid. (Hildesheim 1978); J.D. Cooney, *Amarna Reliefs from Hermopolis in American Collections*, Mainz, 1965.

22 For the royal cemetery see G.T. Martin, *The Royal Tomb at El-'Amarna* I, London, 1974; Aly el-Khouly and G.T. Martin, *Excavations in the Royal Necropolis at El-'Amarna 1984*, Cairo, 1987. The suggestion that the unfinished annexe was for Nefertiti is also Martin's, see *The Illustrated London News* 269, no. 6998 (September 1981), 66–7.

23 Petrie, op. cit., pp. 4–5, Plate XXXV; Davies, op. cit., II, pp. 5–6, Plate I; IV, p. 11, Plate XIII; P. Timme, *Tell el-Amarna vor der deutschen Ausgrabung im Jahre 1911*, Leipzig, 1917, pp. 24ff., and maps.

24 Kemp *et al.*, I–IV; B.J. Kemp, 'The Amarna Workmen's Village in retrospect', JEA 73 (1987), 21–50.

25 A final publication of the Egypt Exploration Society's North City excavations is in progress. For preliminary reports, see J.D.S. Pendlebury, 'Preliminary report of excavations at Tell el-'Amarnah, 1931–2', JEA 17 (1931), 240–3; Pendlebury, 'Preliminary report of the excavations at Tell el-'Amarnah, 1931–2', JEA 18 (1932), 143–5; T. Whittemore, 'The excavations at El-'Amarnah, season 1924–5', JEA 12 (1926), 3–12; M. Jones, 'Preliminary report on the El-'Amarna expedition, 1981–2. Appendix 1: the North City', JEA 69 (1983), 15–21.

26 F.G. Newton, 'Excavations at El-'Amarnah, 1923–24', JEA 10 (1924), 294–8; Whittemore, op. cit., 4–9; H. Frankfort (ed.) *The Mural Painting of El-'Amarneh*, London, 1929, Chapter III.

27 The Central City is fully published in Pendlebury, op. cit., 1951.

28 See the additional discussions, E.P. Uphill, 'The Per Aten at Amarna', JNES 29 (1970), 151–66; J. Assmann, 'Palast oder Tempel? Überlegungen zur Architektur und Topographie von Amarna', JNES 31 (1972), 143–55.

29 See the additional discussions, A. Badawy, 'The symbolism of the temples at ʿAmarna', ZÄS 87 (1962), 79–95; P. Barguet, 'Note sur le grand temple d'Aton à el-Amarna', RdE 28 (1976), 148–51.

30 For an alternative reconstruction, see Kemp et al., IV, Chapter 8.

31 This sequence was determined during the 1987 season of fieldwork, and is to be published in Kemp et al., V.

32 B.J. Kemp, 'The Window of Appearance at El-Amarna, and the basic structure of this city', JEA 62 (1976), 91–2; R. Stadelmann, 'Tempelpalast und Erscheinungsfenster in den Thebanischen Totentempeln', MDAIK 29 (1973), 221–42.

33 Pendlebury, op. cit., 1951, pp. 140–2.

34 P. Ermitage 1116 A, verso, line 118: W. Golénischeff, Les Papyrus hiératiques NoNo 1115, 1116A et 1116B de l'Ermitage Impérial à St-Pétersbourg, Moscow, 1913, Plate XIX, line 118.

35 F.Ll. Griffith, 'Stela in honour of Amenophis III and Taya, from Tell el-ʿAmarnah', JEA 12 (1926), 1–2.

36 Peet and Woolley, op. cit., pp. 109–24; A. Badawy, 'Maru-Aten: pleasure resort or temple?', JEA 42 (1956), 58–64.

37 See Note 19. The Amarna fragment is briefly described by F.Ll. Griffith, 'Notes on Egyptian weights and measures', PSBA 15 (1893), 306. I owe this reference to Dr A. Spalinger.

38 Badawy, op. cit., 1962, has argued for a calendric symbolism behind the designs of the Aten temples at Amarna. Even if one accepts his arguments – and they lie on the difficult borderline between interpretation and invention – they do not provide for the major celebrations of the solar year.

39 E. Uphill, 'The Sed-Festivals of Akhenaten', JNES 22 (1963), 123–7;

40 Davies, op. cit., II, pp. 38–43, Plates XXXVIII–XL, III, 9–12, Plates XIII–XV; cf. also Pendlebury, op. cit., 1951, pp. 22–5, 208–10.

41 Frankfort and Pendlebury, op. cit., Chapter V.

42 EA16: 43ff. The passage is translated in I.J. Gelb, B. Landsberger, and A.L. Oppenheim (eds) The Assyrian Dictionary 16 (Ṣ), Chicago and Glückstadt, 1962, p. 152b(f); also Redford, op. cit., 1984, p. 235.

43 On the Window of Appearances, see U. Hölscher, Excavations at Ancient Thebes 1930–31 (Oriental Institute Communications, 15), Chicago, 1932, pp. 23–8; Kemp, op. cit., 1976, 81–99; R.W. Smith and D.B. Redford, The Akhenaten Temple Project I, Warminster, 1976, pp. 123–32.

44 For the bakery identification, see B.J. Kemp, 'Preliminary report on the El-ʿAmarna survey, 1978', JEA 65 (1979), 7–12; also Kemp et al., I, p. 31; IV, Chapter 9.

45 See Chapter 5, Note 74.

46 Davies, op. cit., IV, pp. 23–4.

47 R. Ventura, 'On the location of the administrative outpost of the community of workmen in Western Thebes', JEA 73 (1987), 149–60.

48 Kemp et al., V, Chapter 1.

49 ibid., III, Chapter 6; IV, Chapter 9.

50 Davies, op. cit., IV, Chapter 3.

51 Building P49.16, Borchardt and Ricke, op. cit., pp. 279–80, Plan 92.

52 Kemp et al., II, Chapter 5.

53 The main excavation reports on Amarna, and most books on Egyptian architecture, illustrate 'typical' houses. A vivid account based on a modern architect's model is S. Lloyd, 'Model of a Tell el-ʿAmarnah house', JEA 19 (1933), 1–7; also C. Tietze, 'Amarna. Analyse

der Wohnhäuser und soziale Struktur der Stadtbewohner', ZÄS 112 (1985), 48–84; Tietze, 'Amarna (Teil III). Analyse der ökonomischen Beziehungen der Stadtbewohner', ZÄS 113 (1986), 55–78.

54 Kemp *et al.*, III, Chapter 1. A valuable discussion of the artistic evidence for reconstructing Egyptian town houses is H.A. Assaad, 'The house of Thutnefer and Egyptian architectural drawings', *The Ancient World* 6 (1983), 3–20.

55 P.T. Crocker, 'Status symbols in the architecture of El-ʿAmarna', JEA 71 (1985), 52–65; Tietze, op. cit. 1985 and 1986.

56 Labib Habachi, *Features of the Deification of Ramesses II*, Glückstadt, 1969.

57 T.E. Peet, 'Two letters from Akhetaten', *Annals of Archaeology and Anthropology* (Liverpool) 17 (1930a), 82–97. For the Aten as an element in private names see V. Condon, RdE 35 (1984), 57–82.

58 Pendlebury, op. cit., 1951, pp. 10, 12, 188–9, Plate LX.5–8; H. Frankfort, 'Preliminary report on the excavations at Tell el-ʿAmarnah, 1926–7', JEA 13 (1927), 210, Plate XLVI.

59 See Note 24.

60 Davies, op. cit., V, pp. 9–11. A man of the same name and title was commemorated in hieratic in two pieces of stone found in the Central City (Pendlebury, op. cit., 1951, p. 189).

61 A good selection is illustrated in Frankfort and Pendlebury, op. cit., Plate XXXV.

62 Borchardt and Ricke, op. cit., pp. 111–12, Plan 28.

63 ibid., p. 222, Plan 64; S. Seidlmayer, 'Zu einigen Architekturinschriften aus Tell el-Amarna', MDAIK 39 (1983), 204–6.

64 Peet and Woolley, op. cit., p. 25. The original field notebook lists parts of two figurines rather than just one.

65 G. Pinch, 'Childbirth and female figurines at Deir el-Medina and el-ʿAmarna', *Orientalia* 52 (1983), 405–14.

66 Kemp, 'Wall paintings from the Workmen's Village at El-ʿAmarna', JEA 65 (1979), 47–53; Kemp *et al.*, III, p. 25.

67 Kemp, 'Preliminary report on the El-ʿAmarna expedition, 1980', JEA 67 (1981b), 14–16; Kemp *et al.*, IV, pp. 136, 139.

68 D. Valbelle, 'Eléments sur la démographie et le paysage urbains, d'après les papyrus documentaires d'époque pharaonique', in *Sociétés urbaines en Egypte et au Soudan* (Cahier de Recherches de l'Institut de Papyrologie et d'Egyptologie de Lille, 7), Lille, 1985, pp. 75–87, summarizes the basic documentation available, including the ancient census lists from Deir el-Medina, although it has to be remembered that the specialized character of this community could well have led to an atypically small presence of adult males.

69 The first is in Kemp, op. cit., 1981a; the second in J.J. Janssen, 'El-Amarna as a residential city', BibOr 40 (1983), 273–88.

70 Borchardt and Ricke, op. cit., pp. 87–100, Plan 27; R. Hanke, 'Bildhauerwerkstätten in Tell el-Amarna', *MDOG* 110 (1978), 43–8; R. Krauss, 'Der Bildhauer Thutmose in Amarna', *Jahrbuch Preussischer Kulturbesitz* 20 (1983), 119–32.

71 T.E. Peet, *The Great Tomb-robberies of the Twentieth Egyptian Dynasty*, Oxford, 1930b, pp. 93–102.
Cf. C. Aldred, 'More light on the Ramesside tomb robberies', in J. Ruffle, G.A. Gaballa, and K.A. Kitchen (eds) *Glimpses of Ancient Egypt: Studies in Honour of H.W. Fairman*, Warminster, 1979, pp. 92–9.

72 Omitting the one householder without a title.

73 For a recent discussion of the various levels of meaning attached to this word, see J.J. Janssen, *BibOr* 43 (1986), 351–66.

74 Perhaps the now partly filled and swampy remains of Amenhetep III's great basin, the Birket Habu, see Chapter 5.

75 For Hekanakht see the references in Note 20, Chapter 6. On his household see D. Franke, *Altägyptische Verwandtschaftsbezeichnungen im Mittleren Reich*, Hamburg, 1983, pp. 231, 275.

76 It must be remembered that it was no mere bureaucratic exercise but part of a major criminal investigation which involved intensive questioning and searching.

77 Kemp *et al.*, V, Chapter 2.

78 Detailed calculations of silo size are given in Tietze, op. cit., 1986, 67–74. The conclusions on the numbers of people supported are, however, vitiated by failure to include the incalculable additional quantities of grain stored in the rectangular granaries which some large houses preferred.

79 K.A. Kitchen, *Pharaoh Triumphant: the Life and Times of Ramesses II, King of Egypt*, Warminster, 1982, pp. 128–9.

80 Sir A.H. Gardiner, 'A protest against unjustified tax-demands', RdE 6 (1951), 115–24.

81 P. Anastasi IV, cited in R.A. Caminos, *Late-Egyptian Miscellanies*, London, 1954, pp. 137–8.

82 T.G.H. James, *Pharaoh's People: Scenes from Life in Imperial Egypt*, London, 1984, Chapter 4, covers well the rural ideal that lay so deeply within Egyptian consciousness.

83 See Note 85 below, Note 81, Chapter 5, and especially also D.B. O'Connor, 'The geography of settlement in ancient Egypt', in P.J. Ucko, R. Tringham, and G.W. Dimbleby (eds) *Man, Settlement and Urbanism*, London, 1972, pp. 681–98, esp. pp. 691–5.

84 Sir A.H. Gardiner and R.O. Faulkner, *The Wilbour Papyrus* I–IV, The Brooklyn Museum, Brooklyn, 1941–52; also Baer, op. cit.; O'Connor, op. cit.; S.L.D. Katary, 'Cultivator, scribe, stablemaster, soldier: the Late Egyptian Miscellanies in light of P. Wilbour', *The Ancient World* 6 (1983), 71–93; Janssen, op. cit., 1986.

85 Sir W.M.F. Petrie and G. Brunton, *Sedment* II, London, 1924, Chapters VII, VIII.

86 K.P. Kuhlmann, 'Der Felstempel des Eje bei Akhmim', MDAIK 35 (1979), 165–88.

87 Peet, op. cit., 1930a.

88 Known from the famous texts of Hapdjefa, see Chapter 3, Note 21.

89 See the diagram in Kemp, op. cit., 1977, 132, Fig. 4.

90 P. Anastasi IV, cited in Caminos, op. cit., pp. 164–5.

91 Crocker, op. cit.

92 Conveniently translated by J. Bennett, 'The Restoration Inscription of Tutʿankhamūn', JEA 25 (1939), 8–15; also Schlögl, op. cit., 85–8.

Epilogue: Onwards from the Bronze Age

1 K.A. Kitchen, *Pharaoh Triumphant: the Life and Times of Ramesses II, King of Egypt*, Warminster, 1982. The other two books are Claire Lalouette, *L'Empire des Ramsès*, Paris, 1985; Franco Cimmino, *Ramesses II il grande*, Milan, 1984.

2 Adams, W.Y., *Nubia: Corridor to Africa*, London, 1977.

Addition to Chapter 2

Since completing the text the Coptos pottery sculptures have been published by Barbara Adams, *Sculptured Pottery from Koptos in the Petrie Collection*, Warminster 1986, who concludes that Old Kingdom and later dates are likely for most of them. She draws a conclusion similar to the one presented here: 'There seems to have been an early and continuing temple tradition for the model human and animal figures, perhaps as a swiftly manufactured votive object.'

INDEX

Page numbers in **bold type** indicate illustrations or their captions. The definite article el- does not affect the alphabetization.